Byron and Newstead

Byron and Newstead

The Aristocrat and the Abbey

John Beckett

with Sheila Aley

DELAWARE

Newark: University of Delaware Press
London: Associated University Presses

Associated University Presses
440 Forsgate Drive
Cranbury, NJ 08512

Associated University Presses
16 Barter Street
London WC1A 2AH, England

Associated University Presses
P.O. Box 338, Port Credit
Mississauga, Ontario
Canada L5G 4L8

The paper used in this publication meets the requirements of the American National Standard for Permanence of Paper for Printed Library Materials Z39.48-1984.

Library of Congress Cataloging-in-Publication Data

Beckett, J. V.
    Byron and Newstead : the aristocrat and the abbey / John Beckett with Sheila Aley.
        p. cm.
    Includes bibliographical references and index.
    ISBN 0-87413-751-9 (alk. paper)
        1. Byron, George Gordon Byron, Baron, 1788–1824—Homes and
    haunts—England—Nottinghamshire. 2. Aristocracy (Social
    class)—England—Nottinghamshire—History—19th century. 3. Country
    homes—England—Nottinghamshire—History—19th century. 4. Poets, English—19th
    century—Biography. 5. Nottinghamshire (England)—Biography. 6. Newstead Abbey. I.
    Aley, Sheila. II. Title.

PR 4384 .B43 2001
821'.7—dc21
[B]
                                                                                    2001027635

PRINTED IN THE UNITED STATES OF AMERICA

Contents

List of Illustrations

List of Tables

Preface

Byron: the single word has been all that biographers, scholars, and poetry lovers across the world have needed to identify the greatest romantic poet of his generation. And Byron was the single word the man himself needed for purposes of identification, because, by convention, English peers sign themselves simply by their titular name. It is easily forgotten that the poet was no less than a full member of the English aristocracy, inheriting a title from his forefathers that he passed on to future generations and that still survives today. He had a seat in the House of Lords, which he occasionally occupied, and he inherited landed property in Nottinghamshire and Lancashire, which he subsequently sold. Yet he was also a confused aristocrat, brought up until the age of six in the expectation that he would inherit his mother's Scottish title and what little money she had kept from her profligate husband. His prospects altered out of all recognition only in 1794, when twenty-two-year-old Lieutenant William Byron of the Eighteenth Regiment of Foot was killed by a cannonball at the siege of Calvi. This particular engagement on the Mediterranean island of Corsica is not one of the better-known British military engagements. It lasted for some weeks during the summer of 1794, and is perhaps best recalled as the occasion on which Nelson lost the use of his right eye. It also claimed the life of William John Byron, heir to the estates of his grandfather, the fifth Lord Byron of Rochdale, and it transformed the prospects of George Gordon Byron (1788–1824), who now unexpectedly became heir to the family estates and title.

Byron, as an English aristocrat, was not a great success. He lacked the requisite interest in estate management, and he parted with the family patrimony for his own short-term gain. At his death in 1824 the title, shorn of any property, passed to a cousin because he had no direct male heir. Had Byron not been a great poet he would have been forgotten, expunged from the family record for selling the chief seat and estate, and reducing the Byrons to a state of virtual landlessness almost unheard of among the English aristocracy.

The reality is that today Byron's poetry is read across the world, and Newstead Abbey, the house that inspired some of his finest poetry but that he sold to fund his debts, is a shrine to his memory. All this has happened because of the lasting importance of Byron's poetry, but in this process Byron the romantic has been substituted for Byron the landed aristocrat. We too easily forget that his passage into "society" was smoothed by his social standing, and that to contemporaries he was, first and foremost, the current representative of a long-established English landed aristocratic family. As Wilfrid Scawen Blunt commented in 1909, Newstead was "a splendid possession, much larger and more important than I had imagined, and one can well understand how the sudden inheritance of it by Byron and his mother turned their heads, and helped to give him that exaggerated pride of birth and position which was his weakness."[1] We may forget also that his friendships with Lady Melbourne, with Lady Caroline Lamb, and with Lady Oxford, as well as with so many other contemporary socialites, were facilitated by his status as an aristocrat. We may also forget that his European tour of 1809–11, from which came *Childe Harold's Pilgrimage*, was possible because he enjoyed the rental income from an aristocratic estate. Even his marriage, however disastrous, was possible in the first place because he was a suitable social match for Annabella Milbanke.

Byron the poet was and is an international success. Byron the aristocrat was not. Over time the memory of Byron the romantic poet has triumphed over Byron the flawed aristocrat: this book tries gently to redress at least some of the balance, and it does so by setting the sixth Lord Byron into his landed and financial context.

In preparing this book I am particularly grateful to the British Academy and the University of Nottingham for providing the initial funding that made the research possible. Subsequently my work has been greatly facilitated by various people who have helped in all sorts of ways, among them Geoffrey Bond, Deborah Bragan Turner, Peter Cochran, Maureen Crisp, David Crook, Malcolm Fraser, Adam Green, Adrian Henstock, Haidee Jackson, Dorothy Johnston, Philip Jones, Virginia Murray, Annette Peach, Colin Phillips, Ken Purslow, Charles Robinson, and Susannah Wade Martins. I am also grateful to the archivists and their staff at the numerous repositories at which Sheila Aley and I worked. Finally, particular thanks are due to Sheila Aley, who was a meticulous research assistant; to Janice Avery, who put the text into shape for publication; and to Dr. Rosalys Coope and Professor Barbara English, both of whom read and commented on an earlier draft of the text and made numerous helpful comments that have saved me from committing unforced errors.

Acknowledgments

For permission to quote from the Lovelace Papers in the Bodleian Library, Oxford, and to reproduce the illustration on p. 181, Laurence Pollinger Limited and the Earl of Lytton. For permission to quote from the John Murray Archive, and for the reproduction of the illustration on p. 144, John Murray (Publishers) Ltd. For the reproduction of illustrations on pp. 30, 45, 73, 90, 127, 176, 197, 276, 290 and the portrait of Byron on the book cover, Nottingham City Museums and Art Galleries (Newstead Abbey).

Introduction

Newstead Abbey is one of Nottinghamshire's best-known country houses. About ten miles north of Nottingham the visitor leaves the main road to Mansfield, and turns into Newstead Park. This is Nottingham sandstone, the territory of Sherwood Forest, covered today, as the Forest has been for hundreds of years, with silver birch and scrub land rather than with the mythical great oaks and dense woodland preferred by Hollywood. After what always seems an unexpectedly long drive, the road bends to the left, and there, nestling in a dip, is Newstead Abbey, with its magnificent thirteenth-century west wall from the great priory church and its adjoining house built around and growing from the earlier monastic buildings. Visitors today come by car or public transport, but the scene that greets them, and that never fails to inspire, would have been recognized by Washington Irving when he visited by post chaise in the 1830s. Irving recalled his carriage rolling heavily along a sandy road until it swept around an angle of a garden wall and "brought us full in front of the venerable edifice."[1] It is a sight that, year in and year out, greets the hundreds, perhaps thousands, of pilgrims from across the world who come to see the ancestral home of the greatest of English Romantic poets, Byron. Despite changes in the abbey and the grounds, for a few moments visitors can empathize with the man whose work is still read today across the globe. They can see the Great Hall, in which he practiced his pistol shooting, walk through the rooms in which he spent time reading and writing, pass through his bedroom—still adorned with the bed in which he slept—and stroll on the grounds as he strolled on them two hundred years ago. Above all, perhaps, they can see the house that inspired so much of his poetry and, in front of it, the "lucid lake" so memorably described in *Don Juan*.

Byron died at Missolonghi, Greece, in 1824, seven years after selling the house and estate to an old schoolmate Thomas Wildman, but in truth Byron has never left Newstead. After Byron's death Wildman turned the abbey into a shrine to the poet's memory, and it was subsequently maintained as

15

such. When Sir Julien Cahn presented Newstead to Nottingham City Council in 1931 to be kept "for all time . . . in safe hands,"[2] this was purely because of the Byron heritage; indeed, with great houses being closed and often demolished in the 1930s it was arguably *only* the Byron connection that helped to ensure that the house survived.[3] And it is as the home of the poet that Newstead continues to attract visitors from far and wide—many of them from Greece, where Byron is a national hero, famed for the support he gave to their fight for independence from the Turks during the last months of his life in 1823–24.

Shrines attract myths, and Newstead is no exception. The Byrons acquired the house and estate in 1540, in the wake of the dissolution of the monasteries. By the late seventeenth century they were substantial landowners, not perhaps in the first rank of the English aristocracy but sufficiently well endowed to have acquired a peerage and to be considered as a major county family. So far so good, but now the story begins to take an unconventional twist. Having carefully built up their Nottinghamshire estates between the sixteenth and eighteenth centuries, the family, it is suggested, was undone by the so-called Wicked Lord, or Devil Byron. This was William, fifth Lord Byron, and his reputation was permanently colored when in 1765 he killed a relation in a duel and was subsequently tried before the House of Lords. He was also financially improvident, and he allowed the estate to go to ruin. In the words of the Irish poet Thomas Moore, Byron's friend and first biographer,

> At Newstead both the mansion and the grounds around it were suffered to fall helplessly into decay; and among the few monuments of either care or expenditure which their lord left behind were some masses of rockwork, on which much cost had been thrown away, and a few castellated buildings on the banks of the lake and in the woods. . . . This eccentric peer, it is evident, cared but little about the fate of his descendants.[4]

Devil Byron, it is alleged, lived reclusively at Newstead, spending recklessly, selling everything that could be disposed of, neglecting house and grounds alike, and leaving to his successor a badly flawed inheritance.

Nor does the myth end here. The sixth Lord Byron, the story continues, was misled by his land steward and innocently fell into the hands of rapacious creditors until he was forced through no real fault of his own to sell the great house. "How Byron cherished Newstead Abbey, and how he loved it is proved by his constant efforts to save it from the hands of his clamorous creditors, and to preserve its beauties for his own and his friends' enjoyment," the Greek prime minister told an audience of two thousand when Newstead was officially handed over to the Nottingham City Council on 16 July 1931.[5] This was, to say the least, taking something of a liberty with the truth, but the audience clapped enthusiastically before adjourning to take tea in a marquee.[6.]

Myths, of course, contain an element of truth, and a combination of the timelessness of Byron's poetry and the accessibility of Newstead—which as a fixed point in the Byron universe has perhaps inevitably turned it into a place of pilgrimage—has tended to embellish the reality. Byron has effectively been absolved from responsibility for what happened at Newstead: the blame has been laid instead at the feet of his great-uncle, William, the fifth lord, for ruining the estate; John Hanson, his solicitor and steward, for duplicitous management; and an assortment of unnamed and perhaps unknown creditors who exploited the gullibility of a young man and left him penniless. Such an explanation may satisfy a literary stereotype, the golden boy whose poetic genius is a blanket excuse for all and any excesses, but it is not likely to have been one that Byron himself would have recognized, nor is it one that can easily be squared with the reality. Byron, a recent biographer has written, "loved Newstead Abbey because it was a ruin, something on which to exert his imaginative powers, seeing it as it once must have been."[7] Doubtless this was so, but it was also the case that he spent little time at Newstead, that he found it a financial burden, and that he sold it. Byron may have been a famous poet with a rakish reputation, but he was conscious also of being an aristocrat, and that by selling Newstead he failed his caste. In 1811 he told his mother that should he be forced for financial reasons to part with Newstead, he would not return to England, "as my only tie to England is Newstead."[8] He was not quite true to his word, but he did live abroad from 1816 until his death, and he showed rather less remorse than his wider family at the loss of the family house.

English aristocratic families accepted that selling the family seat and the core property was not simply to act out a tragedy for the particular family involved, but to fail the class. From the seventeenth century ways had been found of enshrining this unwritten code of practice in a protective coating provided by the law, so that almost every landed family offered work to a bevy of lawyers whose task was to limit the powers of the owner in possession at any one time. The strict settlement, as it was conventionally known, was designed to ensure that a spendthrift owner desirous of liquidizing his capital assets for whatever nefarious purpose he may have had in mind was prevented from achieving his aim. Instead he was legally bound to ensure that the property was passed intact to the next generation. Until the First World War it was a convention that worked remarkably well. Benjamin Disraeli, the nineteenth-century Conservative prime minister, commented in the 1860s that even families that appeared to be beyond financial recovery always seemed to pull through.[9] The landless nobility who figured so prominently in European society had virtually no equivalent in England. John Bateman, in a survey of great landowners published in 1883, was able to trace only a handful of aristocratic families that had been forced to part with their estates.[10]

Yet there had inevitably to be the exception who would prove the rule. George Gordon, sixth Lord Byron, inherited an unsettled estate. He was free, in other words, to do with it as he wished. Had he been the serious and responsible young man that landed families longed for, Newstead and the estate might have been rescued from the neglect into which it had fallen by 1798. As it was, Byron inherited all the worst family characteristics when it came to money, and because the estate was unsettled the usual safety traps could not be sprung. Young Byron had the freedom to do as he wished with the property: the decision to sell Newstead was his alone, a position few other aristocrats enjoyed. This makes an understanding of his finances of great significance for interpreting his lifestyle. Nearly thirty years ago Doris Langley Moore recognized this omission and tried to fill the gap in *Lord Byron: Accounts Rendered.* Without doubt this is a splendid and highly entertaining book, written in Langley Moore's own elegant style, but she too willingly accepted many of the myths about Byron's financial position. In particular, she paid little or no attention to the context in which he inherited the estate, she dismissed Byron's own understanding of his role as a landowner, and she tended to accept an overly negative view of Byron's land agent, John Hanson. Langley Moore's book remains a key text in appreciating Byron the landed aristocrat, but it has not really influenced thinking about Byron in this role. Biographers since the 1970s have continued to show little real appreciation of the social and economic milieu in which Byron lived.[11]

Byron was sufficiently conscious of his standing among contemporaries that he expected to be the object of biographical study. He thought correctly that one image of him would be that of the "*amiable*, ill-used gentleman, 'more sinned against than sinning,'" a portrayal that began with Thomas Moore's edition of his letters and journals published in 1830.[12] In the matter of his estate affairs, this is indeed the image that his biographers have been happy to promote. Yet it sits ill at ease with contemporary views of the English aristocracy, views that Byron undoubtedly shared. We need to rescue Byron from his reputation, to view him as a member of the English aristocracy, and in this context to search for a satisfactory answer to the obvious question: why, when he died in 1824, was this scion of the English landed aristocracy no longer landed?

Not surprisingly, many of the details from which we might have hoped to piece together the fortunes of the Byrons have been missing since Newstead was sold. Indebted families seldom kept good records, and the fifth and sixth Lords Byron were no exception. Yet we can trace the Byrons as they established their landed credentials and settled upon Newstead as their chief seat. This provides the necessary background against which to investigate the activities of William, fifth Lord Byron, as we begin the process of sorting out myth from reality. Chapters 2 and 3 recreate the Newstead story in the eighteenth century, and permit us to assess just how flawed an inheritance it was that the sixth Lord Byron inherited in 1798. In chapters 4 to 11 we view the poet as a landed aristocrat, hoping thereby that he can emerge from the long shadow of Byron the poet, a man of means who mishandled the family fortunes but who still died wealthy. Finally, in chapter 12 we look at how the spiritual presence of Lord Byron has lived on at Newstead. Ironically, the link between Byron and Newstead has grown rather than weakened since 1817. In many respects this is a reflection of the way in which subsequent owners have consciously maintained or even promoted the poet's legacy, but that is all the more reason to try to disentangle the myth from the reality.

Our image of the English aristocracy is one of continuity and stability. We look to the stately homes—to Chatsworth, or to Hatfield House, to Petworth or to Alnwick—and to the families who have lived in them for centuries. They provide a sense of permanence, of the stability of rural England. Of course families came and went, and even those which are still with us have sometimes rescued themselves from imminent catastrophe by the blatantly artificial means of persuading an indirect heir to adopt the family name. What we like is the myth, the idea that generations untold have lived in these great treasure houses, which, since the 1970s, have acquired a special status as England's greatest contribution to Western civilization.[13] It has not always been like this, and Byron demonstrates why not.

Byron and Newstead

1

The Byrons and Newstead

The land running north from Nottingham through much of the west side of Nottinghamshire is an extensive formation of the Sherwood (formerly Bunter) Sandstones, which give rise to poor-quality sandy soils. The natural vegetation is open oak-birch wood, scrub, and heath. It is easy to clear for cultivation, but the soil is rapidly exhausted unless regularly fertilized. Traditionally the land was cultivated in temporary "brecks" for a few years, with the surrounding wood and heath used for hunting and sheep grazing. Permanent settlements were few, and usually small. After the Norman Conquest most of the Sandlands were absorbed into Shire Wood, or Sherwood Forest, and made subject to "forest law" even though the land was not necessarily covered by trees. The Forest was ideal territory for a monastic community, and it was at Newstead that the Augustinians built a complete house, with church, cloister, and ranges, in the late twelfth and early thirteenth centuries. The magnificent west wall of the ruined priory, which dominates Newstead even today, reminds us of the great swathe of history that this site encompasses.

West Nottinghamshire was favored territory for monastic foundations. It was in this same area that the Cistercians settled at Rufford in 1126, the Augustinians at Worksop (1123–40), and the Premonstratensians at Welbeck (1154–70). Newstead was an Augustinian house, founded about 1170 by Henry II, and despite its modern name it was always a priory, an establishment of clergy living a common life of prayer and devotion. When Archbishop Gray visited Newstead in 1252 he found "the prior and canons alike earnest in their religious observance, and lovers of peace and concord both among themselves and towards others."[1]

The first building on the site was a small church, and domestic accommodation was added subsequently. Evidence of the original twelfth-century buildings can still be seen at Newstead. In the thirteenth century the Norman church was replaced by a much larger building with transepts, side chapels, and a north aisle. During the fourteenth and fifteenth centuries

23

further building took place, including the cloister walks and the Prior's Hall (now the much-altered Great Hall) and Prior's Parlour, probably to provide adequate accommodation for visitors to the priory. Repairs to the buildings were carried out regularly.[2] Despite later alterations, the thirteenth-century rebuilding is still well represented, notably in the magnificent west front of the church, standing in its ruinous state as proud today as when Byron immortalized it in *Don Juan* in 1823.

Newstead was not a wealthy foundation, and it was often to be found in deep financial trouble. In part this was because of the numerous visitors. The road to Mansfield ran much closer to the priory than it does to the modern complex of buildings, and the archbishop of York noted the impact in 1320:

> The same priory, which is situated in a wood near the public road is, by reason of the distances of the villages on every side, so grievously and continually burthened beyond the resources of its possessions, which are notoriously slender and scanty, by hospitality to rich and poor, that the very things which are in readiness for its daily victuals have to be made common and set before guests who come unexpectedly to the priory.[3]

The rich included numerous royalty, visiting the (royal) forest to hunt. Edward I visited in 1280, 1290, and 1300, Edward II in 1307 and 1315, and Edward III in 1327 and 1363. When hospitality and building costs are added together, the financial difficulties of the priory are not perhaps surprising, and the position was compounded by corruption and good living. Over time, the financial position of the house fell into some disarray, although the prior and canons seem to have been reasonably successful in their efforts to increase income from landholdings. As a result, by 1535 Newstead had a gross taxable income of £220, although this was reduced by necessary deductions to £168.

Newstead's future seemed secure until Henry VIII set about plundering the monasteries in the 1530s. With a net income below the £200 threshold, it was ripe for dissolution in 1537. Instead, in 1538 it paid £233 6s. 8d. for toleration and the continuance of the house, although as it transpired this was simply delaying the inevitable. On 21 July 1539 John Blake, the prior, together with the eleven canons, surrendered the priory to the Crown commissioners. In a final desperate act, the canons hid the bronze eagle lectern and two candlesticks in what is now the Eagle Pond at Newstead. After 368 years the monastic foundation came to an end, and the prior and canons were pensioned off. The man who received the surrender was Sir John Byron (1487–1567).[4]

After some negotiation, on 28 May 1540 Newstead was granted to Byron together with 750 acres of surrounding land that had been part of the monastic foundation. This included the adjoining manor of Papplewick and the common or waste lands of Ravenshead and Kighill (ancient tracts of Sherwood Forest granted by Henry II to Newstead in the twelfth century), Bulwell Wood, and other land in Linby and Hucknall. Sir John paid the king £810. Thus began the Byron occupation of Newstead, which lasted until the nineteenth century.

By 1540 the Byrons had been living in England for five hundred years. The family arrived at the time of the Norman Conquest, bearing a name that is supposedly derived from Beuron, near Nantes in northern France. They enjoyed some of the spoils of the Conquest and, by the time of Domesday Book in 1086, Ralph de Burun, ancestor of the Newstead Byrons, held manors spread through Nottinghamshire and Derbyshire. In Nottinghamshire these included Ossington, Kelham, Costock, Ompton, Hucknall, Lamcote, and Cotgrave. His principal manor was Horsley, near Belper, in Derbyshire, and he also held land in the county at Weston Underwood, Denby, Kirk Hallam, and Duffield. Hugh, Ralph's son and heir, was a benefactor of the Cluniac Lenton Priory, near Nottingham, founded in 1109–14.

Over time the family widened its property portfolio. Through marriages in the twelfth and thirteenth centuries the Byrons acquired estates at Clayton, Rochdale, and Butterworth in Lancashire. Clayton Hall, near Manchester, became the family's chief seat, and properties in Nottinghamshire and Derbyshire were sold, exchanged, or given to religious houses. However, the family never lost interest in Nottinghamshire, and with the marriage, probably in the 1370s, of Richard Byron (d. 1379) to Joan, daughter of William de Colwick, they acquired an estate at Colwick, just to the east of the county town. In turn, at some point during the fifteenth century this became the chief seat. In 1462 Sir Nicholas Byron acquired a Crown lease of the manor of Rochdale for the length of his life at a rent of £18 6s. 8d., and subsequently the stewardship of the manor.

John Byron supported Henry VII at the Battle of Bosworth in 1485, and was rewarded with the position of constable of Nottingham Castle, steward and keeper of Sherwood Forest, and sheriff of Nottinghamshire and Derbyshire. He was knighted in 1486, and was succeeded in the family properties by his brother Nicholas, high sheriff of Nottinghamshire and Derbyshire in 1493. Nicholas Byron died in 1504 and left the property to his nephew John, the Byron who was to acquire Newstead in 1540. John Byron was knighted in 1522 and served as M.P. for Nottinghamshire in 1529, and probably also in 1536 and 1542. He was sheriff of the county, and of Derbyshire, several times in the years from 1523 onward, and commissioner for the Dissolution of the Monasteries in the northwest.[5] In 1536 he played a prominent role in suppressing the Pilgrimage of Grace, and for his loyal service to the Crown he was in prime position to take advantage of the great land disposal into which Henry VIII entered, following the dissolution of the monasteries, in order to replenish his depleted treasury.

Byron certainly knew what property he was acquiring, although it can hardly be said to have been in prime condition in 1540. John Leland, writing at about this time, referred to "the ruins of Newstead." Byron clearly saw the property as a challenge, and set about the task of turning the monastic space into a domestic dwelling. It must have been a costly business, since he did not go in for half measures. Many lay owners of former monastic property were content to use the abbot's or prior's dwelling, especially if it had recently been modernized, and to pull down everything else, but Byron utilized the entire claustral complex. He destroyed the body of the church, and converted the prior's lodgings and the Great Hall (probably part of the fifteenth-century building) into his own accommodation. It was expensive, although these alterations were certainly cheaper than entirely rebuilding on an adjoining sight. Byron's chief seat remained at Colwick, and as he was regularly away from the county there was no particular hurry to complete the work, although he seems to have taken up residence by 1545.[6] He died in 1567, and was buried at Colwick.

The Byrons flourished under the later Tudors. By the 1570s they were able to enjoy moving between their various seats: Newstead and Colwick in Nottinghamshire, Clayton Hall near Manchester, and Royton (or Ryton) Hall near Oldham, an estate they sold in 1620. In 1585 Sir John Byron, son of the purchaser of Newstead, and known as "Little Sir John with the Great Beard," acquired a thirty-one-year lease from the Crown of the manor of Rochdale. He set about trying to improve the wastes to defray his costs. In Nottinghamshire he purchased Bulwell Hill, or Rise, in 1597 to enlarge the Bulwell Wood estate, on which he built Bulwell Wood Hall (destroyed by fire in 1937). All this activity stretched the family's resources, and when Sir John died in 1604 he left his son and heir in some financial difficulty.

Sir John Byron, who succeeded to the family estates in 1604, was advised by the earl of Shrewsbury to reduce his Newstead establishment and to live instead in Lancashire: "[Y]ou are in great debts, and unless you take some present and speedy course to free yourself of debts [they] will eat into your state like in a moth in your garment."[7] Byron, acting on the spirit of this advice, made available parts of the Lancashire estates for sale, and the Rochdale lease was allowed to revert to the Crown when it expired in 1616. The extent of Byron's estates is known from Richard Bankes's survey of Sherwood Forest undertaken in 1609 (table 1.1). He may have owned more, since some properties could have been attributed to his tenants. Whatever the case, the survey was prepared for the Crown commissioners charged with compounding for defective titles, and after a prolonged legal

Table 1.1. The Byron Estate in Nottinghamshire, 1609

	Acres	Roods	Perches
Newstead	1,813	3	22
Papplewick	490	3	26
Linby	770	3	34
Bulwell	326	3	2
Bestwood	85	2	16
Thoresby	2	3	16
Colwick	402	1	16
	3,893	1	12

Source: S. Mastoris and S. Groves, eds. *Sherwood Forest in 1609,* Thoroton Society Record Series, 40 (Nottingham, U.K.: Thoroton Society, 1997)

case Byron was forced to compound. The estates were regranted to him for the payment of £1,000. To raise the money he had to sell land, and estates at Clayton in Lancashire, including the hall, were disposed of in 1621, with other parcels of land in Lancashire being sold subsequently.[8]

Sir John Byron's son, also John, was just twenty-five when he inherited the estate in 1625. He had studied at Cambridge and been on the grand tour, and in 1624 had been elected M.P. for Nottingham. He was to have an active political career, but his first priority was his property and houses, in both Nottinghamshire and Lancashire. His set about reacquiring the Rochdale lease, which he bought back in 1638 for £2,500. Within the enormous parish of Rochdale, which ran to nearly 42,000 acres, the property was in the hamlets of Butterworth (5,998 acres), Clegge (872 acres), and Hollingworth (1,866 acres), and some of it remained in the family until the 1820s. Also in the 1630s Byron was busy refurbishing Newstead, building the outside entrance stair and the porch (which survived until Colonel Wildman's day), and raising and redecorating the ceiling of the Salon. The outlay involved was more than he could afford. By 1642 his debts amounted to over £20,000, and to rectify the position he sold the 1,190-acre Colwick estate to Sir James Stonehouse for £23,000. Stonehouse paid either £14,000 or £16,000, which was distributed among Byron's creditors. The balance may never have been cleared.[9]

By now, in any case, other events were taking precedence. Byron was a major supporter of the Royalist cause in the English Civil War and, for his loyalty, on 24 October 1643 he was created Baron Byron of Rochdale by Charles I. Fortunately, as it transpired for the future of the title, the grant included remainders to each of Byron's six brothers. Why he decided to take his title from the Rochdale estate is not clear. Perhaps he still regarded this as his main property, or perhaps he feared for the future of Newstead, given that he was a Royalist in a county dominated by the Parliamentary cause. He certainly had cause for concern, because on 9 January 1644 Newstead was pillaged by forces loyal to the Parliamentarians. Any resistance must have been slight: Wildman was to comment many years later that "much mischief and destruction was done by Cromwell's troops, who probably demolished all that remained of the Abbey church (except what is now left) and smashed the saints etc."[10] By the end of the Civil War the Byron fortunes were at a low ebb, and the first Baron Byron, childless and disappointed by the outcome of the conflict, went into exile. He died in Paris in 1652.

It fell to Richard, second Lord Byron (c. 1605–79), eldest brother of the first Lord Byron, to try to pick up the pieces. He compounded for the sequestered estates on 2 June 1646. However, like his brother, the second baron remained unwaveringly loyal to the Stuarts, and in 1652 he was committed to the Tower of London. Newstead was neglected: Sir John Evelyn, visiting in 1654, recorded that it was "capable of being made a noble seat, accommodated as it is with brave woods and streams." However, in 1658 the second baron recovered the Rochdale estate, and after the Restoration he set about reassembling the rest of the property. He petitioned King Charles II to restore the confiscated territory in view of his "great losses, sufferings and services for and to your Royal Father and your self."[11] Subsequently he succeeded in making Newstead habitable again, although his efforts were not universally applauded: Wildman considered that "the attempts at restoration by subsequent Lords Byron since the Restoration of the monarchy were of a piece with that auspicious event—most heterogenous, barbarous and unnatural."[12] With forty-one hearths Newstead was the third-largest house in Nottinghamshire when assessments were made for the hearth tax in 1674, behind only Welbeck Abbey (eighty-eight hearths) and Rufford Abbey (sixty-one hearths), both of which were, like Newstead, on the sites of former monastic properties.[13] Byron died in 1679, when he was succeeded by his son William as third baron.

William (1636–95), third Baron Byron, the new owner of Newstead, had married Elizabeth Chaworth of neighboring Annesley, and settled at Bulwell Wood Hall in his father's lifetime. When his father died in 1679 Byron moved with his wife and three surviving children to Newstead. There he lived in the style and comfort befitting an aristocrat. Although not a great deal is known of the third baron, he seems to have continued the work of restoring the family fortunes after the bleak years of the 1640s and 1650s, and as a result to have placed the Byrons on a financially sound footing. He died in 1695, and was buried in the family vault in Hucknall Church. The estates passed to his twenty-six-year-old son, William.

William, fourth Lord Byron (1670–1736), was brought up to understand the family fortunes, and he seems to have taken some responsibility for estate affairs from the later 1680s. In 1700 his right to cut down trees in Sherwood Forest was questioned, but he successfully proved his claim to "ancient grants" permitting such activity. An active landlord, Byron was intent on improving the Newstead estate. He applied to the Crown for a grant of five hundred trees out of the Sherwood Forest woodlands of Birkland and Billhagh toward the repair of the abbey and the enlargement of the park. By the influence of his neighbor and political ally, the duke of Newcastle, he was appointed in 1717 chief ranger of the purlieus. This was an office in which he had control of forest land still subject to forest laws, particularly in regard to hunting, and he told Newcastle that he intended to do "all that lies in my power to serve you, whatever commands you're pleased to lay upon me." It certainly brought him troubles: in 1726 he learned that "there was great complaints against my under Rangers, that I had given 'em powers to be game keepers over their estates etc." The accusation was, he told Newcastle, a malicious invention:

[A]t the time they made this complaint I had employed no man, nor have I any that has any orders from me to go into the Purlieu, the reason I have employed mine was the Brigadier's acquainting me he had the King's Royal Warrant to kill what ever deer he pleased in the purlieus so by the power of this warrant my office as Ranger was destroyed, or worse, for I was to be but Keeper to the Brigadier.

He clearly disliked having his authority undermined and hoped Newcastle would support his case.[14]

At Newstead, Byron enlarged the house and improved the grounds. He must have been aware when he inherited Newstead that it was not simply a bleak and rather uncomfortable house, but that it was out of date and out of fashion. The trend was away from great halls; in fashionable houses the hall was increasingly only an entrance, and the emphasis was instead on a series of formal "apartments" based on French and Dutch models. Byron set out to follow these models and to impose symmetry and "polite" living on a house that was ill fitted for such renovations. Some of his alterations can be traced from drawings and engravings of this period. Samuel Buck's engraving of the west front, dating from 1726, is the earliest known view of Newstead, and by this date alterations were in progress. They can be seen on a painting of the same front by the Flemish artist Peter Tillemans, of about 1730, and a watercolor of the south front by Byron himself. None of this was especially impressive: Byron's additions were neither very extensive nor particularly notable from an architectural viewpoint.

West View of Newstead Abbey, by Peter Tillemans, c. 1726, oil on canvas. Tillemans (1684–1734) was art master to the fourth Lord Byron, who is thought to have collaborated in the production of this picture. Note the "Gothic Fountain" in the foreground, placed here by the fourth Lord Byron, and later immortalized by the poet in canto 13 of *Don Juan,* but moved by Colonel Wildman to its present position in the cloister garth. (Nottingham City Museums and Art Galleries [Newstead Abbey].)

Inside the house between 1726 and 1730 Byron moved the fireplace from the east to the west wall of the hall, almost certainly rebuilding the original chimneypiece. He introduced family apartments into the house, and he was probably responsible for a new block on the southwest corner of the building, which was already in place by 1726. Byron may also have built the southeast wing, possibly on the site of the monastic infirmary, as a suite of family rooms. The uncertainty arises from the fact that it is not easy to reconstruct the interior of Newstead before the nineteenth century.

Only the medieval ground-floor rooms remain essentially the same, and with one or two exceptions these were never living rooms.[15] The house was filled with pictures, maps, and other wall hangings, as well as chairs, tables, and beds. Sidney Evelyn, who visited in 1738, noted that

> it is famous here for the great variety of pictures that the house is stocked with; several of them of the grotesque kind being painted by the late Lord, and some by the present Lady. Among my Lord's there is a good pretty one of all his servants dancing together done so exactly that the housekeeper could point out every one, there is a fine picture of Mrs Trevanion but not very like, and another very much admired of the late Lord on horseback with his dogs about him going to hunt done by Tillemans. There is a pretty gallery goes all round the house full of prints.[16]

Byron was an accomplished artist who drew creditable watercolors in a style similar to that of his drawing master, Tillemans.[17] Byron also composed music. Several pieces of his have been performed at Newstead in the recent past.

Although there were numerous pictures, in some respects Newstead was a rather sparsely furnished house. The furnishings in the Great Hall were valued at £12 5s. 6d., and while there were oil cloths in several rooms, and fashionable marble tables with mahogany frames in the Blue Gallery, few of the rooms had clocks or other contemporary symbols of wealth such as musical instruments or candlesticks. There were numerous looking glasses, while the groom's room was described as "a room with a large clock in it and a bell." In one passage there was an eight-day clock. The total valuation of furnishings at £829 in 1738 was hardly excessive for a peer, although no books are listed in the inventory from which this figure comes, and references to pictures are generalized. Plate was valued at a further £889.[18] Byron's library collection included an album of Smythson drawings, acquired from Bolsover in 1725 and now in the library of the Royal Institute of British Architects.

Beyond the abbey, Byron laid out the formal garden to the east, and he greatly improved the setting, particularly in regard to the east and west prospects. He reflected the spirit of his age when he laid out the formal garden to the east of the abbey, perhaps under the direct influence of the French designer Le Notre, with whom the earl of Portland (his second father-in-law) had a connection. To the west Byron created the "stepped cascade," and probably also the "steep" cascade that runs directly from the medieval Upper Lake. Evelyn noted that "in front of the house there is a fine cascade, that tumbles over about 30 steps out of a very large bason, that makes a fine shew from the Hall." It has been altered many times since. In addition, Byron was probably responsible for at least starting the terrace gardens and made what was probably one of the priory's fishponds into the formal square piece of water now known as the "Eagle Pond."[19]

Byron was a landlord of his time, active in running his estates, anxious to acquire property that might help to consolidate the landholdings, looking after the house and grounds, and at the same time worrying about the succession. It was partly because of the succession that he married three times, and it is in the complexity of his domestic arrangements that we can locate the background to events in 1798 when Newstead passed to the sixth Lord Byron. The first marriage was tragically short: in 1703 the fourth lord married Mary, daughter of the third earl of Bridgewater, but she died of smallpox only eleven weeks after the wedding. Her portion was £11,000, although whether it was ever paid is not known.[20] Three years later he married again. His second bride was Lady Frances Williamina Bentinck, daughter of the first earl of Portland. Her portion was £10,000, of which £1,000 was assigned to pay off a mortgage on Bulwell Park, £4,000 went to trustees for the benefit of younger children, and £5,000 went to Byron.[21] The alliance was a significant indication of Byron's social and political standing, since his new father-in-law was a nobleman whose family had come to England with King William III following the Glorious Revolution in 1688, and the Portlands were shortly to be established at Welbeck. Lady Frances died in 1712, leaving Byron with a son, George—born in 1707 while Byron was a gentleman of the bedchamber to Queen Anne's husband, Prince George of Denmark—and a daughter, Frances. Two other sons died in infancy. Byron remained on terms of social intimacy with the family.[22]

Byron married for the third time in 1720, spurred on this time by the need to secure the family inheritance. George, his twelve-year-old heir, died in July that year, and within five months Byron had gone to the altar with Frances, the daughter of Lord William Berkeley. Her portion was £6,000, £2,000 of which went to Byron and £4,000 to trustees as portions for younger children. The jointure, the annual sum payable from the estate to the wife should she outlive her husband, was to be £600. Her father was not particularly flattering about the match, telling a correspondent, "I am going to dispose of one of my daughters to Lord Byron, a disproportionable match as to their ages, but marriages not offering every day, I would not miss an opportunity."[23] Byron was, after all, fifty. However, if the object of the exercise had more to do with children than love, and they must certainly have been a significant consideration, the marriage can be counted a success. A daughter, Isabella, was born eleven months after the wedding, and sons followed: William in 1722, John in 1723, Richard in 1724, Charles in 1726, and George in 1730. Only Charles did not survive infancy, dying in 1731. When the second son, John, was born in November 1723, the duke of Newcastle agreed to stand as godfather.[24] George II stood godfather to the youngest son, George, and gave Byron a present of 110 ounces of gilt plate worth £65 to commemorate the event. Byron was already (from 1729) in receipt of a £1,000 annual pension from the Crown that continued until his death in 1736.

Byron's third marriage provides an opportunity to look at the estate in 1720. After the changes of the seventeenth century Byron's estates were now centered primarily on the manors of Newstead and Hucknall and the surrounding area, with only the manor of Rochdale outside of Nottinghamshire. Apart from the two manors, the Nottinghamshire property included the rectorial tithes and advowson (right of clerical appointment) of Hucknall, the parks of Newstead and Bulwell, and manorial rights over Hucknall, Linby, Newstead, Bulwell, and Papplewick. The property included sixty messuages, a water corn mill, five dovecotes, sixty gardens, twelve hundred acres of land, one thousand acres of meadow, a thousand acres of pastures, a hundred acres of woodland, and five hundred acres of furze and heath. Much of the latter was assart lands and breaks in Sherwood Forest (i.e., lands cleared within the Forest for short-term cultivation). Approximately 1,236 acres lay in Hucknall. In Bulwell, Byron owned an iron forge called Bulwell Forge with related lands in Papplewick, commons, common of pasture, watercourses, and various other rents. The income from the property was £1,242 12s. The Rochdale estate brought in £370, together with a further £290 10s. 10d. from coal and slate pits, fair tolls, commons lettings, copyhold rents and fines, and sundry other sources. In total, Byron's landed income in 1720 was £1,903 2s. Although substantial, this hardly placed him in the first rank of English landowners.[25]

Byron actively built up the estate. Early in 1725 he acquired houses and about 130 acres in Hucknall from John and Francis Barber and Lionel Pogson for £600. In 1728 he inquired unsuccessfully after a lease of Harlow and Lindhurst, two estates on the eastern edge of the Newstead property, and in October 1731 he bought further Hucknall property from Daniel and Elizabeth Harding of Nottingham for £200.[26]

The strict settlement agreed upon in 1720 also helped to determine the succession to the Byron estates during the eighteenth century. Strict settlement, either on marriage or on the coming of age of the heir or by will, or by any combination of these three methods, became common practice among landed families in post-Restoration England. It was a device designed to protect the transmission of property to future generations by restricting the current owner to a life tenancy, with limited powers of disposition, but with specific powers to look after the financial interests of his family. Technically, the estate was "entailed" on future generations in an attempt to

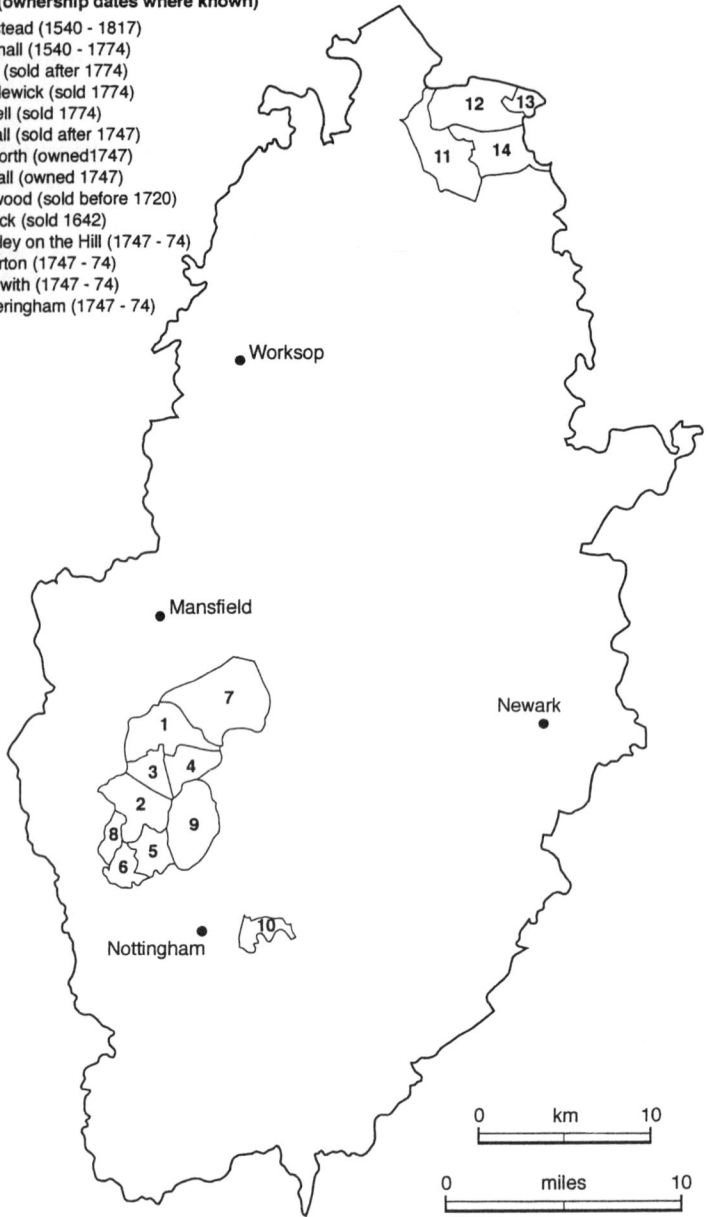

Parishes (ownership dates where known)

1 Newstead (1540 - 1817)
2 Hucknall (1540 - 1774)
3 Linby (sold after 1774)
4 Papplewick (sold 1774)
5 Bulwell (sold 1774)
6 Nuthall (sold after 1747)
7 Blidworth (owned 1747)
8 Watnall (owned 1747)
9 Bestwood (sold before 1720)
10 Colwick (sold 1642)
11 Gringley on the Hill (1747 - 74)
12 Misterton (1747 - 74)
13 Stockwith (1747 - 74)
14 Walkeringham (1747 - 74)

Worksop

Mansfield

Newark

Nottingham

Nottinghamshire Parishes in which the Byrons owned property

prevent its potential dismemberment by a single owner. However, settlement was concerned also with the wider interests of the family. When it took place prior to the marriage of the eldest son, settlement included arrangements for the payment of sums of money to younger children (male or female) of the marriage for their future advancement. It also secured a sum of money, called a jointure, payable annually to the wife during her widowhood, should she outlive her husband. The settlement was secured by the appointment of trustees, whose task it was to ensure that the terms were honored. Under the terms of Byron's 1720 settlement, the trustees' responsibilities related to the use of the £4,000 assigned to the younger children, and the payment of the new Lady Byron's £600 annual jointure entitlement should she outlive her husband.

The 1720 settlement was designed to protect the interests of Byron's new wife; his anticipated, but as yet unborn, children; and Frances, the surviving daughter of his second marriage to Lady Frances Williamina. Frances was nine at the time of the 1720 marriage, but died in 1724 shortly after her thirteenth birthday. Partly as a result, Byron took the opportunity of making a new will on 17 April 1725. In this, while confirming the 1720 marriage settlement—he had no choice in the matter legally—he took the opportunity to grant additional portions totaling £6,000 to his younger children, to be paid from his personal estate. Byron was in fact dividing the portion previously earmarked for Frances among the younger children, born and as yet unborn, of his third marriage. Also in his will he specified that property he had bought in Hucknall, but that was not included in the 1720 marriage settlement, should go with the estate to his eldest son and heir, William.[27] Isabella, born in 1721, subsequently received her portion of £3,600 when in 1743 she married at the age of twenty-two the forty-nine-year-old earl of Carlisle.[28] He died in 1758, and the following year she married Sir William Lawson of Hayton Castle in Cumberland, when she was thirty-eight and he was twenty-two.

Byron's legal arrangements of 1720 and 1725 showed the strengths of the strict settlement as a mechanism designed to ensure the financial fortunes of the family while at the same time maintaining the estate for future generations. As the law stood, land could not be settled in perpetuity, and to achieve continuity of inheritance between generations it was necessary periodically to break the entail and resettle the estates on the next prospective heir. Since, by his third marriage, Byron had several sons who stood to succeed in turn to the estates, no further settlement was needed in his lifetime; indeed, the breaking of the entail and resettlement was not required again until his eldest son married in 1747. Until then the estate was governed by these arrangements; indeed, technically they governed the descent of the estates until the sale of 1817.

How much time Byron spent at Newstead after his third marriage is not known. His new wife disliked the abbey, much preferring to live in London, where from 1707 he had a leased house in Westminster. Why she showed distaste for Newstead is not clear. When one of her friends, Lady North, paid a visit in 1739 she was astonished to find "a glorious fine park, and a fine old house. I am amazed how my Lady could hate it so much." The children were baptized at Newstead by Byron's chaplain, Rev. Thomas Sheppey, but no register was kept "except on a pane of glass belonging to one of the windows of the said Abbey . . . in the handwriting of the said Frances Lady Byron."[29]

It was at Newstead that William, fourth Lord Byron, died on 8 August 1736. He was buried in the family tomb in Hucknall Church on 12 August. Under the terms of the settlements of 1706 and 1720 (on the fourth lord's second and third marriages) and his will of 1725, the estate passed in its entirety to the eldest son of his third marriage, William, who became the fifth Lord Byron. The new owner of Newstead inherited an estate yielding approximately £2,000 a year net, as well as his father's liquid assets: £14,588 8s. 7½d. in ready money, securities, rent arrears, stock in the public funds, and other goods and chattels. From this he had to meet funeral and other expenses, as well as the education and maintenance of his younger brothers. By 1740 these debits had amounted to £4,316 18s. 11d., leaving a balance of £10,271 9s. 8½d.[30] It was an estate well in credit.

By the time the fourth Lord Byron died, the Byrons had been at Newstead for two hundred years. They had rebuilt and extended the house. For a long time their interests had been divided between Lancashire and Nottinghamshire, with some debate as to where they might locate their chief seat. After the difficulties of the 1640s and 1650s the family reemerged if not unscathed, certainly not permanently damaged. With a peerage, and with most of their estates recovered, the Byrons enjoyed a period of stability in the post-Restoration years under the careful guidance of the third and fourth Lords Byron. For centuries they had played the role of landed gentlemen, as justices of the peace, occasionally as M.P.s, and as sheriff of the county. Their estates were not sufficiently sizable to put the family into the first rank of the English aristocracy, and the fourth Lord Byron played no major political role that might have implied a search for promotion in the peerage. Yet he was the head of a long-established, wealthy aristocratic family, with a secured succession, a modernized house, a fashionable garden, and a debt-free estate—except necessarily for the unpaid portions of the younger children. The family fortunes seemed well set in 1736.

2

William, Fifth Lord Byron:
Landowning Aristocrat, 1743–70

On 26 January 1765 William, fifth Lord Byron, was dining at the Star and Garter Tavern on Pall Mall with a group of Nottinghamshire gentlemen. Such events took place regularly when Parliament was in session, but on this occasion the evening turned sour. Byron was sitting close to his neighbor and kinsman, William Chaworth of Annesley Hall, and an argument broke out about the best way of preserving game in west Nottinghamshire. As tempers rose, Chaworth said something that Byron interpreted as a veiled challenge. Subsequently the two men agreed to fight a duel. Contests of this sort were not uncommon among aristocrats who felt their honor had been impugned. Against their better judgment, the two men entered an empty room lit only by candles. In the gloom Byron ran Chaworth through the stomach, a wound from which he died the following day. The coroner returned a verdict of willful murder, and Byron was sent to the Tower of London. By claiming his rank as a peer he was entitled to trial before the House of Lords, and his fellow noblemen assembled in Westminster Hall on 16 April to hear the case. Byron admitted to the irregularity of fighting a duel in a dimly lit room, but he defended himself in terms of Chaworth's provocation and the fairness of the combat. After two days 119 peers found him guilty of manslaughter, and 4 voted him not guilty. He was released, since, on account of his rank, he was excused punishment for manslaughter.[1]

The bloody events of 1765 are not in question, but what happened next is a matter of contention. Byron became the subject of stories that grew into a legend that after the duel he was ostracized by society in London and Nottinghamshire alike, hated and feared by tenants and neighbors and, by now in financial difficulties, forced to live as a recluse at Newstead for the last thirty years of his life. In reality this was an exaggeration. As the sixth Lord Byron told a correspondent in 1823, his great-uncle had not retired from the world after the duel in 1765, but after his son offended him by marrying "contrary to his duty." Unfortunately this was a barbed defense, for in attempting to exonerate his great-uncle on one score he introduced a further complication in respect to his son's marriage, which was equally unfounded. By 1830 the myth was growing: in his biography of the poet Thomas Moore rehearsed in print a string of tales, among them the fifth lord's supposed conduct in pushing his wife into a pond and shooting dead a coachman.[2] Washington Irving, visiting Newstead in 1835, was captivated by such stories, and wrote of how Byron "retired after this to the Abbey, where he shut himself up to brood over his disgraces; grew gloomy, morose, and fantastical, and indulged in fits of passion and caprice that made him the theme of rural wonder and scandal." Nor was Irving content to leave it at that:

> [I]t was said that he always went armed, as if prepared to commit murder on the least provocation. At one time, when a gentleman of his neighbourhood was to dine tete-a-tete with him, it is said a brace of pistols were gravely laid with the knives and forks upon the table, as part of the regular table furniture, and implements that might be needed in the course of the repast. Another rumour states, that, being exasperated at his coachman for disobedience to orders, he shot him on the spot, threw his body into the coach where Lady Byron was seated, and, mounting the box, officiated in his stead. At another time, according to the same vulgar rumours, he threw her ladyship into the lake in front of the Abbey, where she would have been drowned but for the timely aid of the gardener.

Irving added that "these stories are doubtless exaggerations of trivial incidents which may have occurred," but simply by repeating them in print he was helping to perpetuate the myth.[3]

There were attempts, even among contemporaries, to correct the record, notably the publication in 1847 of a ballad entitled "Devil Byron" together with a memoir by Luke Adams, who had been for many years a forgeman in the charcoal bloomery at Newstead. His view was said to "differ from the received and accredited one. 'Devil Byron' appears to have been, on the whole, rather a kind man. His rich neighbours sneered at him because he was poor, and hated him because the poor loved him." Adams, so the account went, believed the duel had begun because Chaworth was in the habit of calling Byron "a poor little lord." This defense of Byron was little regarded.[4] The "official" record repeats the usual stories. According to the *Complete Peerage*, Byron "encumbered his estate, sold the property at Rochdale, co. Lancaster, together with the family pictures, and completely dismantled the mansion at Newstead, and was known as 'the wicked Lord.'" The *Dictionary of National Biography* notes that after the 1765 trial, "he lived in seclusion at Newstead Abbey, ill-treated his wife, was known as the 'wicked lord,' encumbered his estates, and made a sale of his property at Rochdale, the disputed legality of which led to a prolonged lawsuit."[5]

Modern biographers of the poet have restated in one form or another the legends surrounding the fifth lord. André Maurois, in the 1930s, repeated the same salacious details and concluded that "his pleasures were those of a mischievous child."[6] Leslie Marchand wrote of how, "during his later years of seclusion, when fantastic popular legends grew out of the common gossip about the 'Wicked Lord,'" he took part in "unspeakable orgies"; and "he always carried pistols, and it was reported on one occasion that when his neighbour Sir John Warren came to dine he found them placed on the table as if they were a customary part of the dinner service."[7] Elizabeth Longford concluded that "though the House of Lords acquitted him, he lived henceforth as a scandalous recluse at Newstead Abbey."[8] According to Phyllis Grosskurth, "the Wicked Lord epitomised the profligacy and irresponsibility of the Byrons . . . he neglected the property but held lavish parties. . . . He kept the sword with which he had killed Chaworth in his bedroom at the abbey."[9] Even the current guidebook to the abbey is not immune to exaggeration, claiming that the fifth lord exercised "wilful neglect of the house and grounds, in a deliberate act to ruin the inheritance of his son, who married against his father's will."

Such stories have been recycled many times and, like all myths, include an element of truth. Yet they contain contradictions that have seldom been fully investigated. Why, for example, if Byron was in such financial difficulties, did he not simply sell up rather than live in the Newstead kitchens in poverty? We have to try to understand the constraints that governed Byron's life if we are to disentangle the man from his myth. His financial difficulties were certainly not mythical, but Byron's alleged depravities are often cited as evidence that his great-nephew, the poet, inherited an estate that was heavily indebted, badly run, and a serious encumbrance rather than a source of wealth. We shall return to these accusations later, but first we are concerned with establishing what sort of a man William, fifth Lord Byron, really was, whether his reputation was deserved, and how he ran the family estates. In this chapter we shall look at the years up to about 1770, and in chapter 3 at the period when, supposedly, he shut himself away at Newstead and deliberately ruined the estate. As we shall see, 1770 was an important date in this story.

I

William Byron was fourteen years old when his father, the fourth Baron Byron, died in 1736. He had been at Westminster School for the previous four years, but his life, together with that of his younger siblings, was to be severely disturbed by the loss of his father. The school holidays spent pleasantly at Newstead came to an abrupt end when in September 1738 Lady Byron let the house to George Bowes of Streatham Castle, County Durham, for five years at an annual rent of £200.[10] That year she removed William Byron from Westminster School and dispatched him into the Navy, where he was appointed a lieutenant on H.M.S. *Falkland* in May 1738. This was a strange move. A young man of Byron's standing could have been expected to proceed from a public school to one of the universities, and perhaps then to undertake the Grand Tour before returning to take up his inheritance when he came of age. In the circumstances a profession was unusual, and a commission in the navy rather than the army even more unexpected. While there were certainly naval peers in the eighteenth century, serving officers were more likely to be the younger sons of aristocratic families who needed to find a career. This was not William Byron's situation.

If this move disturbed the young lord, worse was to follow. In 1740 his widowed mother married Sir Thomas Hay of Alderston, East Lothian. Whatever her personal happiness, the impact on her children was considerable due to the arrangements for their upbringing laid down by their late father. The fourth Lord Byron's will of 1725 made clear and careful provision for his young family. At the age of fifty-five Byron doubtless recognized that he might not live to see them all into adulthood, and he made specific provision for a guardianship should he die before the children came of age. He named three guardians: his wife; her father, Lord William Berkeley, baron of Stratton; and the duke of Kingston, a landed Nottinghamshire neighbor at Thoresby. Kingston died in 1726, and, since he was not replaced, only two of the nominated guardians were available in 1736. That was not in itself a problem, but the subclause in Byron's will was rather more draconian. He stipulated that if his widow remarried while the children remained underage, she was to forfeit her guardianship, and the task would pass to the other named guardians. Naturally this precipitated something of a crisis when Lady Byron remarried, since at least in theory her father should have taken over from her the responsibility for the children. Sensing that such a position was untenable, he refused to act.

The result was an almighty family row, which ended up before the courts. William Byron was eighteen, and so still a minor in 1740, but he clearly considered himself ready and able to take responsibility for the property. He accused his mother of refusing to provide him with information about rents and profits on the estate—a charge that she denied—and his grandfather of failing to act to secure his rights, and those of his sister and younger brothers. Technically he was a ward of court until the age of twenty-one because the Court of Chancery was responsible for his welfare as a minor, but Byron was clearly unhappy with the existing situation. A bill of complaint was filed in Chancery on behalf of the children by their uncle, the Honorable John Berkeley, in an attempt to sort out what was becoming a bitter row. The court ordered that an inventory should be drawn up of all moveable goods and chattels at Newstead that were the inheritance of the fifth lord, and over which neither Lady Byron nor her new husband were to exercise any control. In his will the fourth lord had specifically bequeathed the household goods, furniture, and pictures at Newstead to such of his sons as should be for the time being entitled to the house "to the intent the same might go as heirlooms for the benefit of his heir male." Hay and Lady Byron were to recognize that the goods mentioned were the rightful property of the fifth lord at his coming of age, and that they had no power of sale.[11]

It was a messy business, and lurking behind these legal maneuvers was family discord, brought on no doubt by a combination of disapproval among the children of their mother's remarriage and her apparent haste in sending William and his brother John as far away as possible. John, the second son, also went to sea and was shipwrecked in South America on his first long voyage in 1741. William Byron spent the rest of his minority at sea, and only his younger brother Richard (1724–1811) pursued a conventional aristocratic course by going to Oxford. He later entered the Church of England, a favored profession for the younger sons of aristocrats. This was after William had come of age in 1743, the year that also saw his sister married and Newstead recovered when the Bowes lease came to an end. Byron left the navy in 1744 and began a new life as a landed aristocrat.

When not at sea William Byron already enjoyed the reputation of a man-about-town. He was a most eligible bachelor within the aristocratic marriage ranks even if, by one account, he could boast of little but a title and "an agreeable face."[12] He regularly bet on horse races, and he probably attracted numerous hangers-on as he sought to make a reputation for himself in London society by spending more than his estates were earning. We do not know precisely what the estate was yielding in 1743. It was probably about £2,000 net, but this was not enough to feed Byron's habits. Besides which, it was not all his to spend. From 1736 the estate had to fund his mother's jointure payments of £600 a year, and from 1743 it was responsible for funding his sister Isabella's portion on her marriage. Funds had also to be found for the maintenance of Byron's younger brothers, and the payment of their portions. By 1747 these had cost Byron £6,845 (John £2,977, including a legacy from his aunt Juliana payable from the estate, Richard £1,931, and George £1,937).[13] Outflows were soon outpacing income, and Byron's father's liquid assets rapidly disappeared. Byron was soon in difficulties, but he had few means of raising additional money. He had inherited a strictly settled estate, subject to the marriage settlements of 1706 and 1720 and his father's will of 1725. He had no powers to sell property, or even to raise money on a mortgage.

If his father had still been alive when Byron came of age, a resettlement of the estate could have been anticipated, designed to protect the property into the future while in the meantime affording William the opportunity of escaping the pecuniary embarrassments into which he had already run. But his father was dead, and Byron had instead to exercise powers available to him as tenant-in-tail under his father's marriage settlements to suffer a "common recovery." This was a legal device to break the entail on his estate and give him restricted powers over the property. Legally he was tenant-in-tail, in other words the owner of the property subject to the settlements of 1706 and 1720 and the will of 1725. He was not free to sell any of the property, and he had to meet unavoidable outflows in relation to portions and jointures. However, by suffering a common recovery (to use the legal language) in November 1743, he was able to raise a mortgage on the estate. He used these powers to borrow £2,000 from Barnaby Backwell, a London banker, on a mortgage secured on the property. Backwell increased the loan by a further £700 in May 1745.[14]

Byron's legal position changed again when in 1747 he became engaged to Elizabeth Shaw, the eighteen-year-old heiress of the late Charles Shaw of Besthorpe Hall in Norfolk. Miss Shaw had inherited from her late father estates in the Norfolk manors of Besthorpe, Plashinghall, Pages, Bridghams, and Curzons, with related property, yielding £624 net annually; Tibenham, which brought in about £300 annually but which was currently assigned to her widowed mother as her jointure estate; part of the manor of Stretham, Cambridgeshire, worth £115 a year; part of the manors of Wymondham and East Dereham, yielding £125 annually, but held on a ninety-nine-year lease expiring in 1765; and the manor of Gringley in Nottinghamshire, with related estates at Misterton, Walkeringham, and Stockwith worth about £580 annually, from which court expenses and a fee farm rent had to be met. Altogether the property yielded around £1,750.[15] It was an excellent match for Byron, but Miss Shaw was a minor. Her guardians, responsible for their actions to Chancery, expected a settlement of both her property and Byron's. Since she was under twenty-one, resettlement could be brought about only by an act of Parliament, and the required legislation was passed in the spring of 1747. Both Byron's property, and his fiancée's estates, were settled on the putative eldest son of the marriage, and the trustees appointed to oversee the settlement were the earl of Carlisle (Byron's brother-in-law) and Lord Berkeley, his mother's brother.[16]

Once the lawyers had completed their negotiations, the couple were married at Miss Shaw's London house in Albemarle Street, by the rector of Linby, on 28 March 1747.[17] Four children arrived in rapid succession. The eldest, William, born in June 1748, died in May 1749. Five months later another son was born, also christened William. Henrietta born in 1751 and Caroline in 1755 completed the family.

II

William, Lord Byron, was an aristocrat, and unless they had fallen on particularly hard times English aristocrats did not normally run their estates personally. Few had any formal training in estate management. During school holidays they might ride round the estate with the steward, and after their coming of age they often took control of an outlying property, as was the case with the third and fourth Lords Byron. Even so, they had far too many roles to play to be concerned purely with the minutiae of rents and leases. The task could be, and usually was, devolved to a steward, whose job was to collect the rents, negotiate leases, ensure the good husbandry and running of the estate, look after the great house, and generally act as a man of business, ultimately with the responsibility of raising the money to support the owner's lifestyle. Thus released, the landowner was free to come and go between his country seat and his London house as and when he pleased, to participate in the legislative process if, like Byron, he automatically commanded a seat in the House of Lords—although Byron was an irregular attender at the House—and to enjoy the delights of the London season, the society of Bath, or any of a multitude of alternative pursuits that he might choose.

The fifth Lord Byron was no exception, although since his father died when he was fourteen and Newstead was subsequently let he must have had less opportunity than most of his contemporaries to learn the business of estate management. We know little of how Newstead was managed in the first decade or so after Byron came of age, but the position is much clearer after 1754, when William Daws was appointed steward, a post he held until his death in 1794. Daws was typical of his genre. He was entrusted with overall responsibility for all the estates, but his primary role was in regard to Newstead. He had to keep the house and property in good order. "I would have you send in a brewing of malt," Byron told him at the beginning of December 1763, "I hope to be down at Newstead next week." Similarly, in May 1768 Byron wrote to tell him, "I propose being at Newstead on Monday 6th [June] when you go to Newstead I would have you tell Clayton [the housekeeper] that she may expect a letter from me on

Thursday or Friday next." Daws was also responsible for finding and supervising the tenants, for collecting the rents, ensuring that husbandry covenants in leases were adhered to, and protecting Byron's game at Newstead.[18]

Freed from the burden of everyday responsibility at Newstead, and
buoyed up by the additional income from his wife's inheritance, Byron, his
wife, and his young children were able to move easily in London aristocratic circles, retiring to Newstead for the summer months. Once in
Nottinghamshire he took a particular interest in the abbey, and he was a
man of sensitive tastes. Through the 1740s and 1750s he was adding to his
father's collection of paintings, and he also spent considerable sums acquiring new marble fireplaces, one of which is still in the Great Dining
Room (the Salon) and one in the north gallery. Joe Murray, born about
1737, who lived at Newstead intermittently for sixty years, recalled that
"whenever there were any very rare and costly articles of virtu or art on
sale in London, [he] would order horses to his carriage and set out at a
moment's notice to purchase them." Since the frequently critical Horace
Walpole was "delighted" by Newstead, and particularly by the "very good
collection of pictures," Byron clearly knew what he was doing.[19] Viscount
Grimston, visiting in 1768, also commented on "the very fine collection of
paintings," adding that he admired "the taste that is shewn in placing them
to the greatest advantage."[20] According to Arthur Young, visiting in 1771,
among the artists hung at Newstead were Rubens, Canaletti, Holbein,
Raphael, Van Dyke, and Titian.[21]

Byron was even more active in the grounds. In 1749 he built two forts
near the Upper Lake. One, subsequently known as Folly Castle, had the
date carved over the porch. It stood on a hill to the west of the water, and
was demolished only in 1921. The second, a smaller construction known
as the Battery, was on the western shore, and is clearly shown on an eigh-
teenth-century east view of Newstead. In 1756 Byron began enlarging the
park and the Upper Lake, and he made a lower or Sherwood lake at the
southern end of the park. He reshaped the Upper Lake and masked the
kennels and stables on the east bank with a Gothic castle facade. The forts,
all of which had gun emplacements, were used for mock naval battles. "A
twenty gun ship," Arthur Young noted, "and several yachts and boats lying
at anchor, throw an air of most pleasing cheerfulness over the whole scene."[22]
Parties and concerts were also held in the forts. On his lower lake Byron
made an artificial island with a tower, described in the 1790s as "a kind of
conic ruin," and he may have considered, but been unable to afford, a third
lake where one was later built in the nineteenth century.[23] His naval career
had obviously had a lasting impact. Joe Murray, who had been a cabin boy
when very young and who first appears in the Newstead accounts in 1755
as "the sailor boy," "fancied himself a bit of a sailor [and] had charge of all

Newstead, in Nottinghamshire, the Seat of Lord Byron, **engraved by T. Milton after Paul Sandby, published 1 November 1780 by G. Kearsly. The picture shows the fifth Lord Byron's fortifications on the lakes at Newstead. (Nottingham City Museums and Art Galleries [Newstead Abbey].)**

the pleasure-boats on the lake." Contemporaries found much to admire in Byron's water developments, and years later the poet vividly recalled them in *Don Juan:*

> Before the mansion lay a lucid lake,
> Broad as transparent, deep and freshly fed,
> By a river which its softened way did take
> In currents through the calmer water spread
> Around; the wild fowl nestled in the brake
> And sedges, brooding in their liquid bed;
> The woods sloped downwards to its brink, and stood
> With their green faces fix'd upon the flood.[24]

Byron took an active interest in the management of his estates. "When you go to Nottingham," he told Daws in July 1766, "I would have you ask Mr Evans if he received my letter, in your next I would have you inform me who has been at Newstead, you dont mention whether Mr Stanley has finished the gutters on the kitchen roof, I hope by this you have got most of the hay." Two years later he wanted "to know if you have the old Lancashire lease by you, if you have it must be sent to town for the new one cant be made out until they have seen that." In the severe winter of 1768–69 he had Newstead in mind when he asked Daws: "If you have as hard a frost in the country as we have in town, I would have you tell J. Lee to get out the dung and lead some rocks and stone from the quarry, and in your next let me know what has been done since I have been gone."[25]

When at Newstead, Byron would meet with the tenants to discuss farming conditions. In 1761 he let to Thomas Beardall a farm of 111 acres for a rent of £30, but in 1771 he proposed to double the rent and to remove the right to turn sheep out into unenclosed forest land. Many years later Beardall's granddaughter recalled that "this was more than could be borne at once and my grandfather determined to say so to Lord Byron himself and try to get a reduction." Beardall arranged an interview with Byron and Daws:

> The Byrons were always reckoned good Landlords, friendly with their tenants and willing to redress grievances. Mr Daws of Hucknall was steward at that time and with Lord Byron when my grandfather went to speak to him. Having stated his grievances he told his Lordship he should be unable to pay it if they took the forest right away, and hoped if he did he would take £10 off the rent. Lord Byron asked Mr Daws what he thought would be right he said, "I think 7 my Lord." Well then it shall be so Beardall if I take the forest away, probably I shall take seven pounds from the rent. And he did take the forest in, and they paid £23 many years.

Byron reduced the rent and let to Leonard Halley, a Papplewick timber merchant, the rights to over 550 acres of timber in the forest for twenty-one years at £35 annual rent. Beardall was still paying £23 in 1776, but the lease was renewed in 1781 for £50. "This friendly bearing on the part of the landlord," added Beardall's granddaughter, was reciprocated with "devotion on the part of the tenant."[26]

Byron and Daws regularly discussed business either at Newstead, or on one of Daws's frequent visits to London, and when they were apart Daws was under orders to write frequently in order to keep his employer up to date with estate matters. Byron was an infrequent visitor to his other properties, although he was at Rochdale in 1756 and 1766, and at Gringley (about thirty miles from Newstead) in May 1765, where he and Daws met to look over affairs.[27] Daws was entrusted with overall control of all the estates, and consequently he was a more frequent visitor, particularly to Lancashire and Norfolk. He often visited Norfolk in the spring to be present in person to receive the rents, settle any lease difficulties, and to attend to other estate matters. In late spring or early summer he would visit Rochdale. In June 1766 he was in Rochdale "to let coal mines," and from there he traveled to Norfolk to give the tenants notice to quit, and to negotiate terms with new tenants. Other visits included Norfolk in November 1767 to value timber, Rochdale in April 1769 to sort out errors in the accounts, and Gringley in August 1772 to oversee a valuation. Some visits were of considerable duration. In June 1761 he went to Rochdale to sell wood and coal, and to oversee some land surveying. He was "obliged to stay there a long time," with consequent expenses of £4.[28] In March and November 1769 he was away from home for more than three weeks, on each occasion visiting Norfolk and then traveling to London for discussions with Byron. In between he visited Rochdale, where he was requested in advance to "order your affairs before you come in such a manner as to stay 4 or 5 days." The local bailiff wanted him to "make my house the place of your residence whilst you are here then we can do our business more privately and more properly than we can at any other place." Daws was eight weeks between Rochdale and London in the spring of 1777, and nine weeks on the same route in July 1780.[29] The London visits were normally designed to update Byron on estate affairs, to present accounts, and to have papers signed.

Daws could not be everywhere at the same time, and Byron, like many landowners in a similar position, appointed local solicitors to supervise the everyday running of the outlying properties on a part-time basis. This practice was universally condemned by agriculturalists and just as widely indulged by landowners. Lawyers were accused of knowing nothing useful about agriculture, and therefore of being unable to supervise the tenants adequately. Against this drawback, they were men of education and frequently men of some standing in the community, who would therefore command respect; and they had all the necessary qualifications for dealing with legal matters such as drawing up leases and holding manor courts. They also worked on a contract basis, charging only for the time spent on the activities of a particular estate, and so relieving the owner of the additional burden of a full-time steward, or of employing for the purpose one of the existing tenant farmers. For Daws, the major frustration was that these men were not wholly committed to Byron's interests, and he might find letters were unanswered for days or even weeks as the agent went about his other business. Joseph Smallwood, the local agent at Rochdale, was a particular offender in this respect, but early in 1772 it became apparent that all his business affairs were in a mess, and he himself was unable to carry on. His son-in-law, James Holland, temporarily took over the agency, and in April was awaiting Smallwood's assignment of all his interests, "and I shall then be able to give a due and uninterrupted attention to his Lordship's concerns and that of others with whom I am entrusted. . . . In a post or two I expect you'll have my father's formal resignation to me, and in hopes of his Lordship's acceptation." Smallwood died in June, and Holland was appointed as his replacement. Ironically, he then complained of the difficulty he found in sorting out Smallwood's affairs because of the length of time Daws took to reply to his letters. However, he retained the position until 1782.[30] Daws also corresponded with lawyers and agents acting on Byron's behalf in London. In May 1766 Brackley Kennett, Byron's banker, wrote to Daws from Pall Mall to say that he had now settled last year's accounts with Lord Byron, "who at that time drew on you for £500," which he thought Daws would like notice of.[31] Daws would doubtless have liked notice somewhat earlier.

Isaac Spratt, attorney-at-law, was the man entrusted with running the Norfolk estates in the 1760s. He died suddenly in December 1768, and within a few days Daws had received letters from two other local lawyers offering their services and stating their credentials for this type of work. Daws favored John Edwards of Norwich, but the other serious candidate, Peter Stoughton of Wymondham, tipped the scales with Byron by offering the by now increasingly impoverished peer an advance of £1,000, "providing his Lordship will be pleased to do anything for me respecting the stewardship of the courts." This was agreed to in May 1769, and Stoughton advanced a further £500 in 1770. He was appointed to the stewardship on a salary of £2, although this covered only rent collecting. Edwards rather ruefully reflected that the post had been filled according to financial criteria rather than ability or track record.[32]

Occasionally the Norfolk and Lancashire stewards may have visited Newstead; certainly Smallwood was at Newstead in the autumn of 1768.[33]

III

Daws's overall control of the estates gave him a range of responsibilities that went well beyond the everyday business of letting farms. Newstead lay on poor-quality sandy soils, and it was not especially profitable. During the fifth Lord Byron's minority, farms were let in such a way that the leases would come to an end when he reached twenty-one. In 1737 Lady Byron, as guardian, let Wire Mill Farm to John Hardstaff for six years from 1738. The rent was set at £58 4s. and a wagon load of coal containing fifty hundredweight, which was to be delivered annually to the abbey. The farm was mainly for grazing, since Hardstaff agreed to pay £5 an acre for any land converted to tillage. Once Byron came of age in 1743 the farm was leased to Hardstaff on a twenty-one-year lease; he subsequently renewed the lease in 1764, again for twenty-one years, but this time at £60 per annum. The farm was of one hundred acres, and the lease included stone quarries and the rights to sell stone and to burn and sell lime. Hardstaff was also permitted to search for iron stone. By 1776 the tenancy had passed to George Hardstaff.[34]

Byron preferred twenty-one-year tenancies. The usual terms enjoined the tenant to use all manure on the land, to keep the property in adequate repair, and to carry a load of coal annually to the abbey. Tenants were also expected to keep a hound for the use of Lord Byron when he was hunting in Sherwood Forest. They were usually allowed to plow small areas of land (breaks) for a number of years before returning them to grass. Soil quality was such that the arable rotations of the Trent Valley were inappropriate in the Forest, but once the land had been cropped for the allotted period it had to be laid down for grazing to hay, with rye grass seeds, usually in the last three years of the lease. Sometimes a £5 penalty was stipulated for any land broken for tillage in the last three years of the lease. Timber and coal were usually reserved to Byron.

Other issues also claimed Daws's time. In Nottinghamshire he was confronted with a long-running issue, the enclosure of Gringley. This estate was part of Byron's inheritance at his marriage, and Daws was involved with negotiations over the enclosure of the joint commons of Gringley, West Stockwith, and Misterton. The enclosure proposals were under discussion in 1768. Charles Slater, one of the Gringley tenants, was commissioned to keep a watching brief.[35] He was concerned that Byron would receive "no more common than they think proper to allot us," which he believed would not be an equal share, and "we to be at half expense of the whole . . . they say they will solicit my Lord about it, not doubting my Lord will come into everything suitable to these conveniences."[36] Discussions went on through 1769, but on Daws's advice Byron opposed enclosure of the common, "so that their present plan is only to enclose the open fields and meadows of Misterton, and the North Carr between Misterton and Stockwith, that being a piece of good land worth enclosing, whereas they apprehend the West Carr will not answer their purpose without a general expensive drainage." Robert Gross visited Byron in London early in 1771 to put the case for enclosing Gringley, "as I thought it would be to the advantage of all the proprietors," but in the end only the Misterton commons scheme went through, as a result of Byron's refusal to entertain the wider scheme.[37]

While the enclosure issue was under discussion, in December 1770 Daws was warned by Charles Slater that the promotion was underway of a canal from Chesterfield to the River Trent to link the ironworks of Chesterfield through Retford to the river. This was being opposed by many of the landowners along the proposed course. Since if it went ahead the canal would "affect his Lordship's properties as much if not more than any gentleman from Chesterfield down to the River Trent," Daws was urged to attend a meeting of the landowners at Worksop on 20 December. Daws turned up to voice Byron's opposition. Proponents of the scheme insisted that Byron had been misled by his tenants in the area, who were "afraid of anything being done that may be likely to inform their Lord the real value of his estates . . . but I am sure his Lordship knows better than to believe it as it is very certain that it will be the means of advancing in value all estates through and near which it goes." Byron's financial instincts were clearly well known! Once the bill passed, Byron's anxiety moved to the question of when his land would be cut through, and the compensation he could expect.[38]

The key issues at Rochdale were enclosure and coal mining. As lord of the manor, Byron enjoyed rights over the commons and waste, as well as the minerals beneath the land. Both "rights" were a source of difficulty to him. The enclosure of Rochdale commons was being actively considered in 1767. This was controversial because large numbers of squatters had established residence, and they stood to lose their common rights. Initially, Daws wanted Smallwood, the local agent, to try to persuade the squatters to come to some sort of arrangement with Byron, but this was an impossible commission. As Smallwood told Daws in June 1767, "I cannot get them to come to any terms for payment of any rent at all, I think therefore it will be proper to serve them with ejectments." At the same time, in preparation for the enclosure, he placed an advertisement in several Manchester newspapers asserting Lord Byron's rights to several unenclosed parcels of land in the manor assigned to him in the inquisition postmortem taken in the reign of Charles I. The local freeholders immediately combined to mount a challenge to Byron's claim to sole rights over the commons. In October 1767 Smallwood warned Daws that "as soon as the enclosure is attempted the freeholders will engage the best counsel."[39]

Byron decided to go ahead in defiance of the freeholders. The plan was for Smallwood to make all the necessary arrangements, by hiring workmen and buying fencing ready to commence work in the spring of 1768. On 25 March 1768 he was ready, and once the weather improved "the inclosure shall be made very soon though I expect it will soon be pulled down but of this I shall immediately acquaint you in case anything of this nature happens." William Chaworth of Goxal told Daws on 21 June that he, like most of the freeholders, was agreeable to the intended enclosure, but was worried about the consequences for the squatters:

> I wish I could offer a proposal that would meet with his Lordships and the freeholders approbation, viz. to set apart some of the ground for the poor industrious labourers, stockingers, and others that are not chargeable to the

parish, for a cow, some few sheep and geese, that by this small advantage they may be enabled to support themselves and families. The farmers, as well as the poor who receive pay from the parish, to be excluded from eating the herbage, or having anything to do with the piece appropriated as above.[40]

It took many months to complete the work, and by the time Smallwood's men reached Crankashaw—where Byron claimed one-third of the common and waste—in September 1768, he was expecting trouble: "I am afraid Mr Entwhistle will be very turbulent with the workmen but I will attend them as much as I can." He feared that once the rails were erected "the freeholders will bring actions against the workmen for breaking up the ground or they will pull the rails down when they are put up." He had retained counsel just in case. By early December he was pushing ahead with the enclosure: "I have got everything ready for that purpose except carriage of rails . . . which I intend to do in a week or 10 days time and to have the enclosure then directly made; Mr Entwhistle will be very rude with me, I am very certain, but that shall not retard me." On Christmas Eve 1768 he reported that the enclosure would be completed in a few days, and by mid-January it was finished: "[T]he workmen met with no interruption only young Mr Entwhistle once told them that neither I nor they had any business there."[41]

Smallwood was not convinced this would be the end of the matter. He told Daws in March 1769 that the enclosure stood "at present unmolested," and when a rail or two had been pulled down three weeks earlier he had simply ordered it to be replaced. However, by July 1769 he was reporting "a deal of disturbance by person or persons that cant be discovered, though the workmen is there both late at night and early in the morning. I am told Mr Entwhistle did pull some rails down himself." In September the problems were still continuing: the fencing had "met with very much obstruction by persons at present unknown, but it is now very nearly completed, but I am afraid it will be soon afterwards demolished. I am of opinion that Lord Byron's right to the Commons which he claims in this manor will never be perfectly established without an Act of Parliament and this I would have his Lordship seriously to consider of." The seventeenth-century inquisition was not, in Smallwood's opinion, sufficient evidence of ownership, and Byron would be well advised to obtain legislation to confirm his position. His hope was that Byron and the freeholders would collaborate not just to establish Byron's rights but also "to have the residuum of the Commons to be divided agreeable to their several interests therein in a proportionable manner."[42]

Similarly important to Byron's financial interests were the coal mines at Rochdale. The fact that they presented a problem first became apparent in February 1766 when Smallwood warned Daws that the leases of Brownwardle and Wallnook mines would expire at midsummer, and that in his view both might be relet at a considerably increased rent. He advertised the mine leases in the local press, only to fall foul of Mr. Simon Dearden, who "insisted on a contract with Lomax being fulfilled. He produced me his accounts by which it appears that the Brownwardle mine is [leased] to him [for] £65. He is willing to give up the old rent of £14 in hand for the term of twenty-one years to come, and so have Lomax's agreement cancelled. I could have set the Wallnook Coalpit had not this agreement stood in the way, so please let me know how I am to act in this article." Daws traveled to Rochdale to try to sort things out, but he evidently failed, because only a few days after his return to Newstead Dearden complained to him about Byron's apparent unwillingness to honor this contract, which in his view was an insult to the poor widow and her fatherless children, "and you know that I am considerably out of pocket."[43]

Daws was unmoved, and Smallwood was told to give notice to Dearden and to accept an offer for the mines from John Scott. Dearden was, not unnaturally, upset: "Mr Dearden was surprised at the notice given him, and said he would not give up the mines and would insist upon the articles which Lomax made with Lord Byron being fully complied with in every respect. He will write to you." Smallwood added that he would "demand possession of the mines by 24 June, even if this meant resorting to the legal mechanism of an ejectment." Dearden was not yet finished. On 28 July 1766 he wrote again to Daws asking to be allowed to retain the lease of the Rochdale mines with Widow Lomax. He had, he insisted, invested large sums of money in the pits for little reward, and he hinted at taking legal action to force Byron to honor the terms of the lease.[44]

All these negotiations fell to Daws, whether it was letting farms or sorting out the problems associated with coal mine leases, and of course he was expected to do more than simply manage properties. A poacher caught during the Christmas holidays in 1766 had his dog and gun confiscated. His employer, John Corden of Eastwood, wrote on his behalf to Daws. Godber, the man involved, was no common poacher; rather, he had been lent the gun and dog "to gather in a little money for us but I did not know he was going as far as your liberty or he should not have had either."[45]

IV

The purpose of a landed estate, as far as the aristocratic owner was concerned, was to provide him with an income sufficient to his needs. Byron had a substantial financial appetite that seems never to have been satisfied by the income from his scattered properties. But what was that income, and how was it derived? The full extent of the Byron estates can be established at the time of Byron's marriage in 1747. In Nottinghamshire the property consisted of Newstead (including the park and abbey, forest and mill), the manor of Hucknall, Bulwell Wood with the park and forge, Linby, Papplewick, Blidworth, Watnall, Nuthall, and Gringley. In Lancashire all the property was within the manor of Rochdale, and in East Anglia it was centered on East Dereham, Wymondham and Besthorpe in Norfolk, and Stretham in Cambridgeshire.

Unfortunately we have no ledgers or estate accounts from which income and expenditure on the various properties can be assessed, although an incomplete set of cash books kept by Daws provides a flavor of the expenditures of the estate, including payments for taxation, outrents, and estate expenses, together with incidental costs such as the wages of blacksmiths and gardeners, the costs of fence mending, butchers' bills, and bills for oats and butter, coal and even crayfish. Daws's traveling expenses, and the regular remittances to Byron, also feature prominently. Other recorded payments, the necessary expenses of landownership, included repairs to the chancel of Hucknall Church, which was Byron's responsibility until he sold the advowson in 1774.[46]

When, from the various disjointed accounts, we try to piece together an idea of Byron's actual income, the nearest we can come to a complete set of figures is for 1766. In that year the income from Newstead was £1,165 gross, and Gringley £593 (£507 net). Gringley was let partly on 21-year tenancies bringing in £394 annually, and partly on at-will tenancies which boosted the rental income to £538 in 1774.[47] After 1767 most of the income was assigned to Charles Gould. Income from East Anglia in 1766 was £412 net. In 1747 the Norfolk rental was calculated at £900, with Stretham producing a further £115. Only net income figures survive in Daws's account books. In 1765 the totals were £442 from Norfolk with another £58 from Stretham, and in 1766 £359 and £53, respectively. Nothing was included in the accounts for the Besthorpe Hall property, which was assigned in 1747 to Lady Byron for her life and, subsequently, to whomever she willed. Besthorpe seems subsequently to be sold around 1752, although there is no evidence as to the transaction or the purchase price.[48] However, Lady Byron retained related property at Tibbenham and Wymondham.

Altogether, these figures suggest an income of slightly more than £2,000 a year in 1766. To this sum we need to add something for Rochdale, although we have no contemporary figures. Even if we assume an income of £500 from Rochdale, it seems unlikely that Byron can have commanded a net income much in excess of £2,500, although he claimed in 1772 that the estate was worth £3,500 a year.[49] Whatever the truth, the income was not

all his to spend. Initially the estate had to sustain his mother's £600 jointure, and his mother-in-law's £300. Both women died in 1757. Mrs. Shaw,
his mother-in-law, was also entitled to a one-third part of the rents and
fines of East Dereham and Wymondham in Norfolk, which in March 1755
amounted to £54 10s. 5½d.[50] Byron can never have derived a substantial
income from it because the lease of this property expired in 1765.

Although we do not have a complete set of figures relating to sums of
money remitted to Byron by William Daws, it is possible to estimate something of the magnitude of Byron's income from the land steward's cash
books. Between 1758 and 1766, when the sums payable were at their peak,
the average annual remittance to Byron was £1,809, although it is possible
that he also received money separately accounted from Rochdale and Norfolk. Without much doubt, however, Byron was not particularly wealthy, at
least if he intended to maintain the lifestyle of a peer, with its London
social life, gambling, hunting, and other expensive pastimes. Even before
he came of age it was obvious that he was well able to live beyond his
limited means, and since on top of the normal expenses of keeping up houses
in London and the country he engaged in improving Newstead and collecting art and other treasures, it is perhaps not surprising to find that he ran
rapidly into debt.

V

Byron's financial difficulties started to become apparent in the mid-
1750s. Of the £2,700 he had borrowed from Barnaby Backwell between
1743 and 1745, £2,000 remained outstanding, even though the 1747 estate
act had given Byron powers to sell timber in order to redeem the debt. In
1754 the mortgage was transferred by Backwell's heirs to the Nottingham
bankers Messrs. Abel Smith and Company, again allowing Byron the option of redeeming the mortgage by timber sales.[51] In March 1755 Byron
borrowed a further £1,000 from the bank so that he owed them £3,000
together with £143 1s. 3d. in unpaid interest. In April 1757 the mortgage
was transferred to John Richardson, a timber merchant, and Thomas
Oldknow, a Nottingham timber merchant and mercer. They agreed to advance £6,120, of which £3,143 was to repay the mortgage, and £2,977
went direct to Byron. To repay themselves, Richardson and Oldknow were
given the right to cut down and sell more than four thousand oak trees from
Newstead Park.[52] It was probably this transaction to which Horace Walpole
was referring when in 1760 he noted that Byron had recently sold oaks to
the value of £5,000 in order to satisfy creditors.

Where did the additional sum of nearly £3,000 go? We do not know, but Byron was busy in the grounds at Newstead during these years, and his expenditure must have been considerable. In addition to his fortifications he was also replanting. Walpole was not impressed, noting sarcastically that Byron had "planted a handful of Scotch firs, that look like ploughboys dressed in old family liveries for a public day!"[53] Despite such criticism, Byron continued with the policy, and in 1764 he bought various saplings, including one hundred beech trees, a thousand oaks, and fifty large Spanish chestnuts, although they were still not paid for in December 1767. Arthur Young was impressed by the "extensive park, finely planted," and the "very noble landscape."[54] Byron was also prospecting for coal; indeed, for this purpose in March 1755 he resorted to the expensive, but reliable, annuity loan, obtaining a lump sum of £1,600 from Roger Mainwaring in return for paying him £200 a year from the estate income. The loan, according to the agreement between Byron and Mainwaring, was to help develop coal mining on the Newstead estate.[55] However, no such reasoning was offered when in April and May 1756 Byron borrowed sums of £1,125 and £375 from the London financier Sir Abraham Janssen in return for rent charges (i.e., annual payments) of £150 and £50 from the estate rentals.[56]

By the late 1750s Byron was running out of money, and having tested the waters with Mainwaring he dipped further into annuity loans. These were quick-fix, expensive ways of raising money in which the advantage to Byron was cash in hand. The risk to the lenders was that Byron might die before they had recovered their money through the annuity payments. Mainwaring, for example, made a profit as long as Byron lived longer than eight years from the date of the agreement (£1,600 divided by £200 = eight years). To guard against the risk of having a loss should Byron die, Mainwaring could insure Byron's life to protect his investment. Such loans usually had a buyout clause and, as we shall see, Byron had plans for redeeming them, but in the later 1750s and 1760s his main concern was short-term cash. In 1758 he borrowed £4,200 from William Glanville in return for an annuity of £300. Two years later George Jones of Lincoln's Inn lent him £2,000 in return for an annuity of £150.[57]

Through the 1760s Byron became increasingly ingenious in the ways and means he used of raising cash. When in 1762 he let Bulwell Forge to Walter Mather, a Duffield ironmaster, Byron collected the complete rent for the twenty-one-year term (£945) in advance, on a bond. Two years later he persuaded Major Samuel Zobell of the Seventy-seventh Regiment of Foot to part with £700 in return for an annuity of £100, and in 1765 William Glanville lent him a further £1,050 in return for an annuity of £150.[58] During 1768 Lord Baltimore lent him £2,800 on an annuity of £400, and Edward Cartwright advanced £1,400 in return for an annuity of £200.[59] Yet fast as the money came in, it was not enough, and Byron's reputation was spreading. Abel Smith, the Nottingham banker who had advanced money in the 1750s, told Daws in February 1768, "as I have great payments to make this month, please to acquaint his Lordship it will not be in my power to comply with your request." Polite inquiries by Daws were firmly rebuffed by Lord Middleton (of Wollaton Hall), whose spare money was already engaged.[60] Daws commissioned London agents to acquire a loan of some sort in the City. His first approach in September 1769 failed:

> the people who have money to spare in this town being most engaged in the funds, by which they get a greater interest than they can on land, and I do believe it will not be in my power to procure it. . . . I should apprehend you will be more likely to get it in the country where the state is known.[61]

Daws then approached Lazarus and Saloman, money lenders, but they were equally non-commital:

> [W]e have received your letters of 12th and 13th current but have not as yet succeeded in His Lordship's request though we made application to 2 different monied men on that purpose. You'll however be so kind to give our humble respects to his Lordship and assure him that we shall neglect no opportunity to comply with his request in regard of finding a person to advance the said sum.[62]

Either they, or their commissioned agents, were more successful in November when Henry Boldero, Henry Kendall, and George Adey, Lombard Street bankers, agreed to advance £3,000 on an annuity of £500. At six years return, the terms were tightening up on the impoverished peer.[63]

More substantive support came from Lady Byron's cousin Charles Gould, whose father had been one of the trustees of the 1747 marriage settlement. Gould at some point made Byron a substantial loan, with an agreement that it should be serviced from the rents of the Stretham estate. In October 1767 Gould informed Daws that these were likely to be low, "the fens having suffered extremely by a break of bank in the Hundred Foot Rings, and great expenses incurred in milling to get off the water, which flowed down from that breach, as well as in saving our own banks." Either because Stretham did not yield as much as hoped, or because Gould increased the loan, Byron agreed in 1767 to secure his money on an annuity loan with Gould being paid from the rents and profits of the Gringley estate. He was to receive a minimum of £500 annually from Gringley, plus whatever else the estate would stand. Gould seems at this point to have been happily tolerant of his cousin's misfortunes, telling Daws in October 1768 that "if Lord Byron should be pressing to receive what the Nottinghamshire estates may produce above £500 this year, I shall not object to your paying it to his Lordship, though I fear the Stretham rents will not this year clear the interest."[64]

Over time Gould grew wise to Byron's habits. When he was approached for a further loan in 1769 he excused himself on the grounds that he would be able to oblige only by selling out of stocks at a loss of 10 percent interest. He watched the Gringley income carefully, and as a result the sums paid to him often exceeded £500: in 1771 they totaled £622, and in 1772 the figure was £524. Gould frequently reminded Daws of the need to remit the money. He told him in October 1771 that both he and Byron had been "in daily expectation of your remitting me some monies, upon account of the Gringley Rents, and he has asked me several times about it."[65]

Byron was borrowing heavily, but he was also squeezing tenants and tradesmen alike in an attempt to maintain his cash flow. He demanded that every penny of rent should be remitted to his personal account, and he was happy to leave tradesmen's bills unpaid and sometimes unacknowledged. Aristocrats were seldom refused credit for the simple reason that tradesmen implicitly trusted their creditworthiness. Even when they ignored bills, tradesmen invariably continued to advance credit, and it was often only when they were financially stretched that questions were raised about payment. While it was common practice among aristocrats to leave tradesmen waiting to be paid, Byron took the practice to extremes. Matthew Butcher of Sutton-in-Ashfield was not untypical. He complained in April 1766 that unless outstanding bills were paid his own livelihood was threatened, since he could not satisfy his suppliers. His plea was ignored, and his account was still unpaid in September. Hearing that Byron was visiting Newstead, he presented himself in person and obtained an interview. Byron played the innocent party. He blamed Daws and suggested an arrangement whereby the money would be made available in two weeks' time. Butcher was apparently satisfied, but by September 1767 he was again demanding payment of his bills, urgently requesting "the small sum that is due to me." The following month he threatened to present himself in person at Newstead, unless he was paid.[66] Another case concerned Robert Halifax of Chesterfield. In November 1766 he wrote to Daws:

> I beg you will present my Lord with his account of the wine, to which is added the balance of the old account, some little brandy, and also what is due to me for bottles, which has been collecting for many years having never charged my Lord with any, some of the Butlers have been very good in returning.[67]

Five months later Halifax's tone was becoming more strident. He had not even received a reply to his letter, let alone any money, and he now named mid-May for payment of the account. On 7 August 1757 he received £20. For a while this seems to have satisfied him, but by early 1769 he had retired from business and was trying to collect outstanding debts: "[H]owever trifling the sum may be to my Lord, it is a considerable lot to me." This was the start of a steady stream of letters through 1769 and 1770 requesting his money. By October 1770 he was complaining that "the money has been due so many years and I suffer great inconvenience from the want of it."[68]

Byron and Daws developed strategies for dealing with tradesmen, happily playing off creditors by blaming one another. Lucy Mason wrote to Daws on 27 September 1766 from London:

> I am very sorry that I have occasion to be so troublesome to you but as it has not pleased his lordship to have the account of my late father settled now due to me, obliges me to be further troublesome: but I hope that his Lordship's known goodness will take it into consideration and let the account be settled this Michaelmas, for it is very hard upon me for to let it lie dead so long. When my Lord was in town I had the honour to speak to his Lordship and he told me that you was then to be in London in a fortnight's time and that you was to call upon me, but I have never heard nothing of you. Sir I shall think myself greatly obliged to you if you would be so good as to make interest to his Lordship for me for it would really make me very happy to have it settled.[69]

Doubtless Byron had forgotten to convey to Daws the need to visit Miss Mason. Similarly outmaneuvered was Joseph Outram, who complained to Daws in December 1766 that

> When I was last at Newstead you was so kind to say from My Lord I should have some cash in about 3 weeks, as the time is gone over and have had no opportunity of meeting you, nothing now but a real want of money should have occasioned you this trouble. I beg you will inform his Lordship I have a large sum to pay at Nottingham Saturday next and if it is not convenient to discharge the whole bill if his Lordship would be kind enough to consent to remit me half the sum now and the other half the next spring it would at this time greatly oblige.[70]

Outram's sycophancy cut no ice, and he was still out of pocket in June 1770. He and Daws arranged to meet in a booth at Nottingham races, although the outcome of their rather strange rendezvous is not known.[71] A similar case was that of Clement Ellis of Mansfield. In August 1767 he called on Byron to ask for his money. Byron played the "Daws card," claiming he had inadvertently overlooked the bill, and that Daws had failed to remind him about it. Byron suggested that Ellis should tell Daws to remind him (Byron) of the bill. This elaborate deception was over a bill for £20, outstanding for fifteen months.[72]

The ingenuity used to divert creditors knew no bounds, but perhaps the classic case concerned a firm run by the Mansfield grocers Robert and Charles Wright. Byron was unable to pay their bill in 1767, and instead gave them a promissory note to cover the £100 outstanding. He promised to pay them "as soon as the rent day is over," but since he did not choose to tell them when that was likely to be, they were left without means of following up the remark. They continued to supply goods to Newstead, but by September 1771 the total sum outstanding had reached £182 2s. 3d. Only £11 2s. 8d. had been paid since 1767, and the brothers were growing concerned about their money. They approached Byron, who again promised to pay once rent day was over, but then set out for London without leaving any instructions to pay them. The Wrights were no different from any other creditors; they had suffered "the disappointment of your promise which we confidently depended on," but they were at least willing to take a step many tradesmen fought shy of—they refused to extend credit any further: "[W]e decline your Lordship's favours as Grocers."[73]

Other creditors claimed that Byron's failure to pay represented a threat to their own situation. In December 1766 James Stevens demanded £17 long outstanding from Byron, which he needed in order to pay his rent. Leonard Halley, the Papplewick timber merchant, complained in November 1770 that he had bought timber for Byron's use, but he had not been paid. He was now being pressed for payment, and he needed cash urgently "or otherwise I am undone for ever." He obviously patched up his differences with Byron, since the following year he leased from him timber rights in Sherwood Forest. Ann Mason of Mansfield Woodhouse complained in November 1771 that "unless his Lordship pleases to take my miserable condition into consideration I must inevitably go to prison as my creditors thinks I make neglects they are flying on me every day, and is resolved to force my books from me unless I produce the money in a few days. Therefore I hope his Lordship will relieve the widow and fatherless."[74]

Nor was the situation helped by the bills run up by Byron's son William, who was completing his education in France. Abel Smith complained in February 1768 that a French banker had drawn two bills for £120, payable in London, on account of William Byron, which "exceeds the sum Mr Daws gave orders for." Byron was asked to make arrangements to accept the bills. In April a further bill for £100 arrived from Angers, again drawn by William Byron. In March 1769 a French banker wrote in some concern about a bill drawn on Messrs. Smith and Payne, bankers of London, for £150 by William Byron. He was worried because "I have wrote several times to my Lord Byron, but he has not once honoured me with an answer.

I believe it is his Lordship's intention to pay his son's debts, as Lady Byron ordered him that I should draw for what money I should want on his account."[75]

Buying goods on credit was one tactic, but Byron also needed cash, and when this ran out he simply had to stall. The Gringley estate was subject to an annual fee farm rent payment to Thomas Townshend. Perhaps not surprisingly, this was a casualty of Byron's financial troubles. In August 1770 Daws was reminded by Vincent Mathias of Scotland Yard, Whitehall, acting on Townshend's behalf, that no payment had been made since Lady Day, 1766. Mathias was probably not to know that Byron's financial affairs precluded payment of such accounts, and when this letter elicited no response after nine months he tried again. Once more no money was forthcoming, and in July 1771 he adopted a firmer line, insisting that the debt was too serious for his employer to turn a blind eye any longer, and requesting a date on which the money would be paid. Byron, if not Daws, was always happy to set dates, even when he had no intention of honoring them. The appointed hour was to be Michaelmas (29 September) 1771, but the day came and went, and a month later Mathias complained that "Mr Townshend having complied with the many appointed times for payment, the last of which expired Michaelmas, and thereby done everything which one gentleman has reason to expect from another, his Lordship must not be surprised if Mr Townshend should put himself under the necessity of obtaining some legal way to obtain the large arrear due to him."[76] Maybe faced with legal action Byron complied. Whatever the case, the issue dropped from sight thereafter.

Whether or not Byron retired to Newstead in 1765 as a result of the Chaworth duel, he appears to have had good reason for living in the country, if only to avoid his creditors and to find ways of servicing the ever-rising burden of debt. The fact that he was short of money is one reason he has been accused of deliberately trying to ruin the inheritance and ensuring that by the 1790s Newstead was a serious embarrassment rather than a thriving estate. Yet legend and reality are not always easy bedfellows, and Byron knew what he was about. By the end of 1769 he had borrowed £19,190, for which he had sacrificed £2,100 of the estate income—in theory, since some of the annuities had not been regularly paid.[77] This might look like an escalating form of financial suicide, but Byron had a plan, albeit a somewhat unusual one, which he intended to put into practice in 1770. It was only when the plan went awry that Byron's fortunes spiraled downward and his financial position deteriorated almost beyond rescue.

3

William, Fifth Lord Byron:
The Man and the Myth, 1770–98

At face value William, fifth Lord Byron, looks by the late 1760s to have been heading toward financial disaster, borrowing from all and sundry, often on seriously disadvantageous terms, and clearly living well beyond his somewhat limited aristocratic means. Byron, however, knew exactly what he was doing. In 1770 his son William would be twenty-one and, as at his own coming of age twenty-seven years previously, the opportunity would arise to break the entail and resettle the estates. Just as he had used that opportunity to capitalize part of his assets, so Byron anticipated making similar arrangements in 1770. Unfortunately for his strategic thinking, whereas in 1743 he had only himself to consider, in 1770 he had also to take into account the wishes of his son. It was when the proposed arrangements went wrong that Byron ran into serious trouble. According to the legend, and this was the particular part of the story that the sixth Lord Byron promoted, the fifth lord set about ruining the estate after his son married contrary to his wishes. The legend has been recycled many times, and William Byron certainly did offend his father by his choice of bride, but he died in 1776 before Newstead was the subject of willful neglect. As with the impact of the Chaworth duel, the legend and the reality bear closer scrutiny.

I

William Byron celebrated his twenty-first birthday on 27 October 1770. In any landed family the coming-of-age of the son was an occasion for celebration, and Lord Byron had been planning for months. Newstead had to look its best. William Bell was employed throughout 1768 together with masons and laborers, "getting stone and sometimes working of it and loading and unloading."[1] All the extended family was invited to Newstead for what Joe Murray recalled as "grand doings," during which "open house was kept for many days." In particular, Byron intended to make full use of his water constructions. Murray remembered, perhaps with the benefit of a little exaggeration, that "a vessel, rigged and equipped, was brought overland from one of our ports . . . she had 21 guns and discharged them . . . the report being heard over Nottingham and some of the adjoining counties."[2] It was a magnificent occasion, but once the hangovers had worn off it was time for serious business.

The coming-of-age of the eldest son meant that a landed estate now had an heir legally able to assume responsibility for the property. When the fifth Lord Byron had himself come of age in 1743 his father was already dead and he entered fully into his inheritance, under the terms of marriage settlements and his father's will, which had been agreed many years previously. He retained unrestricted legal powers over his property from 1743, but relinquished them as part of his marriage settlement in 1747. As a result, Byron had not been able subsequently to secure loans against his property on mortgage, and neither could he sell land to raise capital. This was why he had to adopt the more expensive policy of annuity loans, in effect borrowing on his own life interest. William Byron's coming-of-age offered a financial window of opportunity for which his father had been planning, a resettlement of the estate.

Under strict settlement, landed estates needed to be resettled once in every generation. If the eldest son reached twenty-one without marrying, his coming of age represented an ideal opportunity for resettlement. Byron was well aware of this, and he had devised a simple plan. He and his son would agree on a resettlement in which various estates could be freed up for sale. Byron would then be able to raise cash to exercise the buyout clauses in the annuity loans, and put behind him his financial difficulties. The sacrificial properties were to be part of his wife's East Anglian estates. These plans were hardly a secret. Charles Gould had penciled in his name alongside the Stretham estate, from which he was already receiving the rents, and news was circulating by April 1768 that Byron intended to sell Tibbenham and Wymondham. John Buxton of Shadwell was the first to show an interest, "having some estate in that part of this county myself, which are contiguous to them," and a Mr. Collyer was also escorted round the property:

Mr Collyer says he is very unwilling to find fault with any Gentleman's estate, but cant help observing that the estate is very much injured by the great fall of pollard trees as well as timber that it does not appear to him to be a sufficient quantity left on the estate to allow the tenants their yearly covenant wood so that money must be allowed them in lieu thereof which must be a very great deduction.

Byron, apparently, had been as active as in Nottinghamshire in dispensing with timber in East Anglia in search of additional funds. Yet, despite such criticisms, Collyer was still anxious to know the asking price. Nor do his comments seem to have affected estate policy; William Sword, the local carpenter, told Daws in September 1768 that "the wood will very shortly be all cleared at the Tibbenham farms and there is but a little at the other farms."[3]

When Peter Stoughton, the newly appointed Norfolk steward, visited Byron in London early in 1769, he was told in no uncertain terms that his first task was to find a purchaser for the property earmarked for sale. Stoughton wanted the property to be valued by "some skilful person that a price may be fixed thereon for until a price is fixed nothing can be done with propriety." Byron was reluctant to agree, and Stoughton was soon complaining that "the principal things wanted towards an agreement for sale of his Lordship's estates here will be a valuation and price as observed before with the leases to the present tenants." Here the matter stalled, except for a false alarm in December 1769 when Stoughton heard a rumor that Byron had agreed to sell the property to Lord Winterton.[4] Through the early months of 1770 Stoughton continued to urge the necessity of a proper valuation, and by September, with William Byron's majority looming and a potential purchaser lined up, he considered this to be imperative. Daws suggested Stoughton should make the valuation himself. It took a month, partly because he had received incorrect information that one farm, which Daws assured him was all freehold, turned out to be copyhold, and Stoughton was concerned that this might depress the price.[5]

With the valuation completed, Stoughton was in a far better position to discuss terms. John Buxton of Shadwell came back into the reckoning, telling Daws in November 1770 that he hoped to be able to make an offer but "I find the price asked is 30 years purchase without a deduction of Land Tax or the common repairs that all farms want. . . . I am obliged to my Lord for giving me the refusal of his estate, and the price I may offer will I dare say do my Lord no prejudice in regard to any other purchasers." Bad weather hampered his attempts to survey the property for himself, but he concluded that £9,000 seemed to be near the value, given the estimated income of £300 annually clear of all deductions. He agreed to talk the matter over with Daws, after which terms were agreed with Byron at £8,000. However, he pulled out in mid-January 1771, leaving Stoughton to begin the search for a purchaser all over again.[6]

Byron's scheme was already beginning to fall apart. He had planned to have the East Anglian sales agreed in advance of his son's coming-of-age. The properties could then be omitted from the new settlement, the transactions could be completed, and the money raised would immediately be used to satisfy his creditors. The inability of Stoughton to find suitable purchasers ready to fall in with Byron's plans was obviously a setback, but Byron also failed to take into account the views of one key player in this business—his son. Estates were resettled to ensure the future of the property, but also so that the heir, in return for agreeing to the settlement terms, would be guaranteed an income. Portions for daughters and younger sons were specified in the father's own settlement (i.e., the 1747 act in Byron's case) but no provision was made for the heir. Normal practice was for the resettlement terms to specify an income for the son until such time as his father should die and he would succeed to the property. The son, from a mixture of filial duty and common sense, usually accepted the terms. But if, as in this case, the resettlement allowed for the disposal of property, the son needed to think carefully about the arrangement, since his anticipated inheritance might be devalued. By refusing a settlement on what he considered disadvantageous terms, he could try to ensure that the estate would still be intact at his father's death. Without a resettlement land could not be released, and the father could neither sell nor mortgage settled land. Any money his father might borrow in the meantime on his personal security did not become the legal responsibility of his successors.

The dilemma for William Byron, as for any heir with an indebted father, was that to accept resettlement terms in which land was to be sold reduced the potential inheritance, but not to accept might bring down upon him his father's anger. He could be left without an annual allowance, leaving him potentially penniless and forcing him to live by borrowing, perhaps by annuity loans repayable when he inherited the property at some indefinable future date. By then, should his father live to a great age, he might be financially ruined.

It all required careful thought, and William Byron evidently recognized that he had the whip hand because of his father's financial position. Much to Lord Byron's annoyance, having basked in the reflected glory of the family at his coming-of-age celebrations, William subsequently refused the proffered terms. He agreed, while he was still thinking them over, to raise with his father £2,965 6s. 3d. on a bond, but this was not going to last long in the current financial climate, and in January 1771 the two men also jointly borrowed a further £1,450 on the security of four £50 annuities. They also continued to wrangle, and it was not until February 1771 that terms were thrashed out. William Byron agreed to a resettlement in which the Norfolk and Cambridgeshire properties would be released for sale, and the necessary arrangements would be made to secure the putative portion of Byron's daughter Caroline, and the potential jointure of his wife, on other family properties. For his cooperation William secured for himself the promise of a lump sum of £2,000 and an annual allowance of £700 a year. Father and son had made sufficient progress by February 1771 to join in a common recovery of the Nottinghamshire estates in order to break the entail.[7]

II

Lord Byron must have thought he had reached clear water early in 1771, but he was in for a severe shock. He had in mind a lucrative marriage for his son to complement the resettlement. As the heir to an aristocratic estate, William Byron could be expected to attract a bride with a substantial marriage portion—part of which could be employed to help sort out the financial troubles of both father and son. A suitable candidate was lined up, a lady "of large fortune so desirable as it was thought to the Noble house." All the fifth lord's plans seemed to be working out: the resettlement terms had been agreed, and the wedding was about to take place. The financial relief for which he had so long been planning was about to materialize.

Unfortunately William Byron, having negotiated long and hard over the resettlement, now chose once again to upset his father's plans. "On the very eve of the appointed wedding day," Joe Murray subsequently recalled, William Byron eloped to Gretna Green with his cousin Juliana Elizabeth Byron. He left the resettlement documents still unsigned, and the lady of large fortune stranded at the altar. Just what pressure was put on the young man we shall never know, but the atmosphere at Newstead must have been electric, for this was scandal on a grand scale. The events were still fresh in some memories decades later when all the parties involved were dead. In 1809 Joe Murray could clearly recall how William and Juliana "ran away to Scotland . . . they was there married," and Francis Leigh remembered how "Lord Byron was much offended at his said son's marrying his first cousin."[8] It was another story in which Washington Irving could revel: he wrote of the fifth lord's "inveterate malignancy" toward his son, and of how

> not being able to cut off his succession to the Abbey estates, which descended to him by entail, he endeavoured to injure it as much as possible, so that it might come a mere wreck into his hands. For this purpose he suffered the Abbey to fall out of repair and everything to go to waste about it, and cut down all the timber on the estate, laying low many a tract of old Sherwood Forest, so that the Abbey lands lay stripped and bare of all their ancient honours.[9]

Considering that William Byron was reconciled to his father within a few months, but tragically died only five years later, this imaginative account of events beyond 1771 needs some further consideration.

Juliana Elizabeth was the daughter of Lord Byron's younger brother, Admiral John Byron. Her main failing, in her uncle's eyes, was not that she lacked genteel breeding but that she had little by way of fortune. Under the terms of her father's marriage settlement she was entitled to a one-sixth share of £7,000 invested in 3 percent reduced annuities, £1,166 12s. 4d. It was not paid in her lifetime, possibly because she was a major beneficiary in 1773 under the will of her maternal great-uncle, Lord Berkeley of Stratton. This was in the future, and in the meantime Lord Byron was absolutely furious with his son, and it was months before he could once again bring himself to see or speak to him.[10] Yet whatever his personal feelings, Byron's financial position was such that he could not walk away from the situation. He managed in March to secure four further annuities (£1,600 for annual payments of £200), an agreement to which William Byron subsequently added his signature. Once Byron had recovered his equilibrium, tentative feelers were put out in the direction of William Byron with a view to re-opening the negotiations. The young man drove a hard bargain, although as the negotiations proceeded he did join with his father to raise further annuity loans in May (£1,600 paying £240 a year) and June (£2,100 paying £300).[11]

Byron's carefully laid plans were in disarray, and once news of his predicament began to leak out the creditors started to worry. Peter Stoughton, the Norfolk steward, grew increasingly uneasy. He reminded Daws in May 1771 that it was six months since William Byron had come of age, "at the end of which, in case the money advanced his lordship was not repaid, I was to have better security, or [be] at liberty to execute the judgment to be obtained on his Lordship's warrant." It was time, in other words, for Byron to give him adequate security for the loan, or face the possibility of being taken to court by his own steward. Daws assured Stoughton that Byron was "raising money for the payment," but he wanted something more concrete than vague platitudes: "I should therefore be glad if some certain time could be fixed for that purpose, that I might provide myself with another security." Like so many of Byron's other creditors Stoughton was now being dangled on the end of a proverbial piece of string. By late August 1771 he had heard nothing of his loan, and as he had arranged an alternative security to commence on 10 October he wanted to be paid by that date. Of course 10 October came and went, and on the thirteenth he wrote to Daws in disgust:

> As things even out I am sorry I ever applied for the Court [stewardship], for it has been the cause of so much trouble to me and my family, that I find

I cannot long bear therewith, and though it is much against my will to enter up the judgments and have execution thereon, yet I must and will do it, if I have not better security in ten days from this time.

Thirteen days later he repeated the threat. He finally managed in February 1772 to persuade Charles Gould to take a transfer of the loan, which was secured on Tibbenham and Stretham.[12]

Nor was Stoughton alone. A Mr. Brown complained to Daws in September 1771:

I lent my money in expectation of completing a business from which I expected to be repaid and upon the security of some lands which I believed were unincumbered and that the recoverys were good, which is the only foundation upon which my security would be good for anything. I since have found that all his Lordship's estates are incumbered and the recovery badly suffered therefore that security is not any to me. I also expected to be paid certainly at the time limited, that being expired under these circumstances I must insist upon being paid my money immediately, of which you will please to inform his Lordship. I shall expect an answer by return.[13]

Even Charles Gould was worried. Finding by the end of October 1771 that nothing had been signed, he found himself "in a very precarious situation, and I am bound in honour to make good the purchase of the annuities and to discharge the arrears to Mr Robson." To help Byron he had bought out the annuities granted to Sir Abraham Janssen, "yet his Lordship takes no heed towards securing the repayment, and seems equally indifferent about making me a title to the Stretham estate which he has expressly engaged to do." The impasse seems to have been sorted out the following month when Daws was summoned by Gould to London so that he could be present with Byron "at the execution of the necessary deeds and join therein."[14]

Byron recognized that his position during the summer of 1771 was serious. In July he was desperately trying to find a way of raising money without the cooperation of his errant son, but this was mere wishful thinking.[15] To keep the creditors from the door he must have been paying the interest on his debts, since during 1771 he took only £274 from the Newstead estate income for his own use—he had regularly taken more than £1,500 a year in the early 1760s. In an effort to raise cash, he hastily arranged for Christies to sell part of the Newstead picture collection that he had so carefully put together. A sale was advertised for 20–25 March 1772. The catalog noted that the pictures had been "collected by his Lordship and noble Father during the course of a great number of years with great speculation and vast expense." The sale produced about £3,300 for the 460 pictures that were sold.[16] What had once been a house crowded with pictures now had large areas of empty wall space with only the family portraits, heir-looms for a future generation, for Byron's amusement. A showpiece praised by Horace Walpole was denuded of many of its finest exhibits.

Fortunately for Byron, even as the sale was proceeding relations with his son William were on the mend and, for good measure, also with his brother John, father of his niece and now daughter-in-law, Juliana. Peter Stoughton heard from Daws "of the prospect of a reconciliation between my Lord and his Son and the Commodore, which gives me pleasure in-deed, and I hope nothing will happen to prevent the same."[17] In early March 1772 Walter Mather heard from Byron's own mouth "that he was recon-ciled to Mr Byron and that his affairs was or would very soon be settled." Like Stoughton he had reason to be pleased, since he was owed £615.[18] Byron was able to complete the sale of the Stretham and Tibbenham es-tates in Norfolk to Gould for £5,500. Of this sum £2,072 4s. went to paying Stoughton's principal and interest, and £1,870 7s. was to be regarded as the redemption of all debts owing to Gould apart from three annuities he had repurchased on Byron's behalf. Only £1,279 13s. was earmarked for Byron's own use.[19]

Meantime, Byron had been desperately raising further sums of money to keep himself afloat. During June 1772 he raised £3,150 on six annuities paying £500 a year, and a mortgage of £500. He claimed that charges on the estate amounted to £2,200 from an income of £3,500. In fact, the sum cannot have been less than £3,000, because between 1755 and May 1772 he had raised £28,150 on annuity loans secured across the whole estate, paying £3,540 annually, as well as £3,465 on mortgage. It was not at all clear that he was solvent, and the surplus from the Norfolk sale was cer-tainly not going to solve his financial problems. In these circumstances the estate resettlement finally agreed to by Byron and his son turned out to be rather different from the one proposed early in 1771. In order to protect his £700 annual allowance and to make sure his own debts of more than £3,000 were paid, William Byron now had to agree to a further proposal from his father, this time in regard to land sales in Nottinghamshire.

It was clear early in 1772 that extensive land sales were going to be needed if Byron's financial position was to be relieved. The first property earmarked for sale was Gringley, where, in readiness for sale, a common recovery was suffered in January 1772.[20] In 1774 this estate ran to 1,487 acres, and was divided into twenty-nine tenancies. The rental value was £538. In itself this sale was not going to be sufficient. Consequently, also brought forward for sale was the manor of Hucknall (enclosed in 1769), Bulwell Park, and the rectory and advowson of Hucknall. Altogether 2,220 acres went on the market, with an annual rental valuation of £979. The forty-six separate holdings included William Daws's farm and the iron forge.

Altogether, in Nottinghamshire Byron disposed of 3,707 acres yielding £1,517 rent a year. Property in the vicinity of Newstead, measured at 5,543 acres in 1769, was reduced to 3,200 acres by 1774.[21] These were land sales on a substantial scale, and they were an indication to those who knew of his plans that Byron's debts were significantly greater than had been anticipated.

By the spring of 1772 word was already out that these properties were soon to come on the market. George Mason asked for details "that I may be able to lay them before the Duke of Newcastle as his Lordship has been so good as to make his Grace an offer for it."[22] In July Mr. Mellish of the Hodsock family was considering putting in an offer, and in September Abel Smith, the Nottingham banker, made known his interest. Other land agents were also in touch with Daws during the course of 1772, while Daws himself was at Gringley in August valuing the property. Ironically, Gringley was one of the few places at which Byron had acquired additional property: in February 1771 he had bought John Tindall's house for £60—Daws was told to provide the money—but, symptomatic perhaps of his luck, the bakehouse was gutted by fire in June.[23]

In the end the properties went as a single lot to the duke of Devonshire for £50,500.[24] It was part of a deal already struck with the duke of Portland, whereby the two dukes were to exchange properties in Nottinghamshire and Derbyshire in order to round out their estates, although the exchange was completed only in 1814. At the time of Lord and Lady Byron's marriage settlement in 1747, sums of £5,000 and £6,000 had been secured on these estates toward the portions of younger children. Devonshire agreed that the sum of £11,000 should remain as a charge on the estates, paying interest (3½ percent) during Lord Byron's life. These terms were written into the estate resettlement of November 1773.[25] Byron was thus provided with an additional income of £385, at least until 1778, when he "made an assignment of that annuity to answer a present occasion and the purchasor hath requested I would trouble your Grace to accept him as the future receiver." Byron was too embarrassed to make the request in person to Devonshire: "[S]ome pressing business unexpectedly requiring my immediate attendance at Newstead for which place I set off this morning hath prevented me the honour of personally waiting upon your Grace."[26] In fact he assigned £5,000 of the sum, and continued to receive the interest (£210 p.a.) on the other £6,000. When the capital was paid is not clear, although £1,000 was still outstanding as late as 1809.[27]

In view of the complexity of Byron's financial arrangements, particularly the annuities and mortgages, as well as the need to secure his wife's jointure, his son's allowance, and his daughter's portion, it is hardly surprising that the transaction took months to complete. Indeed, it was only in

November 1773 that Lord Byron and his son signed the numerous legal documents required to free the properties from settlement, and it was not until February 1774 that all the outstanding queries were resolved and the transaction completed.[28] As this had been settled land, the trustees of Byron's own marriage settlement insisted that the money from the transaction should be paid to nominated representatives, whose task would be to pay the creditors. The men nominated were Brackley Kennett and John Heaton. As a result, the whole sorry story slowly emerged. It became clear that Byron had borrowed from anyone who would lend, and that he and his son had become "greatly indebted by annuities, judgements etc., the interest whereof exceeding the annual income of all the estates comprised in the [1747] Act."

Kennett and Heaton had a thankless task, but slowly they unraveled the web of debt into which Byron had so thoughtlessly woven himself. In all, they tracked down a total of thirty-two annuities paying £3,900 a year. These cost £37,469 18s. 2d. to redeem. Bond and mortgage debts cost a further £6,458 15s. 8d. to redeem. William Byron was paid his £2,000 lump sum and one and a half year's allowance (£1,050). Debts he had run up on his own account cost a further £2,000, and a couple of other debts of Lord Byron were redeemed for £224. In total the administrators paid £49,300, leaving only £1,200 to Lord Byron himself—for the payment, presumably, of some of the unsatisfied local tradesmen (table 3.1).[29]

Table 3.1. The Trustees' Repayment of Debts, 1774

Type of debt	Number	Total		
		£	s.	d.
Annuities	32	37,469	18	2
Bonds	3	5,073	13	0
Mortgage	1	1,385	2	8
Lord Byron's debts	2	224	2	1
William Byron		2,000		
William Byron's allowance		1,050		
William Byron's debts	6	2,000	9	6
Trustees' expenses		97	2	3
Paid Lord Byron		1,200		
		£50,500	7	8

Sources: Reelig, 705; NUMD, P1 E12/3

Among those with much to be thankful for was Charles Gould. On 15 December 1772, with the new settlement apparently a foregone conclusion, Gould wrote to Daws enclosing Byron's bond for the last £1,500 advanced on the Gringley estate, which was to be canceled when the deeds were executed, and the bond for £550 on which £450 remained outstanding, "the same for which the plate was pledged." Gould had also bought back an annuity from Edward Cartwright for £1,700 in 1773 to add to the Janssen annuities, and altogether he received £3,934 11s. 8d. from the 1774 sale money for these three annuities.[30] Whether at any time he realized how deeply in debt Byron really was must be questionable, although the fact that even precious metals had been pledged in return for cash must have given him good reason to be concerned.

III

Byron now had to live on the profits of a greatly depleted estate. His annual income must have been reduced by well over £1,500 a year: Gringley's £538 (1772) and Hucknall and Bulwell's £979 represented a loss of £1,517, and the Norfolk properties need to be added to this total. In Nottinghamshire, Byron now owned only the Newstead estate, together with property at Linby, Papplewick, and Blidworth, which brought in rent of £415 a year, but this was subject to taxes and was charged with paying (from 1776) £315 annually to Juliana Byron.[31] Elsewhere he owned Rochdale, East Dereham, and Wymondham. Income from Rochdale is not easy to establish, although it seems to have varied quite considerably, with figures varying between £218 in 1773, £158 in 1775, and £148 in 1776. A statement of the rental drawn up in 1795 showed a total of only £292 16s., of which £122 6s. was rents of coal mines and £14 14s. of stone quarries, and £67 3s. came from copyhold rents.[32] Byron's income from his remaining Norfolk properties is not known. His only other income was the £385 interest on the £11,000 charged on the Gringley estate, and he received only £210 of this after 1778.

If these calculations are correct, Byron's income may not have exceeded £600 a year following the 1774 sales, and for a man of his extravagant tastes this was something close to disaster. He began immediately to hunt around for ways of increasing his spending power, notably by exercising his rights as life tenant of the Newstead estate. Although he could not sell any of the property, he could raise money by disposing of those items which were traditionally excluded from settlement, notably timber and the contents of the house and grounds. In December 1774 he told Daws to advertise the sale of further timber from the park, and acting on local hearsay he

had Eagle Pond dredged and found the medieval eagle lectern and candlesticks of the priory. These he promptly sold, together with his "strong beer,"
to Sir Richard Kaye.[33] Kaye gave the lectern to Southwell Minster, where it
can still be seen today.

In the 1760s Viscount Grimston had considered Newstead a "very dreary
park," and Byron could now see little point in retaining it for aesthetic
purposes when he could make money by selling the timber and then letting
the land for rent. He proceeded to parcel it up into three farms. We do not
know quite when they were laid out, and they may have been created at
different dates, but in 1776 James Topham took the Newstead Park Farm—
which included "closes within the Park pales"—the mill and mill pool with
dams, floodgates, and waterworks. The lease was for ninety-nine years at
£375 annual rent, and he had the right to fish in the lake for his amusement,
and to eat but not sell his catch. Other tenants were specifically debarred
from fishing in Byron's lakes, so this was presumably seen as an important
concession. Topham's lease was suspiciously long, but in any case there
was a further reorganization of the park in 1787, and by 1802 it had been
split into three farms totaling 1,332 acres and let for more than £100 a year.
One of the tenants was William Bowman, who was paying £215 rent for
517 acres and the mill.[34]

Some contemporaries regretted the loss of the park. Joe Murray told
Newton Hanson how, "at the best period of his Lordship's life the park and
domain of Newstead was covered with the finest timber." It was in stark
contrast, Hanson noted, with

> the barrenness of the Forest land in the approach to the abbey and going
> hand in hand with the extensive lakes in the sort of haven in which the
> abbey stands must have rendered it one of the most interesting places in
> the kingdom, but alas these fine trees were cut down, even the last one by
> his Lordship and the Abbey with its gardens, lakes, cascades and battle-
> ments . . . had all become dilapidated and neglected.[35]

In 1797, the historian John Throsby wrote rather more prosaically of the
park that it had "retired from its extensive boundaries," to rest "within a
narrow space, leaving only the traces of what it had been, rushy and miry.
The building in a great degree, has resisted the innovation of time; but the
woods which sheltered it are almost no more."[36] A visitor of 1811 was
distressed to find the estate "bare of wood, and presenting a scene rather of
desolation than of improvement."[37] Washington Irving noted that "the fine
old trees" had been "laid low" by the fifth lord.[38]

Be that as it may, letting the land made sense to Byron, given his financial
circumstances, and Robert Lowe, who reported on Nottinghamshire for

New-stead Abbey, lettered: "Drawn by J. C. Barrow F.S.A. from a correct Sketch taken upon the spot by the Late F. G. Byron, Esqr, published 1 November 1793 by J. C. Barrow and C. J. Parkyn." Aquatint. Whatever the accusations leveled against the fifth Lord Byron, there were still plenty of trees left at Newstead in his final years. This is how the abbey must have looked when the poet saw it for the first time in 1798. (Nottingham City Museums and Art Galleries [Newstead Abbey].)

the Board of Agriculture in 1798, approved of the changes in respect of farming.[39] Even Throsby admitted that there were advantages:

> The Park which once was richly ornamented with 2,700 head of deer, and numberless fine spreading oaks, is now divided and subdivided into farms. Agriculture, perhaps more beneficial, has given in their stead, coarse fences and ploughed lands: of the former not one nimble head is to be seen, of the latter their stumps, even with the surface of the earth, remain an impediment to the traveller.[40]

Critically for Byron, the farms brought in rent—no less than £510 by 1802[41]—and this helped to bolster his income, at least temporarily. His income from the Newstead estates fell from £1,510 in 1774 to £616 in 1775, but as the new farms began to yield rent the average was £775 between

1776 and 1780, and £840 between 1781 and 1790. It fell back slightly to £800 a year in the last few years of Byron's life.

This was not all Byron's to spend, and events between 1776 and 1778 served to complicate his affairs even further. The first event was a tragedy, because in 1776 William Byron died. Following his marriage, William Byron did not return to Newstead. He went instead to live at Pinner in Middlesex, where the only child of his marriage to Juliana, William John, was born on 6 May 1772 and baptized on 30 May.[42] In October 1774 he was elected M.P. for Morpeth on the interest of his cousin, the earl of Carlisle. He was in fact following the normal path of the eldest son of a peer, many of whom gained experience in the Commons before graduating to the Lords on acceding to the title. Unfortunately, William Byron was never to reach the Lords; he died just short of his twenty-seventh birthday. He was buried at Twickenham rather than Newstead, an indication perhaps that he and his wife had failed fully to come to terms with his father. In 1783 Juliana married Sir Robert Wilmot of Osmaston in Derbyshire, by whom she had a further son. She died in 1788.

William Byron's death, Washington Irving recounted, was the last straw for the fifth Lord Byron: "[H]e was baffled in his unnatural revenge by the premature death of his son, and passed the remainder of his days in his deserted and dilapidated halls, a gloomy misanthrope, brooding amidst the scenes he had made desolate."[43] This was, like most of Irving's commentary, somewhat fanciful, but Byron was now without doubt in a position of considerable difficulty with respect to the future of the estate. Even while the protracted resettlement negotiations were in progress he had continued to live beyond his limited means. Possibly he envisaged a situation in which he and his son could, at some future date, join in a common recovery to release more land for sale should his creditworthiness demand such a course of action. If this was in contemplation, William Byron's death in 1776 put an end to such thoughts. The heir to Newstead was now Byron's four-year-old grandson, William John Byron. As a minor he could not join in any measures to alter the settlement. In the legal language of the day, William John was now the tenant-in-tail of Newstead. Since the sale of settled land would have been regarded as damaging the future interests of their ward, the trustees of the 1772 resettlement had no powers of disposal. Byron needed to find other ways of raising money.

Timber sales and rental increases were not Byron's only means of increasing his income, because as life tenant he had powers over the house contents. He began the process of emptying Newstead with a six-day sale of furnishings in June 1778. The 429 lots included paintings, mahogany tables, book desks, firearms, brewing vessels, glass and china, featherbeds, kitchen furniture, and a variety of other goods including some exotic items such as "fifteen packs of Lisbon toothpicks." From "Miss Byron's Room" Byron sold the curtains, tables, chairs, the bed and bedding, the carpets, and the mirror. Also cleared were his own bedroom and study, the nursery, the laundry, kitchen, brewhouse, and pantry. The great dining room must have been virtually stripped bare, and a number of paintings by Rubens, Kneller, and Reynolds, which had survived the 1772 sale, now went under the hammer.[44] In 1772 Byron had used Christies to attract the London buyers, but in 1778 he was content to employ the Mansfield auctioneer John Frost, and to rely on a local audience. Purchasers came from miles around. Among them was the Nottingham socialite Mrs. Abigail Gawthern, who drove out from her home on Low Pavement.[45] Some items, presumably unsold at the auction, were disposed of privately; £8 was raised from the sale of household goods in 1778 and £51 in 1779. How much the auction yielded is not known.

Byron's family by now had had enough. Shortly after the 1778 sale, Lady Byron and her daughter, Caroline, Byron's only surviving child, left to live with the widowed Juliana Byron in Twickenham. A formal separation was negotiated, allowing Lady Byron £100 annually and Caroline an annuity of £500 in lieu of her portion. Caroline's income came from the Park farms. Byron saw the departure of his wife and daughter as an opportunity for further fund-raising. "Tho I cant pull down the house," he told Daws in 1779, "I have a power to sell all the materials on the inside." "A little money," he added, "might be made from the inside of Newstead, such as chimney pieces, brass locks, flooring, wainscott etc. etc."[46] He commissioned William Bell to search "the cloisters for a vault or cellar etc," in the hope of finding buried treasure. Bell was not successful. Byron advertised for a tenant for his London house in Queen Anne Street, and proposed also to let the shooting rights at Newstead.[47] Everything, it seemed, had a market value in the relentless search for cash.

This was perhaps not surprising, given the calls on Byron's income. He now had to find £600 annually for his wife and daughter, and his only relief had come from his son's death, as a result of which the £700 allowance was converted into a jointure of £315 for Juliana (as agreed in the resettlement of 1773). He was having to find £915 annually from his estate income, and no relief was in prospect. His daughter, Caroline, died in November 1784, after providing in her will for the £500 annuity to be shared between her godchildren, her cousin, and her mother during her father's lifetime.[48] Lady Byron died in 1788, leaving specific instructions that she should be buried in the family vault at Besthorpe, and assigning her income from the manors of East Dereham and Wymondham.[49] It is hardly surprising to find Byron forced to exist on a much reduced income. Remittances sent to him by Daws fell from a peak of £1,809 in the early 1760s to an average of only £293 between 1775 and his death.

Byron may have largely emptied Newstead, but he had no authority to dismantle the house, and he recognized that the family portraits were settled heirlooms that must be retained for future generations of Byrons at Newstead. "Somewhat incredibly," according to one historian of these years, Byron was contemplating building a temple in the garden;[50] but this was only "incredible" if Byron is viewed as a mindless wrecker. In fact, and as Throsby noted, he did not entirely neglect the house; indeed, he repaired the northwest angle of the abbey, removing the upper and presumably ruinous part of the spiral staircase, altering the roof, and making the stepped gable surmounted by a cross. When he was preparing to travel to Newstead in December 1784, Byron told Daws to make sure Bell was ready "to put up the hall chimney piece whilst I am down," and Daws himself was to "see that there is a good road to the gates, and down to the house." Nor did Byron stop collecting. In 1785 he spent £16 on three pictures for the study and two statues for the garden. To keep warm he ordered Daws to "put up a few bricks in the hall fireplace that I may have a fire there," an arrangement presumably required because the old chimneypiece had been sold.[51]

On the other hand, estate maintenance did undoubtedly slip in these years. Richard Pearson of Tibenham in Norfolk complained to Daws in October 1771 that "when you was over last you promised me that you would give orders for all necessary repairs to be done, but nothing has been done. Master Sword the Carpenter will not do anything unless there be an order from you. The outhouses in such state that I cant make use of them and for want of repair they grow worse daily."[52] On the Rochdale estate the bailiff complained late in 1771 that because Daws was prevaricating over the funding of repairs at Castlehill tenement, Mr. Fletcher had been prevented from "improving and embellishing" it in a manner intended to have "retrieved the bad character which it had gotten by being used as a public house and a disorderly one."[53] Yet while these outlying estates may have suffered, Newstead was not neglected. Throughout his later years Byron maintained the estate. Fencing and hedging continued; posts, rails, and other equipment were regularly acquired during the 1780s, and the farms were soundly run.[54]

Byron clearly expected Newstead to remain in his family, and his actions do not accord well with the legend that he set out to ruin the estate in order to spite his son; rather, they are explicable primarily in terms of his financial needs. Although father and son quarreled, they were sufficiently reconciled to be able to sort out the future of the property. The problem for Byron was that his depleted resources did not match his spending requirements, and potential creditors who had followed events at Newstead became cautious. Daws was constantly being encouraged to find additional resources. In January 1779 Byron urged, "I desire at the receipt of this you will borrow 30 pounds for me till Lady Day and send it up to me." In July 1781 he complained that he had "been obliged this week to borrow 15 guineas which I have promised to return in ten days. Therefore by return of post desire you will send me up what money you can get." By 1783 Daws was fearful of his own salary, and he persuaded his employer to agree to a legal contract admitting to a debt of £150, the equivalent of three years' pay. Byron also turned again to annuities, although the ratio of lump sum to annual payment was now even less favorable, given that he was in his mid-fifties. In 1786 he persuaded Jacob Kirkman of Westminster to part with £525 in return for a £100 annuity, and in 1793 Kirkman's son agreed to advance £213 in return for £35 a year, generous terms given Byron's age. But this was a costly way of proceeding, and Byron was not likely to find many people willing to lend on the security of his life interest as in the 1760s, when the heir was not due to come of age until 1793.[55]

IV

It was only in his final years that Byron became the irascible old man of popular legend. "He has," wrote Lord Fife in April 1785, "spent all his estate so there is no laying hold of this, and he has no principles, but what can you expect from a desperate, bankrupt, bad-hearted man." He had "no view but what his mind and situation suggests . . . one feels hostile to such a fellow as Lord Byron. Thank God, we have few of these."[56] Such sentiments were reasonable enough in view of events that year that showed Byron at his worst, in particular his lack of scruple at seeking out any way he could of raising money. This was his brush with the Robinsons at Papplewick.

The foundation stone for the first of George Robinson's six cotton mills at Papplewick was laid on 23 March 1778. It was built and operating within a year, and work then started on a second mill, Top Mill. A third, Lower Mill, was completed in 1782. Robinson had not yet finished. In 1774 Byron had sold Bulwell Forge together with its dam and surrounding land to the duke of Devonshire as part of his property disposal. Byron's lease to Walter Mather expired in 1783, and in November that year Robinson signed a lease for this property (from Lady Day 1784), with the specific intention of spending at least £2,000 building a fourth cotton mill, Forge Mill. This was to be "to specifications which are to be approved by Mr Arkwright, senior"—the cotton entrepreneur Richard Arkwright. The rent was £45 a year.[57]

All four of Robinson's mills were worked by water power, and the water came from the river Leen.

Byron resented these developments. His exact motives are not clear. Maybe he was annoyed to find the new owner of Bulwell Forge commanding a rent for the Robinson's latest cotton mill, or perhaps he objected to the forge being turned into a mill, or maybe he resented the fact that the fall of water from the river passed through his lakes and then drove the mills, or maybe he just saw a way of making money. Whatever the case, he took steps designed to increase his income, and this led to a crisis. When Byron created the Lower or Sherwood Lake at the southern end of the park, he fitted a sluice and shuttles or floodgates in order to run water into the old river channel. Subsequently Robinson began laying the foundations for his mills, and he applied to Daws for the use and management of the shuttles to enable his workmen to finish and repair the buildings by stopping the water from time to time. Robinson paid five guineas a year rent as an acknowledgment for each application to use the shuttles. On 4 April 1785 Byron ordered that the floodgates and shuttles should be "stopped up and fixed to the top, to a considerable height above the shuttles, several planks of wood in order to collect the waters to an unusual height—causing the waters that should have worked the mills to be totalled withheld and obstructed." Byron also dammed a tributary at Hardstaff's Wire Mill Farm. It was all quite deliberate—the accounts show spending in 1783 and 1784 on the old Dam Head £3, and Nether Dam Head £5, together with income of 10s. 6d. on "stone for floodgates."[58] For Robinson the result was immediate: the water supply was cut off, the mills were effectively stopped, and the added concern was that "the large bodies of water collected in the Lake and by means of the dams, will by their immense pressure and in a short time respectively breach Lake or dam, or both, and by a sudden and violent eruption of water blow up and destroy the mills."

Robinson was naturally alarmed. Six men were set to watch day and night for an inundation and to protect the mills as best they could. Efforts were made to reach an agreement with Byron, who asked for a £10,000 down payment and £6,000 rent a year. Otherwise, he threatened to destroy the mills. Nor was his threat hollow, since on 20 April the floodgates on the Sherwood Lake were partially opened. By 11 P.M. on 21 April Robinson's watchmen noted a rapid increase in flow, and by 1 A.M. on 22 April the Upper Mill dam was already full and beginning to give way. It took forty workmen to repair the breach and save the dam.

Robinson set off immediately to London to seek legal redress. His lawyers had to show that he had ancient water rights on the river, which had been used at his mills prior to 4 April 1785, and that Byron had been aware of his activities. Since Byron had sold him ten acres of fir trees, and offered stone from the garden wall at Newstead for the building work, this was not too difficult. Robinson wanted a return to the status quo as it existed prior to 4 April, in other words that Byron should take down all dams and weirs, and that the court should restrain him from interfering with the flow of water. On 4 May 1785 a temporary injunction was issued, and Byron was told by the court (with the threat of a £50,000 fine should he fail to conform), that he was not to use any means to prevent water flowing down the river Leen in the quantities it had done prior to 4 April. As Lord Fife told his steward, when he heard the news, "[I]t is just as I foretold them; the Chancellor will stop Lord Byron from doing mischief, till his right is cleared up, and when he finds this, he will come into terms." News of the decision was, according to the *Nottingham Journal* "received with the greatest pleasure" in the neighboring villages, where "the following days were spent in expectations of sincere and decent joy," the decision having "restored to the many hundreds of industrial poor—their daily bread."[59]

The results of this case were, to say the least, ironic. Byron, down but not out, contrived to find ways of continuing his obstructive habits until in July 1790 the injunction granted in May 1785 was made permanent.[60] Robinson, with so much at stake, could not trust Byron. Instead he took steps to provide a supplementary power source for the largest of the mills, Lower Mill. The supplement took the form of a Boulton and Watt steam engine, the first successful application of rotative steam power to drive cotton-spinning machinery. The fifth Lord Byron was thus indirectly responsible for introducing steam power into the British cotton industry.

The Robinson case was simply the best known of Byron's actions as he sought in his later years to turn anything to financial account that might pay. In the last decade of his life he lived mainly at Newstead, probably in a few rooms in the southeast corner of the house. It seems never to have become quite the ruin some contemporaries imagined, although Byron did nothing for his reputation when he charged some of his tenants "for the privilege of laying corn in some of the low rooms at the Hall."[61] Converting Newstead into an additional barn inevitably raised local eyebrows.

The depths to which he had sunk is clear from the new will that Byron made in 1785. All the remaining household effects at Newstead, and at a house on Hampstead Heath, were bequeathed to Robert Aisley, the London attorney he appointed as executor, with the instruction that he should sell them to reimburse himself for money lent to Byron and business done on his behalf.[62] He bequeathed £25 each to his nephews John and Frederick George (sons of his younger brother, George) who lived in Nottingham and were the only relations with whom he was still on speaking terms. The residue was left to his servant Elizabeth Hardstaff, popularly known locally as Lady Betty because of the nature of her supposed relationship with him.[63] Even the faithful Daws was omitted, despite a lifetime of devoted service for which he had never been greatly rewarded. He received a salary of £30, raised in 1757 to £50, reduced to £34 in 1774 after the sale of Gringley and Hucknall, but raised again to £50 in 1777, and reduced to £40 in 1781. While this was not generous, he also ran his own farm at Hucknall, which he leased from Byron. By repute, he produced excellent pigs.[64] Daws was an effective and efficient steward, frequently harassed by an employer who was perpetually short of money, and berated by tenants and creditors who continually believed themselves to be overlooked in one way or another. Daws's omission from the will hardly mattered, since he predeceased Byron, dying in 1794. His son, also William, replaced him as steward, but management seems to have fallen into disarray by the time the fifth lord died in 1798.[65]

Nor was any mention made in the will of Byron's grandson and heir, William John Byron. Little is known about the young man's upbringing, although by 1790 he had joined the army and, in true family form, was "rather short of money." Despite being heir to the barony and estate, young Byron received nothing from his grandfather: "I am sorry to say that Lord Byron has not made me any allowance and I am afraid he never will although he has said he would so often." His debts mounted steadily, and exceeded £500 by 1794.[66] That was the year after he came of age, when Lord Byron could have been expected to open negotiations for a resettlement of the estate, permitting—as in 1772—land to be sold to take care of outstanding debts, and then to bring about a resettlement on future generations. In fact, nothing was done. William John Byron was serving abroad, but it still seems surprising that his stepfather, Sir Robert Wilmot, apparently made no attempt to ensure that a new settlement was agreed. Whatever the case, no moves in this direction had taken place when Lieutenant Byron was killed by a cannonball at the siege of Calvi on 31 July 1794.

Quite how Byron viewed this news we shall never know. For the family it was a serious blow, since there was no longer a direct male heir to inherit the estate. At the same time Byron undoubtedly saw this dark cloud as edged with a silver lining. The death of the young heir seemed likely once again to alter his financial position. The estate had not been resettled since 1773. With the death of the heir, Byron assumed that the terms of the 1747 act of Parliament, as amended by the settlement documents of 1773, now lapsed. If so, he expected to acquire the reversion of the fee simple, the absolute right of disposal. He would have had, in other words, complete power over the estate, either to sell or mortgage it as he saw fit. Not surprisingly, he summoned up one last burst of energy, and set off to visit John Hanson, a London lawyer who specialized in work for aristocratic clients.

Byron was in for a nasty shock. At the time, W. S. Haselden was one of Hanson's junior assistants. Many years later he recalled how Hanson had informed Byron that when the settlement was completed in 1773 "by some unaccountable inadvertence or negligence of the lawyers, the ultimate reversion of the fee-simple of the property, instead of being left, as it ought to have been, in the father as the owner of the estates, was limited to the heirs of the son." The heirs of the son meant, in effect, the nearest surviving male. In terms of strict primogeniture, which is what the law recognized in such circumstances, because William John Byron had died intestate, the heirs of the son would be Byron's next eldest brother and his male offspring. Byron found he was still life tenant, "without any legal power of raising money upon [Newstead]" by mortgaging or even selling the estate. Perhaps not surprisingly, "after some daily attendance, pouring forth his lamentations, he appears to have returned home to subside into the reckless operations reported of him." Hanson told him his case was "past remedy": "[H]e had only an estate for life."[67] This was, of course, a retrospective account, and the "unaccountable negligence" of the lawyers was almost certainly a standard clause designed to ensure that if ever a male heir could be found, the property would remain entailed.

Newstead could not be touched, but there was some better news for Byron. At the time of the resettlement, and under the terms of a deed executed in 1773, he was now entitled to the absolute ownership of the Rochdale estate. Byron needed no further encouragement, and he began to sell properties from the estate. In the course of 1795 and 1796 he sold various parcels of land for a total of £2,370. These sales included Brownwardle coal mine, sold to James Dearden for £630, and a small farm sold to James Fielden for £510. From the proceeds the fifth lord was able to repurchase for £1,455 the Kirkman annuities, which were costing him £135 a year.[68] The Rochdale rental of £292 16s. was reduced by £152 2s. Doubtless this aided his cash flow, but it left a problematic legacy for his successor.

V

Byron lived out his last years in solitude at the abbey. Betty Hardstaff continued to attend to his needs, and Joe Murray was his other companion. According to Irving he was the only servant retained by the fifth lord in his later reclusive years at the abbey, having risen to "the dignity of butler" despite being "very lax in his minor morals," expressed by singing "loose and profane songs as he presided at the table in the servants' hall, or sat taking his ale and smoking his pipe by the evening fire."[69]

Byron died on 21 May 1798, and was buried in the family tomb at Hucknall on 16 June, the delay being blamed on "his Lordship's executor." Aisley was certainly not keen to act, "in consequence of the state of [Byron's] affairs, and the supposed smallness of his assets." He eventually proved the will, swearing Byron's personal estate and effects at Newstead at under £599. By the terms of the 1773 settlement the remaining property, including Newstead, passed to his nearest male relative, his great-nephew George Gordon Byron, who now became the sixth Lord Byron.[70]

In whatever light we view the fifth Lord Byron, his essential problem can be expressed quite soberly—he spent more than his estate yielded, and his attempts to find ways of raising additional funding were not always successful. By the later 1760s and perhaps earlier he planned to solve his problems by resettling the estate in such a way as to make land available for sale. This worked in the short term, although at the expense of a substantial reduction in his property. After the death of his son William in 1776, there was no one to collude with (legally) to release further land for sale, and since Byron continued to overspend the only obvious way he had of raising cash was by selling the house contents and the estate timber and by raising loans on his personal security. Byron's case illustrated both the success of the legal device of the strict settlement in keeping an estate together despite the financial problems of one generation, and also the cash-flow difficulties into which an apparently wealthy man could run because he was unable to dispose of his major capital asset, land.

At his death in 1798 the fifth Lord Byron left his estates in considerable disarray. Newton Hanson later wrote of how "the estates were in confusion at the time of the late Lord's death. . . . the farms at Newstead were in a most neglected state."[71] But his later years, particularly after 1785, ought not to be taken as typical of his tenure of the family estates. In general these were run, despite his sometimes desperate financial straits, in the normal manner of a substantial landowner, with his steward carefully controlling events in Norfolk, Nottinghamshire, and Lancashire. William Daws Jr. kept account until Byron's death and, arguably, the estates were far better run before 1798 than was to be the case thereafter, when, with no resident steward at Newstead with the skill and authority to deal with the day-to-day oversight of the property, it was inefficiently overseen from a distance by a London solicitor.

The Byron legend is a myth. It contains an element of truth, and a great deal of exaggeration. The fifth Lord Byron undoubtedly damaged the estate, but largely to fund his own lifestyle rather than to ruin his son's inheritance. He did not retire to live the life of a recluse at Newstead, or at least if he did it was only in his final few years, not during the whole period from the ill-fated Chaworth duel. Byron ensured that the property was carefully managed and properly controlled, at least until his last difficult years, while the law of settlement dictated that he could neither mortgage nor sell Newstead, thus ensuring that there was an estate for future generations of the Byron family. The house may have fallen into a state of disrepair, the great oaks may have given way to farms, and Byron may have ended his life "in a very lonely and reclusive way in the old Abbey upon such small remnant of the rents as his creditors half yearly left him after satisfying their claims."[72] Yet he did not leave the estate "encumbered by debt," nor was it discovered that "there would not even be enough to bury the old lord after all his debts were paid."[73] It was not even subject to any family charges such as jointures and portions, since his wife and children had all predeceased him. His personal debts died with him, even if disappointed creditors might try to persuade his successor to pay them.[74]

English landowners in the eighteenth century did not generally inherit estates that were both debt free and unsettled. Families had too little trust in their heirs to take risks, and in any case settlement was designed to protect the property into the future and, just as importantly, to look after the interests of daughters and younger sons by specifying their portions. The Byron properties were exceptionally rare in 1798 in having no outstanding charges on them, and they were unusual in passing to an heir who inherited not as life tenant (as the fifth Lord Byron had been) but as the owner of the fee simple. The sixth Lord Byron inherited Newstead debt free, and without any legal restraints. When he sold Newstead in 1817 he showed just why landed families did all they legally could to limit any single individual's freedom to maneuver. The careful planning of the fourth Lord Byron through his marriage settlements and his will, the 1747 legislation imposed by the Court of Chancery, and the resettlement of 1773 all counted for nothing. The fifth Lord Byron has been the scapegoat for the failings of his successor; since the 1830s he has been blamed for passing on a flawed inheritance. He did: but English law ensured that he passed on the Newstead property and that it was not encumbered beyond redemption. What happened after that was not his responsibility.

4

The Estate during the Minority, 1798–1809

George Gordon, sixth Lord Byron (1788–1824), succeeded to the family estates in Nottinghamshire, Lancashire, and Norfolk when his great-uncle died in May 1798. By aristocratic standards it was an unusual inheritance. Broken family lines were a common experience, and settlements were normally worded to ensure that there would be a male heir if one could be found within the extended family. What made it unusual was that the fifth and sixth lords had not met, that the fifth lord had made no attempt to provide for his designated successor, and that because he was currently living in Aberdeen the sixth lord did not set eyes upon Newstead until four months after succeeding to the title. It was also unusual because Byron inherited as absolute owner with complete freedom over the estates. He was free, once his minority came to an end, to borrow on the security of the estates or, more drastically, to sell them. Byron took the latter course, and consequently the title descended to the next male heir of the Byron family separated from any property. The blame for this state of affairs has usually been laid at the feet of the fifth Lord Byron on the grounds that he seriously damaged the estate and bequeathed to his successor a flawed inheritance. We have seen that this was true, but as an explanation for what happened after 1798 it is not sufficient. The fifth Lord Byron left the estate debt free and, as we shall see in this chapter, during the subsequent minority of the poet the estate was carefully maintained for his financial benefit.

I

To understand why a ten-year-old boy living in Aberdeen suddenly found himself bearing an English aristocratic title and owning a neglected estate spread through Nottinghamshire, Lancashire, and Norfolk, we have to backtrack to 1736. William, fourth Lord Byron, died in that year leaving the estate strictly settled in the male line. In practical terms this meant that the designated descent was through William, the eldest son of the fourth lord's third marriage, subsequently the fifth Lord, and his male heirs (see the appendix). English law did not permit settlements in perpetuity, so the normal practice was to resettle an estate in each generation to maintain the fiction of continuity. If no resettlement took place, the third generation inherited as absolute owner. In 1794 the fifth Lord Byron expected that with the deaths of his son (the second generation) and grandson (the third generation) the resettlement executed in 1773 would lapse, and he would gain absolute ownership of the property.

What Lord Byron discovered in 1794 was that the 1772 settlement defined the third generation not as Byron's grandson William John Byron, who was his direct male heir, but the *next* male heir within the extended family. By the rules of primogeniture this was Admiral John Byron, the fifth lord's next eldest brother, and his direct male heirs. John Byron, like his elder brother, had left Westminster School in the 1740s and gone to sea. "Foulweather Jack," as he became known in deference to the storms he survived, made his career in the navy, rising to become an admiral. In 1748 he married his cousin, Sophia Trevanion of Carhays, Cornwall, in a chapel belonging to her father in which no registers were kept, thus providing the backdrop to some complex problems over the family succession in later years.[1] Through his mother's brother, Lord Berkeley of Stratton, John Byron inherited property in Hampshire and Yorkshire valued at £20,000, which, together with a small estate in Surrey that he bought, was shared among his children following his death in 1786 and that of his widow in 1790.[2]

John and Sophia Byron's marriage produced six children, two sons and four daughters, one of whom, Juliana, the second daughter, eloped with William Byron. The eldest son was, like his father, named John (1757-91) and, again following in his father's footsteps, he studied at Westminster School. In 1772 he obtained a commission in the army, and made rapid progress through the ranks, serving in America during the War of Independence. He returned to England in 1778 and relinquished the commission. John Byron now adopted the lifestyle of a gentleman about town. Somewhat in the family tradition he became noted for his dissipated life as a gambler, a rake, and a spendthrift, hence his nickname of "Mad Jack." He quickly ran through the £3,000 portion made available to him following his father's death and, short of money, he met Amelia, daughter of the earl of Holderness, and wife of the marquess of Carmarthen. In May 1778, on her father's death, she succeeded to the title of Baroness Conyers, with an estate yielding £4,000 a year. By November 1778 she had left her husband and was living with John Byron. Carmarthen sued for divorce, which was granted on 26 March 1779, and on 9 June she married Byron at St. George's, Hanover Square. She was described in the register as Lady Amelia D'Arcy, Baroness Conyers, and single. The couple had three children, although only their daughter Augusta, later Augusta Leigh, survived childhood. Byron and his wife lived in Paris until her death in January 1784. She was buried in the family vault at Hornby in Yorkshire the following month.[3]

John Byron's lifestyle was such that his expenses easily exceeded his income, and he quickly sought out another fortune. Within a year he had attracted a second heiress, Catherine Gordon of Gight, Aberdeenshire. They met at an assembly in Bath, and she, stout, frumpish, and unsophisticated, was swept off her feet by the still handsome and relatively young suitor. She was captivated, despite his somewhat unusual past, and with neither parents nor guardians still alive to guide her, she plunged rapidly into marriage. The wedding took place at St. Michael's Church, Bath, on 13 May 1785. Catherine Gordon was descended from a long-established Scottish family with considerable estates, shares, and salmon fishing rights, as well as a castle, in Aberdeenshire. By her father's will of 19 December 1777, as the elder of his two surviving daughters, Catherine inherited his land and the barony of Gight. Her father had drowned in 1779 when she was nearly fifteen. Following the wedding John Byron assumed the Gordon surname to comply with the terms of a clause in her parents' marriage settlement of 2 June 1763.[4]

Although articles of agreement designed to protect her financial interests were drawn up prior to Catherine Gordon's marriage, they proved ineffective. John Byron recovered the freehold of Gight, which he promptly sold for £18,690 to Lord Aberdeen. From this £5,000 went toward paying Catherine Gordon's father's debts, and £8,690 disappeared in maintaining the young couple's lifestyle, leaving only £5,000 capital intact by early 1788. For a while they lived in France, but Catherine returned to England for the birth of her child, and her husband followed her, complaining in January 1788 that his wife "has not any [money] to go on with."[5] For her part Catherine Gordon was by now anxious to secure what remained of her fortune: "I must have it as if Mr Byron gets it it will be thrown away in some foolish way or other, and I shall be obliged to apply for more."[6] These were the rather unpropitious circumstances in which George Gordon Byron entered the world on 22 January 1788.

Byron was born in London, but Catherine subsequently traveled north with her baby and settled in her native Aberdeen. Her husband joined her for a while, but soon returned to France, where he continued to spend her money. In 1790 he was "drawing bills upon those whom he could not reasonably expect to answer them,"[7] and he died hopelessly in debt in August 1791. In his will he left £400—which he did not have—to his sister but nothing to his three-year-old son except his debts and funeral expenses.[8] Mrs. Byron was left with few resources. The estate and most of the inheritance had gone, and she seems to have received little help from her family. Only £4,222 of her capital was left. Of this £3,000 was secured on her life, paying interest at 5 percent (£150 a year), and interest on the other £1,222 (£55 11s. 1d.) took the form of a life annuity to her elderly grandmother.[9] She was, even so, unwilling to blame her late husband for her reduced circumstances: "[N]ecessity not inclination parted us, at least on my part, and I flatter myself it was the same with him."[10]

George Gordon Byron was not at this point an heir to anything but his father's debts and his mother's severely reduced inheritance. Mrs. Byron can have anticipated little more than a modest existence in Scotland on her small income, but there was sufficient for George's schooling to begin in 1792 and for him to be enrolled at Aberdeen Grammar School in 1794. It was only with the death of William John Byron in 1794 that George Gordon Byron became heir to an English peerage. Mrs. Byron had little idea of how substantial the accompanying landed estate might be, nor did she know of the fifth Lord Byron's efforts to obtain the fee simple, but she complained with some irritation that no one had taken the trouble to inform her of the change in her son's prospects. Byron, she wrote in November 1794, "is a fine boy and very well and walks and runs as well as any other child. . . . I hear Mr Parker is dead and that your nephew, Lord Byron's grandson is dead but I have not been informed of it from any of the family."[11] The fifth Lord Byron took no interest in his heir, and young George's Scottish upbringing and education continued without interruption until May 1798.

Catherine Byron, as the daughter of a landed family and as an heiress, albeit one who had foolishly squandered her fortune, bided her time. However tranquil her life may have seemed, after 1794 she was preparing for what she recognized sooner or later would be a return south of the border into England. Legally, inheritances needed to be secured, although the heir did not necessarily have to undertake this in person, because a lawyer could be employed to go to the property and, literally, take possession. Mrs. Byron made her preparations. In 1793 she had consulted a London solicitor, James Farquhar, who in turn requested help from John Hanson, a member of the firm of Birch, Hanson and Birch of Chancery Lane.[12] She turned to them again on hearing that the fifth Lord Byron was seriously ill, and during the spring of 1798 the two solicitors agreed on measures for securing the estate on his death.

Once news reached London on 1 June that the fifth lord had died, Farquhar and Hanson put their carefully prepared plans into operation. Hanson went to Nottinghamshire to attend the funeral and "instantly took possession of the estates and secured all deeds and papers for the young

Lord." At the same time he viewed the farms, collected information about the property, and examined "a voluminous quantity of deeds and papers." The information he reported both to Mrs. Byron and to Farquhar on his return to London. Mrs. Byron kept in touch while she hastily sold her furniture (for £74 17s. 7d.—just about sufficient to fund the journey south), sorted out her remaining Scottish affairs, and set out for Nottinghamshire.[13] She and her ten-year-old son arrived at Newstead in late August, to be met in person by John Hanson and his wife.[14]

II

The new owner of Newstead must have found his changed circumstances somewhat bewildering. From the gloom of his restricted Scottish upbringing he was suddenly thrown into the aristocratic grandeur of the great family mansion, and in the late summer sunshine he was able to explore the grounds, meet the tenants, and enjoy the freedom of his own estate. He may have noticed that only the few rooms in which he and his mother lived at Newstead were actually habitable and furnished, but this was of little importance to a boy whose imagination must have run riot. He planted an oak tree that, because of his 1807 poem "To an Oak in the Garden of Newstead Abbey," subsequently became an object of near veneration among visitors. It died in the nineteenth century, but its stump remains, well entwined with ivy.[15]

Under normal circumstances the ten-year-old heir to an aristocratic estate would have been brought up to understand the sense of longevity and responsibility for the family property and title that even a modern aristocrat finds hard to escape.[16] He would expect to live in the family house, or at least to visit it during holidays from school. On such occasions his father would attempt to instill into him something of the grandeur of his position, and to teach him the ways of a country gentleman. The sixth Lord Byron was denied any such training. His great-uncle at Newstead had made no attempt even to meet him, and his Nottingham relations—while occasionally complaining about his behavior—seem not to have tried to direct his course. His mother appreciated some of the social significance of an heir, but she was more interested in her own family, the Gordons, than the Byrons. She was, Byron later recalled, "as haughty as Lucifer" about her line of descent from the Stuarts.[17] As Thomas Moore was to note in his biography of Byron:

> Even under the most favourable circumstances, such an early elevation to
> rank would be but too likely to have a dangerous influence on the charac-

ter; and the guidance under which young Byron entered upon his new sta-
tion was, of all others, the least likely to lead him safely through its perils
and temptations.[18]

Byron was not left entirely to his own devices. Since he inherited an
unsettled estate as a minor, he automatically became a ward of court. From
1660, heirs and heiresses in his position were the responsibility of the Court
of Chancery, which had the task of safeguarding their interests and welfare
until they came of age. The court did not appoint guardians, which was
usually a family matter, but it did expect to maintain an overview of the
property while the minority lasted. Consequently, it was normal practice
for one of the guardians to be a professional agent capable of administering
the estate through the minority. John Hanson was appointed to this position. The other two guardians were Byron's mother and his distant cousin
Frederick, fifth earl of Carlisle (1748–1825). Carlisle's mother was Isabella
Byron, the fifth Lord Byron's sister, but he was not particularly keen to act
on behalf of relations he clearly regarded with some distaste. In fact, his
was to be a minor role: Hanson was the key player in the guardianship, as
he was to be in Byron's life and affairs more generally.

It was John Hanson who met Byron at Newstead in 1798, and who was
to follow his coffin to Hucknall Church twenty-six years later. Between
those two occasions the sixth Lord Byron's fortunes were entrusted to
Hanson in a way that was unusual in an aristocratic family, and that was
almost certainly not in the best interests of either family or estate.[19] The
circumstances that brought Byron to Newstead in 1798 provided him with
Hanson not simply as a guardian, but as a guide, a mentor, and a father
figure. During the minority this was almost certainly what he needed, and
Byron lived with Hanson in London for a short while in 1799–1801, acquiring in the process something of a substitute family. Byron remained
personally close to Hanson for the rest of his life. From Athens in January
1811 he dreamed of how, had he been in England, he might be taking a
bottle of port at Hanson's Chancery Lane offices, and hearing of how his
livestock fared at Farleigh Wallop, the country house in Hampshire that
Hanson used after 1804 in his role of solicitor to its owner, the earl of
Portsmouth. In 1814 Byron recalled that "I have been acquainted with him
since I was ten years old, which gives him a kind of claim upon what good-
nature I possess."[20] Lady Melbourne disliked Hanson intensely. He was,
she told Annabella Milbanke in 1814, an "odious" man, but cautioned her
niece, "dont tell Lord Byron I called him so, for that is a tender subject."[21]

What transpired in the longer term was not so much an employer-
employee relationship in the usual manner of landowner and steward,
but a dependency on a reliable family friend and confidant. This was not

Portrait of John Hanson, by **John James Halls (d. 1834), oil on canvas. (Nottingham City Museums and Art Galleries [Newstead Abbey].)**

necessarily a disadvantage, but it became increasingly so as Hanson's interests widened.[22] Byron, and all those close to him, were to find Hanson's procrastination irritating (to say the least). Hanson, he told Augusta in 1811, was "a good man and able" even if "the most dilatory in the world," and he retained implicit faith in his judgment. In 1814 he admitted that "I have known him since I was a child, as to his integrity or ability I cannot speak, I suppose as all men think 'patrons capricious and mistresses fickle but every one except his own mistress and his own patron' most people except their own lawyer."[23]

In 1814 Byron gave away Hanson's daughter, Mary Anne, when she married the earl of Portsmouth. After he married, Byron considered but rejected the idea of taking his wife to Farleigh, which he recalled as "a large and comfortably retired mansion which I know by having been there some years ago, and I think it will suit us very well." When in 1821 the Portsmouth marriage became a subject of London gossip, Byron admitted that "it is a great disadvantage to me to have such a solicitor," but he added that "he was made so when I was ten years old, and I have no help for it."[24] It was only after he had sold Newstead and left England that Byron began to have doubts about Hanson's integrity,[25] and even then the bond of friendship, although often stretched, never passed beyond the breaking point. Hanson was an executor of Byron's will—as well as a mourner at his funeral.

Chancery appointed Hanson to the position of receiver on the Byron estates. The court required that the estate should be looked after in the best interests of the heir, and consequently the property had to be assessed for its improvement value. While he was at Newstead introducing the young Lord Byron to the tenants in September 1798, Hanson made arrangements for a Mr. Dowland to carry out a full survey and plan of the estate.[26] Subsequently, Hanson was required to submit regular accounts detailing income, expenditure, and profit on the property, and to pay from the profits £500 annually for Byron's education and maintenance. All other profits over and above permitted expenses for estate improvements had to be paid into Chancery to be made available to Byron when he came of age. Byron was later to argue that "ward I was to my cost . . . the Chancery was the plea of the savings being smaller than they would otherwise have been, though small enough in any case."[27] This was something of a gloss on the matter. Although the surviving accounts do not cover the whole period of the minority, we shall see that, far from giving any hint of impropriety, they suggest Hanson managed the estate in such a way that Byron took it over at his coming-of-age in a reasonable financial condition.

Of course, as a London solicitor Hanson could not be expected to manage the estates in person. He could and did visit Newstead periodically.

Apart from greeting Mrs. Byron and her son in 1798, he was also there in
the summer of 1799 to collect the rents, the following December to discuss
a rent rise, and in May 1801 to collect rents again. Day-to-day control he
entrusted to Owen Mealey, who was appointed in November 1798 and
given a house in which to live. Mealey was briefed by Hanson during his
visits, and at other times he was expected to prepare "a regular daily journal of all the work done," to be written up on a Sunday and sent to London
by Monday's post. Hanson would then be able "to give you more regular
directions." Such a system of management was by no means unusual, and
Hanson seems generally to have taken his responsibilities seriously.[28] Unfortunately, Mealey, the man on the spot, lacked the authority to substitute
adequately for his employer, and Hanson did not help matters by being a
reluctant correspondent.

III

The first decision to be taken after Byron and his mother arrived at
Newstead in the autumn of 1798 concerned the future of the abbey. Byron
enjoyed the freedom of his own estate in the first few weeks after his arrival in Nottinghamshire, and he also traveled into Nottingham to see his
Byron relations. The abbey was, of course, in a poor state, and the fifth
Lord Byron had left instructions in his will to sell any furniture remaining
in the house. Robert Aisley, the executor, agreed to let the furnishings stay
in the house for six months, giving Mrs. Byron the option of buying them if
she wished. Aisley died in August 1798, and as there is no evidence of a
sale, or of the furnishings being removed, we may conclude that the commission lapsed with his death, since he was to have been the beneficiary of
any sale.[29] Even so, the dilapidated and semifurnished house was deemed
to be inappropriate accommodation for the young heir and his mother. Early
in 1799 Mrs. Byron installed her son in lodgings in Nottingham with a
nurse. The intention was that he should continue his education and receive
medical treatment, but in July she agreed that he might move to London.
There he attended Dr. Glennie's school in Dulwich. Byron briefly revisited
Newstead in the summer of 1800, before returning to his studies at Dulwich.
In April 1801 Hanson entered him at Harrow, and Byron spent the subsequent summer holiday with his mother in London and the West Country.[30]

Byron did not travel to Nottinghamshire in 1801, because Newstead
had been let. In September 1798, only days after his first meeting with
Byron at Newstead, Hanson began the task of arranging for Newstead, and
the shooting rights, to be leased out during the minority. Obviously the
abbey left much to be desired as a residence, and the annual rent was set at

only £40—rather less than the £200 George Bowes had paid in the 1730s. In 1801 a Mr. Clay took a one-year lease of the house, the garden, and two acres of adjoining land. He left at Lady Day 1802, possibly after breaching the terms of his lease by selling fish caught in the lakes.[31] Clay was followed at Newstead by the two Misses Launder, who arrived in October 1802 and stayed until the summer of 1803. They came from a local family, but Hanson was reluctant to formalize the terms of their stay at Newstead: in his view they were temporarily occupying "what accommodation the house will afford . . . until we can meet with a proper tenant" and they could find a suitable alternative. By contrast, the ladies thought they had been granted tenancy of the abbey for the duration of the minority: "[A]ll their talk," Mealey informed Hanson, "is that they mean to stay until my Lord comes of age." Apparently under the impression that they had the tenancy, the ladies brought in their own furniture and requested various repairs, some of which they were willing to fund. They even persuaded the farmers to present them with gifts of coal normally regarded as part of the landlord's rent.[32]

The eagerness of the Misses Launder to stay at Newstead suggests that despite the neglect of previous years it still provided tolerable accommodation, although Mrs. Byron complained in 1803 that without some attention it would "soon be in ruins, and the Park is in a deplorable state."[33] When a potential tenant looked around in 1803 he admitted,

> I am really quite delighted with the old Abbey and having been taught to expect a most ruinous and uninhabitable place the few comfortable rooms quite reconciled me, and it strikes me that with very little expense I shall be able to make it answer my purpose very well.[34]

No one was pretending that Newstead was in first-class condition, but Hanson told the Misses Launder that they were welcome to live in whichever rooms were habitable, probably in the southeast wing. They were not allowed the run of the place; indeed, in May 1803 they asked Hanson for access to the two rooms "out of the Hall as all our company wish to see the Abbey and you know there is nothing in them, so locking them up is quite unnecessary."[35]

By early 1803 Hanson had found a potential tenant he regarded as rather more suitable for a house of Newstead's stature than the Misses Launder. This was Henry Edward Yelverton, the twenty-three-year-old nineteenth Lord Grey de Ruthyn, who was currently renting Brandon, near Coventry, and who offered to take a tenancy of the abbey for the rest of the minority. The rent was to be £50 a year, and he was to pay all taxes and the gamekeeper's salary. Hanson offered similar terms to the Misses Launder, but they could not afford the rent and reluctantly prepared to move out. When Lord Grey visited Newstead in March 1803 he found the ladies "much annoyed at the idea of quitting," and he feared that they would not take kindly to his preparations for moving in, which included "making the cellar good" and "altering the stables." He told Hanson that they were "equally displeased with you for letting me Newstead."[36]

The situation then became extremely awkward. Lord Grey agreed to let them stay until midsummer, but once his lease of Brandon ran out and the ladies showed no sign of moving, his temper began to fray. While they remained at Newstead, he "must travel about the country and all my servants and family will be thrown into disorder and confusion." In addition, "the stables and many parts of the house are much in want of repairs" that could not begin until he was "possessed of a settled place of residence." In June he sent his wine and some of his furniture to Newstead. Accusations flew in all directions. Mealey told Hanson that the Misses Launder were refusing to pay tradesmen's bills, and they complained in response that Mealey had mistreated their house guests and prevented them from taking pigeons and gooseberries.[37] Mealey, in his own defense, claimed that two boys from the ladies' house party had stolen his guinea fowls and the rabbit hutch had been broken into, "but the whole of the grievance is because I would not let them have our horse to ride out every day." The ladies then told Lord Grey of Mealey's supposed misdemeanors, and Grey in turn informed Hanson that he hoped Mealey "will not be so impudent as to make the attempt to annoy me in the same way as I will frankly acknowledge my temper is not of that quiescent nature as to submit to it." Mealey in turn recounted how, after a visit from Mrs. Byron to Newstead on 26 June 1803 the ladies and their visitors "make game of her." Mrs. Byron apparently treated the ladies' friends "with the greatest insolence" and accused her tenants of being "intruders," which, since they had outstayed their welcome, strictly speaking they were.[38]

After all this strife, the Misses Launder finally vacated the abbey on 23 July and Lord Grey moved in, although initially without much luggage: "[W]e have literally but half a dozen plates and knives and forks are equally short."[39] Although Hanson might have defused some of the tension had he been a little more snappy in dealing with tenants and potential tenants, he was careful to protect the Byron interests when he let the house—hence, presumably, the locked doors. He excluded from the lease the bailiff's house (where Mealey lived), as well as "the yard to keep timber and work up materials in for repairs of the farms and also the use of such parts of the gardens where the young forest trees quick and seeds are now planted and sown." He also reserved the hunting, shooting, and fishing, while expecting the tenant to maintain the gamekeeper. He made it clear that little money was available for improvements either to the house or the gardens. When the Misses Launder asked Mealey to have "the walks and that part of the Garden that they mean to have [put] in repair, and they will keep it so," Hanson refused their request on the grounds that "it is not the intention of Lord Byron's guardians to be at a shilling expense in any repairs. I cannot therefore give directions for anything being done at their expense either in repairs of the house or in the gardens." The Misses Launder brought some of their own furniture, although Hanson offered to sell what was left from the fifth lord's day to Lord Grey, leaving Byron the option of repurchasing on the expiration of the lease.[40]

Byron, meanwhile, had spent his 1802 vacations with his mother, visiting Bath at Christmas. In January 1803 he was reluctant to return to Harrow. Hanson considered the possibility of hiring a tutor "for a year or so," and he smoothly assured the worried mother that her son was "pursuing a course that will lead him on to consequence and fame."[41] He did eventually return, but Mrs. Byron decided that the time had come to leave London, and began making tentative inquiries after a house in the locality of Newstead as a summer retreat. After some discussion she took a lease at Burgage Manor in Southwell, "a handsome new house and very pleasantly situated." Mrs. Byron, acting in the best aristocratic interests, arranged for the family portraits at Newstead to be removed to Southwell for safekeeping.[42] It was to Southwell that Byron set forth to spend his school holidays in July 1803, but he soon grew tired of his mother's company and set off for Newstead, which he had not visited since 1800.

Lord Grey had made it clear in advance of taking the tenancy that the young heir would be a welcome guest at Newstead. Grey had only just moved in, and since he had as yet brought hardly anything to Newstead, Byron lodged with Owen Mealey rather than staying in the abbey itself. He stayed for over two months, and his mother joined him for part of the time. It was, to say the least, bizarre to find the aristocratic owner of the family mansion lodging in the bailiff's cottage, while a tenant enjoyed the abbey.[43] Byron found Mealey's cottage to be convenient for visits to Annesley, where he was busily falling in love with his cousin, Mary Chaworth. He also paid a visit with Miss Chaworth's family to Matlock.[44] In September he refused to return to Harrow.

Grey was away from Newstead for some time in the autumn, but once he returned in November Byron moved into the abbey. Tenant and owner became firm friends, and there was much consequent gossip about him being "tutored by Lord Grey." Mealey was simply irritated, and wrote spitefully to Hanson of how they would "go out these moonlight nights and shoot pheasants as they sit at roost." As a sportsman, Grey is most unlikely to have engaged in such activities, but Mealey wanted the heir out of his way and complained in late November that for four months his work had regularly been interrupted by Byron. Nor did it help that Byron apparently talked of turning the garden into a hare warren, and complained about Hanson not having collected the rents "as he is losing the interest of his money by laying in the farmers' hands for so long."[45] But, as in 1798, Byron was enraptured by the house—although perhaps not of its condition—and wrote in *On Leaving Newstead Abbey:*

> Thro' thy battlements, Newstead, the hollow winds whistle;
> Thou, the hall of my fathers, art gone to decay;
> In thy once smiling garden, the hemlock and thistle
> Have choak'd up the rose, which late bloom'd in the way.[46]

Byron spent Christmas 1803 at Newstead, but he subsequently fell out with Lord Grey and returned to Harrow in January 1804. Later he was to make oblique references to this period, hinting at some reprochable behavior on the part of Grey, to whom he was never subsequently reconciled; indeed, Byron criticized him in verse for neglecting Newstead and allowing the oak he had planted in 1798 to wither:

> Young Oak! when I planted thee deep in the ground,
> I hoped that thy days would be longer than mine;
> That thy dark-waving branches would flourish around,
> And ivy thy trunk with her mantle entwine. . . .
>
> I left thee, my Oak, and, since that fatal hour,
> A stranger has dwelt in the hall of my sire;
> Till Manhood shall crown me, not mine is the power,
> But his, whose neglect may have bade thee expire.[47]

For his part, Grey claimed to have been mystified by the cooling of relations, and he continued to enjoy a good rapport with Mrs. Byron. Mealey reported in March 1804 that he was "very thick with Mrs Byron," and four months later they were "greater than ever." They had dined together several times, "and whatever he says is right with her." Doubtless Mrs. Byron found much to attract her in the young bachelor, although her son was reported to be "displeased at it," fearing that they might be falling in love.[48] When, in July 1805, Grey commented to Hanson on "the shyness which exists between Lord Byron and myself," Hanson responded: "I am extremely sorry that any shyness should exist between your Lordship and Lord Byron, the cause of which I never could learn. I had felt very comfortable that the most perfect cordiality would have prevailed and I yet hope it will when Lord Byron next visits Notts." It was not to be. Subsequently Mrs. Byron's friendship with Grey also cooled, and on later visits to Nottinghamshire Byron stayed at Southwell: he did not return to Newstead until Grey left in 1808.[49]

Grey was a difficult tenant. The problems began in March 1804 when Mealey reported that he had

> drawn the shuttle of the forest pond to run it dry. As soon as I found it out I went to him and told him my orders from you. He seemed very much displeased and ordered the shuttle to be put down. He said he would speak to you and if you was not agreeable to let him run the lower lake and the rest of the pond dry he would not mind spending £1,000 to get every fish out of all the ponds.[50]

Grey also fell out with Mealey, complaining to Hanson in October that "he has not, or will not, exert the necessary power on many points." It was worse than this:

> This light soil is particularly favourable to the growth of weeds and in a garden like Newstead shows little labour had been bestowed, its continually prolific soil had need [of] every encouragement, you will therefore easily credit the assertion that a good deal of expense had been employed not only to eradicate for the moment, but by continual husbandry effectually to stifle this pernicious hinderance, yet after the garden had been completely cleansed of these tormenters, I solicited Mealey's interference amongst your Forest trees to prevent the rest of the weeds invading your garden and which by the by appeared a very just and reasonable request considering they had occupied a larger share of ground for much longer than the time allotted, but I was considerably surprised to hear him say he had nothing to do with it, and that he could not attempt such a thing without Mr Hanson's orders. My reply was that from that moment I should consider Mr Mealey as a nonentity in regard to his stewardship, and that all my applications would in future be made to you . . . he promised to send a man and the work was tolerably executed.[51]

Grey found Hanson equally annoying. He fired off a letter to him on 25 January 1805 complaining about the coal, about trees in the garden, and about Hanson's lack of interest. He then set about Mealey, asking for the trees to be removed from the garden because "he wants the ground for potatoes and cow cabbage." Mealey complained that Grey was breeding hares that were destroying the quicksets, but he did not dare drive them away, "as he has complained of it at Southwell [i.e., to Mrs. Byron] many times." Since Mealey did not have the authority to remove the offending trees, Grey took legal advice and threatened "to throw them over the wall." Mealey negotiated a temporary truce when he assured Grey in regard to

Hanson "that his letters meet with as little attention as mine." Grey wrote again to Hanson asking for authority to remove the trees, which were supposed to have been taken out of the garden by midsummer 1804 and were still there in March 1805. He questioned Hanson's integrity: "It is extremely unpleasant to be obliged to write so often upon one subject and as in future I may have to apply on other subjects I should wish to know whether you have appointed Mrs Byron, my Lord Carlisle, or the Lord Chancellor to such letters of business," a pointed reference to the fact that Hanson was supposed to be the business end of the guardianship.[52]

Hanson was clearly rattled: most unusually, he responded immediately, giving Grey and Mealey authority to move the trees. Grey was not entirely satisfied: "I cannot on matters of business but feel excessively mortified in having repeatedly failed to procure those replies which a common attention to business entitle me to expect." Hanson agreed to have all the trees moved, but complained about Grey's unwillingness to have the hares controlled. Unfortunately for Mealey, now that Grey had managed to elicit replies from Hanson, his truce with the bailiff collapsed. Grey complained in January 1805 that Mealey was "about to destroy the whole of the cover in the only preserve Newstead Manor affords, and which will so very materially injure the preservation of the game that all my care and vigilance will avail little." Hanson at least supported his employee, at the expense of further annoying Grey, whose "anxious wish" it was "to restore this manor to my Lord Byron more plentifully stocked with game than it was on my taking possession of it."[53]

The ongoing conflict between Grey and Mealey was partly caused by the attitude of the tenants. They had delivered a boon, or gift, of coal, as part of their rent, to Grey, who had complained that they had not provided "the usual and accustomed quantity, for Mealey I understand claims an equal share in the labour of these seams as myself." He told Mealey "he would insist upon the same boon as the late Lord Byron." When the tenants refused to conform he complained to Hanson: "I am sorry to trouble you again but these descendants of Robin Hood are extremely unruly. Hardstaff at the Wire Mill and Mr Davys particularly refuse to supply me with fuel, the former has only done half his booning but alleges that having carried coals to the Miss Launders and to Mealey is a sufficient release from his engagement." This time Hanson did not reply.[54]

Despite these difficulties, Grey clearly grew rather fond of Newstead, and in August 1807 Mealey reported that "all the talk of this country is that Lord Byron means to sell Newstead as soon as he comes of age." The rumor appeared to have originated with Grey, who "means to buy it." By November 1807 the rumor had reached Doncaster, and various people were asking Hanson for first refusal on the property. In December Mrs. Byron was convinced that Grey had no intention of leaving: "I may be mistaken but I believe there will be some difficulty in getting him out, and I know when the time arrives Byron never will rest till he is out. Therefore you must take that business entirely on yourself as I would not have them meet on any account as they hate each other, and I am sure they would quarrel which might end very seriously." Hanson smoothed her ruffled feathers: he had, he assured her, purposely limited Grey's tenancy to midsummer 1808 "in order that it might be open for Lord Byron when he came of age."[55]

Grey's ploy had failed, and in January 1808 he told Mrs. Byron that "she might do what she pleased with the garden." Mrs. Byron in turn instructed Mealey to "get all sorts of vegetables in soon, also the fruit trees cut, wall trees nailed. The trees has not been cut these two years, and the grounds is in a worse state than it was when I first came to Newstead." Grey organized a sale in March, preparatory to leaving at midsummer. He departed in July, leaving outstanding rent arrears.[56]

IV

What of the estate during Byron's minority? Hanson's first task was to take a long and careful look at the financial position his client had inherited. During a protracted visit in the autumn of 1802 he examined the whole property and left detailed instructions regarding fencing, ditching, and draining, tree planting, and tenancy arrangements. As a result, a drain was cut in the Mill Meadow, a dike was cut in Limekiln Wood, fencing was erected at several farms, 20,500 oaks were planted, and buildings—including some rooms in the abbey—were put into repair. Mealey was encouraged "to go round the new plantations and replace any of the plants that may have died or been injured"; he was to preserve the game and ensure that the ponds were fully stocked with fish (Mealey reported acquiring "60 brace of trout," which he put into "different ponds that had been cleared"); and he was to supply Mrs. Byron (spending Christmas at Bath) with game for her son's birthday celebration on 22 January. Hanson regularly sent Mealey money to pay for the work, although he commented early in January 1803 that "this makes eighty five pounds so there ought to be a great deal of work done."[57]

After a visit to Newstead in April 1803 Hanson left Mealey with orders relating to felling oaks and other trees. As a result, in July Mealey supervised the felling of 652 oak pollards, and 3,300 alders. Much of the timber was used for making rails and posts for new fencing, and work continued through the autumn and into the spring of 1804. Repairs were also carried out to the stone wall at the entrance to the abbey grounds. Mealey was not short of timber, but by early 1804 he was running out of money to pay the workmen. In February 1804 he gave Hanson a description of the work in progress:

> I have sent you an account of what work is done in the yard. Likewise the account of Slaney's draining, plashing and fencing. There is a great deal more posts and rails in the yard yet to mortice and tenon, which you will have an account of it all when you come down. Slaney and his man is at work in the yard, and would wish to know where you would have any more fence set down as it gets far on in the season now.

Mealey added that Lord Grey was pressing him as to "when the fencing will be got out of the yard or the oaks out of the garden."[58]

At Easter 1804 Hanson traveled to Newstead partly to collect the rents but also to inspect the work Mealey was supervising. By October Mealey was encouraging him to pay another visit, "as the oaks in the yard wants planting out very bad, and likewise the ash." On 12 December Mealey reported that "as the park fence is done I think it would be a good plan to continue the two plantations one as far as the tollbar, and the other towards Whiteheads. It would make room for as many oaks, and we could put many thousands of ash on Sherwood." This work continued through 1805.[59]

Generally, Mealey seems to have done a satisfactory job, although he did not always enjoy Hanson's confidence. In March 1804 he told Hanson that one area of quicks they had recently planted had been ruined by hares, but Lord Grey would not allow him to run a dog in the area to scare off the hares because this would upset the game. In other areas rabbits and sheep were doing the damage: "If I was to run from one fence to the other from morning until night they would be in every time as they [i.e., the farmers] never offer to turn them out." The appeal fell on deaf ears, since the only response he received from Hanson was to lay the blame at his feet:

> I am very much vexed at your last letter to find that all the expense that we have been at is likely to be thrown away, but you must take the necessary means to prevent the Quickset and Plantations from being destroyed. They are under your care, and you have nothing else to do and I shall hold you accountable for the proper care of them.[60]

Grey also created problems in regard to the water supply through the lakes to the Robinson mills. In July 1804 Mealey reported that the main sluice of the mill pond was leaking, and urgently needed repairs. Mealey was caught between Mr. Robinson, "who wants water," and Lord Grey, who "wants it dry to get the fish." Nor was it only Grey who interfered. In January 1803 Captain Byron visited Newstead and found "a great deal of fault about the few trees that was felled, the garden he said he would talk to you about it when he went to London."[61] And in September 1804 Mealey complained that "Mrs Byron abuses me very much . . . because I could not raise the sum of £400 for her at Newstead. She threatens to turn [the farmer's] off of their farms as soon as Lord Byron comes of age."[62]

What Mealey was overseeing in these years was the managerial result of the transformation of park land into individual farms carried out in the fifth Lord Byron's time. Although the fifth lord had sold considerable quantities of timber, the park was evidently not entirely denuded. Hanson ordered the felling of much of what was left to make fencing for the three large farms carved out of the park. By the time Newstead was sold in 1817, only twelve acres of enclosed abbey grounds remained as park land, and the estate was described as good wheat and turnip land, particularly adapted for the Norfolk system of arable husbandry. At the same time, like any good steward, Hanson had commissioned a timber-planting program to benefit future generations.[63]

V

Hanson's management seems to have worked well in respect to estate affairs over which Mealey had control, but to have been less successful in relation to the tenants. When a landowner had a small estate detached from his main property, on which he could not justify maintaining a full-time steward, he could either hire a lawyer (as the fifth Lord Byron had done in Lancashire and Norfolk) or he might appoint one of the more substantial farmers as bailiff. The bailiff would collect the rents and remit them to the owner, and check that the tenants were conforming to the terms of agricultural leases. Once or twice a year he could expect a visit from the agent, much as William Daws had visited Rochdale and Norfolk in the 1760s and 1770s. Mealey was neither a lawyer nor a substantial tenant. He evidently had some knowledge of farming, because on one occasion he recommended a scheme proposed by William Beardall on the grounds that "he brings more manure to his farm from Nottingham than all the tenants at Newstead besides." Yet in general terms, Mealey failed to command the respect of the Newstead tenants; indeed, while in effect he performed the role of bailiff, he was known both by Hanson and the tenants as the gardener. William Palin recalled many years later that "there was no bailiff or resident agent" at Newstead, and Hanson's orders "were sent through Owen Mealey, the gardener."[64]

Mealey's problems in persuading the tenants to treat him seriously can be traced through his letters to Hanson. In February 1804 Mealey reported,

"I called on Whitehead and Palethorpe according to your orders. [William] Whitehead has paid his half year's rent and I believe was very much put to his shifts. [John] Palethorpe has not paid in yet. He said he would let me know when he would. I fear you will have some trouble with them." Whitehead's rent was £145, which he paid for the year 1803–4, but in 1804–5 he paid only £18. He paid £137 10s. in 1805–6, leaving £134 10s. outstanding as arrears. Palethorpe had been in financial difficulty for a while. He had a farm rented for £98, and a stone quarry for £21. In January 1803 Mealey had reported him to be "very much involved in debt, I know of between 3 and 4 hundred pounds that he owes in one place." Palethorpe paid his rent in 1803–4, but in April 1804 he was committed to Nottingham Gaol with debts of £300. Mealey inspected his farm and found "neither corn nor hay. On the premises there is 18 beasts young and old, a few sheep. His horses is very old and that's all there is." He was not discharged until September, and then Mealey was at considerable pains to ensure that as he sold his stock the cash was paid into Hanson's account at Smith's Bank in Nottingham to cover his outstanding rent. By January 1805 he had paid in £144, but he was again in financial difficulties in 1805–6. Nor were Whitehead and Palethorpe alone: in November 1804 Mealey told Hanson that "there is many of the tenants that would be glad if you would put off the rent day until Christmas."[65]

When Hanson himself took a lead, Mealey had few problems at Newstead. Hanson was strict with the tenants. When one of the Park farmers, Elizabeth Darby, let it be known that she intended to quit her farm and pass it on to a farmer from Blidworth who was going to add it to the two farms he already worked and to keep a laborer at Newstead to run the farm, Hanson made it perfectly clear that he would not accept a tenant "who rents any other farm."[66]

Left to his own devices, Mealey tried to sound confident, but his (often semiliterate) letters hint rather broadly at his difficulties. "Old Bell," Mealey told Hanson early in 1803, "says them that set the new road out [he] wished their head may be put in porridge pot and boiled for two hours. He say there has been no body employed about Newstead since the late Lord Byron died but a set of fools." When in August 1805 he reported to Hanson on Mrs. Bowers, he asked that the information should be treated confidentially for fear "she would pull my eyes out." On another occasion he told Hanson, "Young Whitehead he says that you are an encroaching fellow, and as for me I am nothing, he will pull me to pieces anyday and old Bell says that his head is too bold for yours, this is their speeches behind your back but not to me." This problem of respect also emerged in a case Mealey reported to Hanson in January 1806:

There is a deal of dispute between Rushton and Hardstaff about the fence down the Hawk lawn. Rushton's sheep get into Hardstaff's turnips, and did him . . . damage . . . valued at £4. Rushton will make no recompense, but threatens Hardstaff with law, and I cannot learn that Hardstaff ever made that fence, besides Rushton is so overbearing that he will do nothing but what he pleases. He even told me that you could not settle it that it should be left to a jury.[67]

What really undermined Mealey's position was Hanson's increasingly ambivalent role at Newstead. He either could not or would not devote time to the Byron estate. Planned visits came to nothing—there were none between 1805 and 1808[68]—and potential tenants sometimes went to London in search of Hanson. William Palin, who was after a Newstead tenancy in 1805, later recalled how he had to go to London three times during that year to negotiate his lease with Hanson, who, for one reason or another, seemed incapable of completing the business speedily. Others had similar experiences. When Hanson refused Elizabeth Darby permission to pass the lease of her farm to a man from Blidworth, she had to look for someone else. Mealey thought she would have difficulty finding a replacement, "as the farm is in such a bad state." In fact, Samuel Rushton came forward with an offer, which Mealey was anxious to see accepted. Hanson was in no hurry: on 6 February 1803 Mealey complained that "Rushton has called three times to know if you had sent any answer about Darby's farm."[69]

Mealey had insufficient authority to take important decisions, and often could not elicit from Hanson a speedy answer to his queries. He also found it difficult to persuade Hanson to send him money to pay workmen on the estate. Almost all his weekly digests included requests for money: on 1 March 1803 he told Hanson that there were various men at work, and "they are crying out for money. I have not one shilling to give them on Saturday without you sending some money."[70] These kind of difficulties multiplied the longer Hanson was absent from Newstead, because just through his absence he effectively transferred power to Mealey, but without doing anything to improve his status. When John Howett of Newstead Warren gave notice in February 1805 to quit at Lady Day, Mealey was given the task of interviewing prospective replacements and reporting back to Hanson. However, several candidates, unwilling to trust their fate to Mealey, applied direct to Hanson. On other occasions Mealey had more complex problems with which to deal. He told Hanson in August 1805 that

Mrs [Ann] Nicholson . . . means to marry her servant man. He has lived with her eight years. He has a hundred pounds in her hands which she cannot pay him without selling off her stock which if she does she will not be able to carry on the farm. The man is not willing to marry before he knows whether you will accept him as tenant upon the farm or not. Sir you are the best judge what to do in it. They beg you'll please to send your answer as they are asked in Church.[71]

Given Hanson's track record on answering letters, the couple would have been wise to avoid publishing banns of marriage quite so precipitously.

Nor did tenants, and potential tenants, stop with Hanson. Having by-passed Mealey, if they failed to receive a response from Hanson, or one that they considered adequate, some were happy to carry their case to Mrs. Byron in Southwell. This brings us back to William Palin. George Bowers, tenant of The Hutt, died in 1806, and his widow announced her intention to marry William Palin. Mealey told Hanson of Mrs. Bowers's unruly behavior, but he had an ulterior motive. He painted a rather unflattering picture of her because he wanted the tenancy for himself. Mealey successfully persuaded Hanson to give Mrs. Bowers notice of eviction. For his part, Palin had agreed to marry Mrs. Bowers, who was much older than he was, partly in the expectation of obtaining the tenancy, and in some alarm he appealed to Lord Grey and to Mrs. Byron "to intercede for them." Unaware of the promise to Mealey, the couple requested friends to supply them with references as to their suitability for the tenancy, which they forwarded to Hanson. They even traveled to London to visit Hanson, and when this failed to bring the desired result they consulted a lawyer and then threatened to stay put, and force Hanson to evict them.[72]

In the last days of July 1806, Palin and Mrs. Bowers heard that Byron was visiting his mother at Southwell. They went direct to Burgage Manor and there obtained an audience with the young heir, who was down from Cambridge for the summer vacation. The interview was evidently satisfactory, because Mealey heard that they had "got Lord Byron to promise that he would write to you for them to continue, and sent me word by them that they were to continue." He was, not surprisingly, alarmed by this intervention, and within a day or two had followed Palin to Southwell: "I went over to Lord Byron and reminded him of his promises to me even so late as last June." Byron, busily preparing *Fugitive Pieces* and taking more than a passing interest in a number of young Southwell ladies, was not really in the mood for business: "[H]e seemed confused but told me I might write to you that he was agreeable for you to settle it as you thought proper, that he would not interfere of either sides." Mealey implored Hanson to "stand my friend this time . . . my lord deviates from what he has promised so many times that I have little hopes for the time to come." A few days later Byron left for London after a furious row with his mother, but for Mealey the damage had been done: on 12 August Mealey told Hanson that the Palins "make their braggs now that they can stay without your consent and call me every where they go worse than a dog. If it was only during Lord Byron's minority to keep them out I would be satisfied. Mr Clark has spoke to Lord Byron for them, but he says he will not interfere that it all rests with you."[73]

Subsequently the matter stalled, and the following June Mealey was still complaining that Palin and Mrs. Bowers had retained The Hutt, despite the promise to him of the tenancy. "Lord Byron and his mother says that you told them in London that you would put me into it, and they say it is all up to you and they wish me to have it." He implored Hanson to help him "to what was proposed," so that should his employment be terminated after Byron's coming of age he would at least have somewhere to live. He had, he added, lost his cow, had to see the doctor, and was owed a year's wages. Eventually he triumphed: the Palins were given notice to quit at Lady Day 1808, and The Hutt was let to Mealey with thirteen acres in addition to the public house.[74]

The Hutt case involved Mealey personally, but keeping the tenants under control at Newstead proved increasingly troublesome while Hanson stayed away. Three tenancies came up for discussion in the course of 1807, one through the death of William Bell Sr., and the others because both William Whitehead and John Palethorpe were still struggling financially. Bell's farm caused Mealey a particular headache. The farm had, in Mealey's view, been badly managed, and now Bell's widow wanted to retain the tenancy while his son "will make a better warrener than he will a farmer. He is very idle and a great slovern." The farm stock was auctioned in February 1808. The livestock was described as consisting of three useful draft horses, cows (including ten in calf), two store pigs, and one fat pig. The farm machinery included a roller, a winnowing fan, a straw engine, harness for six horses, plow pads and traces, and a number of good sacks. In the farmyard were hay, clover, wheat, and oat stacks, together with quantities of thatch, rakes, forks, spades, wagons, ropes, and other equipment. The sale also included furniture from the farmhouse. William Bell Jr. bought some of the items, and was granted the tenancy.[75]

The Whitehead case was more straightforward. He had accumulated considerable arrears in 1805–6, and in July 1806 Mealey reported that

> Mr Whitehead is in my opinion and many others making bad work with his farm. The piece of land that he broke up last year next Papplewick Gate and sowed with corn he has sowed again this year with corn which should this year have been fallowed and sowed with turnips.

He had also plowed up at least forty acres, although he had sufficient farmyard manure only for ten acres: "[H]e has sprinkled what he had over part of the fallows and the rest he has sowed with turnips without lime or manure of any sort." This was poor practice and he was likely to reap only a thin harvest: "[W]hat few turnips that grows there he will eat off with his sheep in the autumn and then sow with rye and next season with skeggs without any manure which is his way of farming." This was simply robbing the goodness of the soil without restoring the fertility, and Mealey hardly needed to add his final sentence: "Sir will you please to judge what state his farm will be in when my Lord comes of age." Since Whitehead was also very poor, and "his livestock is bad," Mealey recommended a discharge.[76]

Hanson was unmoved, but in the summer of 1807 Whitehead announced his intention to pay only £39 of his rent. Mealey was not convinced he had any way of finding the rest: "[H]is corn is all thrashed out and gone, his stock is very little, and his crops very bad this year." He managed to pay a further £33 10s. early in August, and asked for time to pay the rest. Mealey thought him unlikely to be able to pay, and Hanson finally agreed to an eviction. Mealey was entrusted with the task of negotiating the terms of his compensation for leaving the farm:

> [T]he following is what he wishes to be paid for: all the manure and straw that is upon the farm, the seeds that was sown last spring and sowing of them, wheat that was sown last autumn and ploughing, rye that was sown this winter and ploughing, the fallows ploughing . . . five times and manuring that is now sown with turnips, the park fence he says that you promised to pay him for, the Brandriffs in the stackyard and all other things that he has a right to be paid for on the premises. You chose one man and he another [as referees].

The news spread, and it was not long before requests were coming in for the vacancy.[77]

William Johnson wrote to Hanson from the Black Bull Inn, Mansfield, to inquire after Whitehead's farm. "I think it lies in my power to manage it well by having a large flock of sheep, and I have all other implements in Husbandry." He added that his lease was up at Mansfield, and he had reserved a large quantity of manure with the intention of using it on a new farm. He quoted Mealey as a referee, but more importantly John Parkinson, Lord Scarbrough's agent at Rufford. A Mr. Taylor who applied for the tenancy was not considered suitable by Mealey:

> I know the old tenants at Newstead cannot bear the idea of his coming. They all say he has money but his principles are bad, and he will make a bad neighbour. As for my part, he was the last man that I expected to solicit for any favour at Newstead for it is not four years since he called the late Lord Byron a dog and damned the present lord and said Mr Robinson's son was as good a gentleman as Lord Byron and worth more money. He always took an active part in Mr Robinson's behalf against Lord B. I could

tell you several other mean things which I will defer until I see you, and no doubt when you come to Newstead you will find others to tell you the same.

By early February 1808 no replacement had been found, and Whitehead wrote directly to Hanson to say he had been unable to find another place and asking to be allowed to stay a further year.[78]

Just as Whitehead had managed to keep going despite his financial difficulties, so the other embarrassed tenant, John Palethorpe, remained at his farm. On 2 August 1807 Mealey told Hanson that Palethorpe needed an extension to the time permitted for paying his rent: he "begs you will look over him for six weeks and in that time he will get his Lime Bills in. He says you may depend on his paying." Mealey was willing to recommend leniency, as "he certainly has been at great deal of expense in improving his farm which he has made a great deal of alteration for the better." He was ready to pay almost anything to keep the tenancy, and was doubtless worried by news that Hanson was also intending to visit Newstead "very shortly." In the event, as was by now usual, the steward did not appear.[79]

VI

Hanson was responsible during the minority for all the Byron estates, including the Rochdale properties, and even before he set off for Newstead to attend the fifth Lord Byron's funeral in 1798 he wrote a "long letter to Mr Milne, the steward at Rochdale, for information on various particulars respecting the Lancashire estate." A couple of months later, on his return from meeting Mrs. Byron and her son at Newstead, Hanson was "perusing several voluminous deeds and many papers respecting the Rochdale estate . . . and sundry letters from the agents to the late lord on the subject of Rochdale concerns." Late in 1799 he traveled to Lancashire to meet Mr. Milne and to "examine the different court books," as well as to discuss with him "various matters relating to the Rochdale estate." Hanson's concern was to establish what the sixth lord actually owned in Lancashire, and whether the fifth lord had acted legally when he parted with a number of properties in the wake of William John Byron's death in 1794.[80]

Hanson's job was to ensure that his client's income was maximized, and his property protected, during the minority, and his study of the Rochdale documentation in the summer of 1798 had been largely "in order to ascertain the late Lord's right to sell the parts thereof he had sold." His conclusion was that the resettlement of the Byron estates in 1773 had left the fifth lord only as tenant for life of the properties with the fee simple resting in his son William, who died in 1776. The sixth lord, he argued, was the legal heir to William Byron, and consequently the fifth lord did not have the powers he claimed. If this was so, the sales were illegal. In particular, Hanson was concerned that young Byron's financial interest in the Rochdale coal mines had not been protected, which is why he paid particular attention to the sale of the Brownwardle mine to James Dearden. After a visit to Rochdale over New Year's 1802–3, Hanson decided to test the issue in the courts by bringing ejectments "to recover the estates in Lancashire." The courts did not move with any speed, and the case was heard at Lancaster Assizes only in 1806, when Byron's cause was upheld on a legal technicality. The fifth lord, the court decided, could not legally make the sales, because he needed the assent of his wife and son. Both were dead by 1795, and so could not give the required consent. Hanson was jubilant. He predicted to Byron that he would be £30,000 richer at the age of twenty-one because of this victory, and by early in February 1807 Byron was excitedly telling his Southwell friend Elizabeth Pigot that success in the courts meant that he would soon be £60,000 better off.[81]

Celebration would as yet have been premature, because the chances of such a verdict going uncontested were small. Dearden duly filed his response in the form of a bill in the Court of Exchequer in Easter term 1807. As a result, Hanson was ordered to desist from carrying out further ejectments until the case had been heard. The case, Hanson informed Mrs. Byron,

> hangs upon our judgements upon the late trials, they will have recourse to every expedient the law will allot to keep possession till the latest time, and it is a lamentable thing that the law will allow them to do it, but I trust they will ultimately pay dearly for it. I have persons employed to keep an account of all the coals they get that we may be able to charge them ultimately with all the profits upon them.[82]

His words were designed to cheer up Mrs. Byron, but by November 1807 she was beginning to fret: "[P]ray what is going in the Lancashire business," she asked Hanson, and when he did not reply she asked again a few days later. Just before Christmas Hanson finally responded: "[I]t is impossible to say when the trial of the Lancashire matter will come on in the Court of Exchequer. They have it in their power to procrastinate it very much and I make no doubt they will avail themselves of it to the utmost."[83] His prediction was to prove all too accurate.

Mrs. Byron was far from happy with Hanson's response. She fired off a reply by return of post: "I am extremely sorry at what you tell me concerning the Lancashire business, can nothing be done to get it forward by those employed for my son?" Her worry was that they wanted "to procrastinate the business till Lord Byron comes of age (which God forbid they should have the power of doing) and that they think in that case to get him to agree to a foolish and unprofitable compromise."[84] Her concern increased in the spring of 1808 when she heard disturbing reports from Rochdale, which she outlined in long letters written on 23 May to John Birch and to her son. Birch, a partner in the same practice as Hanson, had been in Lancashire at the time of the recent court case, and she hoped he could therefore give her a fuller account of affairs than Hanson. She had learned that the Rochdale property had been mismanaged and that depredations had been committed amounting to "the immense sum of two hundred pounds a week at least." Her information was that one hundred colliers were daily engaged in mining and double that number were busy in the quarry, and that "the part of the estate sold by the late Lord Byron was not near so valuable as what never was sold and what my son has an undoubted right to, and if it had been properly arranged Lord Byron ought to have had more than thirty thousand pounds saved out of that property by the time he comes of age." She was not amused, and she intended to be blunt: "I will speak the truth, why is my son permitted to be thus plundered by you and Mr Hanson; why dont you prevent it; what reparation can you ever make to him?"

Nor had she finished. From another correspondent she had heard that "the mismanagement of Lord Byron's property there has long been the subject of conversation and astonishment to all the noblemen and gentlemen in the county of Lancashire, and that those who have the management of my son's affairs are greatly unsound and blamed for permitting a minor to be so plundered." She gathered that Richard Milne, the agent, had not had his accounts audited for six years, and that he had been a bankrupt several times. How, she wanted to know, had Hanson managed to dress this up in his annual accounts to Chancery? Mismanagement, she added, appeared to include the underrenting of farms. Worse still, she believed that for all his soothing words, Hanson was responsible for the delay in settling the legal case, and that the property sold by the fifth Lord Byron had been given up and ought to have been repossessed. "I entreat one or both to awake from your lethargy, and not force me to take steps that would be very disagreeable to myself as well as to you."[85] What these steps were she did not say.

To Byron she wrote in much the same terms. She had heard from Mr. Shaw, she told him, "that you ought to have had clear thirty thousand at least when you came of age from [Rochdale], and you will not have anything or very little." The land not in dispute, had it been correctly managed, ought to be yielding around £8,000 annually. The disputed land produced £4,000 annually from the coal mines alone. She had been reliably informed that if Byron's Lancashire affairs were well managed, in the first five years after he came of age he could expect to "be one of the richest peers in the kingdom." She added that she was ready to take other measures to protect his interests, but since he was relatively close to coming of age she was reluctant to intervene further.[86]

Byron's faith in Hanson was momentarily shaken, and he went off to the solicitor's office, letter in hand. Not surprisingly, the lawyer spun him a rather different yarn. Shaw was "not to be depended on," since he had been the solicitor and confidant of the people most clearly resisting Lord Byron's claims. Now solicitor and clients had quarreled, and "no doubt he is stimulated by revenge against them." Shaw's antipathy toward Hanson was explained as resulting from Hanson's refusal to appoint him as Rochdale steward. All therefore could be explained, and he, Hanson, would visit Rochdale in the summer to put Byron's affairs in order.[87] Birch replied to Mrs. Byron in much the same tones. Shaw's information was "not to be depended upon." She had much maligned Hanson, whose "zeal . . . on behalf of Lord Byron" was such that his "disposition to serve his Lordship to the utmost cannot be matter of doubt." Birch claimed that Hanson's health had prevented him from paying to Rochdale the attention he might have. He had intended to travel to Lancashire in the summer of 1807, but was prevented by his wife's indisposition. However, he had kept in touch with developments through Milne, and he would travel north in the summer of 1808. Birch assured her that should Hanson be unable to travel, he would undertake the journey himself.[88]

Hanson, following his conversation with Byron, also wrote to Mrs. Byron, and reiterated the point about Shaw's lack of reliability: "I have already been deceived by them, and if I had given credit to his representations your son would have been involved in endless suits which must have involved every farthing of his fortune and had he died under age it must have fallen upon you." Shaw, he added, had been solicitor to the parties resisting Byron's claims. There had been a quarrel, Shaw had been fired, and he was now trying to extract revenge. He had a particular grudge because Hanson would not appoint him as steward. He added, "Mr Dearden and his Partners had obtained an injunction to restrain the verdicts we had obtained. Nothing more could be done than to have an account kept of the quantities of coals gotten by them that we might be able to resort to them for the value of them in case the Court of Equity should confirm the verdicts. . . . I am taking all the measures I can to get rid of the injunction, and I am in hopes I shall be able soon to do it." He expected to visit Rochdale in July 1808 and would visit Mrs. Byron in Southwell en route.[89]

Hanson's haste to defend his reputation on this occasion, by contrast with his usual pace of doing business, points in the direction of injured pride, but Mrs. Byron was not much moved by this silky lawyer's talk. She replied immediately. Even if Shaw was a rascal, she had no doubt that "he is the person on earth most likely to honour the real value of Lord Byron's property in Lancashire." She would not be in any way satisfied until either Hanson or Birch traveled to Lancashire "to ascertain the real value of this property which ought to have been done long since." She had evidently touched a raw nerve with Hanson, and she was not to be denied. On 4 July she asked him to name the day on which he would be at Rochdale, and when she had received no reply by 19 July, she wrote to Birch again: "[A]s he [Hanson] seems to be a sleeping partner in the firm, I desire you will inform me when either you or Mr Hanson intend to go to that place." Finally, on 28 July Hanson wrote to tell Mrs. Byron he would be traveling to Rochdale early in August, as soon as a Chancery case in which he was involved was completed. Once again he promised to call at Southwell and explain everything to her.[90]

When Hanson had still not appeared on her doorstep by 2 October, Mrs. Byron was understandably annoyed: "[I]t is now four months since you wrote me that you or Mr Birch would certainly go down to Rochdale in a month. Why dont you go there?" It was a simple question to which Hanson apparently did not have a simple answer, but he did finally set out for Rochdale shortly after this, although he traveled north via Newstead, and not via Southwell. When, on his return journey, he invited Mrs. Byron to meet him at Newstead for a full report she understandably declined, claiming she was not well enough to travel, let alone to discuss business. She refrained from pointing out that he had offered to call at Southwell, adding that "my son being now so nearly of age I think you ought to inform him exactly of his situation in all respects and let him know the best and the worst of everything."[91]

Hanson hurried back to London, where the Rochdale case again came before the Exchequer. Byron's guardians, led by Hanson, applied for the lifting of the injunction restraining them from ejecting Dearden and others. By early December it was rumored in Lancashire that the Exchequer court had decided that the lessees under the late Lord Byron were entitled to hold the collieries till the expiration of their current leases. The report reached Hanson from none other than the much-maligned Shaw, who was in turn assured by Hanson that the report was false: "[O]ur motion to dissolve the injunction was resumed this morning"; and the court had decided that the whole case needed to be heard and that no change in the possession of the property should be agreed to before this had happened: "[T]hey have ordered the injunction to be continued to the hearing of the cause." This, he added, decided nothing, although he expected Dearden to claim it as a victory. Nothing more could be decided until there had been a full airing of the case before the court.[92]

When Hanson informed Byron of this further delay, the young heir grew gloomy. Byron feared the lucrative Rochdale coal resources would never be his: "I do not know if our best method would not be to compromise if possible as you know the state of my affairs will not be much bettered by a protracted and possibly unsuccessful litigation. However, I am and have been so much in the dark, during the whole transaction that I am not a competent judge of the most expedient measures." Byron's meek acceptance of the outcome contrasted with Mrs. Byron's much firmer stand. Early in January 1809 she told Hanson that she was for "no compromise, no sacrifices," but she returned to an old theme, her concern that the Lancashire people were deliberately protracting the business until Byron came of age "merely that they might get him to agree to some compromise very much to his disadvantage." With the coming of age only a few days away she feared the worst: "[I]t is impossible to say what a young man may be induced to do that knows nothing of business, more particularly if he wants a little ready money."[93]

VII

During the minority Hanson was required to make returns of the annual accounts for the estate into Chancery. These have not all survived,[94] but there is sufficient information from which to build up a picture of the value of the property in these years. On first inspecting the property in 1798, Hanson estimated that "the net income of the Newstead and Rochdale property and of any other property [the sixth lord] succeeded to did not exceed £850 a year." The Newstead survey he commissioned showed that there was scope for some rent increases, which Hanson initiated when he visited Newstead late in 1799. "As soon as possible," Newton Hanson recalled, his father "relet the farms at nearly double their old rents and upon covenants for their permanent improvement." This was something of an exaggeration, but John Davy's rent was increased from £130 to £155, and the overall rental was raised to £1,230.[95] The rent rise was in line with national trends.

By 1802 (table 4.1) the Newstead income had increased significantly. Five of the farmers paid rent in excess of £100, and the rental, including the quarry and the abbey (during the initial letting to Mr. Clay), produced nearly £1,300 a year. This was all profit to the sixth lord, because Caroline Byron's £500 a year, which she had assigned to others beyond her own lifetime, lapsed with her father's death in 1798, and there were no other charges on the estate. Consequently, the new owner of Newstead enjoyed a significantly increased income, although only £500 was available for his

Table 4.1. The Newstead Rental, 1802–6

Tenant	Annual Rent	
	£	s.
William Beardall	100	
William Bell Sr.	62	
William Bell Jr.	22	
Ann Trueman	34	
John Davy	155	
William Bowman		
– farm	160	
– mill	55	
Elizabeth Darby*	150	
William Whitehead	145	
Ann Nicholson	55	
John Hardstaff	32	
Richard Hardstaff**	105	
George Bowers	12	12
John Howett (late John Stocks)	45	3
John Palethorpe		
– farm of late		
George Hardstaff	98	
– quarry	21	
Hall Garden and two acres		
to 1802 only	40	
	£1,291	15

Source: BL, Addit. Mss. 62, 910
  * 1803–4 Samuel Rushton replaced Elizabeth Darby as tenant of the Park Farms.
 ** 1805–6 John Hardstaff succeeded Richard Hardstaff, deed, at Wire Mill, and
    William Hibbert replaced John Howlett.

use, through the guardians. Some of the farmers were not in a position to pay their rent in full each year. Table 4.2 provides a better indication of annual income. The figures show clearly how Newstead provided the core income on which the family depended. In 1802–4 some tenants were obviously catching up, but from gross income Hanson had to pay taxes, repair allowances to tenants as required by their leases, quit rents, Owen Mealey's salary of £31 10s., the additional costs of keeping up the estate, £500 to Mrs. Byron for her son's maintenance, his own charges (which Chancery allowed at the rate of one shilling in the pound on rents), and Chancery's

Table 4.2. Income from the Byron Properties, 1802–7
(£-s-d)

	1802–3	1803–4	1804–5	1805–6
Newstead	1,912-6-0	1,449-16-7	1,052-6-0	1,326-9-5
Norfolk	372-1-9	110-18-9	36-2-8	–
Rochdale	84-12-0	16-0-0	96-9-0	31-7-0
Interest from Duke of Portland		300-0-0	45-0-0	–
Bark sales		24-0-0	20-2-0	
Carthorse sale				20-0-0
Total	2,368-19-9	1,900-15-4	1,249-19-8	1,377-16-5
Disbursements	1,486-19-7	1,020-19-8	1,118-19-9	1,384-19-5
Profits paid into Chancery	882-0-2	879-15-8	130-19-11	[7-3-0]

Source: BL, Add. Mss. 62, 910.

legal costs. In 1802 this left a balance of £882 0s. 2d., which was paid into the court for the benefit of Byron when he came of age. The figure was £879 15s. 8d. the following year.

Among Hanson's achievements was the recovery of a backlog of outstanding rent from the remaining Wymondham rents (Norfolk) in 1802, but these could obviously not be repeated. The Rochdale estate was producing very little net income, considerably less in fact than would have been anticipated even after the fifth lord's sales, and the position was worse than the figures imply because a quit rent (in effect a ground rent) was payable to the duke of Buccleuch. In 1802, when two years' worth was remitted, this amounted to £124 17s. 4d. Rochdale may, at this point, have been losing money, which explains why Hanson was pinning so many hopes on the outcome of the legal case. The requirements of Chancery ensured that overall the Byron family property was profitable, and while Hanson undoubtedly prepared the accounts in a manner designed to show the estate's financial affairs in the best possible light, they still bear witness to a relatively successful period of administration. Hanson reckoned that Chancery in 1808 held about £3,000 profit from the estate, over and above outlays during the minority.

But ought the profit to have been more? Byron was later to claim that "I was in Chancery to the last drop of my Wardship and minority,"[96] and the frequent complaints of Mealey and Mrs. Byron suggest that all was not well. Hanson's work in sorting out the estates early in the minority paid subsequent dividends, but his increasingly remote management certainly had unfortunate consequences. As the daughter of one of the tenants during this period was later to recall, following the death of the fifth Lord Byron the estate "fell into the hands of agents who held it for a child and who did not care to manage things in the best manner, the rents were not regularly collected one time, three rents were collected at once, at other times as soon as they became due."[97] Hanson ran out of steam at Newstead, and his confident beginnings under the close scrutiny of Chancery gave way to a rather lax regime in which Mealey was often left to his own devices. Hanson's primary responsibility to Chancery was to make a profit, and this he achieved, although it was already in steep decline by 1804–5 (table 4.2). Unfortunately, figures for the last three years of the guardianship have not survived, but we can be fairly certain that when the sixth Lord Byron came of age in 1809 the estate was in the black. Guardianships frequently provided much-needed breathing space when estates could be reorganized and improved under the watchful eye of the Court of Chancery.[98] This one was probably no exception.

5

Lord Byron Comes of Age:
Funding the Heir, 1803–9

On 22 January 1809, George Gordon, sixth Lord Byron, came of age. It was thirty-nine years since Newstead had last hosted coming-of-age celebrations, when William Byron had reached his twenty-first birthday in 1770 to joyful acclaim from tenantry and family alike. Once again the house and grounds were decked out for celebration, and nearly four thousand people arrived at the abbey for the occasion. In the grounds they feasted on "a fine large fat ox" and six sheep, which they washed down with six hogsheads of ale. Inside the house five hundred invited guests sat down to dine in the Great Hall on venison, game, hams, fowls, roast beef, and plum pudding suitably lubricated with 150 gallons of punch. They were entertained by a band hired for the occasion and then, when all the tables had been cleared away, two hundred couples enjoyed a dance that went on late into the night.[1] It must have been something of a squash, given the state of the house, and how five hundred people got into the Great Hall, which was smaller in 1809 than it is today, is anybody's guess.

The coming-of-age of the heir was a public event, symbolizing the continuity of the family as another generation was declared ready to carry the estate into the future. It must, therefore, have been something of a surprise to the assembled company to find that the young man on whom all the attention was being lavished was notable by his absence. Having celebrated Christmas at Newstead with a group of friends, Byron had returned to London, where he spent his birthday in a hotel, dining alone on eggs and bacon.[2] Nor was his mother present: she stayed put at Southwell and was simply "very sorry to hear of the great expense the Newstead fête would put them to."[3] Instead, it was John Hanson who presided over the company, substituting, as he had done since 1798, for Byron's father. However, while Hanson may have led the feasting, there was little else for him to do.[4] As we saw in 1770, the coming-of-age might be used away from the spotlight

116

to resettle the property as further confirmation of the innate stability of landed families and their commitment to maintaining their property into the future. Hanson's legal skills were not required because there was to be no resettlement.

Absent or present, it made little difference to the two important issues that Byron was well aware required his immediate attention in January 1809. He had to secure his financial position, and he had to decide the future of his property. The most significant change in his circumstances as of 22 January 1809 was that the estates came out of Chancery and passed into his direct control. How prepared was he for this change of role?

I

Until January 1809 Byron's finances were largely determined by his position as heir-in-waiting to an estate that was in Chancery. Under the conditions agreed to in 1798, Chancery made an allowance of £500 annually toward his maintenance and education. Since his mother was responsible for his upbringing, this sum was paid to her until he left Harrow in 1805. By then it must have been obvious to Mrs. Byron that her son was not all she might have hoped. He had clearly inherited his father's good looks, his way with young women, and his extravagance. His mother can hardly have forgotten how quickly and easily John Byron had run through most of her own fortune; indeed, it cannot have been comfortable for her to watch her son mirroring the faults of his father. She had already borrowed, discreetly, £300 from one of the Newstead tenants, which went toward her son's expenses.[5] At least while she controlled his income Byron's financial habits could be contained, and after the break with Lord Grey he spent his school holidays either with her at Southwell or with the Hansons in London. Even had he wished to go elsewhere, he lacked the financial independence to break away from her control as both parent and guardian. All this changed in the autumn of 1805.

Byron went up to Cambridge in October 1805 and, doubtless as a result of conversations—arguments?—between mother and son while he was at Southwell through August and much of September, she persuaded her fellow guardians that the £500 should now be paid directly to the seventeen-year-old student. In retrospect this was not a wise decision since, as generations of students have found to their cost since Byron's day, the attractions of college life went straight to his pocket. He boasted to his half-sister Augusta that the £500 was "one of the best allowances in College," so that he was able to "go on gaily, but not extravagantly." Yet he was by no means grateful to his mother for her largesse, because she had "refused to fit out a single thing for me from her own pocket." As a result he had been forced to buy his own furniture from the allowance.[6] His hopes of living "not extravagantly" quickly evaporated. Since he insisted on keeping three horses and a carriage, and then on spending whatever he needed and simply sending the bills to Hanson, he soon accumulated a deficit. After only one term at Cambridge his debts stood at around £1,000. He asked Hanson to increase his allowance, to which his guardian responded with "much advice, but no money."[7]

Perhaps it is not surprising that Byron should have found plenty of fair-weather friends to help him spend his anticipated aristocratic inheritance. From his earliest days at Cambridge Hanson knew Byron was living well beyond his allowance. In December 1805 he sent him £50, adding that "I would not have you entertain any uneasiness about your future supplies as you will ever find me more a friend than a lawyer." "I hope his Lordship's good sense," he rather optimistically told Mrs. Byron, "will be the means of keeping him within prudent bounds."[8] In fact, by the first Christmas vacation Byron was already well beyond prudent bounds, not simply in terms of what he was spending but also in the way he was funding his outlay. The nature of Byron's inheritance made him a much sought-after client. Under normal circumstances the estate would have been strictly settled. Consequently, Byron would have approached his majority with his financial resources firmly controlled. Since his father was already dead, the position would have been much as in 1743 when the fifth Lord Byron inherited at age twenty-one, and suffered a common recovery to release land from settlement for the purpose of raising a mortgage to cover debts he had run up while still a minor. In fact, the sixth Lord Byron's situation was even more straightforward than this, because he had the absolute ownership of the family estates, and potential creditors knew that once he reached twenty-one he would be in a position to pay his debts, either by raising mortgages secured on the property or, in extremis, by land sales. They were willing to lend him money on this assumption.

The key financial instrument was the annuity loan, the funding method so greatly exploited by the fifth lord prior to 1772. Byron could borrow a sum of money secured on his life (hence the reference to living to reach his majority), in return for paying an annuity (an annual sum to the lenders during their lifetime). Byron did not intend paying; rather, he would allow the payments, and interest on them, to accumulate until he came of age, and then exercise the option to repurchase as of January 1809. This was exactly the way in which the fifth Lord Byron in the 1750s and 1760s and latterly his son had kept themselves financially afloat until William Byron's coming-of-age. Whether Byron knew this past history is unclear, but he certainly understood his own position. As he made plain to anyone who would listen, "if I live to the period of my minority expires, you cannot doubt my paying, as I have property to the amount of 100 times the sum I am about to raise."[9] In theory this was indisputable, but as Byron recalled in canto 2 of *Don Juan*, written in 1818 when he was still struggling to repay debts from these and later years:

> 'Tis said that persons living on annuities
> Are longer lived than others,—God knows why,
> Unless to plague the grantors,—yet so true it is,
> That some, I really think, *do* never die;
> Of any creditors the worst a Jew it is,
> And *that's* their mode of furnishing supply:
> In my young days they lent me cash that way,
> Which I found very troublesome to pay.[10]

As a minor, Byron needed a trusty accomplice to sign as joint security. His choice fell on Augusta, his half-sister. Since she was five years his senior, by 1805 she was already of age. Byron wrote to her admitting he was "in want of money." During the Christmas vacation following his first term at Cambridge he answered a newspaper advertisement from a money-lender. He had, as he told Augusta, been forced to apply to "one of the money lending tribe," but as he needed the joint security of someone already of age he intended to bestow the honor upon Augusta. She declined the invitation and the two fell out.[11]

Fortunately for Byron, Augusta's scruples were not shared by Mrs. Elizabeth Massingberd. Mrs. Massingberd came from Lincolnshire gentry stock.[12] Byron first met her in 1800, and lodged with her at 16 Piccadilly, London, during the Cambridge vacation of 1805–6. She and her eldest daughter were ready to sign as collateral security, and with their support Byron dipped in for "a few hundred pounds in ready cash." Nor did it stop at that. Between 1805 and 1808 Mrs. Massingberd and her daughter signed numerous joint guarantor forms with Byron. They were doubtless confident, as they had good reason to be, that he would redeem all his debts when he came of age, but they also had a game plan of their own, because Mrs. Massingberd extracted a price for her signature. In January 1807 she persuaded Byron to borrow £3,000 on her behalf to repay annuitants to whom she was herself in debt. It was an expensive loan, since he guaranteed to pay £5,000 once he came of age in order to redeem the debt. Byron would later have cause to regret his willingness to help her, although at the time the arrangement seemed mutually beneficial—if rather expensive. Altogether they borrowed about £5,000, and in return Mrs. Massingberd allowed

Byron to use her premises for some of his less reputable liaisons, with both usurers and young ladies. This was during a period when, by his own admission, he was "leading a loose life about town."[13]

Once "dipped," Byron was unlikely to withdraw, and during the three years until his coming-of-age he lived on the assumption that he could pay tomorrow for what he could not afford today. Mrs. Byron realized early in 1806 that he had begun to borrow money to tide him over, and her temper was not assuaged when he refused to return to Cambridge. Instead he stayed in London running up bills he had no funds to pay, finally descending on Southwell in July in a coach and four with a male valet and Boatswain, his Newfoundland dog. Mrs. Byron was anxious to control his financial waywardness. She asked Hanson for a loan of £500, which she intended to fund herself by paying the interest until it could be secured on Byron's coming-of-age in 1809. She recognized that there was a risk involved, "which I shall guard against by insuring his life till he is twenty-one." So far so good, but Hanson's reaction can only be imagined when, further on in the letter, she added that "I will trust to my son's honour." She also complained that her own quarterly pension of £50 was overdue, that some of Byron's bills were unpaid, and that Hanson had failed to answer her last three letters. Byron meantime was enjoying the company of several young Southwell ladies, he was engaged in "private theatricals" with the Pigots, who lived opposite his mother on Burgage Green, and he privately printed (and presumably funded) *Fugitive Pieces,* which appeared in November 1806. *Poems on Various Occasions* was published the following January.[14]

Mrs. Byron's concern was to keep her son's spending under control until he came of age. She was, after all, one of his guardians, and so, like Hanson, responsible for his financial position to Chancery. Byron found her caution annoying, especially when in 1806 Hanson informed him of the high hopes to be anticipated from the Rochdale estate. With such riches seemingly just over the horizon, Byron was only too keen to strut as an aristocrat should, with his carriage, his groom, and his valet. Unfortunately, capital tomorrow did not pay bills today, an excuse that Byron found convenient to use when he remained in Southwell through the autumn of 1806. He was short of cash, and this became abundantly clear once he returned to London after Christmas. Within days he was appealing to Hanson for an advance on his quarterly allowance due in March. When this failed to move his guardian, Byron simply asked him to take responsibility for bills he currently had no money with which to pay.[15] In London, his social life, his gambling, his theatergoing, and his penchant for fashionable clothes and accoutrements, both for himself and for his retinue of good-time friends, were outrunning his available funds by some distance.

By April 1807 Byron was back in Southwell, and he wrote to Hanson recounting the whole sad story. Bills to his stable keeper, to his wine merchant, and to a lawyer had left him without means. Even his mother was trying to help, by borrowing on her own security £1,000, of which £500 came from his great-aunt, Mrs. George Byron of Nottingham, £300 from Misses E. and F. Parkyns, and £200 from Wylde & Company, Southwell bankers.[16] Byron's proposed solution was to leave Cambridge and to sell his horses in order to pay his debts, although he also recognized that there might be an alternative option, an application to Chancery for a special payment from accumulated estate profits to pay "legitimate" expenses, in this case his college expenses. Hanson's handling of Byron's finances during the minority has often been portrayed negatively, but he could pay Byron more than £500 a year only with the permission of the court, which normally required specific claims for particular approved purposes. Clothes bills and gambling debts hardly came into this category, but the expenses of student life were regarded as legitimate. Byron first suggested to Hanson in February 1807 that an application to Chancery might help him, and the lawyer subsequently drew up a list of approved expenses. These included £2 12s. to a bedmaker, £20 17s. 6d. to a bookseller, £4 3s. 6d. to a brazier, 4s. 3d. to a glazier, £75 10s. 11d. to a joiner, £2 3s. 9d. to a locksmith, and various other fees and payments. The court accepted a claim for £136 7s. 5d., and Hanson also agreed to let Byron draw in advance on his next quarter's allowance of £125.[17]

These attempts at alleviating Byron's financial difficulties provided only short-term relief. By early June 1807 Byron wanted Hanson to advance to him two quarters' allowance (i.e., £250), on which he even offered to pay interest. Since Hanson did not respond, Byron subsequently drew a bill for one quarterly allowance under a false name (Mr. Hannibal Higgins), to which his guardian not unnaturally objected.[18] Byron felt himself able as a result of these financial transactions to return to Cambridge, and on 27 June he went back to the university to renew acquaintances with old friends. Unfortunately, he found most of his friends had moved on, or were imminently to do so. His reaction was to suggest that there was no point in returning to his studies, and that he would pay his outstanding debts and leave the university. However, within a few days he had met John Cam Hobhouse, Scrope Berdmore Davies, and Charles Skinner Matthews, and the prospect of interesting new company persuaded him to reconsider his original decision. He spent the summer of 1807 in London basking in a warm glow arising from some encouraging notices of his early volumes of poetry—*Hours of Idleness* was published in June 1807—and in October he returned to Cambridge. The circumstances were not auspicious. He was, he assured Hanson on the eve of his return to the university, "out of cash."[19]

It is hardly surprising to find that, once again, student life overstretched his resources. He was, or so he assured Hanson on 19 October 1807, "contemplating with a woeful visage one solitary guinea, five bad sixpences, and a shilling, being all the cash at present in possession of."[20] Two months later he was wishing the end of his minority,

> for a reason more nearly affecting my material position, at this moment, namely, the want of twenty pounds, for no spendthrift peer, or unlucky poet, was ever less indebted for cash than George Gordon is at present, or is more likely to continue in the same predicament. My present quarter due on the 25th was drawn long ago, and I must be obliged to you for the loan of twenty on my next, to be deducted when the whole becomes tangible, that is, probably some months after it is expended.[21]

Twenty pounds was not going to go far, and within a few days he was asking for an advance of the whole quarter's allowance to March 1808. His alternative policy was simply to send bills to Hanson, asking him to pay them out of the next allowance.[22] It was hopeless, and he left Cambridge at Christmas with no intention of returning.

Early in 1808 Byron settled at Dorant's Hotel, ostensibly to revise his poems and prepare a new volume, although he was also living the life of a young man-about-town. This was of course expensive, and as he admitted to Hanson in January 1808, "the picture I have drawn of my finances is unfortunately a true one." Shortly after his birthday on the twenty-second, he complained that he was now in his twenty-first year "and cannot command as many pounds." He needed Hanson's help to pay his bills: "[A]t present I could as soon compass the National Debt." His debts included £3,300 to moneylenders, £800 to Mrs. Byron of Nottingham (the loan negotiated by his mother), "to coachmaker and other tradesmen a thousand more, and these must be much increased before they can be cleared." Once again he asked Hanson to lend him £20. Hanson responded by paying his £125 quarterly allowance two months early.[23] In March 1808 Byron admitted to the Rev. John Thomas Becher, Elizabeth Pigot's cousin, that he was "cursedly dipped." He anticipated that his debts would reach between £9,000 and £10,000 before his twenty-first birthday, but by contrast with his mother he did not consider such a sum unmanageable: "I have reason to think my property will turn out better than general expectation may conceive. Of Newstead I have little hope or care; but Hanson . . . intimated my Lancashire property was worth three Newsteads."[24]

Whatever Mrs. Byron may have thought, her son clearly believed that he could look beyond short-term necessity toward long-term security, and this is precisely how his actions can be viewed. He spent the early months of 1808 enjoying the vibrant company of Scrope Davies, who had been a friend of Beau Brummell at Eton. Byron suffered setbacks, including vitriolic reviews of *Hours of Idleness* in the *Monthly Monitor* in January and the *Edinburgh Review* in May. However, he was already working on *English Bards and Scotch Reviewers*, which would eventually appear in 1809, and in mid-June 1808 he set off to spend some time in Brighton, having made yet a further arrangement of his affairs. Scrope Davies had nothing approaching Byron's financial prospects, but he had accumulated far more debts: between 1807 and 1809 he raised £14,520 on annuities, with annual repayments of £2,422 2s. 8d. plus interest. His only means of paying such sums was success at the gaming tables, but he clearly tutored Byron in ways of managing his financial affairs. In May 1808 he stood guarantor, with Mrs. Massingberd, for sums totaling £4,500 that Byron was to repay on his coming-of-age. Thus enriched, Byron returned briefly to Cambridge early in July 1808 to collect his M.A., and then went back to the south coast with Davies and Hobhouse. All three gambled and lost, but for Byron this was simply an interlude, because his thoughts were already turning toward his inheritance.[25]

II

Byron was well aware that Lord Grey's lease of Newstead was due to expire in June 1808. He would be free once again to return to his ancestral home, and it was the future of the abbey that was on his mind when in March he asked Rev. John Becher to go to Newstead "and give me your candid opinion on the most advisable mode of proceeding with regard to the house."[26]

Byron may have chosen to exile himself from Newstead, but he had not forgotten the dilapidated house and garden he had explored in 1803 and so vividly recorded in *On Leaving Newstead Abbey*. In *Elegy on Newstead Abbey*, written sometime between 1803 and 1806, and first published in *Hours of Idleness*, he chose to reflect on it as a Gothic ruin, and to allow his imagination to run through its many phases of history. Finally, he reached the present, his own inheritance:

> Newstead! What saddening change of scene is thine!
> Thy yawning arch betokens slow decay;
> The last and youngest of a noble line,
> Now holds thy mouldering turrets in his sway.

He was saddened by what he recalled:

> Thy cloisters, pervious to the wintry showers;
> These, these he views, and views them but to weep.
>
> Yet are his tears, no emblem of regret,
> Cherish'd affection only bids them flow;
> Pride, Hope, and Love, forbid him to forget,
> But warm his bosom, with empassion'd glow.

And, deciding that he preferred the Gothic ruin to "gilded domes," he accepted that to him would fall the responsibility for maintaining the great house:

> Haply thy sun, emerging, yet, may shine,
> Thee to irradiate, with meridian ray;
> Hours, splendid as the past, may still be thine,
> And bless thy future, as thy former day.[27]

These lines reflect Byron's own turmoil about what to do with Newstead, the turmoil that led him to ask Becher to inspect the property, perhaps in the hope of balancing the gloomy reports he had received from his mother. In December 1807 Mrs. Byron told Hanson that she had heard numerous reports

> of the shameful state it is in, all the county talks of it and says it is quite a disgrace for any person in the character of a gentleman to keep a place in such a beastly state (that was the expression that was used). The new windows in the long dining room have disappeared, so I am told that all that must be looked after before his Lordship leaves the place.[28]

Doubtless she had passed on similar tales to her son, and with them maybe her fears that Hanson would advise him to sell his Nottinghamshire estates.

Byron traveled to Newstead in August 1808. It was almost five years since he had last been to the abbey, but he had made up his mind to orchestrate a restoration program. On 18 September he reported that "the house is filled with workmen and undergoing a thorough repair." A few days later he told his mother not to visit because of the work in progress.[29] Hanson, arriving in October, considered the house to be uninhabitable because of the building work. He and his wife lodged in Mansfield. If nothing more, Byron was making a statement of his intentions.

What exactly did Byron do to Newstead in these months? Although at his coming-of-age celebrations in 1809 the abbey was described in the local press as "newly fitted up," this was only partially true. Charles Skinner Matthews, visiting several months later, noted that the house was "sadly fallen to decay . . . every part of the house displays neglect and decay, save those which the present lord has fitted up." The last phrase is significant.

Byron concentrated his attentions on a few rooms, rather than on a general renovation. He told his mother in November 1808 that he was "fitting up the green drawing room, the red (as a bedroom), and the rooms over as sleeping rooms, they will be soon complete."[30] These two rooms were behind the hall in the northwest corner of the abbey, next to the ruined west front of the church, and they were refurbished in such a splendid manner that when Francis Hodgson stayed at Newstead in 1811 he found them "glowing with crimson hangings and cheerful with capacious fires." The rooms were physically separate—deliberately so—from those Byron renovated in the southeast wing, which were intended principally for guests. Byron also built a plunge bath. Nathaniel Hawthorne, who visited Newstead in 1857, commented that "Byron's bath" was "a dark, and cold, cellar-like hole which must have required good courage to plunge into." It was removed shortly after 1860. Plunge baths could be filled with either hot or cold water, but by the end of the eighteenth century they were being replaced by tub baths and shower baths, so Byron might have been considered a little old-fashioned.[31]

Other parts of the house received little or no attention. The main hall was virtually empty, and had been since the fifth lord's sale of 1778. Byron used it for shooting practice, while as for the Great Dining Room (now the "Salon") "he was wont to exercise there his fencing sword and high sticks."[32] A visitor in 1811 commented of the Great Hall that "its only ornaments are two pictures of a wolf dog, and another from Newfoundland, favourites of his Lordship," while the Great Dining Room "is a most noble apartment, presenting a good idea of ancient manners, but now deserted and forlorn." Much of the rest of the house was left in a dilapidated condition. Off the east gallery was a range of bedchambers that were disused, possibly partly roofless, and certainly in poor condition. The visitor of 1811 commented on "a long range of deserted apartments." Other rooms were just about habitable, while the Chintz Room, beyond the Great Dining Room, was Mrs. Byron's home while she lived at the abbey between 1809 and 1811. Hanson thought the building beyond repair. He wrote the 1812 sale particulars (or at least approved the wording of them), which noted that "there are many grand sites for erecting a mansion, and for which there is great abundance of materials in the present buildings."[33]

William Howitt visited Newstead a few years later, after Byron had left, and wrote the following account:

The embellishments which the abbey had received from his lordship, had more of the brilliant conception of the poet in them than of the sober calculations of common life. I passed through many rooms which he had permitted so wretched a roof to remain, that, in about half a dozen years, the rain had visited his proudest chambers; the paper had rotted on the walls, and fell in comfortless sheets upon glowing carpets and canopies; upon beds of crimson and gold; clogging the glittering wings of eagles, and dishonouring coronets.[34]

What is not certain is whether Howitt visited before or after March 1816, when an earthquake in the Newstead-Mansfield area caused the roof and ceiling of the long dining room to collapse. The whole fabric of the house was shaken. Yet Howitt, and earlier visitors, were really making the same point: that Byron spent lavishly on decorating a handful of rooms without providing for the long-term restoration of the dilapidated building.[35]

Beyond the house Byron planned to let the lower lake "for the purpose of stocking my other ponds with the fish therein, but am apprehensive of getting into some law suit with Robinson, who opposes it . . . it is rather hard not to be able to procure myself the contents of my fishponds."[36] Whether his plans were put into operation is not known.

Byron was not alone at Newstead in the autumn of 1808. Hobhouse joined him and together they attended the Infirmary Ball in Nottingham on 12 October. The two men were also invited to dinner at Annesley Hall, where Byron and his hostess Mary Chaworth sat in embarrassed silence for much of the evening. In between supervising the building works, Byron was polishing *English Bards and Scotch Reviewers* and planning with Hobhouse the travels they intended to undertake once he came of age. When Boatswain died, Byron designed a suitable tomb and wrote lines of poetry to commemorate the animal. He had Boatswain and his wolf dog Lyon painted by the Nottingham artist Clifton Tomson, and his own portrait, with his page Robert Rushton, by George Sanders. He wrote poetry, exercised, and made Lucy, one of the female servants, pregnant.[37]

III

Hanson visited Newstead in October 1808 to sort out Byron's finances prior to his coming-of-age, and to determine the future of the Newstead estate. Byron calculated that his debts did not exceed £12,000. Mostly they were secured on his life interest in the estates, repayable at his coming-of-age, so that the financial position was in many ways reminiscent of the situation in 1770 when William Byron reached twenty-one. Byron had several options. One was to marry a wealthy bride. Although he had shown as yet no great inclination to marry, he was aware that as an aristocrat and a landowner he could anticipate marrying "a Golden Dolly," whose portion could be steered toward paying some or all of his debts. It was a view shared by his mother, who wrote to Hanson early in 1809 recommending

Byron and Robert Rushton, 1807–8. Engraved by William Finden after George Sanders (1774–1846). The original picture was given by Byron to his mother in 1809. Subsequently it passed to Hobhouse after Byron left for the Continent in 1816. It was sold by Hobhouse's daughter to King George V in 1914. Robert Rushton was the son of William Rushton, one of the more substantial Newstead tenants in Byron's day. In 1808, when he was about fourteen, Robert was in service at the abbey as Byron's page. Byron took Rushton on his first European travels in 1809, but sent him home from Gibraltar and paid the fees for him to be educated in Newark. In 1816 Rushton traveled with Byron as far as Geneva. (Nottingham City Museums and Art Galleries [Newstead Abbey].)

that he should mend "his fortune in the old and usual way by marrying a Woman with two or three thousand pounds [a year]."[38]

A second possibility was to sell land, as his great-uncle had done in the 1770s. Byron was happy to agree upon the disposal of the remaining property in Norfolk, but this was not likely to be sufficient to cover his debts. Rochdale was a possibility, but it was tied up in a legal case. The only other alternative was Newstead, and at some point during his visit to Nottinghamshire Hanson proposed that it should go on the market.[39] Mrs. Byron was subsequently to recall that "his wish has been for you to sell Newstead ever since he first saw the place. I dont know for what reason, but one there must be."[40] She was being a little economical with the truth. Newton Hanson recalled years later that "although Lord Byron was fortunate in succeeding to the title and estate the latter came to him under circumstances as unfavourable as ever could be." John Hanson's estimate was that the total income of the estates, even when supplemented one day by the remains of Mrs. Byron's fortune, was inadequate for the task ahead: "The condition of the Abbey and estate was such that to restore them even to a limited extent the whole fortune of Lord Byron would have been insufficient." Nor could this be disputed. John Murray, the publisher, visiting Newstead some years later, thought it would cost £100,000 to repair, and this is approximately the sum Wildman subsequently spent on restoration after 1819.[41] Hanson's reasoning in 1808 was much as it had been in 1798, that the likely cost of restoring the abbey would eat up any surplus income and leave Byron perpetually short of money.

Just how much Byron knew of Hanson's thinking is not known. Mrs. Byron was certainly well informed, and whether it was the disagreement between mother and agent that was in Byron's mind when he wrote his *Elegy on Newstead Abbey* we shall never know. Nor have we any idea what advice John Becher had given him the previous spring. What we do know is that however sound the economic reasoning behind Hanson's proposal, Byron flatly refused to entertain the idea of selling Newstead. He proposed instead that Rochdale should be sacrificed.[42] This was awkward. To sell Rochdale with the legal case unresolved would mean accepting a low price, whereas to wait until the case had been won would ensure Byron of a small fortune. The argument for selling Newstead and retaining Rochdale might have carried more weight had there been any sign of the legal case being resolved, but when it came before the Court of Exchequer again early in December 1808 no judgment was reached.

In any case, Byron's preferred course of action in 1808 was to raise money on a mortgage and use the capital to repay his creditors. Hanson was commissioned to raise a mortgage as of 22 January 1809, and it was to be sufficient to cover Byron's outstanding debts and to make available cash for his planned European tour. Mortgages could not be raised on settled land except for the purposes of paying children's portions, but Byron's land was unsettled and legally nothing stood in his way. Many of the men he joined on the benches of the House of Lords in 1809 knew all about debt, and particularly about the flow of money into landed securities from the insurance companies: the Sun Fire and the Equitable had £776,000 lent on mortgages in 1800.[43] It seemed sensible to secure a mortgage on the estate at 4 or at most 5 percent. The annuitants and other moneylenders would be paid off, and in time Byron could expect to redeem the mortgage when the Rochdale legal wrangle was resolved. Hanson had, after all, assured him that this would make him a rich man.[44]

The difference of opinion between Byron and Hanson became clear as soon as the lawyer returned to London. Before Hanson left Newstead he agreed to allow Byron £500 in place of the £125 quarterly allowance then outstanding, but it was symptomatic of the difficult relationship between the two men over subsequent months that he apparently forgot to complete this arrangement once he reached his chambers. Byron complained that Hanson simply did not move fast enough when it came to resolving his financial difficulties. In particular, no progress was made over the mortgage. Hanson may have encountered problems in trying to find a potential lender. Capital loans secured on property could be difficult to obtain in wartime, when investors preferred the higher returns on paper securities. Certainly when a further attempt was made to raise a mortgage in 1811–12 it again proved almost impossible to arouse much interest. In view of the difference of opinion between Hanson and Byron in 1808, however, Hanson may not have tried very hard. Possibly he really believed he could resolve the outstanding legal issues at Rochdale in order to relieve Byron of his debts. Possibly he calculated that a mortgage secured on Newstead would compromise Byron's marriage prospects, since less equity would be available for strictly settling the estate. We do not know.

Byron doubtless believed that following the discussions at Newstead Hanson would return to London, secure the mortgage, and arrange for it to come into force and the debtors to be paid on or about 22 January 1809. If so, he was to be sorely disappointed. Even with his birthday imminent he was short of cash, and he wrote to Hanson asking to borrow £300 "payable on 1st February which I hope it will be convenient to honour, as I shall then be twenty one and I have several Bills due which I need to pay." Hanson agreed to the loan.[45] For his part, Hanson complained that he could not persuade Byron to concentrate on business. Shortly after the coming-of-age celebrations he told Mrs. Byron that although Lord Byron has involved himself certainly to a very considerable extent his Lordship goes too far when he says that he is ruined, for he possesses from his rank and abilities the means of redeeming himself whenever he can bring himself to the resolution to do so, and I think he will soon do it, and I verily believe he will do it effectually when he turns his mind to it.

Hanson had proffered plenty of advice, and would have been happier "if he would follow it more." There was, he added, about £3,000 due to Byron from the Court of Chancery: "I make no doubt he will then discharge many of his small debts and particularly those at Southwell which certainly ought to be paid." He hoped Byron would have no further need to resort to "those rascally moniers," and he condemned Mrs. Massingberd "in the severest terms" for encouraging him in the "incurring of them." He added, "I wish his Lordship to bring his mind to business, but I incline to think he means soon to adopt the course you have recommended."[46]

At this crucial point the difference of opinion between Byron and Hanson was a problem, and Mrs. Byron was caught in the crossfire. In January 1809 she wrote to Hanson, "I have no doubt of his being a great man, God grant that he may be a prudent and happy one also." By March she was less sanguine: "I can see nothing but the road to ruin in all this which grieves me to the Heart and makes me still worse than I would otherwise be." She already anticipated that he would be a great speaker and a celebrated public character, "but that wont add to his fortune but bring on more expenses on him and there is nothing to be had in this country to make a man rich in his time of life."[47]

IV

Hanson's second purpose on his autumn visit to Newstead in 1808 was to discuss the future management of the estate if, as was the case, Byron refused to contemplate sale. Byron had been heir-in-waiting for ten years, during which period his estate had been administered by guardians and his ancestral mansion tenanted. Landowners inherited the job of running the estate with the land; they did not necessarily have natural aptitude for the task, and they frequently had little training. What many of them had was the experience of growing up on the estate and seeing how it functioned, frequently learning from their fathers as time progressed. Byron had none of these advantages. He not only lacked the sense of destiny with which many such young men grew up, but he had little knowledge of either house or estate.

Although in 1798 the decision to let Newstead had seemed a reasonable course of action, there were drawbacks. Letting the house was not a move designed to develop the sixth lord's instincts as an aristocrat. Byron could hardly acquire a sense of the importance of his position when he spent vacations lodging with his mother in a rented house in Southwell or—almost literally—camping out with the Newstead bailiff, Owen Mealey, or as a guest of the abbey tenant. He did not inherit, or learn to shoulder, the burden of responsibility for his family and its property, particularly the importance of conserving the estates for future generations, and he showed little aptitude for estate management. During the months he spent in and around Newstead during 1803, Mealey was disappointed to find that he took "very little notice of the improvements that has been done."[48] Mrs. Byron recognized the same inattention to business. She was anxious to have the Rochdale question resolved before January 1809:

> I much fear they wish to procrastinate the business till Lord Byron comes of age (which God forbid they should have the power of doing) and that they think in that case to get him to agree to a foolish and unprofitable compromise. Now although I have as high an opinion of my son's abilities as anyone can have, yet I am sensible that clever people are not always the most prudent in regard to money matters. Therefore I must own I should be glad for many reasons the affair was settled before he came of age.[49]

As with so many of Mrs. Byron's judgments, this one proved to be correct in time: she, like Mealey and others, had good reason to recognize in her son's behavior a worrying lack of interest when the business of the estate was under consideration. Hanson must have been aware that inattention to business was paralleled by lack of training.

Even before Hanson arrived at Newstead in October 1808, Byron had met and talked to the tenants. If he was to retain Newstead he needed to act like a landlord, and he set about supervising a rent collection. His inexperience soon became apparent when he upset the tenants because "he would not allow the property tax."[50] His lack of confidence was apparent after Hanson returned to London. Writing to him on Christmas Day 1808, Byron relayed the gist of his discussions with three of the tenants—Hardstaff, Truman, and Palethorpe—about Mr. Chaworth's proposal to close a road as part of an enclosure. However, he added "I know nothing of the matter but beg you will ascertain the truth and write to Mr Chaworth and say to me what is to be done."[51] After two or three months in Nottinghamshire Byron had learnt little about running an estate and, remaining in innocence, he placed his faith firmly in Hanson with, in the longer term, unfortunate consequences.

The fifth Lord Byron had run his estates in a way that contemporaries would have regarded as entirely regular, entrusting responsibility to a steward, William Daws, who lived locally and enjoyed the respect of the tenants. The change of arrangements from 1798 had been partly inspired by Mrs. Byron's wish to be guided by someone on whom she felt she could rely, and on the need to satisfy Chancery. John Hanson qualified on both counts, but as of 21 January 1809 his legal responsibility both to Chancery and as a guardian came to an end. Byron should have taken over the effective control of the property, and at the same time it would have made sense to appoint a full-time steward in the mold of Daws. The experience of the previous decade ought to have sounded alarm bells. Hanson had been able to find less and less time for Newstead, either by way of correspondence with Mealey or visits. Now was the time for change.

In the event, Byron's nerve failed him. He had no stomach for estate business, and rather than take his own decisions he chose to leave his affairs in the hands of his trusted mentor. There was some logic in adopting such a strategy. Byron still intended to use Hanson's expertise to sort out his financial difficulties and his legal troubles at Rochdale. He was anxious to travel, and consequently he did not want to be burdened with learning estate matters or settling in a new steward. But Hanson tended to prove the rule of contemporary agricultural commentators that lawyers did not usually make good estate managers. While Byron might be forgiven for lacking the interest and expertise required to run an estate, he was neither the first nor the last landowner to find himself in such a position. Owners, even if they hardly knew one end of a cow from the other, had a responsibility to their family and their heirs to appoint an able, respected, and capable steward. The fifth Lord Byron had done this by appointing Daws.

It is easy in retrospect to see what went wrong in 1809. Hanson wanted Byron to sell Newstead, so he had little interest in advising him to set up a new administrative structure. Once he had rejected Hanson's strategy, Byron needed to replace him (and Mealey) with a permanent steward. In fact, his only positive move was to persuade his mother to abandon the relative comfort of Southwell to live in the drafty abbey and look after his affairs while he was abroad. He also commissioned her to raise the tenants' rents, a somewhat dubious honor, given the well-known difficulties of collecting *any* rents when landlords stayed away from their estates for long periods.[52]

From 1809 estate management at both Newstead and Rochdale can most accurately be described as having slowly descended into chaos. Hanson, freed from the constraints imposed by Chancery, could find little time to devote to Byron's affairs. His occasional visits to Nottinghamshire and Lancashire virtually ceased, and the Rochdale legal wrangle remained unresolved. At Newstead Owen Mealey, never able to command the respect traditionally afforded to a steward or even a bailiff, was increasingly found wanting. Mrs. Byron complained in 1810 that he "seems always stupid with ale, he has about £90 of Lord Byron's money to account for, and God knows if he can give a proper account of it."[53] Maintaining any semblance of order became difficult. The celebrations at Newstead in January 1809 proved to be not the prelude to the new owner coming to claim his inheritance, but to confusion, muddle and, finally, sale. It was, in retrospect, poignant that the heir breakfasted alone in London on 22 January 1809.

6

Lord Byron as Landlord, 1809–12

The Childe departed from his father's hall:
It was a vast and venerable pile;
So old, it seemed only not to fall,
Yet strength was pillar'd in each massy aisle.
Monastic dome! condemn'd to uses vile!
Where Superstition once had made her den
Now Paphian girls were known to sing and smile;
And monks might deem their time was come agen,
If ancient tales say true, nor wrong these holy men.
                              —*Childe Harold's Pilgrimage*

Byron's plan when he came of age was to travel. For young aristocrats of his generation the final stage of their education was usually the Grand Tour, a great sweep through Europe in search of culture and experience before settling down to learning the business of running the family estates. Traditionally the itinerary included Paris and the great Italian cities of Venice, Florence, Rome, and Naples, but the outbreak of European war in 1793 brought to an end the Grand Tour in its best-known form. For many young men of Byron's generation, travel was out of the question, unless they were willing to take a rather different route. Some took a more southerly route through the Mediterranean. Byron, naturally, intended to do more than the average: he planned to take "a route of a more extensive description," perhaps taking in Persia and even India.[1] It was a plan of which neither Hanson nor his mother approved, not because they objected to him traveling, but because they wanted him first to sort out his financial affairs. Byron, predictably, could not see a problem. He had entrusted his affairs, financial and estate, to Hanson, who was expected to sell the Norfolk copyholds, to raise the required mortgage, and to remit to Byron such sums of money as the estate could afford—or, more honestly, as he requested. The changes he anticipated after 22 January 1809 were straightforward. His debts would be redeemed into a mortgage and his existing creditors satisfied. Interest

134

on the mortgage would be paid out of estate income, but this would not be a great burden, as he would now receive the whole sum rather than the £500 annual allowance permitted by Chancery. Such was the theory; in practice things turned out rather differently.

I

Byron returned to London in January 1809 intent on completing a number of unavoidable tasks before starting his travels. Chief among these were to take his seat in the House of Lords and to see through the press *English Bards and Scotch Reviewers*, to which he had been putting the finishing touches during his months at Newstead. He finally entered the upper house on 13 March after a delay caused by some controversy over his right to the Byron title. He considered this dispute to be worth resolving, since he had been reading political memoirs and history and, as he told Hanson, "if I return my judgement will be more mature, and I shall still be young enough for politics."[2] A few days later the new satire was published. It was a savage attack on the state of contemporary English poetry, and although Byron's name was not on the title page he was quickly identified as the author. In April he prepared a second edition, which appeared in May. *English Bards* brought Byron notoriety, and damaged his relationship with Augusta because of the attack it contained on the earl of Carlisle, his ex-guardian. He made no money from it, permitting Cawthorne the publisher to keep the profits. This was at a time when he was pressing Hanson for funding to enable his travels to begin.

While these events were unfolding in London, Byron assumed Hanson was quietly sorting out the required mortgage. It was annoying to all concerned that this had not been completed by 22 January, particularly to Byron, who was importuned by creditors. To his displeasure they approached him—not Hanson—for their money now that the estate was out of Chancery. As he complained early in February:

> I am dunned from morn till twilight, money I must have or quit the country, and if I do not obtain my seat [in the Lords] immediately I shall sail with Lord Falkland in the *Desiree Frigate* for Sicily. I have an unriddable yen to pay tomorrow morning and not five pounds in my purse, something must be done.[3]

Nor was Mrs. Byron impressed by the delay, particularly when he asked for a loan of virtually all the money left in her Scottish fortune, at a time when he had still failed to secure the £1,000 she had guaranteed on his behalf, and when "there is some tradespeople at Nottingham that will be completely ruined if he does not pay them, which I would not have happen for the whole world." She wanted Hanson to convince Byron to "impower you and me to act for him when he is abroad, but he is so unsteady and thoughtless with the best heart in the world."[4] She did however agree that he should have £1,222 10s. of her Scottish capital, the sum freed up by the death of her grandmother. This was paid to Byron in February 1809.[5]

During the delays of these months Byron made a will. "My property," he told Augusta in April 1808, "I can leave to whom I please, and your son shall be the legatee."[6] She was pregnant—with a daughter—but in any case by the time Byron drew up his will they had become temporarily estranged as a result of *English Bards and Scotch Reviewers*. In November 1808 Byron told Hanson he intended Newstead to go to "the next lord," presumably his cousin George Anson Byron, the male heir to the title while Byron remained unmarried and therefore without legitimate children. This was still his intention in February 1809, and he assured his mother he would not "barter the last vestige of our inheritance."[7]

Since Hanson was apparently experiencing some delay in raising the mortgage, Byron took a group of friends including Hobhouse and Matthews to spend a short vacation at Newstead. They amused themselves, imitating the monks and imbibing liberally from the contents of the Newstead cellar. Charles Skinner Matthews wrote from Newstead:

> It was frequently past two before the breakfast party broke up. Then, for the amusement of the morning, there was reading, fencing, single-stick, or shuttlecock in the great room [Salon]—practising with pistols in the hall [Great Hall]—walking, riding, cricket—sailing on the lake—playing with the bear or teasing the wolf. Between seven and eight we dined, and our evening lasted from that time till one, two, or three in the morning. I must not omit the custom of handing round, after dinner on the removal of the cloth a human skull filled with burgundy. After revelling on choice viands, and the finest wines of France, we adjourned to tea, where we amused ourselves with reading, or improving conversation, each, according to his fancy, and after sandwiches, etc., retired to rest. A set of monkish dresses which had been provided, with all the proper apparatus of crosses, beads, tonsures, etc often gave a variety to our appearance, and to our pursuits.[8]

Hobhouse, revisiting Newstead in 1823, hardly recognized the recently refitted gallery:

> It was there that Lord Byron placed the old stone coffin found in the cloisters; and I well recollected that, passing through the gloomy length of it late one night, I heard a groan proceeding from the spot. I went to the coffin, and a figure rose from it, dressed in a cloak and cowl, and blew out my candle. . . . It was my friend C. S. Matthews.[9]

Washington Irving was doubtless somewhat disappointed when he met Nanny Smith at Newstead and she "contradicted the report of the licentious life which he [Byron] was reported to lead at the Abbey, and of the paramours said to have been brought with him from London. 'A great part of his time used to be passed lying on a sofa reading. Sometimes he had young gentlemen of his acquaintance with him, and they played some mad pranks; but nothing but what young gentlemen may do, and no harm done.'"[10]

The Newstead house party made no difference to Byron's hopes regarding his finances. He wrote in frustration to Hanson on 8 April 1809 "it is of the utmost consequence I should learn whether you have procured me a mortgage on Newstead, or if not, or if I do not hear from you directly, I must raise money on very bad terms next week." Four days later he asked Hanson to pay the £264 due to the stonemason at Newstead, and then on 16 April he added: "I am pestered to death in country and town and rather than submit to my present situation I would abandon everything."[11] Just as creditors had sought him out in London, so unpaid tradesmen called at Newstead when he was known to be at the abbey. Annoyed at the lack of progress, he set off back to London, where he arrived on 25 April and booked a passage for 6 May from Falmouth. Next day he told Hanson:

[M]y debts are daily increasing and it is with difficulty I can command a shilling . . . my securities for their annuities must be paid off soon and the interest will swallow up every thing, come what may, in every shape and in any shape I can meet ruin, but I will never sell Newstead. The Abbey and I shall stand or fall together, and were my head as grey and defenceless as the Archbishop of the Friary I would abide by this resolution.

He was willing to procrastinate no longer. If Hanson could not procure the mortgage he was to borrow £3,000, and to "place two in Hammersleys funds for letters of credit at Constantinople; if possible sell Rochdale in my absence, pay off the annuities and my debts, and with the little that remains do as you will, but allow me to depart from this cursed country."[12]

Threats did not work. No money was raised and Byron was forced once again to delay his departure, from May until June. When, on 23 May, he found Hanson was out of town he complained that "I have not five pounds in my possession." He wandered around London, impatient to be away, buying books and leaving the bills for Hanson to pick up. When news reached him that the proposed sale of the Wymondham copyholds had been twisted into a story that Newstead was to be sold, he wrote hurriedly to his tenants to allay their fears. He fixed on 5 June as his date of departure, even if he had "no cash to pay my passage." With time on his hands Byron found other reasons to be annoyed, including the delay in receiving money due to be paid out of Chancery. In April he had asked Hanson why it had taken so long to complete his minority accounts, so that the surplus funds due out of Chancery were still unrecovered. When he saw the accounts he was astonished that at a time when "I must have cash any way I may," £1,000 was still outstanding from the duke of Devonshire as a result of the Gringley sale in 1774. When the Chancery funds had still not been recovered by late May, Byron became abusive toward Hanson for treating him like a child—an indication of the difficult transition for Hanson from guardian to employee. Hanson apologized, but warned Byron he stood to receive only about £700 after all expenses had been paid from the Chancery funds.[13]

By late May there was news of a loan. Hanson had negotiated the promise of £6,000 in return for an annuity of £467 from Wanley Sawbridge, a friend of his partner Birch, although only £2,000 was available at once, and then not until 12 July.[14] This was far from ideal, but it was enough to be going along with, and early in June 1809 Byron set off to Falmouth to board ship. His departure was delayed, and while he was busy kicking his heels in Cornwall he had time to consider further his finances. He told Hanson on 19 June that from necessity he had bought an annuity from George Thomas, a moneylender with whom he had previously had dealings, and that he had also taken up other money on annuities at seven years' purchase, totaling £400 a year (including Thomas's bond). He asked for more cash. Two days later he added that "when the £6,000 is paid which it ought to have been by this time, at least a considerable part of it, you will deduct the sum for the annuities till Rochdale and Wymondham can be sold." He was annoyed that Hanson had refused to accept a bill from a bookseller, believing that he had left either £297 or £397 in Hanson's hands. Hanson's figure was £197, but in any case he considered that annuity payments of £537 10s. took precedence over other debts.[15] When, subsequently, the outstanding £4,000 from Sawbridge was paid, Hanson consequently used £3,000 to clear annuities, and made available only £1,000 for Byron's travels.[16]

Byron also had to deal with the fears of Scrope Davies, who, on having sight of a copy of the recently completed will, found no arrangements had been made in respect of the loans he had guaranteed in 1808. Davies, complaining he could not sleep, demanded that Byron should find a means of protecting him against claims from the creditors. Byron agreed to add a codicil to the will:

> The codicil supersedes the necessity of a bond to Mr Davies, who professes himself merely to be anxious for security in case of my demise, besides it is for £10,000 and Mr Davies only stands pledged for £6,000. It is true I offered to sign any satisfactory instrument for Mr Davies, but I

think the codicil sufficient, without a Bond of Indemnity, which shifts the responsibility completely. I see no reason why it should not stand in its present state, as the annuities are fully intended to be redeemed the moment the estates are sold.[17]

Hobhouse, at Byron's instigation, wrote to Davies on 24 June to tell him that the codicil "by which a particular acknowledgement is addressed to the executors to see that the sum be properly discharged" had been signed. Byron himself wrote that "I have received a codicil from Hanson, which I trust will prevent the sad catastrophe of the triple suicide, yours, Mrs and Miss Massingberd."[18]

With the promise of money on the horizon Byron could no longer be restrained. He posted a last set of instructions to Hanson before going onboard ship at Falmouth, reminding his lawyer that while he was away the Wymondham copyholds were to be sold, the legal case over Rochdale was to be resolved, and he was to sell the property. Then,

When [Rochdale] is sold I wish the purchase money to be applied to the liquidation of my debts of all description, and what overplus there may be (if any) to be laid out in securing annuities for my own life, at as many years purchase as it may be lawful and right to obtain.[19]

In the light of later events much of this seems fanciful in the extreme, but with his instructions and a general power of attorney posted to Hanson on 2 July, Byron embarked, with Hobhouse, on the *Princess Elizabeth* bound for Lisbon. Hanson, meantime, told Mrs. Byron that "the state of his affairs leaves one not a little embarrassed how to act for the best."[20] It mattered little to Childe Harold.

> Adieu, adieu! my native shore
> Fades o'er the ocean blue . . .
> My native Land—Good Night.[21]

II

Byron and Hobhouse landed in Lisbon on 7 July and spent two weeks in the town and at Cintra. Out of sight Byron may have been, but his troubled finances were not out of mind. Cash-flow problems were usually uppermost in his thoughts, but the issues that he and Hanson had discussed prior to his departure also loomed large. It was his custom, he told Hanson in April 1810, "to write to you from every seaport on my arrival and previous to my departure."[22] Not all of these letters reached England, since most of

Europe was, after all, embroiled in war, and it seems inevitable that some of Hanson's replies suffered the same fate.

Hanson's immediate task had been to travel to Norfolk "to sell the small estate at Wymondham which was recovered from Sir Charles Morgan." This was the copyhold property of the fifth Lord Byron's wife. In her will she had assigned the income after her death (1788) and during the lifetime of her husband to her own relations. Only after Byron came of age had it proved possible to recover the property, and it was due to be auctioned in July 1809. Hanson hoped, or so he told Mrs. Byron, that "it will sell well," so that "I may be able to quiet his Lordship's creditors."[23] Byron, writing from Lisbon on 19 July, was anxious to hear the outcome: "I suppose you have by this time arranged the Norfolk sale."[24] Hanson had, but, as so often with Byron's affairs, the outcome was less straightforward than might have been hoped. While several lots sold, one remained on the market. Hanson turned down offers of 1500 guineas (£1575) and £1725 because he thought it would fetch the surveyor's valuation of £1800, but although he agreed in August to accept the latter offer, the matter temporarily stalled.[25] Byron, meantime, also hoped that the Sawbridge loan had been completed. From Lisbon he traveled through Spain, spending a few days at Seville and Cadiz, before arriving in Gibraltar on 4 August. He wrote to Hanson optimistically assuming that "the drafts are paid out of the different monies from Norfolk and Sawbridge."[26]

It was possible for Byron to dream of his affairs running along this smooth course while he heard nothing from England. On 16 August he set sail from Gibraltar and traveled via Sardinia and Sicily to Malta. Arriving there on 31 August 1809, he wrote hurriedly to Hanson complaining that "on my arrival here fully expected to hear some account of the sale of Wymondham etc." He had asked Hanson to send letters of credit, although he assured him on this occasion that "I do not speak from any present necessity, but I wish to have all that can be spared remitted, as I shall remain long abroad, provided no accidents occur." He was in no position to complain, which he clearly recognized, concluding the letter with the assurance that "as to my affairs you must manage them as you best can. I have full confidence in your integrity, but expect and desire no favours." In fact, there were clear limits to his confidence, and Hanson's brief did not extend to selling Newstead: "Whatever distress I may encounter I will not sell Newstead, and whether further monies can be advanced or not, I expect at least a letter on the subject." No letter was forthcoming, and in mid-September Byron left Malta for Greece, where he landed on the 26th. Three days later he and Hobhouse went ashore at Prevesa in Albania, and from there Byron sent Hanson a long account of his travels and a reminder to send remittances through Hammersleys.[27]

Byron wrote again to Hanson on 8 November. He had received "not a single letter" since leaving England, and so he could continue only to dream: "[M]y copyholds I presume are sold and my debts in some train." The Rochdale case, he assumed, had been resolved. Yet beyond the dreams there was also a more serious tone to his thoughts. Absence had not made the heart grow fonder; rather, as he fell in love with the warmer climes of southern Europe he began for the first time seriously to wonder whether he should take Hanson's advice about Newstead: "I still wish to preserve it though I never may see it again. I never will revisit England if I can avoid it . . . it is no country for me." What, he added, would be fair prices for Rochdale and Newstead? "And what income would accrue from the fortune if laid out in the purchase of annuities for my life, or good mortgages." By 22 November he had reached Patras, and he wrote again in much the same tone. He hoped that the sale of the Norfolk copyholds and the additional £4,000 from Sawbridge would have "furnished a tolerable floating sum" until the Lancashire estate could be sold, "and if that is insufficient, much as I regret it, Newstead must follow the rest, and the produce be laid out either in mortgage or well received annuities for my own life."[28]

Byron's reflections on his future took place in something of a vacuum, because no letters arrived from Hanson. During December 1809 he visited Athens, Delphi, and Thebes. He settled for a while in Athens, one of the most formative periods of his life. However, he did not forget his problems at home. On 3 March 1810 he complained that he had still not heard from Hanson: "I have written often, in vain, neither letters nor further remittances have arrived. I have no redress but to write again, and again. Remittances ought to have come long ago from my Norfolk copyholds; from the money raised before I left England, and from Newstead or from my Lancashire sale." A few days later he set sail for Turkey, arriving in Smyrna on 8 March, from whence he wrote to "remind you of my existence." He wrote also to his mother from Smyrna, a letter she received in mid-May, when she loyally complained to Hanson on Byron's behalf about the absence of communication from Chancery Lane.[29] By mid-May Byron had visited Ephesus and reached Constantinople, where he imagined—wrongly, as it transpired—that Hanson was at Rochdale completing the Lancashire sale.[30] In mid-July Byron returned to Greece, and Hobhouse left him to return to England.

On 9 June 1810, fearing that his earlier letters had gone astray, Hanson wrote a long letter to Byron setting out the state of his financial affairs. Sawbridge's loan had been completed, and of the £6,000 half had been sent to Byron via Hammersleys, and the rest used to pay off annuity loans. The Wymondham copyholds he had sold for a total of £4,400, but due to a problem with the title he had not yet received any money from the transaction.

As for Rochdale, the legal case was still in progress and no offer worth considering had reached him, "so that at present I am without funds to pay any more of the creditors, and the annuities are coming round again." It was an unhappy situation, and Hanson seized on Byron's suggestions from the previous November regarding Newstead:

> I think I would sell this estate notwithstanding its condition for a good price, such a one as would after clearing all your Lordship's debts would leave you a sum the bare interest of which would produce a greater income than you can get from it, and my advice to your Lordship is to sell it. Land sells very well at this time.[31]

Such a recommendation cannot have come as a shock to Byron, but his musings of November 1809 were, it seemed, not meant to have been taken seriously: "I will not sell Newstead, come what may," he told Hanson from Athens in January 1811, a sentiment he repeated a month later: "I will not hear of the sale of Newstead." In February 1811 he wrote to Hanson, "I beg leave to repeat my negative to your proposal about Newstead," and when Hobhouse reached England his first task was to give Hanson the same message: Byron had commissioned him "to communicate to you he will not now or at any time sell his Newstead estate although he allows and does feel very much the deficit of his ways and means even for present emergencies." "If we must sell," Byron reminded Hobhouse, "sell Rochdale."[32]

This was all well and good for Byron, enjoying himself on his travels, but rather less satisfactory for Hanson, who was faced with his client's creditors. On 5 March 1811, unaware that Byron was already setting his sights for England, Hanson wrote to him in urgent terms. He anticipated payment for the Wymondham copyholds within four to six weeks, "but it will not be adequate to satisfy the pressing claims of so many hungry mouths," and he needed greater powers of attorney to act for Byron. "There is now about a year of the annuities due and they are pressing hard upon Mr Davies and Madam Massingberd and I cannot relieve them." He needed to raise money, and he suggested that Byron should offer him clear guidance about Newstead:

> I trust that if you are not coming home that you will have sent me some directions about Newstead. I am more and more convinced of the good sense of selling that property as a certain means of extricating you from all your difficulties and putting you in the receipt of a much better income than ever you had. Rochdale is not a property that will sell at this time, it is a speculating property and the present times are much against people embarking in it. Terra firma is the security that everyone is seeking for which

is the cause of land selling now for above its real value; and you never can have a better time for selling such a property as Newstead for all great capitals are really now taken out of trade here. . . .

Without greater financial powers, he added in an attempt to jolt Byron from his complacency, "I fear both Davies and Madam Massingberd must go to gaol," while Mrs. Byron was likely to be "sold out at Newstead for I have great difficulty in preventing or rather suspending the sale of all your curiosities there."[33] But Byron was adamant. In July 1811 he repeated the earlier message: he would not sell Newstead, and "by this I shall abide, come what may."[34] The message could not have been more emphatic, but within a year Newstead had been sold.

III

During his time at Newstead in April 1809 Byron traveled to Southwell to see his mother. They agreed that she should move to the abbey, and that since his financial affairs had still to be sorted out he would give her proper securities for the money she had borrowed on her personal interest. She was to recover smaller sums from the Newstead rents. Byron, she recalled, "insisted" that she should purchase an annuity with the £3,000 left of her Scottish fortune, because he wished to have nothing to do with this money, "as money transactions always made relations quarrel and he would not quarrel with me for £20,000." He also assured her that in his will he had made provision for her to live at Newstead and to have sufficient income for her needs should he not return from abroad. Despite these assurances he set off without even securing the loans she had borrowed on his behalf: "[M]y income is so small I shall be ruined if the thousand pound is not paid up."[35]

Mrs. Byron's willingness to move to Newstead as resident manager was laudable if misguided. She had no time for Mealey, and Hanson had no time for her. Many years later he recalled her as "a very foolish, passionate woman, totally ignorant, never reading anything but a novel or a newspaper." In such circumstances, working relations between Hanson and Mrs. Byron were hardly likely to be cordial, and they got off to a bad start from the moment she arrived. Since she would "not put her son to one farthing's expense" it was her intention to pay all her own expenses from an income she estimated at £340 18s. before payment of taxes and the wages of her female servant. Although she considered dispensing with a servant altogether, she decided that if she stayed through the winter it would be vital to have someone to light fires and keep the place in order: "[I]f that

Mrs. Catherine Gordon Byron, by Thomas Stewartson. (John Murray Archive.)

is not done the house is so damp that the furniture will be spoiled." What Mrs. Byron had not reckoned on was having to pay the gamekeeper's wages of twenty-four guineas, board wages for the servants, and wages for the gardeners. She considered gardeners to be an unnecessary extravagance, "as it can be no advantage to Lord Byron's property to have the gardens kept in order as they produce nothing that can sell." She calculated that the estate workers, the gamekeeper, old Joe Murray—who accompanied Byron to Gibraltar but was sent home—and the wolf dog and bear Byron had acquired at Cambridge were costing £385 annually, and in addition Mealey's salary had to be paid. "I wash my hands of all these expenses," she told Hanson.[36]

Hanson replied in terms he was to use many times in subsequent months. It was "a source of regret to me that Lord Byron was determined to go abroad at this critical juncture, and more particularly before he had perfected that arrangement that was necessary for the settlement of his affairs."[37] Yet having reminded her that he was no longer responsible for the young man, and no more able to dictate his movements than Mrs. Byron herself, he also accepted that he still had a role to play at Newstead. She was quite correct, he agreed, and the expenses at Newstead had to be reduced, especially the cost of "the live animals . . . which really is a most unnecessary expense." He also encouraged her to use all possible means to obtain the rest of her Scottish inheritance, even though she proposed (against Hanson's advice) to lend £2,000 from it to Byron on mortgage, and to use the other £1,000 to pay the outstanding debts she had accrued on his behalf to the Misses Parkyns, old Mrs. Byron of Nottingham, and the Southwell banker. Hanson tried, even so, to allay her fears:

> I would not have you be uneasy on the subject of Miss Parkyns or Mr Wylde's debt, for Lord Byron in case anything should befall him which God forbid has made ample provision for payment of all his debts. Nevertheless I cannot help observing that I think if the remaining part of your fortune could be raised and a security given to you upon the Newstead estate to secure you the income of it that it would be the best way of paying off Miss Parkyn's and Mr Wylde and what remains would be desirable to go in discharge of Lord Byron's debts.[38]

Hanson offered to pay the interest on these debts from the Newstead rents. Mrs. Byron's careful accounting was in stark contrast to that of her son who, reaching Lisbon in July, paid £30 for some old saddles.[39]

It was not just Mrs. Byron's own affairs that needed attention when she arrived at Newstead. Byron had commissioned her to raise the rents. She told Hanson:

Lord Byron having charged me before he left England to have the rents of
the Newstead estate raised if possible, I have accordingly written to Mr
Chambers concerning it, and there ought to be no time lost if the tenants
can bear an advance in rent, and certainly malt, corn, cattle, wheat etc. is
treble the price that they were at the time this estate was valued.

Almost everywhere rents had been rising since the 1790s, and Hanson had
raised them at Newstead back in 1799. He agreed with Mrs. Byron, but he
expressed concern that it would not be easy, given Byron's "great dislike to
grant leases." Without leases, in Hanson's view,

it will I fear be difficult to get the full extent of rent unless some money is
laid out in repairs, for tenants will not sink money unless they have leases.
However, that a year may not pass over I have directed Mealey to serve the
tenants with notice to quit at Lady Day next in order that the advanced
rents may take place from that period.

Hanson objected to her employing Chambers for the task, and suggested
instead a surveyor who "does a great deal of business in that line" and who
had valued the Norfolk estate at £4,500, which "was talked of as an enormous valuation and yet we have sold it for within a few pounds of that
sum."[40]
    Hanson's lecture on leases fell on stony ground. In the course of the
years of the Napoleonic Wars tenants were increasingly suspicious of long
leases because of fluctuations in prices. In Nottinghamshire few farmers
wanted leases: Robert Lowe, the local agricultural reporter for the Board
of Agriculture, wrote in 1798 that "the greater part of the lands in this
county are, I believe, let to tenants at will, who in general do not feel themselves uneasy under their tenure, and frequently succeed to their farms
from father to son for generations."[41] Mrs. Byron knew this. While she had
no objection to using Hanson's preferred valuer, she queried his understanding of leases. Although it was her personal opinion that they should
be granted, "it is not done in this county and the idea of granting leases is
much disliked here." Yet despite this show of independence she was reluctant to dispute Hanson's judgment, adding rather pathetically that she realized he should have the final say: "I never will oppose anything that you
think is for Lord Byron's advantage."[42]
    Hanson arranged for his surveyor to visit Newstead, and he recom-
mended raising the rents to about £1,700 a year, although he warned that
this would mean spending considerable sums on repairs to buildings. It
was agreed that the rents should be raised at Lady Day 1810. In fact, Hanson
neither made the necessary arrangements, nor visited Newstead to supervise the transition, and consequently no rents were raised. Mealey simply

instructed the tenants to pay their usual rents directly to Smiths Bank in Nottingham, the normal policy when an official rent day was not held. Hanson stayed away for a good reason: Byron's creditors were gathering. In Mealey's words, the local tradesmen "complain worse than ever as they expected you would be down and pay them part, but on hearing of the rents being paid into the bank very much disheartened them."[43]

Mrs. Byron had been unaware when she moved to Newstead that Byron had failed to pay for most of the renovations he commissioned in 1808. He had complained when tradesmen applied to him for payment during his house party at Newstead in April 1809, but it was only when he was abroad that the full extent of his financial neglect came to light. A joiner called Farnsworth, who had worked many hours at Newstead but not been paid, traveled to London, where Hanson gave him money on account, but by January 1810 he was threatened with prison if he did not pay his own local creditors. Hanson's response was that he had paid Farnsworth £158 10s. when he called at his London office, about half the sum outstanding from Byron, "although about one guinea was all that the Funds then in hand would admit receiving."[44] Farnsworth had more success when he called at Newstead. Mrs. Byron borrowed £120 on advance rents from the tenants to pay him:

> The poor man would have had all his goods sold or been put in prison which would have been his utter ruin and I have not that stoical indifference in my disposition to hear of such scenes without doing something for the relief of the person if in my power particularly as my son was the cause of it.[45]

If Mrs. Byron thought Farnsworth was the only unpaid creditor she was soon to discover her mistake. In February 1810 a painter from Mansfield requested payment of £339 5s. 1d. for work undertaken at Newstead and, while Mrs. Byron was still considering how to meet his demands, bailiffs arrived at the abbey on behalf of the Nottingham upholstery firm Brothers "that furnished the Abbey." Byron had spent £2,100 with the firm, but had paid them only £500. The rest of his account was overdue. She was in a flurry of anxiety, asking Hanson for advice as to what she should do if bailiffs tried to seize her personal belongings from the house, including "plate, linen, wardrobe, and some furniture from my late house at Southwell etc." She was also concerned that Byron was being imposed upon: "Lord Byron had great part of his furniture from Cambridge . . . and I really dont see that Brothers bill can fairly amount to so much money." While she was tangling with the upholsterers, Wylde, the Southwell banker, asked for the repayment of his loan. Mrs. Byron paid some of the interest, but in June he asked for £200 of the capital together with outstanding interest and commission.[46]

Other bills arrived. The Mansfield painter kept pressing for his money, and the upholsterers proposed a sale of furnishings from Newstead to recoup their outlay. Mrs. Byron subsequently discovered that all this activity was partly inspired by false rumors circulating in the neighborhood to the effect that Byron's estates were, after all, entailed, and that this might damage the chances of creditors ever being paid.[47]

None of this was quite what Mrs. Byron had envisaged when she moved to Newstead promising to keep "a very strict eye over things here." "For God's sake," she complained to Hanson in February 1810, "let me have as little trouble in this business as possible for I am teased to death with the one thing and another." By May she reported having "reduced every expense here as much as possible." From farm rents she had paid interest on the loans from old Mrs. Byron and the Misses Parkyns, but she needed £20 to pay Wylde, £10 to pay to her maid for money advanced to the gamekeeper, and a further £18 due on 22 June to Mrs. Byron and the Misses Parkyn. She had paid the gamekeeper because he was owed wages, and his wife had just given birth. She wanted Hanson to visit Newstead, and when she could not even persuade him to reply to her letters she wrote in disgust to his partner. This at least elicited a response, but one that simply confirmed that the two ex-guardians were still in the same boat together. Byron, Hanson assured her, was continually calling for remittances, leaving him "in a situation of infinite perplexity." Hanson did at least send her money to pay the gamekeeper's wages.[48]

Byron, like many a young man far from home, could scarcely believe that there might be any difficulties. If his mother had "occasion for any pecuniary supply," she was to "use my funds as far as they go without reserve, and lest this should not be enough, in my next to Mr Hanson I will direct him to advance any sum you may want, leaving it to your discretion how much in the present state of my affairs you may think proper to require." Hanson's response to such wishful thinking was to point out that he had sent £3,300 to Byron since he left England, and that he had no more money.[49] The straightforward absence of cash was not something that greatly concerned the contented traveler, who happily dispatched instructions about the estate, without much thought about how they could be implemented. When his valet, William Fletcher, returned to England Byron promised him a farm or the mill at Newstead. Fletcher complained to Hanson when Mrs. Byron refused to offer him anything, even a position in the garden at Newstead, "as it is in so ruinous condition." He had even applied without success for the public house at Rochdale, and was soon £20 out of pocket and in some financial difficulty. He complained also to Byron, who told his mother, "I shall separate the Mill from Mr Bowman's farm (for his son is too gay a deceiver to inherit both) and place Fletcher in it, who has served me faithfully." John Bowman, the son, had made pregnant the sister of Byron's page, Robert Rushton, but was refusing to marry her, a situation to which Byron objected because "I will have no gay deceivers on my estate."[50]

Hanson, meanwhile, stayed in London, and the Michaelmas rent day in 1810 again passed without a visit. Once more the tenants were instructed to pay their rents into Smiths Bank, although Mealey pointed out that this was hardly worth the effort since, after various deductions including money diverted by Mrs. Byron to pay her son's creditors, there was hardly anything left. By mid-December the balance of the Smith Bank account stood at 2s. 1d. after rents had been received and bills paid.[51] Mrs. Byron gamely struggled on. As she told Byron in March 1811, any improvements brought about in his absence were largely her work: "As to the Newstead rents I am sure they never would be raised was it not for me"; indeed, she continued, "neither the farms would have been valued nor the rents raised was it not for me. The rents are not raised but ought to have been so before now, but they shall soon." Hanson, she argued, "may and I believe does work you well, but I am neither satisfied with his activity or his diligence." She added, "[T]hings wont go right till your return yourself."[52] She was quite right, and she doubtless had some appropriate words of wisdom for her son that she was destined not to pass on.

IV

Byron, far from home and greatly enjoying his newfound freedom, knew little of the chaos closing in behind him. The annuitants were particularly pressing, since they had expected settlement of their debts following his coming-of-age, and in the course of 1809 and 1810 he was the subject of legal claims in the courts of King's Bench and Common Pleas for sums outstanding running to more than £9,000 (table 6.1). Most of these were annuities he had anticipated redeeming from the proposed Newstead mortgage.[53]

Then there was Mrs. Massingberd. In February 1810 she reminded Hanson that he needed to pay the annual premium on the Pelican Life insurance policy on Lord Byron's life, which was designed to repay the debts for which she had stood surety in the event of his death. Unfortunately for Mrs. Massingberd, not only was Byron alive and well so that she could not claim the insurance money, but he had failed to provide the funding to pay off her annuitants. As a result, as of January 1809 she was personally responsible

Table 6.1. List of Judgments against Lord Byron,
Courts of King's Bench and Common Pleas, 1809–14

Year	Person	Sum involved		
		£	s.	d.
1809	James Milne	1,500		
1810	Benjamin Brothers	1,513	2	0
1810/1814	George Thomas	1,600		
1810/1814	George Orme	1,400		
1810/1814	James Stewart	1,400		
1810/1815	Robert Baxter	700		
1810/1814	John Heron and Samuel King	700		
1814	Samuel Randall	244	10	

Source: Reelig, 706

to some of them, but Hanson was unwilling to help her. On 20 July 1810 she forwarded to him a letter showing that she needed to pay £265, the half year annuities to three of the creditors. Hanson's reply clearly did not please her, because she wrote again on 30 July to say that she expected the annuitants to take out an execution against her if she did not pay, and that she imagined Lord Byron would be most upset by such proceedings. Hanson replied that he had no funds of Byron's with which to help her. On 9 August she told Hanson the annuitants were threatening to take her to court, but Hanson was unmoved by her plight. Mrs. Massingberd's letters testify to an increasing desperation, and in May 1811 she was arrested at the instigation of one of the annuitants.[54]

Early in 1811 Mrs. Byron was still trying to find ways of satisfying the local creditors. Her requests for help from Hanson usually elicited little more than polite sympathy. In January 1811 he suggested that she should secure her £3,000 Scottish fortune on a mortgage to Byron with the farm rents of Hardstaff, Trueman, and Coleman assigned to paying her the interest.[55] But this was no longer her most pressing problem. At the end of January she was expecting Brothers, the upholsterers, to send bailiffs to Newstead if their bill of £1,512 2s. 2d. was not paid. She was worried about Mr. Brothers, who had a wife and eight children and was threatened with prison or bankruptcy or both: "[M]y son will be represented as the cause of this man's ruin whether it be true or not." Hanson thought her real concern was with her own possessions at Newstead, and he calmly assured her that she "need not be under any apprehension for the safety of any property belonging to you at Newstead as nothing but what actually belongs to Lord Byron can be seized under an execution, you have not been rightly informed on that subject."[56]

Mrs. Byron's increasing irritation with Hanson spilled over into her letters. She told Hanson that she believed he could, if he could rouse himself to action, pay Brothers by securing the debt as a mortgage on Newstead or by taking a security on the effects of the house. She warned him that Byron would be most upset if his effects at Newstead were sold, and what he might do if his books were sold she did not care to think: "and it would be a thousand pities that so good a collection, selected with such care . . . should be sold at all, and more particularly for almost nothing which they are sure to go at in this country."[57] Perhaps not surprisingly, Hanson resented her hectoring tone: "You seem to think it was my fault that Lord Byron did not give security for Mrs. Byron's and Misses Parkyns' money before he left England but it was not. I mentioned it to his Lordship more than once but he said he did not think it necessary meaning, no doubt as his Lordship did, to discharge the debts at the first opportunity."[58]

Hanson and Mrs. Byron cobbled together a temporary truce, but this collapsed in May 1811 when bailiffs arrived in the abbey. Mrs. Byron scribbled a hurried note to Hanson: "[F]or God's sake do not let me live in this state something must be done immediately." Hanson failed to respond, so in desperation Mrs. Byron wrote to his clerk in Chancery Lane: "Mr Hutton and three of his men are now in the House and the goods will be sold off immediately unless I can procure a delay." Hanson did finally write on 28 May to say he had been with Mr. Hodgkinson "and have settled with him that the execution which Brothers has sent in shall be withdrawn as soon as I have given him the proper security, which will be done tomorrow . . . in a post or two the men will be directed to withdraw from the house." He added that he "heartily wished" that "Lord Byron would come home that his affairs may be put under some arrangement." A few days later he assured Mrs. Byron that he was "sorely perplexed with the creditors having no means of satisfying them."[59] Surprisingly—or perhaps not, given how difficult it is to be sure how much of the truth he was willing to tell Mrs. Byron—Hanson did manage to pay Brothers's outstanding bills in July 1811.[60]

V

Byron returned to England in 1811 determined to do battle with Hanson over Newstead. He abandoned plans to visit Egypt, Syria, and the Holy Land, and instead set his face toward England with a stream of letters to Hanson, assuring him that under no circumstances was Newstead to be sold; indeed, he went further, telling Hanson that if anyone except him had suggested selling Newstead, "I should have looked on it as an insult."[61] Mrs. Byron was delighted at this display of fortitude: "I am glad you have refused to sell Newstead, stick to that, stick to it, but this I need not urge knowing your firmness." She had no time whatsoever for Hanson's plans, and she had discovered from his clerk that "you are not yet ruined, or much injured if you take care in future of what you are about." Thomas France, the clerk, had told her that the sale of Rochdale alone would be enough to pay off all Byron's debts and still "clear a hundred thousand pounds." He had convinced her that by raising the rents, resolving the legal case, and working the coal mines there, Byron could easily rescue his financial situation: "[W]hen all this is done, which will and must be, you will be rich again. The estate which has been sold [Wymondham], and my money, will pay part of your debts."[62]

Byron recognized that simply refusing to sell Newstead would not resolve his financial difficulties: "[M]y affairs, I must own, seem desperate." Writing from Malta in May 1811 he told Hobhouse that he was "hastening homewards to adjust (if possible) my inadjustable affairs," but during the weeks he spent traveling across Europe the impression is of a young man ready at last to do battle with Hanson. "*He* wants me to sell Newstead, partly I believe because he thinks it might serve me, partly I suspect because some of his clients want to purchase it. I have told him fifty times to sell Rochdale and he evades and excuses in a very lawyerlike and laudable way." Byron had taken to heart his mother's comment that if the Rochdale property was likely to be worth more than £100,000, what was she doing entertaining bailiffs at Newstead, and why was he never able "to raise a shilling"? Hanson had made it seem as if Newstead would need to be demolished to pay Mr. Brothers's bill. To other friends Byron wrote of traveling to Nottinghamshire to raise the rents and to Lancashire to sell his collieries, and then returning to London to pay his debts, "for it seems I shall neither have coals nor comfort till I go down to Rochdale in person."[63] Such fine talk was rather undermined by his shortage of cash when he had to ask Hanson to pay some outstanding bills, and provide £20 "to enable me to proceed from port to London and pay the custom house duties."[64]

Hanson was unmoved. Even while Byron was sailing up the English Channel he was telling Mrs. Byron,

I think when you know of the various and daily calls that are made by Lord Byron's creditors for Bills to the amount of upwards of £10,000, and annuities daily accruing to the amount of between two and £3,000 a year, without any funds to answer a tenth part of them and his Lordship's continued calls for remittances you will allow that I am placed in a situation of infinite perplexity. And if your £3,000 is not to be forthcoming I dont see what can be done to appease the people. . . . I have written to his Lordship very fully on the subject of his affairs and I have suggested to his consideration the only plan which can in my judgement relieve him from all his difficulties . . . in a very few days there will be near £1,000 to pay, which I have not funds to answer.[65]

Hanson could see no obvious way of resolving Byron's financial difficulties unless Newstead was sold.

VI

Byron was back in London on 14 July 1811, and he was immediately hailed by old friends and acquaintances, among them a relieved Scrope Davies. He had brought with him the manuscript of *Childe Harold*, which his distant cousin and self-appointed literary agent, Robert Dallas, carried off to the publisher John Murray. Byron gave Dallas the copyright, apparently on the principle that a gentleman should not derive financial reward for his "work," a principle he subsequently abandoned when money became tight.[66] He found time to pay a brief visit to Hobhouse on militia duty in Kent. He set about sorting out his financial affairs, although Hanson would not have been pleased to hear that he had given away the copyright of *Childe Harold*. Byron saw one of the annuitants, George Thomas, he wrote to Mrs. Massingberd about her annuities, and he made a start on unraveling other debts. He was still in London, delayed by the need to sign some papers, when news arrived that his mother was critically ill at Newstead. He set off almost immediately for Nottinghamshire—after first borrowing £40 in cash from Hanson—but she died on 1 August while he was still traveling.[67] Fate had played a cruel hand.

Byron preferred his mother in small doses, and preferably at a distance, but she had been unfailingly supportive through the trials and tribulations of recent years. It is perhaps not surprising that, once at Newstead, he was discovered by her maid sitting by her mortal remains, exclaiming that he had only one friend in the world "and she is gone." His spirits were further rocked even before the funeral by news that his old Cambridge friend Charles Skinner Matthews had drowned in the Cam. He told Hobhouse on 10 August, "I am really so much bewildered with the different shocks I have sustained, that I can hardly reduce myself to reason by the most frivolous occupations."[68] Mrs. Byron was buried in the family tomb at Hucknall.

Byron stayed on at Newstead. He wrote a poem that reflected his gloom in these August days:

> In the dome of my Sires as the clear moonbeam falls
> Through Silence and Shade o'er its desolate walls,
> It shines from afar like the glories of old;
> It gilds, but it warms not—'tis dazzling, but cold.

The absence of his mother—though he and she had never lived together at Newstead—preyed on his mind:

> And the step that o'erechoes the gray floor of stone
> Falls sullenly now, for 'tis only my own;

Matthews's death made him reflect on the house party he had hosted on his last visit to the abbey in April 1809:

> And sunk are the voices that sounded in mirth,
> And empty the goblet, and dreary the hearth.[69]

Byron told Augusta in September that he was "quite alone and never see strangers without being sick." He was "on good terms with my neighbours, for I neither ride nor shoot or move over my Garden walls, but I fence and box and swim and run a good deal to keep me in exercise and get me to sleep."[70] He spent some time revising *Childe Harold's Pilgrimage*. It was perhaps this gloomy period that he was recalling in canto 5 of *Don Juan*, written in Ravenna in 1821:

> I pass my evenings in long galleries solely,
> And that's the reason I'm so melancholy.[71]

More than anything, Byron had in these months to look into estate business, but Mrs. Byron's death had removed the one person who might have persuaded him to maintain the resolve he had shown in letters to Hanson since the previous November. As it transpired, she was never to provide the account of affairs at Newstead that he had been anticipating, or to express her doubts to him about Hanson. Left to himself, and in such circumstances, Byron was unlikely to mount a fundamental review of his financial affairs, or to hire for himself a sympathetic lawyer who would be able to raise a mortgage on Newstead, or to appoint a proper steward. He told Hodgson that he was going to raise the rents: "I have only to give discharges to the tenantry here (it seems the poor creatures must be raised though I wish it was not necessary) and arrange the receipt of sums and the liquidation of some debts." The rents were to be raised to £2,100, although Byron apparently rejected a proposal from Hanson to turn out the old tenants and replace them with monied men who could pay more: "[I]f I chose to turn out my old bad tenants and take monied men they say, Newstead would bear a few hundreds more from its great extent, but this I shall hardly do."[72]

Byron also had to sort out his mother's affairs, and for this purpose he employed Samuel Bolton, a Nottingham solicitor, whom he invited to Newstead on 3 August. He intended also to make a number of changes to his will, drawn up in 1809 "principally . . . in consequence of the death of Mrs Byron." His plan was to entail the Newstead estate on his cousin George Anson Byron and his heirs, and then on to other members of the Byron family in default of such heirs. He wanted to leave substantial legacies to his friends (notably Hobhouse, Davies, and Francis Hodgson) and servants, and for this purpose he intended that Rochdale should be sold to raise the necessary finance. Bolton did his work thoroughly: his claim for fees included "searching for and perusing pedigree to enable us to entail the real estates according to your Lordship's instructions." The will was quite specific about land sales: "it being my will and desire that my said estates . . . at Newstead shall be disposed of in the event only of the proceeds arising from the Sale of my other estates and property by this my will directed and authorized to be sold proving inadequate to the deficiency in my personal estate." In other words Newstead was to be retained, and strictly settled on the next male Byron, a clear indication to Hanson—who was, after all, not asked to prepare this will—that far from disposing of the abbey, Byron was trying to ensure it had a future in his family.[73]

On the question of cash flow, Byron was pleasantly surprised to find his mother's collection of jewelry was worth £1,130, at which price he promptly sold it to a London jeweler.[74] For the longer term he talked of seeking the easy way out by contracting a lucrative marriage. "I shall marry if I can find anything inclined to barter money for rank within six months," he told Augusta, adding a few days later that "money is the magnet." To Hobhouse he confided his opinion that "I must marry some heiress or I shall always be involved [i.e., in debt]."[75] Perhaps above all, without his mother's influence Byron never had quite the resolve to resist Hanson. Years later he confided in Thomas Medwin that "I never could have ventured to sell [Newstead] in my mother's lifetime."[76]

Hanson joined Byron at Newstead in September, and together they set out for Lancashire to spend a few days on the Rochdale estate. The legal case had been dragging slowly onward over the previous two years, and Hanson had told Mrs. Byron in March 1809 that "I am in hopes we shall be able to come to an arrangement with the Rochdale People. I wish very much that his Lordship would go down with me thither this Spring when he should probably be able to put an end to that business, and I am inclined to think he will."[77] Byron had gone abroad instead, and the head of steam that had built up over Rochdale soon evaporated. The neglect, of which Mrs. Byron had been so worried in 1808, continued. "One thing I am sensible of," Thomas Elliott told Hanson from Rochdale after holding the manor court there in May 1810, is that "Lord Byron's rights demand an active resident steward, and he is daily suffering by incroachments to the other matters." He recommended for the position John Kershaw, a Rochdale attorney, son of a former steward, and "a man of character and property and very active." Receiving no immediate answer, he wrote again a few days later, once more complaining that Byron's affairs had been neglected, that he (Elliott) had been mistaken for the steward—a position he did not want—and enclosing his expenses for holding the courts.[78] Mrs. Byron, writing when Byron was on his way back to England, had also warned him of neglect: "[T]here has been a person from Rochdale at Newstead recently. He says your presence is much wanted there, it would do much good to the people there, and also to yourself as you would get many thousand pounds by it, that is allowing people to build, and you might make a good deal of your manorial rights."[79]

Byron and Hanson left for Rochdale in late September 1811 for what was to be his only visit to the Lancashire estate. He told Augusta before setting out: "My Rochdale affairs are understood to be settled as far as the law can settle them, and indeed I am told that the most valuable part is that which was never disputed, but I have never reaped any advantage from them, and God knows if I ever shall." The visit to Lancashire was planned in the expectation that "something will be decided as to selling or working the collieries. I am the Lord of the Manor (a most extensive one) and they want to enclose which cannot be done without me, but I go there in the worst humour possible and am afraid I shall do or say something not very conciliatory."[80]

Byron's accounts of his visit to Lancashire have to be treated, like all his letters in these years, as being tailored according to the correspondent he was addressing. He stayed at Hopwood Hall, the home of Robert Hopwood and his wife Cecilia Byng. Two of her sisters and a female cousin were also in residence. The result, or so Byron claimed in writing to Hodgson, was that "unluckily receiving an invitation to a pleasant country seat near Rochdale full of the fair and fashionable sex, I left my affairs to my agent (who however managed better without me) never went within ken of a coalpit, and am returned with six new acquaintances but little topographical knowledge."[81] While he may not have seen much of the countryside, Byron had not been inactive. His host recognized that he was "in these parts on business," and that as lord of the manor of Rochdale "he has a large fortune." Byron's understanding of his business affairs is clear from his correspondence with Hobhouse: "If I work the mines myself, [they] will produce c.£4,000 p.a." Since this would mean investing capital that he did not have, the alternative was to let the mines, although this would produce only half the rental: "[S]o we are to work the collieries ourselves of course." He added a few days later, "I believe my Rochdale statement was pretty correct, with this proviso that if I could afford to lay out £20–£30,000 on it, the income would probably be double the utmost I mentioned." He had been assured the figures were correct by several Lancashire gentry.[82]

Back at Newstead Hanson and Byron undertook a detailed study of his debts, estimated now at £20,000. Nothing more was heard of Hanson's plan to sell Newstead; indeed, he even agreed that a further attempt should be made to raise a mortgage on the property. Subsequently he advertised for a mortgage, which brought one or two positive responses, and he made a number of inquiries through his own contacts, but none was forthcoming. The problem now was much the same as in 1809: loans secured on landed estates were simply not attractive to people with money to lend. Wartime never produced good conditions for borrowing on the security of property. Heavy taxation of land, together with the more attractive return on government borrowing, served to channel funds away from the mortgage market. As a witness told the 1818 Select Committee on Usury, during the wars there had been considerable distress among landowners because they were not able to obtain fresh loans of money on land security when mortgages were called in. Arthur Goodeve of the Sun Fire Office, who gave evidence to the same committee, claimed that in some years during the French wars mortgages could not be had at any price. Anyone still willing in these circumstances to lend money on the security of landed property was hardly likely to find Newstead an attractive proposition because the estate was so run down, and the position was complicated by the fact that since it was unsettled a potential mortgager would have no legal guarantee that his was the first or only secured loan. Possibly Hanson should have tried harder, but it was soon obvious that Byron's patience was wearing thin: he was "harassed with this business beyond bearing." "I have been doing everything to raise money by mortgage on Newstead for these last three months to no purpose," he told Scrope Davies; "I have been disappointed in every expectation." As in 1809, so now again in 1811, Newstead was simply not a good proposition in the economic circumstances of the day.[83]

The lure of London soon carried Byron away from Newstead, but his newfound interest in business matters continued for a while. In November 1811 he reminded Hanson that they needed to inform the tenants of the intended rent rise. Yet it was a frustrating business while Hanson was unable to raise a mortgage, and when Byron returned to Newstead at Christmas he told Hobhouse that "my affairs are disordered in no small degree." He took comfort from the fact that "as those of every body else seem no better one has the consolation of being embarrassed in very good company." He was trying to obtain the remainder of his mother's Scottish fortune, he had traveled to Lancashire "to no great purpose," he had arranged for a doubling of the Newstead rents, and he was hopeful of finding a way of sorting out the annuitants.[84] Byron stayed on into the new year ostensibly to sort out the Newstead rental, but more pressingly to continue the liaison he had struck up with one of the housemaids, Susan Vaughan.

Back in London again during January 1812, Byron sent Mealey instructions that those tenants who had been given notice to quit their farms by 25 March were to go on with preparations for planting the spring corn, and to manage their farms properly. He was about to send someone to Newstead to examine the state of cultivation on all the farms. Anyone who could not reach an agreement for continuing their farms at the increased rent would be compensated for their work before leaving. The tenants agreed to these terms, and were in turn informed that Byron and Hanson would soon visit Newstead to examine each of the farms in detail. Mealey reported ill-tidings: "[T]he farmers are making bad work at Newstead for there is scarcely any land at Newstead that will bring spring corn but what is ploughed up."[85]

Unfortunately, Byron's business attention span was limited, and he could always find something more interesting to do. He found London society so much more enthralling than the Nottinghamshire countryside. With ambitions of being a political orator, he resumed his career in the House of Lords on 15 January 1812, delivering his maiden speech on 27 February in support of the Nottinghamshire Luddites.[86] And he craved literary success. When, the following month, *Childe Harold* was published to quite astonishing reviews, Byron was catapulted headlong into literary society. The proposed visit to Newstead to inspect the farms did not take place.

It is easy to be wise after the event, but between 1809 and 1812 Byron had the opportunity to put his financial and estate affairs into some sort of order. The failure to secure a mortgage on Newstead remains a mystery. How hard Hanson tried in the spring of 1809, and again in 1811–12, is unclear. Given his preference for selling Newstead, Hanson was probably not the best agent to employ in the search for a mortgage, and money was certainly not easy to obtain in these years. In the longer term a mortgage would not have prevented Byron from overspending his resources, but it would have put his financial position into clearer perspective because the annuitants would have been paid off. Interest payments apart, Byron would have given himself a clean financial slate, and the sense of financial desperation that pervades the years between 1812 and 1816 would have been avoided. Byron's biographers have been almost entirely gloomy about his financial prospects. Leslie Marchand suggested that Byron's affairs were in the worst state imaginable while he was abroad between 1809 and 1811, and more recently Phyllis Grosskurth has claimed that "Hanson tried to raise a mortgage on Newstead Abbey, which no sensible investor would consider in the light of Byron's dire finances."[87] These were Hanson's views, but they were views expressed with a particular course of action in mind.

Byron lacked experience, and he was not very confident in his handling of the tenants, but for a short while in 1811 he certainly seemed to know his own mind. His ability to persuade Hanson once again to seek a mortgage, together with his new will in which he intended to strictly settle the estate, imply an unusual degree of attention to business, perhaps while the memory of his mother was still fresh in his mind. The reason he seemed perpetually in financial difficulty had everything to do with cash flow. His capital assets far exceeded his debts, but by failing to liquidize part of his tied capital he left himself short of money. As a result, he gave the appearance of being overwhelmed by debt, and lacking the sustained energy and interest that he needed to sort out his financial affairs he passed the burden back to Hanson. He never managed to combine the roles of literary giant and aristocratic owner in the manner of, for example, the bluestocking Elizabeth Montagu, who occasionally slipped away from her London salon to organize her coal miners in County Durham.[88]

7

The Abortive Sale, 1812–14

On 14 August 1812 John Cam Hobhouse, Byron's traveling companion and his great friend over many years, went to Garraway's Coffee House, the London auction rooms for landed estates. They went, Hobhouse recalled,

> to the sale of Newstead Abbey by auction by a Mr Fairbrother, where, having just secured myself with Byron, I bid twelve times, and left off at 113,000 guineas for the large lot, which was bought in at 113,500 guineas, B. having fixed £120,000 as the price. The second was bought in at 13,100 guineas. Never having done the like before, I was, before the thing began, in a complete fever, but was told by Hanson, B's solicitor, that I came off most admirably. I had just then only one pound one shilling and sixpence in the world.[1]

For a man possessed of £1 1s. 6d. to bid for an estate at £118,650 was a risk of considerable proportions, hence presumably his "complete fever," but why was he in this position at all? It was only a few months since Byron had been busily dealing with estate business, and not much longer since he had been adamant that he would not part with Newstead, even if he would allow Rochdale to go. Yet now the course of action urged by Hanson since 1798, and opposed so strongly by both Byron and his mother, had been adopted. Although, as Hobhouse noted, neither Newstead nor Rochdale reached their reserve price, this was not to be the end of the matter.[2] Over the next few years Newstead was put up for sale three times, and it was finally sold in 1817. How are we to explain Byron's change of heart?

I

Byron returned to London from Newstead on 13 January 1812. He was, as usual, short of cash. To raise money he went in search of annuity loans, and informed his friends he was considering selling his furniture at Newstead. He told Hodgson he was taking "some necessary but unpleasant steps to clear everything" before leaving England for good in the spring of 1813.[3] In the circumstances he was, not unnaturally, pleased to hear from Hobhouse that following a truce with his estranged father he was able to pay Byron the £1,323 he owed to him from their European travels.[4] Armed with such prospects, Byron made haste to his tailor, and he paid a number of outstanding bills, although Scrope Davies was told to wait a little longer for financial satisfaction.[5]

These were no more than preliminaries for the main course, which commenced with the publication on 10 March 1812 of *Childe Harold's Pilgrimage*, a romantic Spencerian poem based on Byron's travel experiences between 1809 and 1811. It was an instant literary success, with the first edition selling out in three days. Virtually overnight Byron became the most sought-after person in fashionable London. Everyone wanted to meet him—not least, the prince regent—and party invitations arrived by the score. He was feted at Holland House, where Lord and Lady Holland presided over the prestigious Whig circle at which everyone sharing their interest in politics and literature was welcomed. At Melbourne House, another of the great Whig centers, he met Lady Melbourne, who offered him worldly advice and motherly understanding as he sought refuge from his unexpected fame. He began a spectacular affair with Lady Melbourne's married daughter-in-law, Lady Caroline Lamb. For four months they conducted a scandalous and astonishingly public relationship, which through April and May reached apparently undreamt-of heights of indiscretion, and almost led in late July 1812 to an elopement. Through these months there were regular highly publicized arguments, and almost as many well-attested reconciliations. Byron occasionally managed to escape for a few hours to the House of Lords (twice in March and three times in April), and in June he spent a few days at Newstead with Hobhouse, although even here Lady Caroline bombarded him with letters.

Byron's life was transformed, and there was to be no going back. He was no longer the callow young man dependent on his old Cambridge friends for his London company; rather, he was launched into the heart of literary society, and at some point in the midst of his frantic round of social events he accepted Hanson's advice that he should sell Newstead. Hobhouse knew in March that this was "your lawyer's scheme with respect to Newstead," and Dallas learned "early in the autumn of 1812" from Byron that "he was urged by his man of business, and that Newstead must be sold."[6] When it came to estate business Byron's attention span was short, and in the heady spring of 1812 it disappeared altogether. As he admitted to Scrope Davies in 1817, "I am not a man of business," and his friend Richard Hoppner summed him up accurately when he told Byron in 1819 that "until you can make up your mind to look a little after your own affairs, it will be difficult for you to find a steward who will not take advantage of you."[7] In the summer of 1812 he had no interest at all. He willingly accepted Hanson's advice about Newstead, but insisted on going against his lawyer's wishes by including Rochdale in the auction. He was anxious to be out of land.

Once Byron had taken his decision, Hanson moved swiftly to make the estate available for sale. In June or early July sale particulars were prepared and the estate was offered for sale by private contract. Anyone interested was invited to make an offer. If no acceptable offer had been received by 14 August the estate was to go to auction. How much interest was shown in the estate at this point is not clear. Matthew Robinson Boulton, son of the Birmingham entrepreneur Matthew Boulton, was sent the particulars by his London agent, William Le Blanc. He was interested in what appeared to be "a desirable property," since he was looking for somewhere more rural than Soho, his country retreat near Birmingham. Unfortunately, he did not have the time to view Newstead before the auction date. Boulton's business partner, James Watt Jr., also took a passing interest in Newstead.[8]

Unfortunately for Hanson's planning, the failure of the auction at Garraway's in 1812 looked likely to thwart his immediate hopes of sorting out Byron's financial affairs. Land sales in wartime, when potential investors had many alternatives for placing their money, were always a problem. Since, during the French wars, the interest payable on government securities regularly outran the return on land, new men of wealth preferred to keep their money in higher-yielding government securities, and to enjoy the profits accruing to contractors and industrialists. Consequently new purchasers tended to be looking for relatively modest estates, and for this reason larger properties were often broken up for sale. As a result, while plenty of land came on to the market in the years 1810–14, large estates were not particularly popular. Newstead had the double disadvantage of being both a substantial estate in property sales terms, and also being rundown and in need of improvement. Joseph Bennett, who cast his eye over Newstead on behalf of James Watt Jr., painted a gloomy picture:

> The house, called the Abbey, as well as the pleasure grounds, etc., are in a very bad state and cannot have been much attended to for several years. The lakes and small plantations seem to have been equally neglected. I did not go very near the Abbey, but it appeared at a distance as an old gothic structure, nearly falling in ruins. . . . The fences were wretchedly bad, particularly the pales of the boundary next the Forest. The soil which I examined was extremely light, composed chiefly of red and white sand, and without any prospect of getting marl, which would be the only effectual corrector. . . . The crops I saw were miserable rye and oats. . . . I think for a

gentleman the neighbourhood is bad, and the estate without the smallest degree of beauty. . . . I should think it one of the most unlikely properties for sale I know.[9]

With such a report in his pocket, Watt probably did not bid, but the most worrying part of Bennett's comments concerned the value of the property. Hanson had originally invited offers for Newstead, but when it came to auction he set the reserve price at £120,000. Bennett's valuation was "79 or 80 thousand pounds," although he had heard that the owners of neighboring Annesley and Papplewick Halls both valued it at rather less.[10] In these circumstances the reserve price of £120,000 was probably set too high for the prevailing market conditions. If the whole estate of 3,200 acres had been let for 20.7s. an acre (the average rent for this type of land in 1812), and if it had sold at the average price for 1812, it would have raised £100,000. Of course, these average figures assume the estate was in at least average condition, which it was not, hence the local view that £80,000 would have been a good price. Consequently, the reserve of £120,000 looks to have been optimistic. Hobhouse may have worked up a sweat on 14 August, but arguably Newstead failed to sell because Hanson set the price too high.[11] In later years Byron was to complain bitterly that Hanson had been unrealistic in his expectations about Newstead, although Hobhouse's recall of events suggests that they had come quite close to achieving the £120,000 reserve.[12] We do not know who was still in the bidding when Hobhouse was finally put out of his misery.

In any case, all was not yet lost. Many estates that failed to reach their reserve price on the London auction market subsequently changed hands privately. The morning after the auction Hanson was approached by "a Lancashire gentleman . . . who has made such an offer as deserves attention. . . . His offer is £140,000 for the whole property, including timber and furniture."[13] Given that only the day before potential purchasers valued Newstead at less than £120,000, there was good reason for concern at this "offer," but Byron, acting on Hanson's advice, accepted the proposal. Newstead, it seemed, was sold—to the disappointment of some of Byron's relations. His great aunt, Mrs. Frances Byron, told him in October that she had been "hurt at your having parted with my favourite Newstead." She wished him well for the future, having "heard with real pleasure from Mr Hanson that your Lancashire estate will prove of great value. If so perhaps you will sometime try to regain poor Newstead."[14]

Mrs. Byron's disappointments were premature, because Newstead was far from sold. Two years after the Garraway's auction Hobhouse recorded that "Byron has got back Newstead," adding without explanation that "the buyer, Claughton, has forfeited £25,000."[15] Ostensibly this looks like a remarkable piece of business by Byron, or perhaps Hanson: in effect, making a profit of £25,000 for nothing. It was not quite so simple.[16]

II

Thomas Claughton (c. 1774–1842) of Haydock Lodge near Warrington, the Newstead purchaser in 1812, was not a landowner or would-be landowner in the normal sense of the term; rather, he was an attorney experienced in dealing with landed property. Claughton had been brought up by his uncle, a Warrington attorney, and he soon followed in his footsteps, specializing in land speculation. In this role he came into contact with the landed gentry of northwest England, and he married in 1806 Maria, the illegitimate daughter of Thomas Legh of Lyme Hall in Cheshire. Claughton was a trustee of her (legitimate) brother's interests and lived in one of his properties, Haydock Lodge. He was among a group of Lancashire attorneys who, in the course of the eighteenth century, came to dominate the mortgage market in the county, from which it was only one short step to accumulating substantial property themselves. Hanson assured Byron that Claughton had acted on behalf of "the second son of the late Colonel Legh of Lyme and I have little doubt he has purchased for some part of that wealthy family, so much the better if it be so as it affords additional security for completion." In fact, Claughton seems to have acted alone, although the story of his link with the Leghs remained current in Claughton's family until recent times.[17]

Claughton negotiated for Newstead as a speculation. The sale particulars drawn up prior to the auction described the 3,200 acre estate as "highly improveable," and let at "old and very low rents . . . to tenants who are under notice to quit."[18] Claughton saw an opportunity here that would enable him, by some vigorous estate management, to resell the property at a substantial profit in a rising market. Within a few days of the transaction being completed he was at Newstead surveying the estate, and when he found Joe Murray packing linen and glass to send to Byron he insisted that only the books and pictures had been exempted in the agreement drawn up with Hanson.[19] Hanson was clearly shaken by such speed: "I think your Lordship had better not remove any of your goods and chattels till I go down, when I can arrange what things you would have sent up, and it will be as well to keep the gentleman in good humour with his purchase till we get hold of the deposit."[20]

If Claughton was speculating when he bought Newstead, why did he offer such a high price? Given the timing of his proposal, he must have known all about the auction, and if he attended, or sent an agent, he must also have known the price at which Newstead was called in. As an experienced land agent he must have been able to work out fairly accurately the net worth of the estate, both improved and unimproved. Given these assumptions, he might have been expected to offer around £120,000, at which price he would certainly have secured the property. Yet his offer was greatly in excess of the reserve price at the auction, so did he have other expectations?

One possibility is that Claughton anticipated the coal-mining potential of the property. Coal had long been mined along the Erewash Valley between Ilkeston and Mansfield. By the eighteenth century considerable quantities were being raised, particularly on the Derbyshire side of the valley, where the coal outcropped near the surface and was relatively cheap to mine. The presence of coal in and around Newstead was well known. The fifth Lord Byron had funded trials (by borrowing) in the 1750s, and tenants on the estate made a gift of coal to the abbey as part of their rent. When Byron was snowbound at Newstead early in 1814 he told Lady Melbourne he was quite warm, "being in no want of combustibles (you know that Notts is famous for coals & the fair sex)," to which she responded that "I envy you the good Nottinghamshire coals, which I think the best in the world."[21]

No mention was made of coal reserves in the 1812 estate details, but Claughton clearly knew that there was coal in the area and, having some experience of mining on the south Lancashire coalfield, may have thought that he could exploit the reserves to his own benefit. If so, he was to be disappointed. Profitable deep mining reached this area only during the 1840s, and it was not until the 1850s and 1860s that pits were sunk in the neighboring parishes of Hucknall, Bulwell, and Annesley. W. F. Webb, by then the owner of Newstead, leased the coal seams under the abbey to the Sheepbridge and Staveley Coal and Iron Companies in 1872, and Newstead Colliery opened three years later. Until the 1870s mining in the Newstead area remained small-scale, and by then Thomas Claughton's interest in the area had long since ceased.[22]

In fact, we have no record of Claughton's intentions in 1814.[23] What we do know is that he was not a man of great wealth, and he had no hope of purchasing the property outright. It is even possible that he did not bid for Newstead at the auction, because he was unable to meet the terms and conditions for payment laid down in the further particulars. What he needed was the equivalent of a modern hire-purchase agreement—payment, in other words, by installments. Such methods were not unusual; indeed, much the same policy had been used in the 1770s when the duke of Devonshire bought the fifth Lord Byron's Gringley estate. In the wake of the auction Claughton negotiated with Hanson an agreement whereby he would pay for Newstead over several years. Initially he was to pay a deposit of £20,000 in two equal installments, the first by 29 September and the second by Christmas 1812. He was then to pay a further £60,000 by 24 June 1813, and to leave the last £60,000 as a mortgage secured on the estate for three years. Claughton was to enjoy absolute possession only with completion on 24 June 1813 of the £80,000 payment and £60,000 mortgage. In the meantime he was to collect the rents from 25 March 1813, occupy the abbey, and enjoy use of the furniture, and seed and stock the farms in hand. Specifically excluded from the contract were "the plate, linen, glass, books, fire arms, swords, sabres, pictures, wines and liquors of all sorts which the s[ai]d Lord Byron reserves to himself," and it was a sign of the trouble to come when Claughton objected to Joe Murray packing up linen and glass to send to Byron.[24]

Whatever Claughton's motives, as far as Byron was concerned the transaction seemed to represent a remarkably good deal. His debts, which he now put at "not £25,000," would be paid off and, when the Rochdale legal case was sorted out and the income added to the Newstead surplus, he would be "as independent as half the peerage." Hanson was offered "carte blanche as to Rochdale," and he was commissioned to ensure that, as Claughton paid the installments on Newstead, Byron's creditors were paid off. Byron suggested that Scrope Davies should be at the head of the queue.[25] Meantime Byron could attempt to draw breath, particularly when in early September Caroline Lamb went with her husband and mother to Ireland. He himself departed for Cheltenham, where Davies insisted on being repaid £1,500 without delay.[26] While Caroline plied Byron with letters from her temporary exile, he confided in Lady Melbourne that he had formed an attachment to Annabella Milbanke, one of the many young ladies he had met since the publication of *Childe Harold*. Lady Melbourne proposed on his behalf to Miss Milbanke in October. This might seem rather bizarre, although as Annabella's aunt (she was Sir Ralph Milbanke's sister) she probably considered herself to be playing an important intermediary role. In any case it hardly mattered, since the proposal was rejected.

What was Hanson planning for Byron in the autumn of 1812? Hanson favored Byron selling Newstead, but this did not mean he simply anticipated Byron pocketing all the money left over once his debts were paid. He envisaged dividing the £140,000 into three: £20,000 going toward paying Byron's debts, £60,000 remaining on a mortgage paying 4 percent (£2,400 per annum) or preferably 5 percent (£3,000) in order to provide a regular income; and the other £60,000 being reinvested in property and securities that would be appropriate for the social standing of his client. Within days of sealing the Claughton deal Hanson and Byron were discussing moderate country residences: "I spoke to your Lordship about Mr Wickham's house, Cookham Elms, close by Maidenhead Bridge and on the Thames. It is a most comfortable thing for a residence and I think would suit your Lordship as a beautiful and desirable retreat on a moderate scale, and may be bought upon such terms as would secure you from loss in case you should ever wish to part with it."[27] Even while Byron was thinking over this possibility, Hanson was negotiating to purchase the tithes of the manor of Rochdale for £15,000. Hanson expected the tithes to

> turn out prodigiously advantageous to your Lordship. The landed property in that country is rapidly improving and increasing daily in value and circumstanced as you are as Lord of the Manor without anything but manorial rights attached to it, the uniting of these rights with the tithes gives you a substantial property not inferior to that of any other freeholder in the parish and enhances the value of each in a tenfold ratio.

In layman's terms, the tithes were worth about £475 per annum, but when they were commuted Byron could expect to be recompensed with a substantial share of the commons in the manor.[28]

These putative plans depended on Claughton fulfilling his side of the bargain, and it was soon clear that the optimism of late August might prove misplaced. Once Byron heard from Lady Melbourne his fate in relation to Miss Milbanke, he set out for Eywood in Herefordshire, at the invitation of Lady Oxford. Although sixteen years his senior, she quickly became his new lover, and he was able to tear himself away from her and return to London only at the end of November to spend a few days with Hanson addressing business matters, notably the Newstead transaction. Claughton was due to pay the first £10,000 by 29 September, but Michaelmas came and went, and during October Hanson began to show signs of concern. Eventually Claughton paid £5,000, but not until the end of October. "I always foresaw that Claughton would shirk," Byron told Hanson rather piously on 8 November. Within a few days he was urging Hanson to take legal action if necessary to ensure that the payments were forthcoming.[29] Claughton was later to claim that he should never even have paid the £5,000:

> Had the real state of the title been shown me, as it ought to have been, in the first instance, I should have completed my contract in all respects, but a title in fact defective was only produced, though in reliance upon your Lordship's honour and character I made a payment in the face of that defect.[30]

Claughton had a convenient memory: the articles of agreement had required Hanson to produce evidence of title only by 24 June 1813, but Claughton first raised questions about the title in October 1812. Hanson wrote to him "upon the subject and I trust from what I have said to him he will deem it becoming to make the payment forthwith."[31] He was to be disappointed. Claughton turned out to be

> very stubborn in refusing to pay any more of the deposit until we furnish him with the information called for by his Counsel on the title. I am fully prepared to solve their doubts, but I am satisfied with your Counsel's opinion that no more papers ought to be handed over until he has performed that part of his Contract.

Hanson's view was that these questions over Byron's title were simply filibustering because Claughton did not have the money to pay, "or he never would have allowed himself to be placed in so awkward a situation" in which he could not "take any means to improve or let the estate and any loss resulting from it must fall upon himself." Hanson talked about taking legal action, if necessary, to force Claughton's hand.[32]

After discussing with Hanson what measures they might take in regard to Claughton, Byron escaped back to Eywood before Christmas to stay once again with the Oxfords. He commissioned Hobhouse to find him a London house for the season, and after some negotiation returned to London on 19 January 1813 full of schemes for foreign travel. He had planned with the Oxfords a visit to Sicily—a scheme from which he subsequently extricated himself. In fact any plans he made were likely to run up against the problems caused by Claughton's procrastination. To begin with, he had no income. Byron, like his great-uncle before him, and along with many of his contemporary aristocrats, was happy enough to live with debt, but without an income he lacked cash to pay for necessities. Claughton was due to collect the Newstead rents from 25 March, and Byron was receiving little or nothing from Rochdale. Most of the £2,000 remaining from the initial Claughton deposit (after £3,000 had gone to Davies and as a deposit on the Rochdale tithes) soon disappeared in paying bills to Byron's hatter, his jeweler, his tailor, his saddler, and his swordsmith. When Hodgson asked him for a loan of £500 Byron was able to offer him only a bond: "[W]ith regard to security, as Newstead is in a sort of abeyance between sale and purchase, and my Lancashire property very unsettled, I do not know how far I can give you more than personal security, but what I can I will." He lent him £200 in April, but he could offer nothing to Augusta, who was as usual struggling to make ends meet as a result of her husband's gambling habits.[33]

Byron's intention at this juncture was undoubtedly to resume his travels. When he asked Hobhouse to find him a London house, it was just for the season. Hobhouse's suggestion that he might be willing to buy the lease was rejected on the grounds that it "would amongst other things militate against our travelling schemes."[34] Unfortunately for Byron, without money he could not travel, so to fill in the time he attended the Lords on a number of occasions in February and March 1813, but his taste for politics was waning. In March 1813 he told Hanson to sell Rochdale for "what I can get," and he gave him full powers to organize his affairs during what he was now planning as an extended absence from England.[35]

Claughton, meantime, failed to come up with any further sums of money, and the delay was soon driving Byron almost to distraction. He began to talk recklessly of canceling the contract, resuming control of Newstead, raising the rents, dismantling the house, and selling Rochdale. In one breath he was offering Hanson full control of his affairs, and in the next complaining bitterly about the advice he had been given. "Your father said sell," he told Hanson's son Charles; "I have sold and see what has become of it! I shall tell Mr Claughton he is a scoundrel and have done with him, and I only hope he will have spirit enough to resent the appellation and defend his own rascally conduct."[36] Byron could hardly contain his annoyance when he wrote to Samuel Rogers on 25 March, three months after the deposit should have been paid:

> I have parted with an estate (which has been in my family for nearly three hundred years and was never disgraced by being in possession of a lawyer, a churchman or a woman during that period) to liquidate this and similar demands and the payment of the purchaser is still withheld, and may be perhaps for years.

He was particularly incensed that with Newstead apparently sold he remained beholden to moneylenders. But trying to force the issue by taking legal action simply filled him with dismay at the thought of a repeat of the Rochdale case. Hanson, as usual, attempted to pour oil on troubled water. Byron should not worry about his "cursed concerns" (Byron's words) but leave them to his lawyer. Byron was receptive to such a message—"[Y]ou must at least allow that I have acted according to your advice about Newstead," he reminded Hanson.[37]

Meanwhile Byron's affair with Lady Oxford was continuing. He spent much of April at Eywood, but he was back in London toward the end of the month, and during May Lady Oxford left with her husband for Sicily. Lady Caroline Lamb caught up with him once more, notably with an "incident" at Lady Heathcote's ball. On 1 June he made what was to be his final speech in the Lords, and four days later *The Giaour* was published. Byron's reputation was now assured; and the poem soon ran into several editions, to each of which he added extra lines. By now he was actively planning further travels. Hobhouse left for the Continent on 27 May, and Byron was determined not to be far behind. Through June he was making preparations, buying uniforms he considered appropriate for paying visits to foreign potentates and magnificent gifts with which he intended to impress them—although the gold lids on a set of snuff boxes turned out to be silver gilt! In July he bought camping equipment, a hammock, guns, portable telescopes, and clothes by the trunk load (among them tartan trousers and a tartan jacket, presumably to allow him to appear as a Gordon). His tailor's bill was nearly £900, and he owed his goldsmith close to £1,000. He gave orders for his books to go to John Murray, and for his plate, linen, pictures, and other movable goods not included in the Claughton contract to be disposed of immediately to raise cash.[38]

Hanson was appalled. He was not amused by wild talk of canceling the contract, and he urged Byron not even to think of resuming his travels while the situation remained unresolved. Midsummer's Day (24 June) came and went without Claughton completing the contract, but early in July Hanson reported receiving "an ambassador from Mr Claughton proposing an armistice and negotiation for peace." On 7 and 27 July Claughton paid two installments of £7,500 each, which at least completed the deposit due six months earlier.[39] Byron was not amused when, toward the middle of the month, he heard reports that he was being accused of selling Newstead to a young man "who has been overreached, ill treated and ruined by me in this transaction of the sale, and that I take an unfair advantage of the law to enforce the contract." Such claims were nonsense: Claughton had "bid his own price," and the agreements reached were at his behest. At the same time he assured Lady Melbourne that he was himself the most injured party by the putative transaction, since Claughton had raised doubts about his title to the estate, called his character into question, and caused him to delay his travels.[40]

Although the Claughton transaction remained incomplete, it seems that he was serious about fulfilling its terms as soon as he had the money available, and Byron's cup appeared to overflow when his mother's estate was finally wound up and the £4,500 surplus paid to him during July.[41] All seemed set for his departure after so many disappointments during the previous months. Early in August, being "about to leave the Kingdom," he signed a power of attorney to allow Hanson to take all necessary decisions in regard to Newstead. He also arranged for £3,000 to be available through Hammersley's for travel expenses.[42]

III

Byron did not go. "My intended departure from this country is a little retarded by accounts of Plague &c. in the part of the world to which I was returning," he told Annabella Milbanke, but this was a gloss, since the truth was rather more complicated.[43] Byron had been joined in London during June 1813 by Augusta, and the relationship seems quickly to have developed beyond a platonic friendship. Incest, whether real or imagined, was to Georgian England what homosexuality was to the late Victorians, and Byron's supposed relationship with Augusta created enormous problems for him from 1813 onward. What is not in doubt is that within weeks of renewing his relationship with Augusta he was talking of taking her with him on his travels, perhaps to Russia. Augusta, suspecting she was pregnant, returned to her family, but Byron still did not depart. In mid-September, after leaving instructions for John Murray to find him a passage to the Mediterranean, he set off for Yorkshire to visit Wedderburn Webster at Aston Hall, near Rotherham. Byron first offered to advance his old friend £1,000 on loan (for which he had to ask Hanson to provide the money) and then considered, but rejected, seducing his wife Frances.[44] Instead he returned to London and made a new will dividing his remaining property between George Anson Byron and Augusta. Then, with his mind still in turmoil, he returned to Aston Hall and persuaded the whole party to go with him on a visit to Newstead. He wrote to Lady Melbourne "from the melancholy mansion of my fathers, where I am dull as the longest deceased of my progenitors," but where he still found sufficient energy almost to seduce Lady Frances. He was annoyed to find that, contrary to the 1812 agreement, "Claughton has broken open the cellar," and (in Mealey's words) "helped himself to what wine he wanted, and then put a fresh lock on it." Byron told Hanson to remind Claughton that he was entitled to full possession of the property only when all the purchase money had been paid, and meantime he had only "temporary possession."[45]

Byron returned to London, where he gave Hodgson £1,000 to help free him from his debts and enable him to marry,[46] and he sat down and wrote *The Bride of Abydos*, which Murray published on 2 December. Six thousand copies were sold within a month, and Byron was again the toast of literary London. He was also, as his loans and gifts suggest, a man with money in the bank. He was still restless, writing in his journal on 23 November 1813, "I have no ambition . . . my hopes are limited to the arrangement of my affairs, and settling either in Italy or the East (rather the last), and drinking deep in the languages and literature of both." "Nothing," he told Lady Melbourne on 10 January 1814, "but this confounded delay of Newstead etc. could have prevented me from being long ago in my isles of the east."[47] Lady Melbourne is unlikely to have believed such a transparent gloss, particularly when only a few days later he set out with Augusta for Newstead. On 1 February Murray published *The Corsair*, which Byron had started writing in mid-December 1813, and which sold ten thousand copies on the day of publication.

Claughton, meantime, had failed either to complete the purchase or to suggest when he might come up with the outstanding cash. In mid-January 1814 he proposed an amendment to the 1812 Newstead agreement. He suggested that he might pay a further £20,000 (making a total of £40,000) and then leave the rest, £100,000, on a mortgage at 5 percent interest. This sum would be reduced by annual installments of £20,000. Hanson wanted Claughton to pay £30,000, leaving £90,000 on mortgage, and with this proviso Byron was happy to accept the compromise. On the other hand, since the Rochdale legal case remained unresolved, Byron could not resist a barbed comment: "I do believe this famous sale which was to set all right will perplex me more than ever." Claughton himself arrived at Newstead just before Byron was preparing to return to London in early February, "and we go on very amicably together—one in each wing of the Abbey." They agreed that the terms of the contract should be fulfilled, and Byron returned to London sure that "the Newstead business is set at rest in my favour."[48]

Back in London Byron was still unsettled. During March he refused a request from Wedderburn Webster for a further advance, but he did manage to establish that his debt to Scrope Davies stood at £4,804, which he then paid off when Claughton advanced a further £5,000. Early in April Byron spent a few days with Augusta at Six Mile Bottom, from where he wrote to Hanson asking him to press Claughton to comply with the terms of the agreement they had reached in January.[49] Returning to London he was reunited with Hobhouse, newly returned from his extensive European tour. Byron wrote and published *Ode to Napoleon Buonaparte* within days of the emperor's abdication. Unsure whether to rejoin Augusta or to take up an offer from Annabella Milbanke to visit Seaham, he remained in London, urging Charles Hanson to pursue Claughton: "[H]e should be brought to immediate peace or war—payment—or law." He was at his wits' end over Claughton's "sad shuffling." In May Claughton paid a further £3,000, but even with the £5,000 this was far short of the £30,000 discussed in January. Byron began writing *Lara*. The hero had just returned from abroad to his Gothic seat, where he wandered around the "solitary hall" by moonlight, admiring its "gloomy vaults" and "Gothic windows." Through May and June Byron once again threw himself into the delights of the London season, culminating in the duke of Wellington's grand masked ball at Burlington House on 1 July. Delights or not, he still found time to press Hanson to sell Rochdale "immediately . . . for such is the pressure of my debts that I am unable to describe the perplexity in which they involve me."[50]

Claughton was clearly in no position to fulfill the renegotiated terms of January 1814. Byron told Moore early in July that "he doesn't know what to do or when to pay, so all my hopes and worldly projects and prospects are gone to the devil." The only conclusion to the matter seemed to be for him to take back the estate, "which is as good as ruin," or he would have to "go on with him dawdling, which is rather worse." On 11 July he urged Charles Hanson, who had arranged a meeting with Claughton to try to sort out what to do next,

> Whatever is done must be done now. . . . for years and years I have been sinking gradually deeper and deeper. I do not mean to exonerate myself, my own extravagance has doubtless been the principal cause, but at the same time I must add that delay never ending . . . has materially contributed to assist my own imprudence in adding to my involvements.

It was two months since they had discussed selling Rochdale, but nothing had been done, despite Byron's willingness to dispose of the property "for what it will bring. . . . Why cannot this be attempted at least?" Two days later he had received no reply and was annoyed: he was ready to ignore the lawyers and settle personally with Claughton: "I would sooner lose anything or everything than bear the suspense a day longer." When two further days passed without news he issued his own ultimatum: he would meet Claughton the following day (July 16) with or without John Hanson in attendance. For his part Claughton was less certain: he agreed to meet Byron only if he could be assured that he would be met "with temper."[51]

Claughton had good reason for his apprehension. Byron was preparing to set out with Augusta and her family for Hastings, where Hodgson had arranged for him to rent a house for a few weeks, when news reached him about Claughton that had him fuming with rage. Despite failing to pay the installments on Newstead, Claughton had bought the reversion of Thomas Johnes's Haford estate in Cardiganshire. Like Byron, Johnes had run up considerable debts, and he had funded them partly with loans from the Equitable Assurance Company. In 1813 he devised a plan to sell the reversion of his estate—the ownership after his death—in return for a lump sum paid immediately. Claughton was negotiating the purchase, and Byron got wind of the fact that he was about to conclude a deal along these lines at an agreed price of £90,000. A proportion of the estate, valued at £35,000, was to be conveyed directly to Claughton, with the rest to come into his possession when Johnes died, at which point the balance of the purchase price would be paid to Johnes's executors.[52] In fact, Claughton probably had no intention of fulfilling the transaction as negotiated. As at Newstead, so at Haford, he was speculating, calculating that with the conclusion of Continental hostilities the interest on government stock would fall and, commensurately, land prices would rise. He would make a windfall profit by selling out at a higher price.

Byron was furious. Before setting off for Hastings he berated Hanson in no uncertain terms:

> I am convinced that he is a man of neither property nor credit. He has never once kept his word since the sale was concluded, and at all events I will do anything to be rid of him. . . . *You* will cling and cling to the fallacious hope of the fulfilment, already shown to be so, till I am ruined entirely. Pray think of Rochdale, it is the delay which drives me mad . . . I would rather have but ten thousand pounds clear and out of debt, than drag on the cursed existence of expectation and disappointment which I have endured for these last 6 years, for 6 months longer, though a million came at the end of them.[53]

Once at the seaside with Augusta, Byron tried to relax. He was reading *Waverley*, swimming, and walking on the cliffs, but he was also anxiously awaiting news from Hanson, who was involved in delicate negotiations with Claughton.

The 1812 agreement had included penalty clauses. If Claughton failed to fulfill the stipulated terms, Byron was entitled either to enforce the contract or to annul it by repaying any of the money already given to him by Claughton. Claughton had, of course, been in breach of contract almost from the beginning, and Hanson had been urging Byron to be patient partly on the grounds that if Claughton failed to complete the agreement he would have to pay compensation. "I make no doubt," Hanson told Byron in April 1813, "he would gladly forfeit the £5,000 he has already paid and a great deal more."[54] Once Claughton's financial dilemma became apparent in July 1814, Hanson expected that his chief concern would be the level of compensation that would allow him to escape from the contract. Hanson and Claughton were engaged in talks while Byron was in Hastings. Terms were almost reached by 17 July when Claughton asked for more time: "[H]e thinks he ought not to make so great a sacrifice as is required of him without making further efforts to meet his payments to you." Hanson gave him until 25 July, but Byron was agitated. When by the twenty-ninth he had still heard nothing from London he sat down to write to Hanson, and got as far as to suggest that he would soon be "reduced to the necessity of conducting my treaty with Mr C myself." In the end he scrapped the letter, which was just as well, given that Claughton did not return to London until 30 July.[55]

Hanson and Claughton finally met and reached an agreement in August. Of the £28,000 Claughton had so far paid to Byron he was to forfeit £25,000, with Byron repaying the £3,000 one year hence. Claughton was to be given time to remove any remaining personal effects from Newstead and to reap and gather crops and sell stock from land in hand as of August 1814. Byron was to resume full ownership of the property as of the previous Lady Day rents. The 1812 agreement was to be torn up. For Byron this was a financial windfall, and for Hanson it was a triumph. Byron was elated: as he told Lady Melbourne "on all law points Hanson certainly beat him as the result proved and the said Claughton was also a lawyer." It was, he added, "some proof of his talent."[56]

How was the sum of £25,000 calculated? In the absence of specific evidence some speculation is necessary, but it was presumably assessed according to several criteria. First, Claughton had collected the rents at Lady Day and Michaelmas 1813 and Lady Day 1814, which in theory (if not in practice) should have brought in about £3,400.[57] Second, Claughton had agreed that if he failed to meet the terms of the agreement on 24 June 1813 he would pay interest from then on the £60,000 to be left on mortgage, and the £60,000 payment due at that date. For the period from June 1813 until August 1814, Hanson doubtless calculated the unpaid sum at 5 percent on £120,000 for thirteen months—£6,500. These sums together amounted to perhaps £10,000. Third, the forfeit must have included a notional element for the value Claughton had enjoyed (particularly the house and contents and shooting and fishing rights) and the income from those parts of the estate he had farmed, together with a valuation based on the improvements that he had carried out. Finally, a further sum must have been earmarked for the inconvenience to Byron, and for Hanson's fees. This would not have added up to £25,000, but Claughton was in breach of the original contract and could expect a heavy penalty had the case gone to court. Byron was, under the terms of the 1812 agreement, entitled to enforce the contract.

IV

The terms of the forfeiture partly reflected Claughton's activity in reorganizing the Newstead farms and adjusting the rents. Initially, the 1812 agreement seemed like a recipe for confusion, because Claughton had possession but not ownership during the period set aside for him to fulfill the financial terms of the contract. Claughton arrived at Newstead in August 1812, together with a surveyor, and he began to issue instructions. Hanson visited Newstead in September to finalize the agreement, when he heard that "he is making arrangements for ring fencing the estate with a nine foot stone wall and planting seems to be the order of the day." However, once Hanson returned to London, Mealey found himself in a dilemma. Hanson expected him to look after Byron's ongoing interests at Newstead. He sent him instructions "that the mule and the dogs may be parted with. You will therefore give the keeper directions to part with the dogs immediately and put a stop to all further expense." Mealey replied that he had heard the mule belonged to Mr. Claughton, and in any case he thought it would sell for little or nothing locally and recommended sending it to London on a Pickford's wagon. Claughton also expected Mealey to carry out instructions. He told the erstwhile bailiff to "cut and thin the plantations." Mealey did not know what to do, fearing the consequences if he carried out Claughton's instructions without Hanson's permission. Claughton was "for planting a great deal this winter."[58]

Mealey was caught between two masters, with a watching brief for Hanson and employment from Claughton. His letters to Hanson show a natural tendency to guard his own back by offering a rather disparaging view of Claughton's competence. In February 1813 he wrote that

> unless there is stop put to the farmers in time, I am afraid they will injure the estate very much as they ploughed and sowed more last spring than

West View of Newstead Abbey, c. 1815, artist unknown, watercolor and gouache. A romanticized impression of Newstead. The picture may have been painted for Thomas Claughton before his attempts to buy Newstead fell through. It was in the hands of Claughton's family until they donated it to Newstead in 1954. (Nottingham City Museums and Art Galleries [Newstead Abbey].)

they ought to have done . . . they take no notice of me. We have no labourers at work at Newstead now nor nothing doing in the garden. Mr Claughton sent for me . . . to settle with me, and to ask what I thought was best to be done with the tenants. I told him I thought he must let them stand over as they was until Michaelmas as he could not satisfy them before.

He asked Hanson for instructions about sowing seeds in the garden, and suggested that "it will be necessary to bring these farmers to some regulation as soon as possible," but he had never been able to achieve such an end and now it was no longer his responsibility.[59]

Claughton left no papers about his time at Newstead.[60] As an alternative record Mealey's views are certainly not to be trusted, but we know that Claughton had no intention of accepting the status quo at Newstead. After the relaxed atmosphere since the days of the fifth Lord Byron, his vigorous approach came as something of a shock. Rebecca Heath recalled many years later that Claughton "completely revolutionized" the Newstead estate, paying no regard at all to the established farmers. His first move was to have the whole estate surveyed, with the intention of raising the rents from Lady Day 1813. The tenants were not easily persuaded, and it was only in October 1813 that Claughton was able to reach any agreement with them for the year 1813–14. Rents on five of the eight Newstead farms, separately accounted from the Park farms laid out in the fifth lord's day, were increased and three reduced, leaving the overall total much the same. Critically for Claughton's plans, William Bowman and Samuel Rushton, two of the three tenants of the large Park farms, refused the proffered new terms. They stayed on their farms for the time being—presumably at the old rents—while negotiations continued. In theory, at least, the 1813 rental was £1,784.[61]

Claughton had no intention of being held to ransom by recalcitrant tenants, and he drew up a scheme that amounted to a major reorganization of the farming structure. It was based on two principles: he wanted fewer, larger farms, paying pro rata higher rents, but he also intended to reduce the size differentials between the Park and the Newstead farms (presumably to prevent Bowman and Rushton attempting to hold him to ransom). John Davy's 322-acre farm was to be supplemented with land currently in Bowman's tenancy to total 407 acres. The farms rented by John Palethorpe (158 acres) and Joseph Coleman (106 acres) were to be amalgamated and, together with Hardwick Field currently in Davy's tenancy, form a new farm of 284 acres. William Beardall's 158-acre farm was to be amalgamated with William Bell's 93 acres and supplemented by additional properties to total 311 acres. Wire Mill Farm, of which John Hardstaff Sr. was the tenant, was to go from 188 acres to 320 with the addition of land currently held by Bowman and Rushton. And so it went on: in all, 1,780 acres were to be let in seven separate holdings. Since 2,581 acres were let in 1812 and 1815, Claughton evidently kept back some land from the auction. He subsequently told Hanson that "I have thought it best to agree with Bowman and Rushton, tho to my disadvantage, but I must appeal to Lord Byron hereafter. I have allowed Rushton £63 and Bowman £55 in addition to their advanced rents."[62] Presumably he was trying to keep them, although with smaller farms, but if so his optimism proved premature, since neither man remained at Newstead.

The first that the Newstead tenants knew of Claughton's plans was when advertisements appeared in the local press during December 1813.[63] The new farms were to be let at a public auction at the Hutt, Mealey's public house just outside the abbey gates on the Nottingham-Mansfield road, on 6 January 1814. Attracting new tenants by farm auctions in this way was not approved by agricultural experts, because they feared that individuals would bid up the rent to a point where only by exhausting the land could they hope to farm it profitably.[64] This was hardly a problem for Claughton, since he intended to sell the estate when the land market was sufficiently buoyant, so that his primary concern was the size of the rental, which would determine the sale price. Bidding at the auction was competitive: "[P]eople came and bid enormous rents," recalled Rebecca Heath, whose father, William Beardall, a long-standing tenant at Newstead, "thought he was quite outbid." Beardall, "despairing of taking the farm again at a rent that he could live upon it, took a house at Mansfield and set of malt rooms where he had used to have his malt made." Rebecca's mother thought he would never survive such a move from "his old home," but as it transpired the people who had bid for his farm "did not come up well," and "Mr Claughton sent for my father and let him the old farm again." However, William Bell's farm, which was to be let together with Beardall's— and which he was currently farming—was let instead to William Green, "a friend of one of the new sub-agents, whose friends found places without regard to ought but self."[65]

Beardall's case reflected the problems into which Claughton ran with his auction. It was easy to bid, but signing on the dotted line thereafter took more courage, and Claughton soon found that several of his potential new tenants were not willing to take the proposed fourteen-year lease agreements. Hanson told Byron that "the obstinacy of the tenants, the change of the times in the price of corn, and the season of the year, have all conspired to prevent his letting the farms and he is likely to have the whole estate upon his hands."[66] The latter was scaremongering in the extreme, but when Byron reached Newstead on 22 January 1814 his own inquiries among the tenants convinced him that "his difficulties in letting &c. are of his own making . . . and all the delays are none of ours." Yet he still felt some sympathy for Claughton and, while snowed in at the abbey, sought to lend him a hand:

> I have seen Rushton & have talked him into tractability as far as regards Mr Claughton, though I believe it will cost me something in the way of compensation for the stock &c, but this is a matter of hereafter discussion. In the mean time he promises not to oppose further. Bowman I have not seen and have no notion of seeing. Mr Claughton must deal with him himself.[67]

Since neither Bowman nor Rushton stayed, we must assume Byron's intervention was not successful.

Claughton did not fill the tenancies according to the advertised scheme, although there were various changes in the wake of the auction. John Hardstaff Sr.'s rent for Wire Mill Farm rose from £150 to £200, although the acreage declined from 188 to 178 acres. Joseph Coleman's farm had been due to disappear under the reorganization, but he retained it with the rent advanced from £80 to £200 despite a reduction in the acreage from 106 to 91 acres. William Beardall lost nine acres, but his rent remained unchanged. Out went John Trueman, John Palethorpe, and John Davy. John Hardstaff Jr. took over much of Palethorpe's farm, while Davy's farm disappeared into a new tenancy found for George Wightman (404 acres). Robert Walker (116 acres) and Thomas Heath (211 acres) were other new tenants, while William Green took over what had been Beardall's second farm. In 1812 the three Park farms totaled 1,291 acres, and the eight Newstead farms totaled 1,136 acres. Following the reorganization nine farms were let, totaling 1,502 acres, but at a considerably increased rent. In 1811 2,482 acres were let for £1,777 (14s. 6d. per acre); after Claughton's reorganization 1,502 acres were let for £1,950 (£1 6s. per acre), an 80 percent increase. Conversely, a considerable acreage (1,079) was now "in hand." Bowman and Rushton having refused the revised tenancies, William Palin gave up the third Park farm (356 acres in 1812) to become manager of what was left of the three farms, which Claughton effectively turned into a substantial home farm. Byron was certainly impressed with Claughton's achievements. He admitted to Lady Melbourne in October 1814 that the rents had been raised "beyond what I could have done, because I should not have liked to turn out the old (though stupid) tenants." To Annabella Milbanke he wrote with a touch of exaggeration that "the rents have more than tripled, almost quadrupled."[68]

The figures are important for explaining a number of points about the 1812 transaction. When Claughton bought Newstead, it was let at a notional 14s. 6d. per acre. In other words, the maximum income (assuming all the land was let) was £1,859.[69] Expressed as years' purchase (price divided by rental, the normal calculation in the nineteenth century) this makes the estate look expensive at seventy-five years' purchase, although because it was described as improvable Byron and Hanson had set a minimum price at £120,000 or sixty-five years' purchase. Claughton's reorganization raised the rents to 26s. per acre, well above the national average for these years of 20.7s. per acre. At this level the price he had offered (£140,000) represented forty-two years' purchase. This was still expensive. Although estates in these years regularly fetched thirty or more years' purchase, Claughton needed a considerable increase in price before his speculation would begin to look profitable—unless, that is, he was also anticipating profits from coal mining. By July 1814 he must have been aware that his speculation had failed. Grain prices, which rose through the war years to a peak in 1812, started to fall steeply and continued downward with the conclusion of peace in 1814 (before Napoleon's temporary resumption of the war), and this was one reason why Claughton had such difficulty letting the Newstead farms at the advanced rents he proposed.

Claughton was no fool. As an experienced land conveyancer he must have recognized that the chance of making a profit on Newstead was now slim. Even if, as he anticipated, land prices rose with the cessation of hostilities, he would have needed an exceptionally favorable combination of circumstances—including rents remaining high (which they did not)—to be able to anticipate making money on a speedy resale of Newstead. In July 1814 he appeared to have accepted that the transaction had overreached him, but it is important not to confuse the issue (as Byron did) with his acquisition of Haford. Whether he could afford the Welsh venture or not, Claughton agreed to the Newstead forfeit because he accepted that he could not expect to make money should Byron insist on holding him to the contract. Ostensibly, the forfeit seemed to leave Byron better off both in financial terms and as the beneficiary of Claughton's truncated reorganization at Newstead, even if it had not produced all the financial benefits he had anticipated. In reality, Claughton had a new agenda. Hanson told Byron that Claughton "begs me to add that he is induced to make this sacrifice from a principle of making every atonement in his power of the disappointments which his own disappointments have been the means of occasioning to your Lordship."[70] This was nonsense: what he really wanted to do was to renegotiate the terms.

V

Byron signed the forfeiture papers in mid-August and went down to Nottinghamshire with Augusta and her children. "Newstead," he told Moore,

Augusta Leigh, Byron's half-sister, who visited Newstead with him twice in 1814 and subsequently regretted the loss of the abbey. She inherited the bulk of Byron's unsettled estate following his death in 1824. (Laurence Pollinger Limited and the Earl of Lytton.)

"is to be mine again. Claughton forfeits twenty-five thousand pounds; but that dont prevent me from being very prettily ruined. I mean to bury myself there and let my beard grow and hate you all." Hobhouse was delighted: "[A]s the event has happened perhaps it will be unsafe to hazard a prediction but something tells me, as it has always, that Newstead will continue to be the scene of iniquities in the same family as have already honoured it with the sight of their sins, for some centuries to come."[71] Perhaps even Byron thought he could be right—after all, he had just acquired £25,000 toward paying his debts. In one of his occasional fits of enthusiasm for estate affairs reminiscent of August and September 1811, he told Hanson on 3 August 1814 that "the next thing we have to consider is something immediate in arrangement as to letting the property &c, somebody must go down and settle the rents, neither the *keeper* nor Mealey, nor any of the old set must remain." The gamekeeper was "the greatest rascal and sells the game . . . we must turn over a new leaf, and since the property is still to be mine at all events it shall not be as it has been." Once at Newstead, Byron swam, fished, rowed on one of the lakes, and even entertained a suggestion that he should pay £1,500 for eighty acres of land at Blidworth that Claughton had proposed to purchase.[72]

Byron found a much altered estate. Two or three of the farmers he had not previously met, and many of the farms had changed since the reorganization of the previous Lady Day. More than one thousand acres were "in hand" as a home farm, run by William Palin, who resided in the abbey. The older farmers, or those who remained, were pleased to see him back since, by contrast with Claughton, he always "shewed a great regard to his tenantry." William Beardall met him clambering out of the rowing boat. Byron shook him by the hand and told him, "Beardall you are one of the oldest friends I've got."[73] Perhaps it was because Augusta was with him at Newstead that he was in such good spirits, but as in 1809 and 1811 his fine talk of reorganizing the estate quickly came to nothing. Augusta told Francis Hodgson on 14 September in respect to Newstead, "[O]f future plans I really can say nothing they are in such a glorious state of uncertainty."[74] She knew that other things were on Byron's mind, and when he left Newstead a week later he did so for ever. Hobhouse's prediction turned out to be wrong.

8

Marriage and Debt, 1814–15

Byron's relaxing stay at Newstead in September 1814 was to be but a temporary revival of his role as an English landed aristocrat. Hardly had he had time to walk the estate, row across the lake, and enjoy the delights of the countryside than Thomas Claughton renewed his offer to buy Newstead. Even while he was considering this possibility, Byron was looking at his personal future and sent an offer of marriage to Annabella Milbanke, which she accepted. By the time he left Newstead for London he had much to think about on both counts, and over the next two years Claughton and Annabella would play quite separate but almost equally significant roles in determining Byron's fortunes.

I

Thomas Claughton's motive in agreeing to the forfeit became apparent only a few days after Byron arrived at Newstead. He received a letter from Claughton offering to renew negotiations. Claughton convinced Byron that he had "already made such a sacrifice . . . he has paid pretty dearly for his non-completion," and Byron agreed to give him further time in which to raise the money. Whatever Hobhouse may have hoped, Byron was still committed to selling the property. As he told Claughton:

> Upon the subject of Newstead I will be explicit with you. It *is* my intention to sell the estate, and I would certainly rather renew the sale with yourself on the same terms than part with it to any other, even should chance or circumstances offer a more advantageous purchase. . . . I hope you are now satisfied that "the channel of Negotiation is left open," nor would it ever have been closed on my part, but for the necessity that existed of some decision one way or the other for the time being.

Byron explained his conciliatory attitude—he invited Claughton to stay at the abbey and shoot over the estate—to Annabella Milbanke:

> [H]e has lost a considerable sum in forfeiture by his temporary inability or imprudence . . . though against the advice of lawyers, and the regrets of relations, I shall not hesitate to give him an opportunity of making good his agreement, but I shall expect, indeed I will not endure such trifling for the future.[1]

Byron proposed to give Claughton until November to see if he could raise the money. Hanson was far from surprised at this turn of events, but he urged Byron to drive a hard bargain: "[I]f he could bring forward on the nail £50,000 possibly your Lordship might think it proper to indulge his predilections." He warned, "I see great danger and always did in your renewing your treaty with Mr Claughton lest it might preclude you from negotiating with others, and you must not give him a hold over you."[2]

Once Byron had agreed to reopen the negotiations there seemed little point in setting about reorganizing the estate. Instead, the old regime was reinstated, and the opportunity of turning over a new leaf was neglected. Mealey returned to his post. On 20 October he assured Byron of his continuing trustworthiness: "My Lord, your orders shall be obeyed in every respect by me." By November he was handling a dispute over unpaid taxes.[3] And Mealey, of course, was beholden as ever to Hanson. Byron's fine words in August had been hollow. He was determined to press ahead with the sale, and in the meantime to worry as little as possible about estate administration.

Even while he was dealing with Claughton, Byron was also considering his longer-term future when on 9 September he posted a proposal of marriage to Annabella Milbanke. Byron's rather unusual courtship of Miss Milbanke, which took place mainly by correspondence, is well known. Anne Isabella (Annabella) Milbanke was the only daughter and heiress of Sir Ralph Milbanke, and Byron proposed to her despite previously admitting that the relationship lacked "one spark of love on either side." She had refused his first offer of matrimony in 1812, and even now she accepted his renewed proposal through an exchange of correspondence—they had not been in personal contact for ten months. Byron received her acceptance on 18 September while dining with Augusta at Newstead, and he turned so pale she thought he might faint.[4] He quickly recovered, and after the meal he sat down to write letters, first to Annabella, and then to Hanson. Since he was now engaged to be married, he needed to see his lawyer for advice on a matter that had not previously been a pressing issue, the settlement of his property. After walking through the woods and crossing the park once more, on 21 September he left Newstead. Whether he knew it at the time or not, he was leaving for ever.

Byron's behavior in the autumn of 1814 seems in many respects to border on the perverse. Far from hurrying north to Seaham to visit Annabella and her parents, he set off in the opposite direction, parting with Augusta at Six Mile Bottom, her home near Newmarket, and traveling on alone to London. It was more than a month before he arrived in Seaham, and even then he stayed only a short while before returning to London. His actions, rather than his letters, suggest hesitancy about his proposal, and there were to be a number of occasions on which both he and Annabella seem to have considered calling off the engagement. At the same time, Byron was faced with some awkward questions relating to his finances, and it is no real surprise to find him running at full speed in the direction of John Hanson. Equally unsurprising is the rather different pace at which Hanson proceeded to investigate his affairs, but at least on this occasion there was a genuine reason for the delay in the form of Hanson's own family troubles.

In March 1814 Hanson's daughter Mary Anne married the third earl of Portsmouth (1767–1853), one of Hanson's clients. Byron gave away the bride. Portsmouth's first wife had died in November 1813, and at the time of the wedding he was forty-seven. He was also mentally unstable. Portsmouth's brother had not been pleased when the wedding took place, fearing that the young wife would produce an heir. In November 1814 he attempted to take out a commission of lunacy: "There is a deal of confusion in Lord Portsmouth's and Hanson's family, the brother of Ld P wants to lunatize him or stultify him, and there is law and all kinds of squabble," wrote Byron. Consequently, just at the point when Byron needed a marriage settlement, Hanson was dealing with a scandal in his own household. The marriage was eventually dissolved in 1823 on the grounds of Portsmouth's mental derangement,[5] but this was far into the future. In the short term Byron found Hanson difficult to pin down to financial business, and even if neither Byron's financial difficulties nor Hanson's family problems are adequate explanation for the time taken for the young lover to travel to his fiancée's home, both were relevant to the way in which events unfolded between September and their marriage on 2 January 1815.

Byron recognized in September 1814 that if Annabella accepted the proposal of marriage his finances would come under intense scrutiny, and even while awaiting her response he was busily totting up his fortune. At Hoare's Bank he had £4,000 or slightly more. He also had Murray's promissory note for £700 paid on the publication of *Lara*. His tangible assets ran to about £5,000, of which, somewhat bizarrely under the circumstances, he intended to put aside £3,000 toward his proposed travels to Italy and the east with Hobhouse (he does not appear to have told Hobhouse of this arrangement). He had recovered full ownership of his estates, and he could look forward to enjoying the rents due from Newstead on 29 September. The situation looked quite encouraging, partly because, as he told Annabella on 3 October, his debts had been "reduced very much within the last three years, and a few thousand pounds will cover the rest, considerably above half have been already paid." Once she accepted his proposal, the dream of further travel with Hobhouse had immediately to be dispelled, but Byron was confident as to the future when he returned to London to discuss with Hanson "the state of my affairs."[6]

Byron's calculations as he sat in the tranquil isolation of Newstead were back-of-the-envelope guesses. He sent a copy to Hanson, who replied diplomatically that they could "talk the matter over . . . very fully," which was a euphemism for marking the figures incorrect when the two men met on 7 October. Byron's debts, it transpired, were far from paid, and this raised the question of what had happened to the £28,000 he had received from Claughton between 1812 and 1814? The fate of this money can be traced, because most of it passed through the account at Hoare's that Byron opened in October 1812 to receive the first installment of Claughton's deposit. From this sum of £5,000 Byron paid Scrope Davies £1,500 and John Hanson £1,500. The latter sum was the deposit on the Rochdale tithes, which was returned with interest in June 1813 when the transaction fell through. Over the first six months of 1813 Byron paid a series of bills totaling £2,135. Many of these were for clothes and other items of maintenance. By the end of June 1813 the account showed a net deficit of £85.

Once Claughton paid £15,000 in two installments during July 1813, financial troubles disappeared as a subject of Byron's correspondence, and as evidence of his newfound affluence in early 1814 he moved into a larger London home in the Albany. The first Claughton payment of £7,500 was largely accounted for by £4,500 Byron withdrew for his own purposes and £2,840 he loaned to Hanson on account of his unpaid legal bills.[7] Of the £4,500, Byron transferred £3,000 to his account at Hammersley's towards his projected travels with Hobhouse. The rest of the Claughton money disappeared in a number of large payments over the following six months, including £1,000 to Augusta on 16 August, £1,000 to Wedderburn Webster in October, and £800 to Scrope Davies. Substantial sums were also paid to his valet William Fletcher (£1,275), presumably for maintenance, and to Owen Mealey (£117 4s. 6d.) for estate expenses. Altogether £13,963 was paid from his bank account in the second half of 1813. In the fifteen months since Byron opened the account he had received £20,000 from Claughton, and made payments of just over £19,000. Since the Rochdale tithe money was repaid with interest (£1,541), this left a credit balance of about £2,500.

During the first six months of 1814 Claughton made further payments of £5,000 and £3,000. Most of the first payment (£4,804) was diverted to repaying Byron's debts to Scrope Davies. The £3,000 paid in May 1814 went directly to Augusta (or strictly speaking to her husband) and did not pass through Byron's Hoare's account.[8] Byron's bills, some of which represented interest on loans, amounted to £2,395. The balance on the account by the end of July 1814 was approximately £200. Only Davies had been repaid his capital, although with various sums lent at interest Byron could in theory call in other money to redeem his debts. However, as he admitted to Hobhouse, a great deal "was swallowed up by duns, necessities, luxuries, fooleries, jewelleries, 'whores and fiddlers.'" He also admitted that "some of the tradesmen's are largish sums, but the coachmaker, tailor, and others have received a few hundreds."[9] There was still much to be paid out.

What Byron discovered from Hanson in October 1814, as he later recounted to Hobhouse, was that his capital debts had scarcely been reduced. They included

> six thousand charged on Newstead to a Mr Sawbridge, a thousand to Mrs Byron at Nottingham, a Jew debt of which the interest must be more than the principal, & of which Hanson must get an amount from Thomas, another Jew debt, six hundred principal, and no interest (as I have kept that down) to a man in New Street . . . a good deal still before majority . . . a good deal of tradesmen &c &c.

The Sawbridge debt was £6,200; debts we can identify, including Thomas, amounted to £5,800; and to Mrs. Byron he owed a further £1,000—a total of £13,000. The Claughton money had gone without paying any of these, and he also had to repay £3,000 to Claughton himself. Apart from £1,050 from Murray for the copyright of *Ode to Napoleon Buonaparte* he had no other income. The £700 Murray paid him for the copyright of *Lara* took the form of a promissory note that he had not banked, and there is no evidence to suggest he was receiving any income from Rochdale. There was nothing left. Byron was exaggerating when he later told Hobhouse that his debts could "hardly be less than thirty thousand"—Hobhouse replied that "I can't for the life of me make out thirty thousand pounds or even twenty thousand. . ."—but they were certainly substantial. He explained the situation slightly more rationally to Annabella on 14 December: his debts had been "lessened during the last year, and might perhaps have been done away with, were it not that there were others whom, it was in some instances my duty and in other my inclination, to assist."[10]

Byron's finances needed to be put into some sort of order, because his wealth was an important consideration when it came to drawing up the prewedding property settlement. Marital alliances between landed families required careful thought on the part of the parents and the lawyers,

particularly the latter, because it was necessary to "settle" the estates of
both parties. Until 1814 Byron had enjoyed unrestricted powers over his
estate, but this situation could no longer continue. He was well aware that
his fiancée's family would demand as much to ensure the future financial
interests of Annabella and of any children born to the couple. This, inevitably, brought into question the status of Newstead. For the first time since
his mother died in 1811 Byron had a reason to keep the property as a family home for the present, and as an inheritance for his children (should
there be any) in the future. Such reasoning was clearly in his thoughts when,
writing to Hanson immediately after Annabella had accepted his proposal
of marriage, Byron noted that among the affairs he needed to sort out was
"the expediency of retaining or selling Newstead or Rochdale."[11] What had
once been a certainty—the sale of Newstead—now needed to be reconsid-
ered in the light of changing circumstances.

Byron had never given up his hopes of selling the problematic Rochdale
estate as a way of resolving his financial difficulties. At the time he signed
Claughton's forfeiture documents in August 1814 he told Hanson that with
Newstead back in his hands the sale of Rochdale became urgent: "I suppose you will look about for a purchaser there," he suggested, "no matter
what, or who, I would sell it for half its value so that I could extricate
myself once *clear* with the creditors."[12] He subsequently told Annabella
that it had long been his intention to sell the Rochdale estate rather than to
part with Newstead:

> [M]y Lancashire inheritance consists merely of a very extensive and
> uninclosed manor with the mineral and all other rights. I wished to have
> sold it instead [of Newstead], but was dissuaded, and still am, and told that
> it will ultimately be very valuable, perhaps more so than the other, on ac-
> count of the collieries which have never yet been worked to the proper
> extent because I could not spare the requisite sum, and at the same time
> discharge my debts till Newstead was sold.[13]

In other words, in his own mind the preference was still to sell Rochdale,
but the realistic course of action was to sell Newstead.

Was Byron being honest? It is probably not possible to explain his
behavior in the weeks following his engagement in any rational manner.
Byron's biographers have assumed that he had no option but to sell
Newstead,[14] but was this actually the case? To Annabella he offered excuses. "We should find Newstead sufficiently spacious," he told her on 19
October, "but not quite comfortable in its present state for a permanent
residence, besides, we should certainly grow fond of it, and it would then
be disagreeable to part with it." Writing to Thomas Moore in February
1815 he was more direct: "[I]t is uninhabitable for my spouse." Just in case

his fiancée should be surprised that at this significant point in his life he intended to sell the family home, he explained that "when I had once determined to sell that estate I conquered or stifled those feelings which attach one to an old patrimony in the conviction that it was better for many reasons it should be so."[15]

These claims did not convince her. When the marriage was over Annabella visited Newstead incognito. She was fascinated by the place, and she carefully noted what she was told by her guide, a woman who had been employed by Byron. The woman, Annabella noted, commented that "he should have lived there, particularly after he married, but his Lady had never come there."[16] Nor was Hobhouse convinced: when in July 1815 Newstead again came up for auction he was shocked by the eagerness of Byron's mother-in-law, Lady Milbanke, "in pushing Lord Byron, after having married a reputed heiress, to part with a property which had been in his family since the reign of Henry VIII."[17] Byron never took Annabella to Newstead: his last visit to the house in September 1814 was with Augusta. Perhaps the real reason he pressed ahead with the sale had more to do with his emotional attachments than his financial needs.

Whatever Byron's true motives, he had little difficulty justifying the decision. He told Annabella in words that sound suspiciously as if they originated with Hanson that "the income is still far short of what I should derive from the produce of the sale, besides the expense of keeping up the place in any kind of order." He was less coy when addressing Lady Melbourne: "Hanson is decided for the resale of Newstead," he told her, "because although the rents are nearly quadrupled, yet the income is much short of what would arise from the purchase money, and the house requires too much keeping up." And if he needed a fallback position, Byron could argue that he had a gentleman's agreement with Claughton on which he could not renege, although he did suggest to Hanson on 1 October that in view of his engagement Claughton should be hurried: "[H]is determination must be immediate one way or the other, and clear and the funds in part and security for the rest, equally palpable and tangible." He suggested to Hanson that he should write to Claughton on these lines and to add "that the reply must be prompt, & clear, & decisive."[18]

Byron's touching faith in Claughton was much like his touching faith in Hanson, and Claughton's response was, as Byron ought to have predicted, neither prompt, nor clear, nor decisive. It was not until 5 December that he replied, and now for the first time his real motives came into the open. Claughton's original offer of £140,000 was, as we have seen, extremely generous. By the time he agreed to the forfeiture he was aware that with falling agricultural prices and unlet farms he was not going to make a profit on his investment in the foreseeable future. Rather than forgo all his outlay, what he really wanted was a new agreement, and when he wrote to Byron early in December he proposed to pay back a total of £92,000. Since he had already paid £28,000, and Byron had yet to pay the £3,000, this amounted to a reduction in the price from £140,000 (the 1812 agreement torn up in August 1814) to £120,000. This was the price Hanson thought it was probably worth in 1812, but in Claughton's view—and he was un-doubtedly right, given the trend in rents and land prices—this was now an overvaluation. He proposed to pay £10,000 immediately, and a further £22,000 at a date to be agreed, leaving £60,000 on mortgage as in the pre-vious agreement. Hanson regarded these terms as being "quite inadmis-sible," and he suggested to Byron that a purchaser at £90,000, promptly paid, would represent a better deal (in view of the £25,000 forfeited to Byron).[19]

Byron was apparently dissatisfied: the proposition was "inadmissible as it not only involves reduction of price but delay in payment. I have ordered the flattest of all possible negatives in reply and there's an end." Overlooking entirely the problems of selling Newstead in 1812, he added, "I shall have it sold to some other purchaser, from whom at all events, whether we obtain more or less I can have the whole sum paid down." Hanson, translating this into more temperate language, told Claughton that "as you seem so wide apart there appears to be little prospect of your com-ing to any agreement and his Lordship considers himself at liberty to treat with any other person."[20]

Byron's words on this occasion, and his subsequent actions, were at variance. Claughton certainly did not receive "the flattest of all possible negatives," and Byron's own claims quoted here were in a letter to Annabella prior to a suggestion that under the circumstances a "further delay in our marriage" might be advisable.[21] Since this was written at one of the points when he is known to have been having severe doubts about going through with the wedding, we must interpret this as an excuse. The reality, as he was well aware, was quite different. It was not the sale of Newstead that was vital to the drawing up of the marriage settlements, but the decision as to whether it should be sold or retained. If it was to be retained, then the property would need to be named in the settlement and the financial ar-rangements organized accordingly. If it was to be sold, part of the putative income from the sale could be assigned to trustees for the benefit of Lady Byron and future children with the actual sale taking place at a later date. Hanson had already told Byron this, and Annabella was well aware of the various contingencies that were built into the settlement.[22] Clearly it was not possible to put the property on the market and hope for a completion prior to the wedding, which, as was normal at the time, was likely to occur within a few weeks of the engagement. In addition, the experience of 1812 suggested that potential buyers were likely to be in short supply, and disposal could take months. Byron was simply looking for an escape route.

II

Byron's proposal to Annabella Milbanke raised eyebrows among contemporaries who thought he was more interested in her cash than in her person. Hodgson claimed stories were circulating that Byron was fortune hunting.[23] Subsequently, Byron's apologists have dismissed such motives. Hobhouse, who clearly heard the stories and could always be relied upon to spring to the defense of his old friend's reputation, claimed:

> No! if Lord Byron had married for money he would have attached himself elsewhere . . . he did not marry for money. He married because he thought he should marry, and because he thought Miss Milbanke, on the whole, a suitable person, and one with whom the experiment might be made with the best chance of success.[24]

Byron himself professed disinterest. He wrote blithely to Lady Melbourne that "whether Annabella is to have any fortune or not I do not know and am not very anxious . . . the only thing is this, if she has nothing I had better sell Newstead again as I can thus give her a better settlement . . . I will settle on her all I can . . . her circumstances will make no difference to me." He told Thomas Moore on 7 October, "[H]er expectations, I am told, are great, but *what*, I have not asked."[25]

Such high-mindedness might strike a chord with Byron's literary friends, although Lady Melbourne was doubtless sufficiently worldly-wise to treat them as at best the musings of a distracted lover, but Byron knew perfectly well that there could be no wedding until the financial terms were agreed. Under normal circumstances his family would have wanted to know something of his intended wife's fortune long before any engagement was announced; indeed, as a young man he could have expected to be steered—although not forced—into the company of young ladies of suitable standing. Forty years earlier the fifth Lord Byron's son William had demonstrated all too vividly the consequences of marrying without his family's blessing. The sixth lord had no close family to guide him, and if he paid less attention to his wife's financial affairs than he might have done in other circumstances this did not mean that he ignored them. He claimed to have passed the responsibility to Hanson, who was "a little more inquisitive than I have been about Annabella's expectations," but even this was disingenuous because Byron knew that potentially Annabella Milbanke was a considerable heiress.[26]

Sir Ralph Milbanke (1747–1825) owned estates at Seaham in County Durham and at Halnaby Hall in Yorkshire. He was life tenant of the Halnaby estate, but absolute owner of Seaham, which had come to him from his mother. As the outright owner of Seaham he had secured considerable mortgage debts on the property to raise money for election expenses, and in 1821 it had to be sold to pay his debts. Milbanke had, in fact, done to Seaham precisely what Byron had failed to do at Newstead, although in Byron's case it would have been to pay his personal debts rather than election costs. Halnaby was strictly settled, as Newstead had been until 1798; in other words, it was entailed on the next male Milbanke heir. However, it was charged with a portion of £16,000, which was to be raised for Annabella on her marriage. Annabella was the only child of Milbanke's marriage in 1777 to Judith Noel, eldest daughter of the first Viscount Wentworth. His bride was also potentially an heiress, in her case to the Noel family estate at Kirkby Mallory in Leicestershire, worth about £5,000 annually. This was the estate of her uncle, Viscount Wentworth, which he had settled on his eldest sister, Lady Milbanke, Annabella's mother, with Annabella as the third generation in the entail.

As matters stood in 1815 Annabella had considerable prospects. She was heir to her father's Seaham estate, and she stood to inherit Kirkby Mallory on her mother's death. In these circumstances it is no surprise that she had already received at least two firm offers of marriage, both of which she had rejected. Nor was Byron unaware of her position. Only five days after he had assured Lady Melbourne that Annabella's prospects were of little significance to him, Byron told Hanson:

> Upon the subject of my own affairs it will be proper that you should submit their state with the necessary documents to Sir R. Milbanke's solicitor. . . . Miss Milbanke will actually be Baroness Noel and inherit certain property with that title from her uncle Lord Wentworth. There is also something settled from her father's estates and she will have Seaham and all that he can give her, but *entre nous* I believe Sir R. is much involved by electioneering &c & that her present portion will not be considerable.

Not only did he know these details, but Byron framed his offer to Miss Milbanke's father accordingly. Hanson proposed that £50,000 raised from the anticipated sale of Newstead should be assigned to the trustees to make adequate provision for any children and to fund a jointure if Annabella outlived her husband. Byron persuaded Hanson to make it £60,000 since "it was best to do things handsomely."[27]

In reality, he was not just doing things "handsomely," he was taking a calculated risk. The usual ratio of portion to jointure was ten to one, and even after Sir Ralph agreed to supplement his daughter's portion in order to raise it to £20,000, Hanson's proposal of settling £50,000 to yield £2,500 still seemed generous. Byron's counterproposal of £60,000 was even more liberal, since it would be expected (on the basis of 5 percent interest) to raise £3,000 a year, a ratio of 6.6 to 1. It was much more than he needed to offer, particularly as he recognized that there was an element of chance in his proposal. He told Lady Melbourne that "I must run the risk of Sir Ralph's 'possibility' nevertheless devoutly praying for Lady Milbanke's long life or a young and pretty step-mother in law in case she should leave us."[28] What Byron meant by this became clear years later when he told Douglas Kinnaird that he had left "both her father Sir Ralph, and her Uncle Lord Wentworth . . . perfectly free to leave their property as they liked, instead of requiring a previous settlement upon her." In other words, had Lady Milbanke predeceased her husband, and had he remarried and started a second family, Annabella could have been superseded in the inheritance— and Byron would doubtless not then have been so enamored of a pretty stepmother-in-law.

In subsequent years, as he brooded on what had gone wrong, Byron at least convinced himself that "I certainly did by no means marry her for her fortune," and he complained to Kinnaird about

> the comparative smallness of her then fortune (twenty thousand pounds, and that never paid) when surely as a young man with an old title, of a fortune independent enough at that time (as Newstead would have made me had the purchaser kept to his bargain) with some name and fame in the world, I might have pretended to no worse a match than Miss Milbanke anywhere, and in England to a much better whether you take into the balance fortune, person or connection.[29]

That was in retrospect: at the time the generosity of his offer reflected the prospects he foresaw, notably the expectation that having sold Newstead he would secure a regular income that would one day be supplemented by the residue of his Rochdale property and by Annabella's inheritance of Seaham and Kirkby Mallory. Seaham was sold, and Rochdale resolved only shortly before he died, but had the marriage been a success Byron would in 1822 have become the squire of Kirkby Mallory.

Byron had not exactly rushed to his fiancée's side once the engagement was announced. He had left Newstead in September for London rather than for Seaham, explaining to Lady Melbourne that "surely you cannot wonder that I should wish to arrange my property first, & not proceed hurriedly in a business which is to decide her fate & mine forever." Lady Melbourne was not alone in questioning his behavior: "[T]he noble poet does not appear to have been too grateful for [Annabella's] acceptance," Anne Romilly told her sister on 7 November, "for although it took place six weeks ago, he has lingered in town. . . ."[30] This was hardly romantic, and the pace at which his affairs could be sorted out was undoubtedly slowed by Hanson's own family difficulties. Aristocrats, however, did not normally wait for mere commoners to sort out their own problems: Lady Melbourne told Byron on 19 October that "were I to judge from appearances, I should say he [Hanson] has been unpardonably dilatory in this business from the beginning."[31] Byron was no more sympathetic. On 23 October Hanson wrote to Byron from Ilfracombe, Devon, where he was unwell. Whether or not Byron had received his letter, the following day he complained that it was taking Hanson far too long to schedule a visit to Durham to consult with the Milbanke family lawyers. He reminded him that it was

> now *five weeks* since Miss Milbanke's resolution and mine, and since that period little or nothing has been done towards the object of our wishes . . . I have written to you three times to press your departure, but without an answer. I certainly did hope that on an occasion not the least important with regard to my present as well as future prospects and happiness there would not have been so much necessity of urging you.

Hanson offered to send his son Charles to undertake the negotiations, an offer Byron flatly rejected: "[I]t is impossible he could give the explanations required, or that any but yourself should be sufficiently master of the subject."[32] Was Hanson really dilatory, or was Byron using the situation to play for time? It could have been either, or both.

Byron finally set off for County Durham on 29 October, by now sufficiently embarrassed by the passage of time to abandon a planned visit to Newstead. His cousin George Anson Byron went there to await his arrival—in order to convey his personal thanks for the loan of £100. George was astonished at his cousin's nonappearance, and as he found the place rather dull on his own he invited a friend over and they amused themselves by catching poachers in the park:

> I hope by now you are thinking of coming as you will perceive I have been among the poachers already, though today was wet, there being no books I took a walk with my gun and fell upon two fellows covering with three greyhounds. They killed a hare before my face which of course I took, and I enclose you their names and hope you will make them pay for it as they gave me and the keeper a devil of a time up two hills after them. I am convinced the Duke of Portland's keeper was with them but he having set off with their horses I could not prove it.[33]

He waited in vain, enjoying the comforts of "this blessed spot," while Byron passed through Newark, taking the more direct route north along the Great North Road.

Byron arrived at Seaham on 2 November, and after spending a few rather difficult days with his fiancée and her family—he took an immediate dislike to his future mother-in-law—returned to London to complete the business preparations. In the meantime Hanson had set off for the north on 31 October, and in Durham he sorted out the settlement details with the Milbanke lawyer, William Hoar. A few outstanding queries were resolved by late November,[34] and the settlement deeds were finally signed on 29 December 1814.

Under the terms of the settlement Sir Ralph Milbanke was to pay his daughter's £16,000 portion assigned under the terms of his own marriage settlement, and a further £4,000 in view of Byron's generosity in relation to the ratio of portion to jointure. Newstead was to be sold, and £60,000 paid to the marriage settlement trustees, Douglas Kinnaird and Thomas Bland. The total of £80,000 was to be invested in 3 percent consolidated annuities until the trustees could find a suitable opportunity for lending it as a mortgage secured on landed property. The investment income was to be paid to Byron, who was in turn to pay Annabella's pin money of £300 a year. If she survived Byron, the trustees were to pay her a jointure of £2,000 a year from the income. Subsequently, in his will, Byron earmarked £16,000 of the capital as his daughter's marriage portion.[35]

The arrangements were designed to fund Byron's outstanding debts so that he could begin married life with a clean slate, and to provide an investment income for the newlyweds. Assuming Newstead sold for £120,000, £60,000 would go to the trustees. Together with Sir Ralph's £20,000 this would be invested to yield an income of £2,400 a year. The trustees were to pay £20,000 to Byron "for his own use and benefit" (i.e., to pay his debts), leaving £40,000 for additional investment. From the beginning these plans were hypothetical. Not only was Newstead unsold, but Sir Ralph admitted to being unable to pay all of Annabella's portion immediately. He proposed to pay £6,200, and to leave £13,800 outstanding. On the latter sum he would pay interest of £690 a year, of which £300 was earmarked for Annabella's pin money. The couple would therefore have an income of £3,090 following the Newstead sale, plus the interest on the extra £40,000, or whatever the final sum turned out to be.[36] It was not a princely income, but Byron was relieved of the problems of running Newstead, and the long-term prospects were encouraging.

Of course there were many possible pitfalls, but any agreement would have carried an element of risk. Byron could have kept Newstead, and offered to settle £2,000 of the estate income in return for Annabella's portion of £20,000 (the usual ratio of 1:10). He could have left the rest of the Newstead estate out of settlement, enabling him either to sell or, more appropriately, to raise a mortgage to pay his debts. However, the Milbankes might have demanded more than £2,000 (or, in effect, a more favorable balance in their favor of the jointure-to-portion ratio) in view of Annabella's standing as a future heiress. Byron would also have had to resume the role of estate owner, which he clearly disliked, and to rely on a rather uncertain future income from Rochdale if he was to raise capital to redeem his secured debts. Meanwhile, he would have had little spare income to spend on Newstead, especially as he must have been aware that Sir Ralph could not actually pay his daughter's portion. The future would have looked far from secure. He himself subsequently justified his actions on these grounds: "I still think it upon the whole much better to sell [Newstead], more particularly as I believe Lady Byron's title by heritage is older than mine (though that is ancient) and consequently our son (if we have one) would be Lord Noel."[37] This was all speculation: by the time Byron finally tied the knot with Annabella, Hanson had negotiated precisely the deal he had been urging on Byron since 1808—the sale of Newstead with the money raised invested to produce a regular income. Even Hobhouse was confident:

> [I]n a year's time . . . if your property is in land you will have a regular steward at 30 or 40£ per annum to receive your rents on the spot and transmit them to your banker—if in money you will employ your banker in London to receive and give you credit for your dividends. At all events I foresee golden days for you.[38]

III

Byron and Miss Milbanke were married on 2 January 1815 in a private ceremony at Seaham. Hobhouse was best man. Hanson was not present. The newly married couple went first to Halnaby Hall in Yorkshire, then returned for a while to Seaham.[39] Avoiding Newstead, they traveled to London to take up occupancy of the duchess of Devonshire's house in Piccadilly Terrace, which Lady Melbourne had rented for them at £700 a year.[40] Once settled in London in March, Byron threw himself back into the literary and social life he had so much enjoyed in the past. He met and conversed with Sir Walter Scott, and in April *Hebrew Melodies* was published. Ten thousand copies of the first and second editions were sold. As a married couple Byron and Annabella got along tolerably well, although Annabella was soon having considerable doubts about Byron's relationship with Augusta, doubts that were exacerbated in April when Augusta joined them in Piccadilly Terrace.

In theory, with the marriage settlement details agreed, and with their vows sworn, Byron and Annabella could look forward positively to—at least in the immediate term—a London-based life among their friends and

Anne Isabella (Annabella) Byron, by Mary Anne Knight, watercolor on paper. The poet's wife, whom he married in 1815 but refused to take to Newstead. She visited the abbey incognito after the separation. (Nottingham City Museums and Art Galleries [Newstead Abbey].)

in the midst of his literary acquaintances. When they wanted to escape from the hustle and bustle of London they could retire to Seaham or Halnaby or, following the death of Viscount Wentworth in April 1815, to Sir Ralph and Lady Milbanke's new home at Kirkby Mallory in Leicestershire. All seemed set fair, and yet storm clouds on the horizon soon became downpours over Piccadilly Terrace, and mostly they rained financial problems. Byron's suspicions had first been raised when he and Hobhouse were at Seaham for the wedding and they discussed Hanson's handling of his financial affairs. From Halnaby Byron wrote to Hanson warning him that Hobhouse would be in contact on his return from the north. Hobhouse found Hanson less willing to listen than he was to talk, but they finally met on 20 January.[41]

At Seaham Byron and Hobhouse had discussed two key issues involving Hanson. The first was his fees. He seems not to have presented Byron with an account since the minority ended in 1809. The sums outstanding, and the relationship between these and the money lent by Byron to Hanson in 1814, were unclear. Second, and more important, was the question of Rochdale, and particularly the long delay in achieving a legal settlement. Hobhouse convinced Byron that he needed a second opinion as to how he should proceed, and he told Hanson as much at their meeting:

> Hanson talks magnificently of the sum which Rochdale, if the business was settled in your favour, would produce—40, 50, nay 60, or 70,000*l*. The more necessity, said I, for bringing the matter to an issue and the worse misfortune its being so long delayed. Appoint then, I pray, the counsel, this moment.

Hanson was not convinced of the need for an independent assessment, but Hobhouse would not be put off, and by mid-February 1815 he had asked Benjamin Winthrop of Lincoln's Inn to undertake the commission. Byron did as Hobhouse asked him and requested Hanson to make available any information required by the barrister: "[I]t is my particular wish that no time should be lost in this."[42]

Hanson ignored both Byron and Winthrop. "[S]uch omissions must lead to an end of all confidence and intercourse between us," Byron thundered, "being not only professionally negligent, but personally disrespectful . . . I am at a loss to conjecture what can have prevented your immediate compliance with my request." Hanson knew his client too well: Byron was soon telling Hobhouse, "I have not heard from Hanson . . . I have talked of 'an end to all confidence,' and still he answers nothing." By the time he reached Six Mile Bottom in March on his way to London, Byron was in better temper, and nothing more was heard of Mr. Winthrop, although Hobhouse continued to urge a change of solicitor.[43]

Byron stood by Hanson partly out of sentiment, and partly because the

Newstead sale still had to be completed. While it was unsold Byron's debts remained unpaid, and the terms of the marriage settlement could not be implemented. Claughton, far from being given the flattest of all possible rejections, as Byron had seemingly proposed in December 1814, still appeared to be the most likely purchaser, and he agreed to take the tenancy of the vacant Newstead Park farmland at £350 a year rent with an option to purchase the estate. Owen Mealey was not amused at this turn of events: he complained in May 1815 that Claughton's stock was "doing a great deal of injury to the farm than the ploughing and sowing will do good."[44]

Negotiations with Claughton continued while Byron was on his honeymoon. For his part, Byron continued to blow hot and cold. On 2 February he suggested that Claughton should remove his belongings from Newstead, since they seemed unlikely to conclude a deal, only to assure Hanson the following day he was "willing to go on with Mr Claughton." A week later Hanson told him that agreement was close, which Byron interpreted to Hobhouse as Claughton being "about to complete."[45] After so many disappointments, Byron's optimism was naïve, to say the least. By 17 February he was assuring Hobhouse, "I am disposed to give up, and not hold out with Claughton upon the present conditions." But continue he did, even though Claughton was now requesting an abatement of £5,000 in the price, and to take the rents for 1814.[46]

Negotiations with Claughton dragged on. Byron agreed to accept most of the terms set out in his letter of 5 December, whereby he would pay a further £32,000 to obtain the property, leaving £60,000 on mortgage. Byron's only condition was that he should pay the £32,000 in a single sum, but Claughton refused to meet a proposed deadline of 25 March, offering to pay on 1 May 1815 or, preferably, 1 June. Claughton claimed to have "so fixed my heart upon Newstead that I would make great exertions and some sacrifices to obtain it."[47]

All this looked like the usual, prevaricating Claughton, and back in London in March Byron was able to adopt a new tactic. Hanson was in York for part of the month attending the assizes, but he returned to his chambers to find a letter

> from Mr Fountayne Wilson, the nephew of the late Mr Montagu and lord of Papplewick. . . . I have answered that you do intend selling Newstead if you can get your price for it, and any proposal he might think proper to make I would communicate to your Lordship. I have also noticed to him that it was before sold for £140,000. I thought it best not to name any price but to hear his proposal and requested to hear from him.[48]

For Byron this was a gift horse not to be looked in the mouth. He wrote immediately to Claughton to tell him he had received "proposals from a highly reputable quarter to treat for Newstead. . . . I had and have every disposition to give you the preference, but the delays and demurs in treaty and payment justify me in giving attention to other offers." To Hanson he wrote, "I think it will be proper to intimate to Mr Claughton that we have other offers for Newstead."[49] Perhaps the use of the plural was something of an exaggeration, but Byron had waited long enough for Claughton, and he was willing to grasp at any straws. He broke off negotiations with Claughton for what was intended to be the last time.

While Newstead remained unsold Byron could not complete his part of the marriage settlement, and equally problematic was Sir Ralph Milbanke's position. He had originally intended to pay £10,000 of Annabella's portion by selling a farm at Aldborough. Subsequent to the signing of the settlement he changed his mind, and offered for sale three farms at Moulton. They were auctioned on 1 February 1814. Only one of the farms was sold, Moulton Hall Farm, which Colonel Dalbiac purchased for £7,350 although he did not have the money at hand.[50] Consequently, none of Lady Byron's portion was paid to the trustees. This in turn meant that no money was invested by them from which to supply Lord and Lady Byron with an income, or from which Byron could begin to pay his debts. All he had to rely on was the income from Newstead, where rents were proving to be almost uncollectable.

Claughton's attempt to reorganize the farm structure early in 1814, and the difficulties he had subsequently encountered in finding tenants, were the background against which Byron had reinstated Mealey and the old administrative structure when he resumed ownership of the property in August. Mealey had never found it easy to exert any authority, and he was now faced with new tenants selected by Claughton who refused to listen to him, and with the older (Byron) and newer (Claughton) tenants willing to play off "owners" against each other. Mealey claimed that the longer-serving tenants were able to pay their rents as demanded, but that "Wightman and the rest of his new tenants says that they have no right to pay any advanced rent as Mr Claughton did not stand to his agreement with them, nor will they pay any until your Lordship sends down." He added, "As to what I say they take no notice of so that your Lordship had better order Mr Hanson write down to them to pay it immediately and what sums to pay or they will not pay this side of June."[51]

When Mealey tried to collect the Michaelmas rents in the autumn of 1814, three of the new tenants—Green, Wightman, and John Hardstaff Jr. (in respect of Palethorpe's old farm, which he had taken over at Lady Day)— "stopped part of their rents according to some agreement they had with Mr Claughton to pay out so much money yearly in manure. Mr Hibbert says he has laid down his rent for your Lordship's taxes."[52] Byron, who had never had much time for Mealey, now appears to have thought he was stalling. In December 1814 he began to inquire as to the fate of the rents, and on the thirty-first he complained to Hanson that he had received "a damned twaddling cheating account from Mealey, so for Godsake send down executions directly on all the defaulters, there is no bearing this."[53]

Byron might sound off to Hanson from the safety of Seaham and then Halnaby, but Mealey was the man in the firing line, and getting any sense of order into proceedings was becoming impossible. On 27 January 1815 he told Byron that George Wightman—a Claughton tenant—was about to cut a wagon road through one of the plantations, "which will be a pity to cut down such thriving trees and to no purpose for I am afraid he never will be able to pay his rent. He says Mr Claughton promised him he should have a road there." Mealey asked Byron to give orders to put a stop to the road, but Byron had lost interest. On 3 February he simply passed Mealey's letter on to Hanson, commenting that he did not know what answer to give. Tenants were defaulting on their rents since he had resumed control of the estate, and, as Mealey told Hanson on Lady Day (25 March) 1815, when they ought to have been paying, or preparing to pay their rents:

> As to Newstead estate God knows what will be the end of it, for the land and fences is going to rack and ruin every day, and nobody durst speak a word but Mr Palin. He pretends to be master of Newstead, and all the rest of Mr Claughton's new tenants backs him and says the estate is still Mr Claughton's so that no body else has no chance but them, but be aware of the rent this Lady Day or else you will have as much or more trouble to get the rents than ever you had for Hibbert cannot get his taxes off them. . . . Sir, I hope to God you will please to give some orders how we are to go on, and please to let us know who is our master. I hope my Lord Byron.

Hanson responded by sending letters to all the tenants demanding the rent. In response Mealey found them unwilling to pay before mid-May.[54]

For Mealey the position was impossibly difficult. Byron had resumed ownership, but neither he nor Hanson had attempted to stamp their authority on estate affairs, and in a worsening economic climate the tenants' intransigence was increasingly combined with real inability to pay. By mid-May 1815 several of them had paid none of the Lady Day rent, and in some frustration Mealey wrote direct to Byron, who passed the letter on to Hanson with the comment that "some immediate step must be taken to compel the remaining tenants to pay their rents." He also suggested an arrangement for Smiths Bank, which traditionally received the Newstead rents in the absence of Hanson, to pay the remittances to his own account at Hoare's. Hanson was not disposed to treat Mealey's concerns too seriously, but the difficulties into which some of the tenants were running were put into sharp perspective when on 13 June 1815 bailiffs entered George Wightman's farm in search of goods to repay a debt of £200. Mealey asked Hanson to supply instructions to the sheriff to seize goods in lieu of Wightman's rent: "[T]here is the stock upon the ground at present, and as you are coming down so soon I hope things will be safe until you come down." On 29 June Byron complained rather lamely to Hanson that "everything is standing still on account of your absence . . . the rents remain unpaid."[55]

IV

Under the circumstances that prevailed during the first six months of his marriage Byron's financial position deteriorated rapidly. He was soon all too obviously living beyond his means. During the second half of 1814 his Hoare's account shows no income, but expenditure of £2,851, while in the first six months of 1815 his bank deposits of £1,873 were more than matched by outlays of £1,965. Of the £1,873 only £500 came from rents. Byron found it expedient to cash Murray's £700 promissory note for *Lara*, and to wonder whether some opportune deaths in his wife's family might alter his financial position. On 3 February he was speculating that if Sir Ralph Milbanke or Viscount Wentworth, or even both, "being elderly" should die, "the plans about Newstead might be so materially changed."[56] Wentworth actually obliged by dying on 17 April, but his property passed to Lady Milbanke. She and Sir Ralph took the surname Noel in deference to Wentworth's will. Lady Byron received nothing. Strictly speaking she was entitled to nothing, since technically she was heiress to her mother in the Wentworth succession. Byron was well aware of this, although it had not stopped him from hoping for some "pecuniary advantage . . . as he has been most kind to me & mine both before & since the marriage." Unfortunately, some of Byron's creditors took the opportunity of calling for payment after newspaper reports had suggested that he was a beneficiary of the estate through his wife. Byron sought to contradict the reports.[57]

Byron's problem throughout 1815 was the one that had dogged him since his Cambridge days—cash-flow. Desperate times required desperate measures, and early in June Lady Byron on his behalf approached her family solicitors for a loan to be secured on her portion:

> I understand that there are various impediments which will for some time delay the raising of the whole £16,000 settled on me, and though a lesser sum is not adequate to relieve Lord Byron from all embarrassments, yet it is of the utmost importance to him to have £6,000 before the expiration of six weeks from the present time. If you could therefore devise means for

hastening the payment of that sum from Col. Dalbiac or if that be imprac-
ticable of obtaining it upon Lord Byron's offered security, you would ren-
der me a great service.

Six weeks later she wrote again, and when in mid-August she had still to
receive a positive answer she pressed him further without success.[58] Nor
was her concern surprising, given that her father had as yet contributed nothing of her portion, and Newstead had once more failed to sell at auction.

By the end of April 1815 Byron was anxiously scouring the daily papers for Newstead advertisements, and when they had still not appeared in
mid-May his patience was wearing thin. Hanson's view was that the sale
should be in late June or July, and he had still taken no action when on 1
July Claughton submitted a further proposal that Hanson urged Byron to
consider.[59] This proved to be another false dawn, and in mid-July Hanson
at last put advertisements in the newspapers. Farebrothers, the auctioneers
who had acted in 1812, were again commissioned to organize the sale, and
the catalog details were much the same as three years earlier. The one significant exception was the omission of reference to "old and low rents." On
28 July Byron and Hobhouse were back at Garraway's coffeehouse, almost three years to the day since the abortive sale of 1812. Once again, and
this time without involving Hobhouse's bidding skills, the property failed
to sell. Newstead was withdrawn at 95,000 guineas (£99,750), although
according to Hobhouse the bona fide bidding was only 79,000 guineas
(£82,950). Subsequently Mr. Wilson offered £80,000, which Byron later
regretted turning down.[60] Rochdale was withdrawn at £16,000.

Byron was bitterly disappointed, while his mother-in-law "expressed
herself in terms of much regret thereat to Mr Hobhouse who thought that
the eagerness of her Ladyship . . . had an indecent appearance." In August
a Mr. Walker, who had previously shown interest in buying Newstead, offered to take the property on a lease for the shooting season, an offer Byron
turned down. Claughton let it be known that he was still interested: he was
"as much in love with the property as ever and is straining every nerve to
be the purchaser."[61]

With this latest twist in the long-running Newstead saga Hanson could
no longer avoid a visit to Nottinghamshire. He set out on 31 August with
"not any favourable expectations," Annabella told her mother; "the tenants
all wish to be broken up, and to relinquish their leases which are so much
higher than the farms could now be let for." Nor were Hanson's expectations unfulfilled. On returning to London he told Byron that "I have not
been so successful in the rents as I could have wished, the times press most
severely on your Lordship's tenants though I am not fearful of anything
being lost."[62]

Hanson accepted the tenants' view that the new tenancies introduced by Claughton needed to be reexamined, and to this end he commissioned a Mr. Wilson to carry out a full survey of the property. Wilson arrived at Newstead with a land valuer named Smith, from Leeds, and a Mr. Ward, on 26 September. They spent five days looking over the estate. Mealey "could not learn what they made of it."[63]

Resurveying the estate was not of much immediate help to the tenants, several of whom were now in difficulties when faced with paying wartime rents in peacetime conditions. Robert Walker, one of Claughton's new tenants, was already struggling even before the forfeiture was completed in August 1814:

> There is eight acres of bad wheat about six acres of bad clover all the land where the turnips was is in a state of wilderness and all the land that should be fallowed and sowed with oats is going wild as there has not been a plough put in the grounds since the wheat was sown.

Walker himself turned out to be worth "not one shilling"; his son had become a butcher and "has got shut of what little they had, the old man has done nothing since he left Newstead." By October 1815 he was refusing to pay £115 rent due the previous Lady Day "until Mr Claughton paid him a large bill for improvements upon the farm." Mealey could see no option but to distrain his goods, "for I plainly see that he means to turn rough if he can." Hanson agreed, and the following month Mealey reported that the sheriff's officers had "distrained upon Mr Walker." This at least brought Walker into offering a compromise, to pay part of the money now and be given time to pay the rest. The sheriff's officer wanted to know if sufficient goods were to be seized to cover all the rent, after which, Mealey believed, Walker would have nothing at all left. Walker paid £185 17s. to the sheriff and offered Mealey a bond to pay the rest of the outstanding rent in January. Mealey consulted Hanson, who agreed to give him until 1 February 1816 to pay the outstanding rent, with interest.[64]

Byron did little more than vent his annoyance on the unfortunate Owen Mealey. He complained to Hanson on 9 October 1815 that "Mealey has I understand been doing every thing to impede and discourage the sale of Newstead. I desire therefore that he may have his discharge as a tenant immediately. He shall not remain on that property while it is mine." At the same time he complained about Mealey to George Anson Byron, who had to agree:

> I am not the least surprised at the conduct of Mealey, having long time suspected he was no honest Gentleman, in fact I have often said so, though without proof, but he was always too meeley mouthed for me, and cer-

tainly fit for any situation but that he holds. The fault lies in him that put the worthless fellow there. I shall certainly tell him your wishes and opinion, and I think without being softened, though I shall suffer having at present some of his sheets to lay on.

Whether or not Byron appreciated the barbed comment about Mealey's appointment, this turned out to be another of those unsustained moments of interest in the estate. Mealey stayed in post, defending himself stoutly: "Captain Byron was pleased to tell me that your Lordship has been informed by Mr Boultain that I had under valued your lordship's estate at Newstead. My Lord, such a word never come out of my mouth, I should be a damned rogue and a villain if I ever offered to do the like when I have got my bread."[65]

    Although the estates had not sold in July 1815 Byron was determined to go ahead with the sale of the contents. At the time of the 1812 "sale" Claughton had complained to Hanson that his intentions regarding the contents had not been acceded to, and consequently he had not been given any powers to dispose of linen, glass, and other furnishings. As a result, the contents of the house were still much as in 1812, although the most valuable items had been removed in the spring of 1815. "Your plate and linen of every sort of course you know was sent for by Fletcher last March," commented George Anson Byron, "and not a particle of silver remains here." So when in June and July 1815 Farebrother prepared a catalog of goods and furnishings at Newstead, there was not a great deal to boast about. George Anson Byron was distressed to find just how thorough the valuers had been:

[Y]ou will observe Mr Farebrother has not omitted even a plate or the common old chairs, in fact nothing except what old Joe [Murray] has in his room. I do not know my dear B[yron] whether this was your intention, but I can assure you the fire cooking utensils with some of the chairs and about two dozen cracked plates . . . would not pay by some shillings Mr Farebrother's passage from town, indeed I fear that the better part of the furniture will sell but very badly.

He had been living in the abbey since the previous autumn and now feared that even the furniture and utensils in the couple of rooms he and a friend were occupying would not be permitted to remain:

[T]hese two rooms with enough of the most ordinary furniture suffice for our sitting rooms, with the few cooking utensils that remain is all I will ask of you to leave unsold. They really will fetch little or nothing, and besides myself any other person you might wish to shoot or remain a day or two to see the place there would be always a bed for them. The rest of the house Mr Hanson may strip to the walls.

He was concerned also about personal items, including Byron's mother's belongings and "the skulls that are in the present sitting room as well as the cup once there and also your gloves. . . ."[66]

Newstead was due to be opened on 13 October 1815 for the sale contents to be viewed, and Mr. Palin was to show prospective purchasers the farming stock on the day before the sale. The contents sale itself was to begin on 23 October and to last for four days, during which time "very elegant Furniture (new within a few years)" and "a small cellar of particularly fine flavoured old wines" were to go under the hammer. On day one the sparse contents of various bedrooms and the blue dining room were to be sold, together with a quantity of glass and chinaware, and the contents of the cellar. Day two was to see the contents of nine more rooms sold, including the library, where the bookcases were on offer—the books had, of course, been removed. Day three was to be the last of the furnishings, including the contents of the garrets, the kitchen, and the servants' quarters. Perhaps the most interesting item was lot 131, Byron's own four-post bedstead—which is still at Newstead. The contents of the estate were to be sold on 27 October. They were described as

> the live and dead farming stock, consisting of a fine flock of 500 sheep, of the improved Forest and South Devon breed, ten cart geldings and mares, a yearling colt, a mule, twenty heifers with calves, and in calf; waggons, carts, ploughs, one hundred hurdles, cart and plough harness, 260 quarters of oats, 70 quarters of barley, a stack of rye about 24 loads, 40 tons of hay and various farming utensils. Also the growing crop of turnips on 30 acres.

If nothing else, this list points to the activity of Claughton over the previous couple of years, particularly the sheep breeding.[67] House and grounds were to be stripped bare.

At the last minute the sale was abandoned: Claughton came up with a new offer. His proposal, which was contingent on the auction being called off, was to buy all the furniture from Byron for £1,200 except for several beds, which were to be sent to Byron at Piccadilly Terrace. He was also to lease the house until he could complete his long-projected purchase of the estate. He would continue to hold the farm that he had tenanted since the previous Christmas. Although Mealey reported "a fine deal of grumbling about stopping the sale so near the time," an empty house would have been even less attractive as a sale proposition than Newstead was already turning out to be. Byron accepted. George Byron was asked to supervise the handover to Claughton, who was expected at Newstead on 28 October to take possession.[68]

Once again confusion was the order of the day at Newstead. Claughton did not take up residence, nor is there any evidence that he even visited

Nottinghamshire in these months. Instead he simply reinstated William Palin as his agent on the premises, with a commission to continue running the home farm. As requested, George Byron "sealed up the keys for Mr Claughton and gave them to Palin. He has taken charge of everything." Mealey reported that Palin and his family were living in the abbey by Claughton's orders, and refusing to pay either Joe Murray or the house-maid. Mealey was also having trouble with him: "Mr Palin seems to hint that Mr Claughton will have the estate, which he takes a great deal of author-ity on himself. . . . Sir, I hope you will be down very soon to settle things or send orders down that the tenants may be satisfied who is landlord. Pray, is Palin to have the use of the mule and the cart . . . in short there is nothing going right to benefit the estate."[69] This was certainly indisputable.

V

By the time this transaction was completed Byron had been married nearly a year, his wife was heavily pregnant, and none of the terms of his marriage settlement had been fulfilled. Newstead remained unsold, so he could not pay his debts, which in the meantime continued to accrue interest payments. In the second half of 1815, Byron spent £1,938 from his Hoare's bank account, but until December his receipts were only £1,324, of which £1,050 was probably a delayed copyright payment from John Murray for *The Bride of Abydos*. Byron's available resources were fast disappearing. There were parallels with the days of his minority when he borrowed in the expectation of better times. What he needed was breathing room, and this is what Lady Byron had been attempting to negotiate in July. With Newstead unsold, it became even more important to find some relief. Byron's marital problems have often been blamed, at least in part, on his financial difficul-ties, and these came to a climax when on 8 November he suffered the em-barrassment of having bailiffs enter his London home. Thomas Moore de-scribed Byron's predicament in graphic terms:

> Those embarrassments which, from a review of his affairs previous to the marriage, he had clearly foreseen would, before long, overtake him, were not slow in realising his worst omens. The increased expenses induced by his new mode of life, with but very little increase of means to meet them, the long arrears of early pecuniary obligations, as well as the claims which had been, gradually, since then, accumulating, all pressed upon him now with collected force, and reduced him to some of the worst humiliations of poverty. He had been even driven, by the necessity of encountering such demands, to the trying expedient of parting with his books, which circum-stance coming to Mr Murray's ears, that gentleman instantly forwarded to

him £1500, with an assurance that another sum of the same amount should be at his service in a few weeks.[70]

Byron responded to the appearance of bailiffs by taking to the bottle in an attempt to drown out his problems—not the course of action he seems to have recommended to his mother in similar circumstances at Newstead while he was abroad in 1811. But as ever, the problem was one of cash, not capital. Perhaps if he had gone ahead with the Newstead contents sale he might have raised some cash, but Claughton insisted on a single transaction and then, of course, he failed to pay. Byron proposed to sell his books for fear that with his wife due shortly to give birth he would have bailiffs and midwives in the house concurrently. On the other hand he refused Murray's offer: "[T]he circumstances which induce me to part with my books," he told him on 14 November, "though sufficiently, are not *immediately* pressing."[71] He was not so sanguine in his letters to Hanson, but the true gravity of the situation was at last recognized by the various trustees and lawyers responsible for the welfare of their client, his wife and—imminently—his child.

By October 1815 discussions were taking place between the lawyers with the intention of forwarding to Byron £6,000 of Colonel Dalbiac's purchase money. This was to be considered as part of Annabella's portion, but technically that had to be paid to the marriage settlement trustees for investment. Consequently, the lawyers had to find a way of regarding the money as repayable to the trustees out of the £20,000 earmarked from the Newstead sale for payment of Byron's debts. Lawyers being lawyers, this took an immense amount of time and correspondence through the autumn of 1815, and although the sum was eventually increased to £6,200 it transpired at a late stage that £1,000 of this would take the form of a promissory note payable in six months' time. The deal was finally agreed on 9 December, and the bailiffs had been evicted by the time Augusta Ada was born the following day.[72] From the money Byron assigned £450 to Mealey to pay board wages (£50) and Mansfield tradesmen. Also to be paid from this sum were two men who had been employed by Joe Murray "to trench in the cloisters and in the cellars and the old kitchen." In his search for cash Byron had been reduced to expedients similar to those used by the fifth lord. It was not going to be enough—Joe Murray was still owed nearly £10, and none of the major creditors had been paid—but it was a start. As on so many previous occasions Byron was short of cash, not capital: liquidizing capital into cash had once again been the essence of the problem, but now he was in funds and he gave Augusta £70 on 20 December, the first of four payments to her, totaling £720 in the months preceding his departure from England.[73]

English landlords rarely flourished if they did not pay attention to their estates, particularly if they failed to put in place an adequate management structure. Improvement at Newstead, such as there was, resulted from Claughton's activities between 1812 and 1814, but after he defaulted having reorganized the estate and raised the rents, Byron simply allowed the old managerial structure to return. What little authority Mealey could muster was compromised by the willingness of the tenants to play off Byron against Claughton, which was itself a result of Claughton's continuing interest in the estate. Neither Byron nor Hanson attempted to stamp their authority on Newstead with a personal visit. Byron regularly sounded off about Mealey, but for all the failings of the bailiff appointed by Hanson as long ago as 1798, he was still in post at the close of 1815. Meantime Hanson stayed in London and the estate descended into chaos, with the tenants virtually refusing to pay rent. It was a sorry tale highlighting the all too familiar story of how financial disaster might be just around the corner for those landlords who depended too much on their servants without taking a real personal interest in their affairs.[74] Maybe if Byron had taken Hobhouse's advice about Hanson in the spring of 1815 the predicted golden days might have arrived.

Byron, aged 27, by James Holmes (1777–1860), watercolor on ivory. The artist's copy, c. 1824. The original was painted for Scrope Davies in 1815–16, and was probably given by him to Hobhouse when he left England in 1818. From Hobhouse it passed to Augusta Leigh, who owned it by 1824. (Private collection.)

9

The Sale of Newstead

On the morning of 23 April 1816 seven men set out by coach from London for Dover. Byron was accompanied by Hobhouse, his old traveling companion from 1809, and Scrope Davies. The other travelers were William Fletcher, Byron's faithful valet, and Robert Rushton (both of whom had undertaken part of the 1809 tour), a Swiss guide named Berger, and Dr. John William Polidori, a personal physician hired for the journey. Byron traveled in style. In the manner of an aristocrat he was accompanied on his journey by personal servants, including his doctor, and he traveled in a specially built carriage designed along lines similar to the one Napoleon captured at Genappe. It had cost £500, which Byron had not paid. The party paused briefly at Canterbury to see the cathedral, and arrived in Dover at about 8 P.M. Hobhouse arranged for the coach to be loaded aboard ship—fearing it might be seized by bailiffs—but contrary winds delayed departure by twenty-four hours. Byron had time on the twenty-fourth to scribble a note to Hanson: "I hope that you will not forget to seize an early opportunity of bringing Rochdale and Newstead to the hammer, or private contract." And then, when the wind changed direction, Byron shook hands with Davies and Hobhouse and sailed for Ostend, "waiving his cap . . . as the packet bounded off on a curling wave from the pier-head at Dover."[1] Hobhouse and Davies walked along the pier and then returned to London.

I

It was almost seven years since Byron and Hobhouse had set out from Plymouth for Lisbon. On that occasion Byron had waited with ill-concealed patience for Hanson to arrange his funding. It was a journey that he had planned for months, but despite occasional comments to the contrary he had always intended to return. And he had done so, with a flurry of letters assuring Hanson and his mother that whatever other course of action might

211

be necessary he would not sell Newstead. Now, after two failed attempts to dispose of the estate, it was still in his thoughts as he waited at Dover. This time there would be no change of mind, and no return. Yet in one respect the circumstances of 1809 and 1816 were similar: on both occasions Byron left behind him a trail of unpaid debts and unsatisfied creditors despite being, at least on paper, a wealthy man. Newstead was unsold, Rochdale was unsold, the rent on Piccadilly Terrace was unpaid—bailiffs seized the contents after he set out for Dover[2]—and numerous creditors were left unsatisfied. For a man of Byron's literary fame and capital assets it was an ignominious flight, but it was not caused primarily by money.

Byron's troubles were also about marriage, and it was for both financial and marital reasons that early in January 1816 he had proposed to his wife that their expensive Piccadilly establishment should be given up. Lady Byron and their daughter were to go temporarily to live with her parents, who had moved to Kirkby Mallory in Leicestershire following Viscount Wentworth's death. Byron assigned her sums of £400 on 2 January and £300 on 16 January to cover her pin money and other necessary expenses. She left London on 15 January, by now convinced in her own mind that he was probably insane. Initially there was every expectation that the couple would come together again shortly, but when her parents learned the full extent of Byron's mistreatment of their daughter over previous months, this came increasingly into doubt. On 2 February Sir Ralph Noel proposed an amicable separation. Byron was shocked. He wrote a number of letters designed to elicit his wife's real feelings on the matter, and purportedly planned—but did not carry out—a visit to Leicestershire. But on 12 February he decided there was no turning back, and he instructed Hanson to put the necessary legal proceedings into operation.[3]

Byron tried several times, perhaps rather unconvincingly, to effect a rapprochement. He blamed himself for the failure of the marriage, admitting to Thomas Moore that part of the trouble was probably brought on by his "strange and desultory habits which, becoming my own master at an early age, and scrambling about, over and through the world, may have induced." Lady Byron apparently questioned his financial motives, but Byron denied that the Wentworth inheritance had ever been a consideration: "[W]hen I married you I settled all I could and about all I had upon you, and though strongly advised and justified in demanding a settlement of your father's dispensable property I would not and did not, solely from delicacy to you and to your family."[4] If this claim contained an element of self-justification it was, broadly speaking, an accurate portrayal of the facts.

In the eyes of the law Lady Byron's case for a permanent separation and custody of her child was relatively weak, particularly as both she and her family were anxious to prevent the case going into open court. The fact that she achieved her objectives was at least in part owing to the skill of her legal adviser, Dr. Stephen Lushington. For his part, probably unwisely, Byron relied on Hanson, with help from advocates in Doctors' Commons.[5] Although Byron initially refused to sign the separation papers, whether he liked it or not there could by now be no turning back. Not only was it clear that the marriage was over, but he was increasingly the subject of rumor and innuendo over a range of alleged offenses including murder, incest, homosexual and heterosexual sodomy, adultery, and brutality. "You can hardly have forgotten the circumstances under which I quitted England," he reminded Scrope Davies in December 1818, "nor the rumours of which I was the subject, if *they were true* I was unfit for England, if *false* England was unfit for me. You recollect that with the exception of a few friends (yourself among the foremost of those who staid by me) I was deserted and blackened by all, that even my relations (except my Sister) . . . despaired of or abandoned me." It was a theme to which he returned in an article published in *Blackwood's Magazine* in 1820.

> The fashionable world was divided into parties, mine consisting of a very small minority—the reasonable world was naturally on the stronger side—which happened to be the lady's as was most proper and polite—the press was active and scurrilous. . . . I was accused of every monstrous vice by public rumour, and private rancour; my name which had been a knightly or noble one since My fathers helped to conquer the kingdom for William the Norman, was tainted. I felt that, if what was whispered and muttered and murmured was true—I was unfit for England,—if false—England was unfit for me. I retired from the country perceiving that I was the object of general obloquy . . . I perceived that I had to a great extent become personally obnoxious in England, perhaps through my own fault, but the fact was indisputable; for the public in general would hardly have been so much excited against a more popular character, without at least an accusation or a charge of some kind actually expressed or substantiated—for I can hardly conceive that the common and every day occurrence of a separation between man and wife could in itself produce so great a ferment. . . .[6]

This was, of course, retrospective, and in the spring of 1816 Byron had no intention of remaining in England to hear his name blackened in every area of literary life. He planned a resumption of his long-postponed Continental travels, and over a few hectic weeks he was to be found paying off a series of debts, including some to moneylenders, and making a gift of £100 to Samuel Taylor Coleridge. In early April his books were sold at public auction. The sale raised £723 12s. 6d.: Hobhouse spent £34. On 16 April Lady Byron was concerned that he would depart without winding up his affairs, and on the eighteenth he was rumored to be preparing to begin his travels the following day. Byron hired Polidori and gave him £332, presumably to stock up with medical requirements for the coming travels. Hardly pausing for breath, he had a brief affair with Claire Clairmont that he would soon have cause to regret.[7]

Meantime the lawyers were completing their task, and one of the key issues to be resolved involved property. Married women had few rights over property. Through his alliance with Annabella, Byron had, in theory at least, obtained the freehold reversion of her property at Kirkby Mallory. This was the estate now owned by her mother, to which Annabella was technically the tenant-in-tail—in other words, the next heir. For her immediate financial needs, Byron agreed to supplement Annabella's £300 pin money by a further £200.[8] The income itself was to be secured on the 5 percent interest Sir Ralph Noel agreed to pay on the £13,800 unpaid part of his daughter's portion. Byron was thereby relieved of the need to fund an income for his estranged wife. Since 5 percent on £13,800 was £690, Sir Ralph also agreed to pay the £190 excess to Byron, although he had regularly to be reminded to do so.

For the longer term, the lawyers had to resolve what should be done about Kirkby Mallory after Lady Noel's death. In theory the income of the property (about £6,500 a year in 1816) would come to Byron. Annabella's lawyers wanted him to agree that it should be divided half and half, which he initially refused, saying only that he would make fair provision for his wife out of the property. After much legal wrangling, the point was submitted for arbitration to the solicitor general, Sir Samuel Shepherd, who decided in favor of Lady Byron.[9] It was agreed that the legal device of a trust would be set up (with Annabella's adviser Stephen Lushington as the trustee) to secure half of the Leicestershire income for Lady Byron after her mother's death. Byron might have forced the issue had he been prepared to take it into court, but Annabella's advisers used the scandalous rumors about his behavior to pressure him into accepting a settlement they regarded as favorable to Lady Byron. Meantime they had also ensured that Ada was made a ward of Chancery, of which Byron was unaware for a further year. The intention was to prevent him from insisting on paternal rights to the child, which could have forced Lady Byron to give her up, or to resume living with Byron.[10]

Byron's "flight" in April 1816 looks in some respects to have been undertaken with almost undue haste, but he was careful to make adequate arrangements for his financial affairs to be looked after in his absence, however long that might turn out to be. On 12 April 1816 he gave powers of attorney to John Hanson and Douglas Kinnaird to run and, if necessary, sell his property. Kinnaird, who was a trustee of his marriage settlement, was to act as a check on Hanson. Hobhouse was instructed to deal with

Byron's bank account at Hoare's. Byron had no desire to sideline Hanson, who was to continue dealing with his property, but he wanted his friends Hobhouse and Kinnaird to be more involved with his private finances, partly so that they would act as a check on Hanson. Hobhouse gradually ceased to play more than a minor role as his political career developed, and Kinnaird, a banker, came to be the key figure. Kinnaird closed Byron's account at Hoare's and transferred his finances to Ransome's bank, in which he was a partner, so that he could keep a careful check on his financial position. He seems to have taken up Byron's cause with almost missionary zeal. "I have often told you," he wrote to Byron in July 1818, "and beg to repeat it again, you have nothing to do but to write for a letter of credit to any amount you wish and it will always be sent out to you by return of post." Nor did his commitment wane: "I have ever regarded your unacquaintance with business," he wrote in July 1823, "as making it my especial duty to keep your affairs so clear as to speak for themselves should anything happen to me."[11] Byron was fortunate in his choice of friends, since not only did they ensure that there was never a reason connected with his financial affairs that might have necessitated his return to England, but they even agreed after his death to say nothing publicly of his lifestyle more generally.

On 21 April 1816 Byron signed the deed of separation. Hanson presented the papers to Lady Byron the following day—and hours later expressed to Sir Ralph "the pain I felt in the performance of my professional duty this morning." Byron transferred £2,504 from his Hoare's account to Hammersley's to fund his travels.[12] Two days later he left London for exile.

II

Byron crossed the channel to Ostend, and traveled slowly through Belgium, visiting the field of the Battle of Waterloo on 4 May. He passed through Cologne, and along the Rhine, to enter Switzerland at Basel on 20 May. Five days later he arrived at Geneva, where he met the Shelleys, and on 10 June he moved into the Villa Diodati, which, with its magnificent view across Lake Leman to the Jura mountains, reminded him that he had left behind some pleasant scenery of his own at Newstead. Byron also began writing *Manfred* while in Geneva, although the reference in act 3 "to levell'd battlements," and "ruinous perfection," which are often taken to be Newstead, were probably written in Venice. As he said in his *Epistle to Augusta*, written at Diodati:

> I did remind thee of our own dear lake
> By the old Hall which may be mine no more—

Leman's is fair—but think not I forsake
The sweet remembrance of a dearer shore.

The upper lake at Newstead hardly bears comparison with Lake Geneva in size, but that clearly was not Byron's point.[13]

The canton of Geneva had become part of the Swiss Confederation following the collapse in 1814 of Napoleon's empire. After Waterloo, tourists (and refugees) from across Europe flocked to what was neutral territory. Byron enjoyed literary contact with the Shelleys—and intimate contact with Claire Clairmont—and his travels with Percy Shelley took them around the lake, which he also crossed regularly to attend Mme de Staël's international literary salon at Coppet. These were altogether more pleasant conditions than those he had left behind in England, and he resumed writing, composing the third canto of *Childe Harold* while he was at Diodati, as well as *The Prisoner of Chillon*—after a visit to Chateau Chillon, where he was later said to have carved his name on a pillar. Hobhouse and Scrope Davies arrived late in August. Davies stayed only a short while, returning to England with Robert Rushton, Byron's page. Byron and Hobhouse first went on a tour of the Bernese Oberland and then, after dispensing with Polidori's services, set off early in October for Italy.[14]

Byron found life in Switzerland rather more conducive than his final weeks in England, but he was never able entirely to divorce his thoughts from his financial affairs. Not surprisingly, at Newstead all was confusion. The house was damaged in an earthquake in March 1816,[15] but it was on the estate that the most serious problems were uncovered. Following Waterloo the downward trend in rents and grain prices had continued. In January 1816 Mealey was concerned that "the stack yards at Newstead has got very thin this winter," and he was far from hopeful that all the rents would be paid. The troublesome Walker had announced his intention to leave his farm at Lady Day, both John Hardstaff Sr. at Wire Mill Farm and William Green were talking of quitting, and George Wightman was struggling. Wightman had been visited by bailiffs three times since Hanson's visit in September 1814, "and I am afraid will have them again soon without Mr Claughton helps him." Shortly after this, Wightman traveled to Lancashire to see Claughton, who owed him money but now refused to acknowledge the debt. William Green gave notice of intention to leave at Lady Day 1816, and Walker was unable to pay his outstanding arrears on 1 February. It was a sorry picture: "[F]arming is going on very bad at Newstead at present, fences are neglected all round." When Mealey tried to press the new tenants he was firmly rebuffed: Walker "said his agreement was with Mr Claughton for his farm which was all the answer I could get from him."[16]

Walker finally paid his outstanding arrears on 21 February 1816, but he still had to pay his Michaelmas 1815 rent, and Mealey learned that he was preparing to cut and run: "[H]e means to start by night." Four days later Walker was gone, reputedly into Derbyshire, with a few horses, two wagons, and all his household furniture. He had sold all the hay and straw and left the farm "in a most dissolute state." More optimistically, Wightman had heard from Claughton that he would shortly be at Newstead "to pay him for his estate that he bought of him last year."[17] Hardstaff stayed at Wire Mill Farm, but William Green gave up his farm to William Beardall, Joseph Coleman's farm passed to a Mr. Lee, and Walker's farm was divided into two and tenanted by William Hebbard and Samuel Howett. Either from the state of the farm after he left or due to the fact that he was overassessed for rent, Walker's property was relet at only £127 14s. when he had been paying £240. Mealey, hard though he tried, could still not exert any control. He almost implored Hanson to visit "this Lady Day as I am at a loss to know how to proceed." Hanson, of course, did not visit, and by mid-June 1816 Mealey was concerned that the tenants had come up with a new ploy, which was to refuse to pay their rents into Smith's Bank at Nottingham "without seeing your handwriting." Two months later he reported that a few rents had been paid, but Wightman had not a shilling with which to pay, since Claughton still owed him money. On 28 August Mealey warned Hanson that "without you make the rents safe before Michaelmas there will be a great loss in them. . . . I hope you will be down soon for regulation is very much wanted here."[18]

By now the chances of any improvement had virtually expired. Almost everywhere rents were falling, tenants were renegotiating their agreements, and landlords were making remissions. Rebecca Heath recalled how

Farm produce which had been very high much higher then was ever known in England before or since, and all other things had risen proportionately now began to have a downward tendency and soon got so seriously low that it was impossible for farmers to meet their payments without drawing on their stock many farmers were ruined and my father gave up his malting to continue the farming, which suited him best and he was sure would pay when things got into their regular course in time of Peace. Another source of trouble came, a bad harvest, the worse that has been in my life, the rain, the mists and fogs that followed has never been so bad since. Then came the rot in sheep, the flock of sheep on which my father prided himself kept dying one by one and had to be sold for inferior price. These calamities added to the cares of a family, approaching old age, and ill health, weighed heavily on my father he was never in my memory a healthy man, being subject to liver complaints and one attack followed another in spite of all our care.[19]

These were unpropitious circumstances for collecting the rent, particularly with the owner traveling abroad and his agent firmly settled in London.

"The times," Hanson assured Byron in December 1816, "have sadly depressed the Newstead tenants," and he had been obliged to have crops seized in order to secure any rent. Even Byron despaired. He asked Kinnaird in January 1817 whether Hanson had "been able to collect any rent at all (but little it can be in these times) from Newstead." He added that he would have appreciated receiving any balance left over. He was less sympathetic in May, insisting that "something must now be due, as it is a considerable time since the Newstead tenants paid at all." A month later he told Hanson, "from Newstead there should surely be some balance, it is now a year and two months since I quitted England and the tenants were in great arrear before."[20]

Byron's real concern remained the disposal of the estate, which was a condition of the terms of his marital separation. When he left England, Claughton still had the first option, and with land prices falling Hanson was reluctant to look a potential gift horse in the mouth. As he told Byron in July 1816, "the times are not so far improved as to allow of any prospect of a sale of that property and I am persuaded it would only be a waste of money to attempt an exposure of sale till things improve." By November 1816 Byron realized that there was not much chance of an immediate sale of Newstead, and in December he told Kinnaird, "I suppose any sale of Newstead or Rochdale is hopeless for the present, but I wish it could be accomplished. I have it so much at heart . . . my great object is to pay my debts." To Hanson he wrote simply that "I wish something would be done about Newstead."[21] A falling market was bad news for Byron and his creditors, and Claughton was in no position to push forward his long-promised purchase of the estate.

Claughton's affairs were unexpectedly complicated by the death in April 1816 of Thomas Johnes of Haford. He became liable to pay the outstanding purchase money on the Welsh property of which he had acquired the reversion in 1814. Almost certainly he had intended to sell the property in a rising land market, but the end of the Napoleonic Wars had depressed prices. Claughton could not find a purchaser, nor was he in a position to pay the remaining £55,000 due on the estate. To play for time he reverted to a ploy he had first used at Newstead in 1812: raising objections to the title of the estate, in this case in regard to encroachments by Johnes onto land belonging to the Crown. Johnes's executors brought a case in Chancery to compel Claughton to pay, and there the case remained suitably tied up until 1824 when, just before it came into court, Claughton was declared bankrupt. By then, apparently undaunted by such setbacks, he had contracted in 1821 for the Bolesworth Castle estate in Cheshire. He was declared bankrupt again in 1838, and he died in 1842.[22]

All this was in the future, and despite the crisis over the Haford estate in April 1816 Claughton remained optimistic about Newstead. He told

Hanson that he still intended to be the purchaser "whenever circumstances will permit," and he continued to hold the tenancy of the home farm until the property was sold. Subsequently he claimed that

> During the period I held the farm as tenant I expended upon it about £3,600 and I have received back from the purchaser for the tenant right as 'tis called £3,250 incurring to me a loss of £350, and I implore your Lordship not to add to the great loss I have sustained by the demand of rent for that which notoriously yielded nothing to me, but relieved your Lordship in any event from the expense of keeping servants and paying taxes.[23]

Rent of £820 and £150 of the £1,200 furniture money was still outstanding in 1820, and it was no easy matter to make him pay.[24] In theory Byron could simply deduct them from the £3,000 he had owed to Claughton since 1814, but the situation was complicated by the fact that on 2 March 1819 Claughton sold the bond to Charles Hanson for £1,500. Byron was furious, not only because young Hanson had bought the bond "at a considerable profit," but because it meant Byron was yet further in debt to the Hansons, and because it reduced the leverage they could exert in extracting the outstanding rent and furniture money from Claughton; indeed, it forced Byron to consider legal action to recover the debt. Nor was Kinnaird impressed: "[I]t is a most disreputable transaction for an attorney to become the purchaser of his clients' debts at a depreciated price."[25]

In these circumstances it is not surprising to find that this developed into a long-running saga. In separate letters Byron complained to both Hanson and Kinnaird on 11 January 1821 that they were not pressing Claughton hard enough. "I desire," he told Kinnaird, "that Claughton may be prosecuted and made to pay." Three months later he raised the same issue: "As for Claughton, why don't he pay? I wrote to desire that he might be proceeded with weeks ago." Later in 1821 Claughton paid £460 of the outstanding money; hence Byron's comment to Kinnaird, "If Claughton has paid Hanson, let Hanson pay the money into your bank. . . . Claughton's money should go to the creditors." What did happen to it? Byron was unsure, asking Kinnaird in December 1821, "I wish at least for an account of how Claughton's money was disposed of," given that he had heard it went toward paying his debts. Months later he was still waiting, telling Kinnaird on 26 September 1822, "I see no account of the money lately paid by Claughton."[26]

III

After leaving Switzerland in October 1816, Byron traveled with Hobhouse first to Milan, and then to Venice, where he arrived on 11

November and settled for the winter. Within days of his arrival he had fallen in love with Marianna Segati, and she proved to be a loyal companion after Hobhouse left on 5 December to continue the Italian tour. In London, canto 3 of *Childe Harold* was published on 18 November. Claire Clairmont, by now back in England, gave birth to Byron's illegitimate daughter, Allegra, in January 1817. After enjoying himself immensely during the Venice carnival, Byron set off on 17 April 1817 for Florence and Rome. Arriving in Rome on 29 April, he spent the next three weeks with Hobhouse seeing the tourist sights. Even while enjoying himself, Byron's thoughts often returned to the complexities of his financial arrangements. From Rome he told John Murray that "if I could but make a tolerable sale of Newstead there would be no reason for my return." He encouraged Kinnaird to take Hanson in hand in an effort to sell Newstead in the summer of 1817:

> I do not care for what, I will procrastinate no longer. Make Hanson act upon this and make it be put up for sale, and sold if possible. . . . Pray, press the sale of Newstead and do not answer me that "the times" etc, damn the times, they wont mend in my time, and sold it must be. I would take £80,000 *entre nous*, more or less, or anything, but by the Pope's toe! it must be sold, and this summer, or I shall go mad.

Sale, he added, would enable me "to clear or nearly," and he could live abroad comfortably, "which I have lately done, and to which my ambition is limited."[27]

At the end of May 1817 Byron returned to Venice. Hobhouse had gone south to Naples, but Byron was anxious to avoid the large number of English tourists who congregated there, and so returned via Florence. To escape the Venetian heat, he took a six-month lease of the Villa Foscarini at La Mira, on the banks of the Brenta. He was now more than ever worried about Newstead. "Two years ago," he told Kinnaird, "a Mr Wilson offered £80,000 for it which *(by advice)* was then declined. I do not know that he or anybody else would give so much now, though it is in fact worth a good deal more, or would be in decent times." Hanson, he feared, would not press the sale except for a price "which in these times cannot be obtained." In mid-June Byron summoned up the enthusiasm to write direct to Hanson, expressing his regret at not having accepted Mr. Wilson's offer, and once again urging the sale. He even enlisted help. Augusta was asked "to urge Mr Kinnaird and Mr Hanson from me my request that Newstead be put up for sale and *definitively sold* to the highest bidder *this summer*—as every year would become an additional loss and embarrassment by the delay. I am sick of objections and will hear none . . . it seems useless to wait longer or expect more." Scrope Davies was asked to put pressure on Kinnaird to arrange the sale of both Newstead and Rochdale. Byron stressed again how he now regretted not having taken Mr. Wilson's £80,000 two years earlier.[28]

Shortly after moving into the Villa Foscarini, Byron received a long letter from Kinnaird, who had been trying, with Hanson's help, to establish the extent of Byron's debts. It still weighed on Byron's mind that he had failed to pay the £6,000 outstanding to Sawbridge and—at this date—that he had been unable to reimburse Claughton's £3,000. "This is all (I believe) except the Israelites," he told Kinnaird, adding that "I am fully disposed to sell either or both Newstead & Rochdale for whatever they may bring, at the market, public auction, or private contract." His wider line of argument had not changed. Rochdale had "long been the stumbling block of all arrangements." He had been duped by exaggerated statements as to its value into keeping it from the market, but weariness and experience had finally converted him into believing it should be sold for whatever sum could be raised. Kinnaird was given a free hand: "[T]here will be no obstruction on my part, to whatever you may decide upon."[29]

A few days later, having reexamined the list of debts, Byron wrote to Kinnaird again, this time raising queries about some of the sums he had been told were still outstanding. In particular, he disputed the figure of £9,000 owing on annuities to moneylenders. Since the age of twenty-one, Byron continued, he had raised only one sum of £2,000–£3,000 principal, and another of £600 to £700, which he had repaid just before leaving England, thereby redeeming the annuity: "[T]he sum therefore to the Jews cannot by any means be so much unless he includes Sawbridge's annuity which is not a Jewish transaction." He concluded, "I think it necessary to add that Hanson's notions as to the value of Rochdale must be tempered down—or not attended to. I want to get rid of that manor if only to shake off the anxiety and litigation it has given me the last seventeen years. Sell it for anything, and Newstead the same."[30]

Through the long summer days at La Mira, Byron amused himself with Marianna Segati, began writing the fourth canto of *Childe Harold*, and looked on appreciatively as back in England Murray published *Manfred* (for which Byron asked three hundred guineas). Hobhouse rejoined him late in July, and Kinnaird visited him in September. Although Byron tired of Marianna, he found a new infatuation in Margarita Cogni, a baker's wife. Despite these liaisons he continued to write, and his mind was never entirely closed to business. Once he heard Kinnaird had left London for Italy, Byron found the energy to write to Hanson on 26 August, insisting that both Newstead and Rochdale should be sold: "[A]ny sale of both or either of these properties must be far more advantageous to me if immediate, than any possible future profit or increase of price from delay." He added that "if the product of the sales should not do much more than cover the settlement of £60,000 after the surplus has been applied to the liquidation of my debts, a part of the income can be set aside for a series of years, to the adjustment of the remaining claims."[31] This was all very high-sounding, but the truth was rather less palatable. As would become clear in succeeding months, Byron had grossly underestimated his debts, thus justifying Hanson's insistence on holding out for the best possible deal. While Byron regretted not having taken £80,000 from Mr. Wilson, in the event the £94,500 for which it finally sold was insufficient to cover all his commitments. He would undoubtedly have regretted a sale for £80,000.

In any case, Hanson was not inactive. On 26 August 1817, the very day Byron was berating his lawyer for not pressing the sale more actively, Newstead came once again under the auctioneer's hammer. It was offered for sale by Farebrothers at Garraway's coffeehouse. By contrast with 1812 and 1815, Byron and Hobhouse were not present, but it made no difference: the estate failed to reach its reserve price and was withdrawn. Byron must have heard about the auction when Kinnaird arrived in Venice in mid-September, and he certainly heard from Charles Hanson both that Newstead had failed to sell at Garraway's and also that there was the possibility of a private contract being concluded. Since this seems to have been a further proposal from Claughton, it was perhaps wise of the Hansons not to admit too much to Byron.[32]

By October news was circulating in London that Newstead had been sold, but Byron had heard nothing by the time he vacated the villa at La Mira and returned to Venice in mid-November, having, in writing *Beppo*, put himself on the road to lasting literary fame. Furious at what he took to be another instance of the neglect of his interests by Hanson, Byron fired off a letter to Charles Hanson asking for information. He insisted to Charles, as he had previously insisted to his father, that Newstead should be sold at "any price . . . do not hope for a high price as that has been the fatal error of the former auctions and the cause of the property remaining unsold; sell it by lots in any shape or form, but let it be sold." He also wrote to Kinnaird, by now back in England, that he had heard nothing about Newstead since their meeting in Venice. Early in December he heard that the estate had at last been sold.[33]

Newstead had gone to auction three times since 1812 and on each occasion it had been withdrawn because it failed to reach the reserve price. On each occasion a private offer had subsequently been received by Hanson, and in 1812 this had gone as far as the abortive sale to Claughton. Once again the purchase involved sale by private contract, but this time the purchaser was not a speculator but a man of means who seemed likely to be able to raise the purchase money. His name was Colonel Thomas Wildman, and the agreed price was £94,500. At face value this looks like a deal made out of desperation, given that Claughton had contracted for £140,000 only five years previously. In fact, during the time that had elapsed conditions had changed. First, as we have seen, Claughton had offered an unrealistically high price even in 1812. As Byron told Hanson in August 1817, "I trust that neither you nor I are now so insane as to expect anything like the price for Newstead which Claughton proposed and could not make good." Second, the post-Napoleonic War agricultural depression had a significant effect on land prices. There was now no possibility of selling in a rising market, which had been Claughton's aim, and so Wildman was, of necessity, looking to pay a reasonable price given the economic conditions. According to the 1817 sale catalog, 1,502 acres were let at an annual average rent of £1.4s. The total estate was measured at 3,226 acres, which suggests a rentable value (assuming all the land could be let for £1.4s. an acre) of £3,871, or twenty-four years' purchase (£94,500 divided by £3,871), which was more or less the going rate for land in 1817. Wildman, in other words, was offering as good a price as Byron could hope for in the circumstances, particularly given the state of the abbey. This was certainly Hanson's opinion: he told Byron in July 1818 that they had "secured for your Lordship every sixpence due on a high rental and from a precarious tenantry."[34]

Byron was pleased to discover that the property was passing into reliable hands. He had last encountered Wildman at Dover while awaiting favorable winds for his crossing to Ostend in April 1816, and he had not forgotten him. "I recollect [Wildman] as my old school fellow and a man of honour," he told Hanson, adding that "I need hardly say that I shall gladly concur in every proper measure to bring the treaty to a satisfactory conclusion, and that I am obliged by your exertions and rejoiced by their probable success." Wildman bought the abbey as it stood, that is, virtually as Byron left it—and therefore as he had renovated it in 1808. He agreed to advance £20,000 almost at once—the paperwork was completed on 25 November 1817—as a deposit, which the trustees immediately invested in exchequer bills. The rest of the money was left at interest until January and February 1819 while the details were worked out. Byron expected the interest to be paid directly into his account. The total eventually received by the trustees was £97,972.[35]

IV

One of the more engaging features of Byron's personality was his generosity. He was always willing to help fund needy projects and to support ailing friends when he knew that behind his temporary cash-flow problems lay substantial capital assets that could one day be called upon to supply his needs. Sometimes his actions seemed foolhardy, as when in March 1809 he gave Lady Falkland £500 at the baptism of her son, despite having failed to pay tradesmen who had supplied him with goods at Newstead.[36] He could act like an aristocrat, refusing to take an income from his poetry and giving away the copyright (*Childe Harold* to Dallas, for example) on the grounds that aristocrats enjoyed an unearned income and did not need to work for their living.

Such piety had already been abandoned by 1814, and once he began to travel in 1816 he became increasingly careful with money. His past scruples about earning what he was apt to call "brain" money soon faded away.[37] He told Wedderburn Webster, who still owed him money, that "my own worldly affairs have had leisure to improve during my residence abroad, for things with time and a little prudence insensibly re-establish themselves, and I have spent less money, and have had more of it, within the two and a half years of my absence from England, than I have ever done within the same time before." He added that "my literary speculations allowed me to do it more easily."[38] Among those literary earnings were £1,050 for *The Siege of Corinth* and *Parisina*, published together in February 1816, £2,000 for the third canto of *Childe Harold* and *The Prisoner of Chillon*, 600 guineas for *Manfred* and *The Lament of Tasso*, and 2,500 guineas for three cantos of *Don Juan* and three plays. Murray suffered the indignity in August and September 1817 of being berated for miscalculating what he owed for canto 3 of *Childe Harold*, *Manfred*, and *Tasso*.[39]

The same concern is obvious in Byron's response to news that Newstead had been sold. After so many false dawns it would not have been surprising had he been unwilling to take any action until he knew the paperwork had been completed. In fact, when on 11 December he sat down to write to Hanson he could hardly spare time to comment on his schoolboy friendship with Wildman before plunging into a long account of his debts. "The first step in the event of a satisfactory conclusion," he told Hanson, "will be the liquidation of my debts."[40] Kinnaird had, of course, provided him with a list during his visit to Venice. This had been only Byron's starting point for weary dredging in the recesses of his mind to add names and amounts, in the absence of the paperwork he had left with Hobhouse in England. It was clearly a more serious business than the vague calculations made at Newstead in September 1814. The list included the Sawbridge transaction of 1809 and other annuities from moneylenders amounting to £12,800, a sum that, by his calculations, ought to have been £12,500. Another £3,300 was still outstanding on annuities contracted with the help of Mrs. Massingberd, but these "may wait as they are minority debts and must only have interest at five per cent at any rate they shall wait for the present till a fair arrangement can be made." Other creditors could not be postponed in this way, particularly the annuitants, including George Orme, George Thomas, and Robert Baxter. In addition, Claughton's £3,000 had yet to be repaid, and Baxter the coachmaker was still owed £500.

There was also his great-aunt, Mrs. Byron of Nottingham, to whom he still needed to repay the £1,000 borrowed on his behalf by his mother (originally in three loans, now consolidated into one). She had been very patient, just occasionally inquiring about the possibility of at least being paid the interest on her loan. Hearing he was in funds early in 1814 she reminded him that she had "hitherto refrained from asking you to pay the interest due upon the money lent you, when at Cambridge, to be paid on your coming of age, or as soon as convenient after." She asked for £99, the outstanding interest, because she had "real occasion for the money to satisfy some demands that we must discharge next Lady Day." She asked again in March 1817, and Byron passed on her request to Hanson: "[I]f there is any residue from the rents, let her have what you can, her and poor Joe Murray poor old man." Murray's wages had been stopped by Hanson when Byron left the country.[41] The list of creditors to be satisfied from the Newstead sale was a long one, but Byron was happy to think that many of these people would see some reward for their patience. "I am quite contented & pleased with the terms of the sale," he told Hanson, but he threw in a proviso that clearly arose from his experiences since 1812: "if acted upon and complied with."[42] The ghost of Thomas Claughton still haunted him.

Byron had plenty of time to compile and correct his lists of debts, because the Newstead paperwork took months to complete. Naturally this was attributed to Hanson's usual procrastination, but the lawyer was up against obstacles over which he had little control. Lady Byron's signature was required on the documents, and her parents insisted on taking legal advice before she so much as lifted a pen, "as Hanson may play tricks." William Hoar, the Durham solicitor who had helped to draw up the marriage settlement, also had to be consulted; but since the Noels had fallen out with him since the wedding, the pace at which he worked was Hansonesque. Wildman's solicitors also conducted business in a fairly leisurely fashion.[43]

Byron had never for a moment intended returning to England to sign the Newstead documents. He had spent a second winter (1817–18) in Venice. Hobhouse had remained with him until early in January 1818, when he set out for England carrying with him canto 4 of *Childe Harold*. Byron's expectation was that a clerk would bring the papers to Venice sometime in March 1818 for his signature. He was by no means amused when the Hansons proposed, with Hobhouse's support, that he should meet the messenger in Geneva.[44] He refused to move, and his position was quickly justified by the inability of the Hansons to name a date when their man would set out. In

May Byron took a three-year lease on a house on the Grand Canal within sight of the Rialto Bridge, having already sent for Allegra, his illegitimate daughter by Claire Clairmont, whose upbringing he now intended to supervise.[45] In England, *Beppo* was published anonymously in February 1818, and canto 4 of *Childe Harold* on 28 April.

Byron soon grew annoyed at the delay in receiving the papers. To Charles Hanson he wrote on 10 June 1818 that "I am very much surprized indeed at not receiving any advice of the papers being forwarded, in preparation so long ago, and so far forward that you pressed me to go to Geneva to meet the bearer of them." Writing to Hobhouse he added that "had I been at Geneva I should have had to wait months for the ragamuffins." Hobhouse tried not to take the bait: "When Spooney's man sets off you shall know," he wrote breezily on 5 June 1818, but the tone was soon to change.[46] In the weeks that followed, Byron peppered his English friends with complaints about the delays. "When will he come, or even set out?" Byron asked Charles Hanson on 18 June; "Where is Spooney's messenger?," he wrote to Hobhouse ten days later. Kinnaird was told to "spur him, kick him," and even take him to court. Hobhouse, embarrassed because he had recommended the Geneva rendezvous, took it upon himself to chide Hanson. At the end of June he promised Byron, "I shall send to Spooney tomorrow what the devil detains his lawyer from commencing his journey." By mid-July Hobhouse had started regular visits to Chancery Lane. A month later he was hoping any day "to be able to announce to you that Spooney had sent his messenger or had set off himself with the papers. . . . I have presented myself to Chancery Lane so often as to be a nuisance and an eye sore to his retainers below stairs." Still the waiting went on. By late September Hobhouse reported that "Hanson's folk are tired of my repeated visits and I myself am almost sick of asking for the fiftieth time if either father son or company is set out with the papers."[47] Byron, meantime, had begun writing *Don Juan* in July, and he was enjoying the company of Percy Shelley, who arrived in Venice in August 1818 and left in late October.

Eventually Hanson decided that he must himself meet Byron, and after a further attempt to lure his client to Geneva he set off on 12 October with his son Newton and a Mr. Townsend, Wildman's solicitor. They reached Geneva on 21 October, where they found Byron's final refusal to stir from Venice, and being now so far committed, they traveled on across the Alps to arrive on his doorstep in Venice on 12 November. It was not an easy reunion: Newton Hanson recorded, "At their meeting, I could not help observing a nervous sensitiveness in his lordship, which produced a silence for some minutes. It was broken by his lordship observing, 'Well, Hanson! I never thought you would have ventured so far. I rather expected you would have sent Charles.'" The tension was not eased by the fact that Hanson had brought only one of three parcels given to him by John Murray, and this turned out not to contain the books Byron was looking forward to but "only a few different-sized kaleidoscopes, tooth brushes, tooth powder etc., etc. At this Lord Byron was greatly annoyed, and would not be pacified for some hours." "He brought nothing," Byron complained to Murray, "but his papers, some corn-rubbers, and a kaleidoscope."[48]

Byron's relationship with Hanson deteriorated once he left England in 1816. He entrusted part of his affairs to Hobhouse and Kinnaird, although Hanson continued to be responsible for his property (including its sale). His reliance upon Kinnaird had been growing since 1815; hence his appointment as joint trustee with Hanson in April 1816. Eventually Kinnaird became Byron's literary agent, and by ensuring that Byron was paid for the copyright of his poetry he was able to help keep him in cash.[49] Just as importantly, Byron grew to trust Kinnaird simply because he found him more reliable: "I apply to you in preference to addressing myself to Hanson, firstly, because you are acting for me equally and secondly, I know your promptitude and ability in the dispatch of business, when you choose to set about it."[50] Byron urged Kinnaird to watch Hanson carefully: "Pray, look very sharp after Spooney, I have my suspicions, my suspicions, Sir, my suspicions." Kinnaird, he hoped on another occasion, would "extract a positive answer from that knave or blockhead Hanson." He accepted Hobhouse's view that Hanson was "a damned dawdle if not a rogue." When Kinnaird warned him to count the number of signatures he was required to place on documents during Hanson's visit to Venice, Byron responded angrily, "[H]ow was I to dream that any of those blasted parchments might be garbled or falsified? or that Hanson was so damned a rogue as you hint him. You might at any rate have said all this before."[51] Byron might just have asked himself why he seems to have been the last person to spot such a possibility but, if he ever did, the answer he offered is probably in a letter he wrote to Kinnaird early in 1817: "With regard to Hanson I know not how to act, and I know not what to think, except that I think he wishes me well."[52]

Neither Kinnaird nor any of Byron's other friends ever persuaded him to break with Hanson, partly from loyalty and friendship and partly because of Hanson's legal position in regard to his marriage settlement, his will, the general power of attorney he had given him before leaving England, and the Rochdale case. He might suggest to Kinnaird that Hanson could be hurried, but only occasionally could Byron bring himself even to chide him, as when he wrote from Ravenna in April 1820 suggesting that he should see out the Rochdale business one way or the other, "and if you could for once be a little quicker about that or anything else it would be a great gain to me and no loss to you." Even when Byron was advised that Hanson's claims for legal expenses might be fraudulent he could scarcely be brought to offer criticism. In 1821 he wrote that "it is a great disadvantage for me to have such a solicitor. However, he was made so when I was ten years old, and I have no help for it." He told Kinnaird in December 1822, "It may not be my interest and it is not my wish to quarrel with him." Byron found in Hanson a substitute father for legal and financial matters, a man in whom he placed his trust and of whom he could never quite bring himself to believe ill.[53]

Hanson's arrival in Venice in November 1818 stirred many memories for both men, but what were his motives for traveling so far at such a late stage in the year? Clearly financial matters were important, but Byron was surprised Hanson had traveled to Venice himself rather than leaving the visit to his son and junior partner, Charles. The main reason, according to Newton Hanson, was that

> My father's object in undertaking the journey *himself* was to ascertain his lordship's sentiments relative to his lady, and, in the course of his stay at Venice, took upon himself on two or three occasions to endeavour to promote a reconciliation.[54]

However, when Byron made plain to Hanson that he had no intention of being reconciled to Lady Byron, the subject was dropped. Instead, the two men concentrated their whole attention on business matters. The first item on their agenda was the Newstead sale. Byron had to sign various documents before it could be completed, and Hanson explained how the purchase money from Wildman would be assigned. From the £94,500, £60,000 was to be paid immediately to the trustees of the marriage settlement in conformity with the agreement signed in December 1814, and reconfirmed in the separation papers of 1816. A further sum of £6,200 was also given to them, representing the advance to Byron in December 1815 secured on Annabella's portion. Consequently, £66,200 was accounted for immediately. This left £28,300. Under the settlement terms, £20,000 had been assigned from the Newstead sale toward paying Byron's debts. Of this sum, £6,200 had been advanced to him in December 1815. Consequently, in theory only £13,800 was available for debt payment: in practice, and presumably after negotiation undertaken by Hanson before he set off for Venice, the whole of the residue (£28,300) was now assigned toward paying Byron's debts. "The remaining £28,300 I shall conceive it to be the duty of Hobhouse and myself to apply to the payments of your debts," Kinnaird told Byron in December.[55] Such an arrangement was legally possible because the terms of the marriage settlement had now been fulfilled (by Byron, although not as yet by Sir Ralph Noel) as to the investment income, and because under the separation arrangements Lady Byron's annual income had been secured.

Once Byron had signed the Newstead papers the key question was whether the residue of £28,300 would cover his outstanding liabilities. Ever since he had received Kinnaird's list, Byron had a fair idea of the extent of his commitments, but Hanson's concern in November 1818 was primarily with the secured debts, particularly the annuities. He had negotiated terms for some of these. Sawbridge's annuity cost £6,656 to repurchase, and those owing to Baxter (£431 15s.), Orme (£792 17s. 6d.) and Thomas (£906 2s. 9d.) cost another £2,130 (table 9.1). From the £28,300, a total of £8,786 had to be deducted to pay these debts, leaving £19,514. These were the initial calls on the purchase money. They did not include various other annuity debts and bonds totaling £6,683 6s. 4d. (with interest). The latter included the £1,000 owed to Mrs. Byron of Nottingham and the £3,000 outstanding to Claughton.[56] It was a complex business: Hanson told Hobhouse in January 1819 that "I have been battling the annuitants, and have got four of them to abate something of their usurious claims, and I am in hopes the last of them will come in. Claughton we have had some trouble with." In fact, Claughton had asked to have £5,000 of the £25,000 forfeit returned to him: "[T]he man surely has not yet recovered his senses."[57]

With the annuitants and bondholders paid, just under £13,000 was un-assigned. Account had now to be taken of Byron's simple contract debts, including Hanson's own bill. Hanson had not been able to complete this list before he left England, and how much he admitted to Byron about the size of his own bill is uncertain. In fact, he was Byron's largest creditor. He was owed (or so he claimed) £9,178 3s. 1d., of which Byron agreed that £5,000 should be paid immediately on account, although he queried why the bill exceeded £8,000.[58]

Hanson stayed only one week, long enough to complete the business matters and for Byron to grow heartily sick of his guest.[59] Then, with Newton and Mr. Townsend in tow, he set off for the long return journey to Chancery Lane. Once back at his desk, his first task was to acquire the necessary countersignatures required to complete the Newstead transaction. Lady Byron's solicitors demanded sight of the documents before she signed anything, and even when this was agreed and she had put pen to paper, her mother continued to interfere. Just before Christmas, Hanson's clerk and Wildman's solicitor traveled to Warrington to obtain Claughton's signature to the various deeds, and they then went on to Kippax Park in Yorkshire, where Thomas Bland, the other trustee of the marriage settlement, was to add his endorsement. When she heard what was going on, Lady Noel commissioned her own agent to go to Kippax Park "to caution Mr Bland against signing the deed without first having the money paid to himself and Mr Kinnaird." The agent told Lady Noel a letter would be sufficient, "but this she would not hear of, as it was a matter, she said, of such immense importance."[60]

Table 9.1. The Newstead Sale, 1817–19

Income		£
Newstead estate		94,500
Interest		3,472
Total		97,972
Expenditure		
Trustees of the marriage settlement	60,000	
Repayment of loan to Byron, Dec. 1815	6,200	
Sawbridge annuity	6,656	
Baxter, Orme, and Thomas annuities	2,130	
Total	74,986	
Loss on interest	418	
		75,404
Balance paid by Wildman		22,568

Source: Reelig. 705; Murray Mss.

Despite Lady Noel's distrust, the details were sorted out quite quickly in the early weeks of 1819. Late in January the £66,200 was paid to the trustees of the Byrons' marriage settlement and invested by them—as required by the terms of the settlement—in 3 percent consolidated annuities (£84,174 17s. 7d.). In February the annuitants were paid off, as was old Mrs. Byron of Nottingham; the Newstead transaction was completed, and all the interest was accounted. Wildman acquired full possession of the Newstead estate—including the dilapidated abbey. "The little Major Wildman," Kinnaird commented, "has behaved like a prince."[61]

V

Among the papers Hanson carried back to England from Venice in November 1818 was a sealed letter addressed to Kinnaird and Hobhouse. In it, Byron expressed his concerns about the size of his debt to Hanson, and asked Kinnaird and Hobhouse to keep a watchful eye upon the lawyer.[62] Nor was the matter inconsequential. Kinnaird told Byron on 20 December 1818 that while £28,300 was available for debt repayment, the sums outstanding amounted to £34,162, leaving a shortfall of £5,862:

> But the lawyer's bill is stated in this to amount to no less a sum than between nine and ten thousand pounds. It is my decided opinion that not one farthing of this should be paid till the whole bill up to the date of its delivery is given in by . . . Hanson.[63]

Put in another way, Hanson's bill was the difference between Byron clearing his debts and being left with sums outstanding, and Kinnaird decided that they should take a stand on this particular issue. On 28 December, Kinnaird entertained Hanson, Hobhouse, and Hobhouse's father to dinner. "We had a very satisfactory conversation," Hobhouse told Byron, during which they agreed—against Hanson's advice—"that no composition is compatible with your honour." In other words Byron should act like an aristocrat and pay his bills in full, although they thought it made sense to postpone as many of them as possible until after Lady Noel's death, whenever that might occur. Baxter the coachmaker, Griffiths the wine merchant, and Newman the horse jobber were all agreeable to these terms. Less satisfactory to the lawyer was the agreement "that Spooney must wait." He was also relieved of some responsibilities, with Kinnaird and Hobhouse countersigning payments for "all the larger bills."[64] Not surprisingly, Hanson was less impressed by the way he was being sidelined, and dropped hints about keeping the Rochdale documentation as security for the sums he was owed. He had previously told Kinnaird that it would take nine months to prepare a detailed account, and that in any case he had agreed with Byron when they were together in Venice to take an interim payment of £5,000 "which I had fully relied on in consequence of what you [Byron] told me you had written."[65]

These were hardly ideal conditions under which Kinnaird and Hanson were supposed to be working together for Byron's good, but Kinnaird was not to be moved. On 16 February 1819 he told Byron that Hanson

> this day requested I would sign a draft for £5000 to him, but I told him I considered myself bound to have his account delivered before I paid a farthing even on account. I so read your letter of instructions to Hobhouse and myself. You say you have agreed to pay him £5000 on condition of his delivering in his account to us. Now I take it for granted you mean that this agreement to pay him £5000 was to operate as a quickener of the production of the account. . . . Hanson asked to see your letter to us, but I see it is marked private. We are quite good friends, but I am sturdy on matters of business.

Kinnaird was taking a tough stance because Byron had written that "I have agreed to pay him *five thousand* pounds, but on condition that his bill be *submitted* to *you twain*." He had not said when this was to be, and Kinnaird's reluctance to advance the £5,000 to Hanson left Byron distinctly uneasy. On 6 March he told Kinnaird that it was his intention that the £5,000 should be advanced to his lawyer.[66] In fact, even before his reply arrived in London, Kinnaird had agreed to advance £670 to Hanson, which he was determined should be seen as part of the £5,000 but which the Hansons wanted to be regarded as additional. Subsequently, following a "long and not very agreeable discussion," Kinnaird refused to pay the Hansons more than the balance of £4,330.[67]

Aggrieved he may have been, but Hanson continued with the task of locating Byron's debts, and in September 1819 he finally submitted to him through Kinnaird a detailed listing (table 9.2). Hanson had prepared the original list before he set out for Venice, and he and Byron discussed its contents at their meeting. Hanson added a further £679 of debt that came to light on his return to England, making a total of £28,476, of which £17,622 had been paid, leaving £10,854 outstanding. Hanson suggested that £6158 could be put off, denied, or converted into bonds. That left unavoidable debts of £1,480, which he rather optimistically suggested could "nearly be paid out of Mr Claughton's debt of £970 and £200 arrears of Newstead rents to be received."[68] Hanson hoped the list was complete, but many of the creditors were unhappy: "[W]e have done all in our power to bring about an arrangement with the Mansfield creditors honourable to Lord Byron and satisfactory to them, but they appear so slow into coming in any that we submit, the best course now will be to pay those bills as they stand."[69] Kinnaird distrusted Hanson's motives:

> [I]t was manifest that the more he could knock off the more would remain for him. As to the merits of the claims, we could not be judges. . . . He proposed to leave the county creditors to shift for themselves. To that I objected in the name and on behalf of your character. Having sold your estate it would not have been proper to have left your debts around it unpaid.[70]

While these financial transactions had been in progress, Byron had remained busy. Both Kinnaird and Hobhouse had their loyalty to Byron stretched to the limit by the arrival in London during the last days of 1818 of the first two cantos of *Don Juan*, which included numerous autobiographical references implicating Annabella in a manner not thought appropriate for the London reading public. Despite their objections, it was published in July 1819, and although the expensive folio editions did not sell very well it circulated in cheaper, pirated editions.[71] Meantime, in Italy

Table 9.2. Lord Byron's Debts in 1819
(£.s.d.)

	Debts	Paid	Unpaid
Annuities (principal)	3,270 0 0	3,270 0 0	—
Annuities (arrears)	1,961 12 10	1,451 1 11	[a]
Bonds	4,704 10 0	4,342 18 3	403 15 3 [b]
Contract debts	18,540 8 7	8,555 3 4	10,450 12 8
	28,476 11 5	17,622 3 6 [c]	10,854 7 11
Sums available for debt payment		22,300 0 0	
Debts paid		17,622 3 6	
Surplus		4,677 16 6	
Unaid		10,854 7 11	
Deficit		6,176 11 8	
Debts commuted or renounced		6,158 9 11 [d]	
Payment available		4,677 16 6	
Unavoidable debts		1,480 13 5	

Source: Murray Mss. The list was enclosed with a letter from Hanson to Kinnaird, 7
   September 1819.
[a] Although there appears to be a discrepancy between debts and sums paid, nothing
   is given in the unpaid column, presumably because these were considered
   closed when Hanson visited Venice.
[b] The sums do not add up because some of the interest payments are greater than
   the sums given as due.
[c] The actual figure is £17,619. Hanson seems to have totalled the list incorrectly.
[d] Hanson does not explain the difference between this figure and the deficit.

during April 1819 Byron began his long affair with Teresa Guiccioli. Early
in June he followed her to Ravenna, passing through Padua, Ferrara, and
Bologna en route. It was while he was at Ravenna that Byron hired Lega
Zambelli, the Italian who was subsequently to act as his secretary and ac-
countant and whose business instincts helped Byron to live within his means
for the rest of his life.[72] On 9 August Teresa and her husband left Ravenna
for Bologna, and Byron followed them a day later. He stayed in Bologna
until 12 September, and shortly before he left the definitive list of debts
reached him from London.

Despite the fact that he had seen most of this list nine months earlier, Byron's initial response was one of outrage. He claimed that the list was much longer than he had anticipated, and in his view included a good deal of fiction: "[D]epend upon many of these having been paid before or are originally impositions," he wrote in the margin of the list; "many names are quite unknown." In a covering letter returning the list to Kinnaird he was forthright: "I have marked on this paper many names of creditors whom I do not know and deny them thrice. There is no Hopkinson of Southwell, and if there were I owe him nothing."[73] Whether he liked it or not, many of these bills went back a long way, which was partly why he had forgotten them; indeed, several of them were to Nottingham and Mansfield tradesmen still unpaid from the Newstead refurbishment of 1808. Some may have been bills Mrs. Byron had been anxious to pay in 1811. His questioning of such small sums strikingly paralleled his great-uncle's behavior in the 1770s.

Byron's most scathing criticism was reserved for Owen Mealey, who was owed £400. Byron annotated the list by inserting after Mealey's name, "a damned rascal," and adding in the covering letter to Kinnaird, "Mealey is the greatest scoundrel in the world." It is perhaps ample commentary on Byron's love-hate relationship with estate management that the man who had shown him around the estate in 1803, who had served him before and after the minority often without receiving his wages, and pre- and post-Claughton, and whom he could never get around to firing should continue to evoke such strong emotions. Poor Mealey was still owed money in 1820, when Charles Hanson thought it prudent that he and Kinnaird might sort out how much he should actually be allowed. Byron's anger had not abated: he suggested in November 1821 that Mealey might be paid £10 and no more, because "he is the greatest rascal that ever emptied a brandy bottle. Pay *him!* quotha! what do you take me for."[74]

Mealey died on 7 November 1822 leaving his debts to his widow, whom he also appointed as sole executrix. Kinnaird, while writing to Byron on 15 November, answered a knock at the door and found Widow Mealey, newly arrived from burying her late husband. He resumed the letter after this unexpected interview:

> I really think you ought to pay the Widow. Mr Orme, Col Wildman's and Lord Rancliffe's steward, whom I know for an upright man, says he has examined all the books and that there does not appear anything overcharged in amount. I never could learn on what distinct ground Hanson advised you to object to paying this bill.

Kinnaird urged payment, or "I must be at charges for an extra porter to keep the woman out of my house. She has a tongue like a mill." Six months later he was still awaiting instructions: "[P]ray authorize me to pay Mealey. The widow is very clamorous. Something might be paid." He again asked permission to pay Mrs. Mealey in July 1823: "I have, from every source I have probed, found reason to believe that the articles in Mealey's bill were really furnished, and are not overcharged." Byron was not to be moved, perhaps displacing onto the unfortunate Mealey the frustration occasioned in reality by the failed father-figure Hanson. Kinnaird was still trying to get authority to settle with Widow Mealey in March 1824.[75]

Byron had recovered his temper by the time he returned to Venice toward the end of September 1819: "[M]y affairs in England are nearly settled, or in prospect of settlement," he cheerfully told Hobhouse. Subsequently he joked to Kinnaird that "it is very iniquitous to make me pay my debts."[76] Typically, Byron's thoughts were already moving onward. During September he had considered eloping with Teresa Guiccioli to France or America, and during October he was seriously considering settling in South America. Periodically he also talked of returning to England.

VI

Byron showed an astonishing lack of judgment when he tried unsuccessfully to persuade Hanson to consider accepting an offer of £80,000 for Newstead, but how, in the end, did he actually feel about parting with the family estate? When Byron left England in 1816 he assured Augusta that Newstead would never fade in his memory. In his *Epistle to Augusta* he reminded her of their time at "the old Hall" and "our own dear lake," and added,

> Sad havoc Time must with my memory make
> Ere *that* or *thou* can fade these eyes before—
> Though like all things which I have loved —they are
> Resigned for ever—or divided far.[77]

Newstead may have been resigned, but the fear that it would fade proved unfounded, even if this was not quite how it seemed when the Wildman transaction was completed. In the immediate aftermath of the sale, and at a time when he was simply glad to see a possibility of paying his debts, his relief was palpable. As he told Kinnaird in January 1818, "I am as you may suppose very well pleased so far with regard to Newstead, it was and will be a great relief to me, at least I hope so."[78] Augusta had made no secret of her regret that Byron had sold "poor, dear Newstead,"[79] but in the euphoria of the moment Byron seems to have valued the opportunity of being rid of his debts rather more highly than the loss of the abbey.

Subsequently he seems to have been keen to justify the decision. He told Augusta that had his daughter been a son,

> I do not think that I should have parted with it after all, but I dislike George Byron for his behaviour in 1816, and I am unacquainted with the others who may be in the line of the title, and being myself abroad, and at feud with the whole of the Noels, and with most of the Byrons except yourself, of course, these concurring with other and pressing circumstances, rendered the disposal of the Abbey necessary and not improper.[80]

This was a remarkable claim because of the way it twisted the facts to suit his conscience. Byron had agreed to sell Newstead long before his daughter was born, and only by altering the marriage settlement could he have reversed that particular decision. It had not been a decision taken to deny the succession to his cousin George, who had sided with Annabella against him when the marriage broke up; indeed, had Newstead been settled in the normal way he could not have prevented the estate passing (as did the title) to George after his death. No self-respecting aristocratic family would have regarded the sale of Newstead as "not improper," and Byron knew this. Thomas Medwin, whose conversations with Byron when he was at Pisa in 1821–22 were published after his death, recorded how he had learned that "I was compelled to part with Newstead. . . . As it is, I shall never forgive myself for having done so." However, Medwin also noted that Byron put financial considerations above those of property, in that he considered the estate inadequate for his needs: "Newstead was a very unprofitable estate, and brought me in a bare £1,500 a year. The Lancashire property was hampered with a law suit which has cost me £14,000 and is not yet finished."[81]

Byron came up with one further justification. As he told Kinnaird some years later, "I have always preferred my mother's family, for its royalty." Given the opportunity, he claimed, he would have attempted to buy back her Scottish estates rather than to worry about those of his father's family. This was interesting, coming from someone who never even returned to Scotland after 1798, but it was in line with his view following his marriage that as Noel was an older title than Byron, it was the one to which a son would have succeeded had there been one.

In the end this was all rationalization. Byron sold out because he placed his own financial needs and desires above the social considerations that had maintained the Byrons at Newstead for the previous 277 years, and because he had never understood that he should see himself as a trustee of the estate with the responsibility of passing it on to future generations. Just as his father had ruined his mother's inheritance for his own financial gain, the bottom line was that the sixth Lord Byron cashed in his family's inheritance to pay his creditors.[82]

Yet whether Byron regretted the sale or not, he never forgot Newstead. Early in 1823, by which time he was once again a landowner—albeit purely in the role of estranged husband—and after several months when he had been immersed in trying to sort out his financial affairs, Byron allowed his imagination to return to the great house that he had last seen nearly nine years earlier. Perhaps by now it was the ideal rather than the reality of Newstead that mattered to him, but it made a scarcely disguised and memorable reappearance in canto 13 of *Don Juan*. The detail of the description was so fresh that it seemed almost as if Byron was again walking in the park when he put pen to paper.

> To Norman Abbey whirled the noble pair,—
> An old, old monastery once, and now
> Still older mansion, of a rich and rare
> Mixed Gothic, such as Artists all allow
> Few specimens yet left us can compare
> Withal: it lies perhaps a little low,
> Because the monks preferred a hill behind,
> To shelter their devotion from the wind.

No one who had visited Newstead could mistake the description, but Byron had much more to say. The "Norman Abbey" "stood embosom'd in a happy valley, / Crown'd by high woodlands," with, in front of it, a "lucid lake" with "a steep cascade." The great west window was described in detail:

> A glorious remnant of the Gothic pile
> (While yet the church was Rome's) stood half apart
> In a grand Arch, which once screened many an aisle.
> These last had disappear'd—a loss to Art:
> The first yet frowned superbly o'er the soil,
> And kindled feelings in the roughest heart,
> Which mourn'd the power of time's or tempest's march,
> In gazing on that venerable Arch.
>
> Within a niche, nigh to its pinnacle,
> Twelve saints had once stood sanctified in stone;
> But these had fallen, not when the friars fell,
> But in the war which struck Charles from his throne,
> When each house was a fortalice—as tell
> The annals of full many a line undone—
> The gallant Cavaliers, who fought in vain
> For those who knew not to resign or reign.
>
> But in a higher niche, alone, but crown'd,
> The Virgin Mother of the God-born child,

With her Son in her blessed arms, look'd round,
Spared by some chance when all beside was spoil'd;
She made the earth below seem holy ground.
This may be superstition, weak or wild,
But even the faintest relics of a shrine
Of any worship, wake some thoughts divine.

A mighty window, hollow in the centre,
Shorn of its glass of thousand colourings,
Through which the deepen'd glories once could enter,
Streaming from off the sun like seraph's wings,
Now yawns all desolate: now loud, now fainter,
The gale sweeps through its fretwork, and oft sings
The owl his anthem, where the silenced quire
Lie with their hallelujahs quench'd like fire.

And so the description continued as Byron recalled in detail the "Gothic fountain" (moved by Colonel Wildman from outside the front entrance to its current location in the inner courtyard), and then went on to describe the house:

The mansion's self was vast and venerable,
With more of the monastic than has been
Elsewhere preserved; the cloisters still were stable,
The cells too and refectory, I ween:
An exquisite small chapel had been able,
Still unimpair'd to decorate the scene;
The rest had been reform'd, replaced, or sunk,
And spoke more of the baron than the monk.[83]

Byron's description of Newstead in these verses of *Don Juan* astonished Thomas Moore when he visited the abbey on 21 January 1828 while gathering material for his planned biography of the poet. He was, he recorded,

Much struck by the first appearance of the Abbey; would have given the world to be alone; the faithfulness of the descriptions in *Don Juan*, the ruined arch, the Virgin and Child, the fountain etc.[84]

Nor is his response surprising. Byron's lack of remorse over the sale of Newstead jars with these verses. It suggests, perhaps, that while he undoubtedly sold the estate for material gain, and while he made all sorts of attempts subsequently to justify his behavior, Byron also retained an affection for the old house that never left him. By the time he wrote these lines

Byron was living far from home, but he was once again a landowner, he was dissatisfied with having his capital tied up in stocks rather than mortgages, and he was seriously trying to sort out his financial affairs. It was the nearest he came to admitting that Newstead had, after all, retained a special place in his heart despite events since 1812.

10

An Exiled Aristocrat, 1818–23

The sale of Newstead was like the removal of an albatross from around Byron's neck. As he told Shelley in September 1818:

> [M]y own worldly affairs have had leisure to improve during my residence abroad. Newstead has been sold and well sold I am given to understand. My debts are in the prospect of being paid, and I have still a large capital from the residue, besides Rochdale, which ought to sell well, and my reversionary prospects which are considerable in the event of the death of Miss Milbanke's mother. . . . I have spent less money, and had more of it within the 2½ years since my absence from England, than I have ever done within the same time before.[1]

The irony is that as he shed his landed property, Byron became increasingly careful with money, and it was only in the last months of his life, which he spent in Greece, that he began once again to display the largesse of his youth. In 1811 Byron told Hanson that "one thing is certain, if I should ever be induced to sell [Newstead] I will spend my life abroad."[2] Whether or not he remembered these words, which were written from Athens during his first European tour, we do not know, but he did sell his property and he did live abroad: he became a nineteenth-century rarity, a wealthy, unlanded, English aristocrat.

I

Although Byron and Hanson were primarily concerned with the Newstead sale and the burden of debt, when they met at Venice in November 1818 they also discussed other affairs. Byron's future income was obviously high on their agenda, and this now looked healthy. The invested Newstead capital was yielding him £2,525 annually, to which he could add the £190 due annually from Sir Ralph Noel. In addition, his poetry was a more than useful supplement. Hobhouse noted as much in June 1819: "[Y]ou have got two thousand paunds two thousand shillings for your poeshie, and now, pox rot it what wilt thou do with the money Tam? Your treasury must be in an overflowing condition."[3] For the future he could anticipate his share of the Kirkby Mallory estate on the death of his mother-in-law, Lady Noel. Byron must have been aware by the time he saw Hanson off to England at the end of November 1818 that the prospects he had outlined to Shelley in September were a realistic assessment of his situation, even if many of his debts had still to be paid.

Byron and Hanson also discussed Rochdale.[4] The legal case had been proceeding (or, perhaps more accurately, not proceeding) through the courts since 1808, but in the meantime we know little of what was happening at Rochdale. Although the fifth lord sold several properties, in 1798 Byron inherited cottages, coal mines, and stone quarries. Some of these he still owned when Thomas France inspected them and reported to Mrs. Byron in 1808, but while there is no surviving record of any sales, the advertisement for Rochdale prior to the 1815 auction does not mention specific properties. Byron's rights were those of lord of the manor over approximately 8,256 acres of the 45,000-acre parish. He could hold manor courts (leet and baron), collect the market and fair tolls, exploit the coal resources (had he had the investment capital), enjoy the grouse and game, and receive a small income from copyholds. The townships in his part of the manor were Hundersfield, Spotland, Butterworth, and Castleton on the Lancashire side of the border and Saddleworth in Yorkshire.[5]

Hanson and Byron had differed sharply in their views as to the future of Rochdale. It was Hanson's view that Byron would win the legal case and that this would make him a rich man. By contrast Byron, who wanted money today rather than potential riches tomorrow, had no doubt that the appropriate course of action was to sell Rochdale for what he could raise, as a contribution toward paying his debts. Since it seems to have brought in little or no income—most of it disappeared in legal fees—this was reasonable, although Hanson consistently claimed that winning the legal case should be a first priority, because of the difference it would make to the capital value of the estate on sale. Byron had his way in 1812, and Rochdale was put up for auction at Garraway's. Unfortunately for his plans, it failed to reach its reserve price. Nor did a purchaser come forward when it was readvertised in 1815. According to Farebrother, the auctioneer, Hanson turned down an offer of £17,000 in 1815, although subsequently—under close questioning from Kinnaird—Farebrother admitted that "there never was a bona fide offer of more than £10,000."[6]

Once the Newstead sale was completed, Byron was anxious to be out of landed property and not to wait for the law courts to decide the fate of Rochdale. He told Kinnaird in January 1818, "I wish you would try at Rochdale too, I should then be quite clear," and two months later he was encouraging Hobhouse "to spur [Hanson] into the like for Rochdale." Kinnaird was again urged to "spur" Hanson into selling Rochdale in May, and the same message was pressed on Charles Hanson a few days later.[7] John Hanson would not be moved. He told Byron in July 1818 that

> With respect to Rochdale my humble and earnest advice to your Lordship is to suspend a sale just at present, for I think it extremely probable that when we have proceeded a little further in the suit in the Exchequer it will lead to your obtaining much better terms, and most probably your adversaries will be glad to purchase the property and the suit off at a high rate, at present we have not got to the decided stage to induce such an arrangement but shall in a very few months.

Byron must have groaned at the thought of "a very few months," but with Newstead sold a further delay could be tolerated, and he authorized additional legal expenses of up to £1,000—a sum Kinnaird described as "surely a large discretion." Byron remained committed to sale, and equally sure that any likely profit from the estate would be swallowed up in lawyers' fees long before it reached his pocket.[8]

As Byron could easily have predicted, the very few months turned out to be more than a year, partly because of the death in the meantime of one of the trustees appointed under the 1773 estate settlement. By the autumn of 1819 he was again urging a sale. He told Kinnaird in September that he was "of decided opinion for the sale of the manor, even without waiting for the decision of the Suit." He repeated the same message to Hobhouse, but these were musings rather than real hopes, although Kinnaird reported that Charles Hanson was considering offering £20,000 for the property.[9] Nothing came of this, but Byron was pleased to hear early in 1820 that a conclusion was in sight. "If the claim could be adjusted, and the whole brought to the hammer," he told Charles Hanson, "I could clear everything and know what I really possess." Hanson did not respond, and in April 1820 Byron urged Kinnaird, "Pray follow up the prospect of the Rochdale accommodation (and sale let us hope)," adding in a subsequent letter that since the property was not settled, "a moderate accommodation is preferable to the uncertainty and delay of law."[10] It was not to be; he told Charles Hanson that although "it would have given me pleasure that the Rochdale suit could have been terminated amicably and without further law but by arbitration . . . since it must go before a Court I resign myself to the decision."[11]

The case was heard in the Court of the Exchequer on 5 June 1820. Byron, alerted by Hanson that the hearing was imminent, responded gloom-

ily that "I am by no means sanguine but would wish to be out of the suspense." He was not to be put out of his misery quickly—a letter written by
Charles Hanson to tell him that the chief baron was delaying judgment
seems to have gone astray, and as a result Byron heard nothing more until
Hanson informed him that the case had been heard, but without any indication of the outcome.[12] Hanson was not being difficult. He was simply reporting that the lord chief baron, before whom the case was heard, took a
month to consider his judgment, which he finally delivered on 8 July. Within
a week Byron had heard from Kinnaird "the 'fatal intelligence'" of the
Rochdale decision. The court had found in favor of James Dearden, accepting, in other words, that although he might not have a title in law (a
point established by the courts while Byron was still a minor), he had one
in equity. Charles Hanson had assured Byron in advance, "I am persuaded
they will find it very difficult to establish an equitable one," so it is hardly
surprising that Byron was dismayed by the outcome: "[I]t is indeed a severe blow after fifteen years of litigation, and almost as many thousand
pounds of law expenses with two verdicts in my favour." His immediate
response was to suggest to Kinnaird that preparations should be made for
selling the undisputed part of the property: "I (were I on the spot) should
immediately order the manor, and whatever rights are mine to be brought
to the hammer, and sold to any bidding without consideration of price. This
will at least pay the law expenses and perhaps liquidate some part of the
remaining debt. . . . I have tried the question and will have no more law."[13]

By the same post Byron wrote in similar terms to Hanson, but when, a
day or two later, he heard from Charles Hanson that an appeal to the House
of Lords was being prepared, he agreed that they should at least get a legal
opinion as to the possibility of success. By September 1820 he was having
second thoughts and beginning to wish once again that Rochdale could be
sold without further delay: "I would still much rather sell the manor at any
price than enter into a new and hopeless litigation." A month later he finally
received the long-promised opinion as to why an appeal might succeed, at
which point he somewhat reluctantly agreed to proceed, although without
any great hopes of a successful outcome. He had, he told Kinnaird early in
1821, "had more trouble than profit with it."[14]

II

During his years in Italy Byron controlled his finances more tightly
than he had ever done in the past. This changed attitude came to Augusta's
ears: she heard in July 1818 that he had become something of a miser who
"kept counting his money."[15] He was coming to regard money in a manner

not unlike his great uncle, the fifth Lord Byron; in other words, he wanted those people who owed him money to be hounded into payment, while he was happy to jeopardize the financial arrangements of those to whom he himself owed money. Murray, for example, was offered an accountancy lesson in 1817 when he seemed to have miscalculated the outstanding royalties:

> If I understand rightly you have paid into Morland's [Bank] £1500. As the agreement in the paper is two thousand Guineas, there will remain therefore six hundred pounds and not five hundred, the odd hundred being the extra to make up the specie. Six hundred and thirty pounds will bring it to the like for *Manfred* and *Tasso*, making a total of twelve hundred & thirty, I believe, for I am not a good calculator.[16]

Similarly, in June 1818 Byron issued a series of instructions to Kinnaird regarding debts owing to him and from whom they were to be collected,[17] and in 1820 he asked Hobhouse to take steps to sell Wedderburn Webster's bond of £1,000 (£1,500 with unpaid interest) outstanding since 1813. In fact, this latter sale proved more difficult than he anticipated. It had still not been sold in December 1821, and Byron's memory was jogged again a year later when Webster visited him: "I think that he might at least have paid some of the interest," Byron suggested to Kinnaird; "to say the truth he has behaved shabbily about it, and had the impudence to ask me the other day whether 'my heirs could act upon it.' I am sure that all my creditors have been a good deal less patient." Kinnaird was still trying to sell it in May 1823. Only Augusta was excused the general roundup of debts— Byron refused to entertain any idea of her husband repaying the sums that he had supposedly lent to him.[18]

Byron did not explain what he saw as the difference between Webster waiting for his death and his own creditors being expected to await Lady Noel's demise; indeed, for those people still waiting for Byron to pay their bills, the situation was quite different. Hanson and Kinnaird between them were to pay his outstanding debts as funds became available, but there were clear lines of precedence. Kinnaird was instructed in 1819: "[D]on't pay away to those low people or tradesmen, they may survive Lady Noel, or me, and get it from the executors and heirs, but I don't approve of any living liquidations, a damned deal too much has been paid already."[19] Even so, having expected the Newstead sale to put an end to his financial worries, Byron felt the weight of the continuing burden. He told Kinnaird in July 1820 that "the payment of debts must be now my only object," and when there were still bills to be met late in 1821, he insisted that "you really must not pay anybody, I cant afford it."[20] "I really can't pay Farebrother or any one else more than the *interest* on their debt at present," he insisted to Kinnaird in December 1821; "surely I have paid enough debt for one year. . . . I wonder at your profligate expectations of my paying more just now, can't they be content with the interest until the death of Lady Noel or my own sets my capital free." Kinnaird was less impressed: "I regret your determination not to pay Mr Farebrother at least. . . . He is hardly used and did his duty by you." Kinnaird also wanted to pay Baxter the coachmaker, but Byron was adamant, and this reluctance to pay his debts was a theme that would dominate his financial thinking while he remained in Italy.[21]

Byron's growing concern with money was reflected also in his attitude toward arrangements respecting his marriage-settlement capital. When he heard that the trustees had carried out their commission to invest £66,200 in 3 percent consolidated annuities, he complained to Kinnaird. The interest of £2,525 5s. was payable to him as income, but he was still unhappy:

> I can't say that I approve at all of the funds in which I have no faith whatever, and I wish to have the money either laid out on Mortgage, or at any rate in any thing rather than so precarious a tenure as I conceive the funds to be. And pray why not in the 5 per cents instead of the three for the time being?

"I know nothing of the matters," he added. When Kinnaird told him that "it was your own or Hanson's doing . . . your interest would have been larger in the 5 per cents," Byron was even more irate, complaining to Hobhouse that "Douglas Kinnaird with more than usual politeness writes me vivaciously that Hanson or I willed the *three per cents* instead of the five, as if I could prefer *three* to *five* per Cent! death & fiends!"[22] Neither Kinnaird nor Hobhouse was amused by this outburst, and when Byron continued to complain, Kinnaird was more forceful: "I utterly deny ever having been asked my opinion of the three per cents, in proof of which I beg to inform you that Spooney, as you are pleased to designate your man of law, brought over with him your lordship's fiat to an unwritten order to invest the money in the three per cents."[23] Hobhouse pointed out that Byron's annoyance simply highlighted his financial ignorance: "[T]he *three* per cents are not *two* per cent under the *five* per cents as you ought to know by this time as you are now and have been any time this two months a monied man."[24]

In any case, whatever Byron's complaints the trustees were simply carrying out their commission. They were to hold all the money paid to them under the terms of the 1814 marriage settlement in 3 percent consolidated annuities until they had available the sum of £76,000, consisting of £60,000 from the Newstead sale and £16,000 from Sir Ralph Noel for Lady Byron's portion. Then, and only then, were they permitted to withdraw the money from the funds and invest it in a mortgage. By February 1819 they had the Newstead money, but from Lady Byron's £16,000 portion they had received only £6,200 (the money advanced to Byron in December 1815 and now repaid from the Newstead sale). Sir Ralph had intended to raise the other £9,800 through the sale of Aldborough Farm. This did not sell at auction, where it failed to reach a reserve price of £12,000, but it was subsequently bought privately by a Mr. Barrett for £9,800. Unfortunately, Mr. Barrett failed to pay, and in August 1819 the contract was scrapped and Sir Ralph had to start again in his attempts to raise the missing portion money.[25]

Byron was not placated, and was soon complaining again: "I shall never rest while my property is in the English funds, let it be invested in land or mortgage although at a present loss." Coming from Byron, who had agreed to a marriage settlement in which his landed estate would be sold to provide him with an investment income, this was an interesting new development. Nor had his ingenuity yet been exhausted. "Could not the same," he suggested, "be vested in Sir Ralph Noel's estates (who wants money) he giving mortgage, and paying fair and lawful interest? Thus there might be an accommodation for both."[26] He was, it seems, suggesting that his capital should be used as a loan to his estranged father-in-law. It would certainly have been an unusual arrangement.

This interest in the fate of his capital reflected Byron's long-term unease about keeping money in government funds rather than moving it into landed security in the form of a mortgage. He told Augusta in 1819 that the seeds of his doubts about holding money in the funds were first sown by Kinnaird, who persuaded him that a mortgage would offer greater long-term security on a fixed income. In fact, Kinnaird wrote to him on 19 March to express agreement with his *own* opinion: "I am quite of your opinion that the money should be laid out on mortgage if possible." He warned Byron subsequently that mortgages were not easy to obtain, "not from the wealth of the landed proprietors but they are mortgaged up to the hilt."[27] Byron may have found this ironic in view of his own experiences. Hanson was less sure about mortgages. Byron complained that

> Mr Kinnaird writes that the mortgage is the most advantageous thing possible, you write that [it] is quite the contrary. You are both my old acquaintances, both men of business, and both give good reasons for both your opinions, and the result is that I finish by having no opinion at all. . . . I retain however my bad opinion of the funds and must insist on the money being one day placed on better security somewhere.

Kinnaird was requested to sit down with Hanson and form a joint opinion.[28]

Byron's interest in a mortgage was partly because he was asked to loan money on an Irish estate at 6 percent. This, it was calculated, would yield an increase in his investment income amounting to £1,000 annually. Hanson reluctantly accepted that there might be advantages in turning the stock into a mortgage (although not necessarily an Irish one), although he would probably have preferred to see £30,000 lent to his son-in-law, the earl of Portsmouth or, more accurately in the circumstances, to his daughter. Kinnaird favored a mortgage to Lord Blessington on his Dublin property "to pay for extravagant diversions with his "most gorgeous" lady." Byron approved the deal, but Hanson dragged his feet. In an effort to speed up the negotiations, on 8 June 1820 Byron sent Hanson and Kinnaird his "definitive consent to lend the sum proposed on mortgage to Lord Blessington, without cavil or delay, if there were any form of words stronger than this to express my consent I would use it."[29] In the end, on legal grounds, the trustees opposed moving the money into settled property. Byron was annoyed, "for I would rather sell out [of the funds] at any cost, than trust to the infamous bubble of the British funds in which (had I been on the spot) I could never have entered."[30]

Technically, the marriage settlement money could not be removed from the funds while part of Lady Byron's portion remained unpaid. Kinnaird should, and Hanson probably did, anticipate such an objection,[31] but it was Hanson who took the brunt of Byron's wrath:

> By the intervention of your good offices, Lady B's trustee has declined to ratify the mortgage. I shall content myself with observing that knowing my wishes so well upon the subject, knowing also how frivolous the objection is in fact, whatever it may be in law, that whether as my friend (and I have always shown myself the friend of your family, in circumstances even where others condemned you) you ought to be ashamed of yourself for having suggested the objection.[32]

Despite this setback, Byron continued to urge Kinnaird to investigate the possibilities of transferring the money into a mortgage. Time and time again he complained to Kinnaird about his distrust of the funds: "[S]ell out at all events," he wrote in March 1821; "do something to get us sold out" in June; and "extract me from the said stocks, which sit very heavily upon my slumbers" in August. Kinnaird's attempts to calm him down were useless. "Nothing but a foreign war can do much injury to our funds for years," he wrote in March 1821; "do not fidget about the funds," he added in subsequent letters.[33]

Whatever he may have written, Kinnaird did keep a watchful eye out for a mortgage. In December 1821 he wrote to tell Byron that he had heard of a £50,000 mortgage at 4¾ percent, which he had "written to accept," although he needed Byron's approval.[34] Five months later discussions were underway with a view to lending £46,000 or £47,000 on Lord Le Despencer's estate in Kent, but after several months of negotiation it proved impossible to establish a good title, and the scheme collapsed.[35] Byron could not be placated: he wrote to Kinnaird in 1823 urging him to accept almost any mortgage on offer, "anything to get out of the tremulous funds of these oscillating times. There will be a war somewhere, no doubt . . . get us out of them with all proper expedition."[36] It was an irrational and unfounded fear, but Byron seems to have been unmovable in his prejudice.

III

Byron had returned to Venice in September 1819 with Teresa and her husband, and he stayed at La Mira through the autumn. He continued to contemplate abandoning Italy for England, or for North America or South America. By early December he claimed to be actively preparing to set out for England, but in view of the season and of Allegra's indifferent health he canceled these plans. Teresa and her husband returned to Ravenna in mid-November, and Byron joined them there on Christmas Eve.

He spent the next two years in Ravenna. Cantos 3 and 4 of *Don Juan* were finished and sent to Murray in February 1820, and canto 5 was written the following October and sent to Kinnaird in December.[37] During 1821 he wrote a drama, *The Two Foscari;* started work on another, *Cain;* and completed both *The Vision of Judgement* and *Heaven and Earth. The Vision of Judgement* was subsequently to place his new publisher, John Hunt, in legal difficulties. Teresa left Ravenna for Florence in July, but the following month Byron was joined by Shelley. During a two week stay at Ravenna, Shelley persuaded Byron that they should form an expatriate community at Pisa. Byron was reluctant, but after completing canto 6 of *Don Juan* he finally left for Pisa at the end of October. He arrived on 1 November and settled in the Casa Lanfranchi. Pisa was to be his home for much of 1822, and it was here, early in the year, that his financial position changed once again for the better when Lady Noel died.

Byron heartily disliked his mother-in-law, partly out of personal distaste and partly because her death offered him financial prospects that would relieve the burden of his debts. "So much good would arise from her death," Byron told Kinnaird in May 1819, "that I have little doubt of her immortality. Malice will keep her alive, the bitch is but a bare seventy and a mere minor in longevity." A set of instructions to Kinnaird later in the year included the caustic comment, "[A]sk Lady Noel not to live so very long."[38] Nor did time heal the wounds. In October 1820 Byron complained to Kinnaird, "[T]he bitch will live forever to plague her betters," and in November 1821 he was annoyed that she seemed to be "immortal." When she died Byron admitted to Kinnaird, "I shall not pretend to any violent grief

Byron, by Prepiani, 1819. The original watercolor was given by Byron to Teresa Guiccioli in April 1819. This is a copy of 1860 commissioned by Guiccioli from Giuseppe (Joseph) Fagnani (1819–73). (Private collection.)

for one with whom my acquaintance was neither long nor agreeable."
Kinnaird was disposed to agree: she was, he noted to Byron after her death,
"notoriously a very foolish woman."[39] Crucially for Byron's finances, her
death freed up capital from which he would benefit: Kinnaird was instructed
in December 1821 that his creditors should be content with interest "until
the death of Ly N[oel]—or my own—sets my capital free, or her income at
my disposal, or a part of it."[40] Byron was granted his wish when, on 28
January 1822, Lady Noel died.

Byron's marriage had collapsed in 1816. By modern convention it would
have terminated in divorce with a division of the financial spoils, but the
inexorable logic of English law worked rather differently in the early nineteenth century. Whatever the nature of Byron's marriage and its subsequent breakdown, the agreements signed at the end of 1814 and in the
spring of 1816 remained firmly in place. Byron heard on 15 February 1822
of his mother-in-law's death and, acting on Kinnaird's advice, he immediately adopted the name Noel Byron in accordance with the terms of her
will. Meanwhile Hanson "lost no time in taking the necessary measures to
procure the Crown License for the Assumption of the Noel Name & Arms."[41]
Next, it was necessary under the terms of the separation agreed in 1816 for
Lady Noel's property to be assessed by referees, one appointed by Byron
and one by Annabella, before it could be divided. Byron nominated Sir
Francis Burdett as his referee. Burdett (1770–1844), a radical politician,
was Hobhouse's political sponsor.[42]

The assessment and division of the property was likely to take time,
and Byron was aware that under English property law he had only a marital life interest in the Kirkby Mallory property; in other words, he would
enjoy an income from the estate only while his wife lived. To protect himself against the possibility that she might die in his lifetime, cutting off the
potential income he expected to enjoy from the property, Byron issued
instructions to insure his wife's life for £10,000. His intention was to use
the prospective income from Kirkby Mallory to boost his financial position or, in the event of his wife's death, to use the insurance money for the
same purpose.[43] Consequently, he was far from amused when he heard
from Kinnaird that "I fear much that Lady Byron's is not an insurable life.
She has been living on milk diet for some time." Having set his sights on
this additional income, the prospect of having it whisked away from under
his nose stirred Byron's temper, especially as he feared he might also lose
the annual interest payable on the £9,800 outstanding on her portion.[44] In
fact, this doom-ridden scenario proved to be far too gloomy. Lady Byron's
health was more robust than Kinnaird imagined, and he secured £10,000
on her life in April 1822. Subsequently he, Byron, and Hobhouse discussed
whether this was sufficient. By October they had more or less decided to

raise it to £15,000, and then in November Byron began to talk about £20,000. Kinnaird subsequently raised the insurance to the latter figure in December 1822.[45]

The insurance was important to Byron, but as far as his estranged wife and her widowed father were concerned the key issue was the property division at Kirkby Mallory. Kinnaird was annoyed to hear within days of Lady Noel's funeral that "Lady Byron's trustees expected a great deal of law and hostile proceedings in arranging what is now to be settled on the part of Lord and Lady Byron." Byron was, he insisted, hopeful of settling "on the most amicable and honourable footing," and to this end he had no intention of requesting possession of Kirkby Mallory. Kinnaird learned that neither Lady Byron nor her father wanted to live in the house, which was "in a sad state and will be considered a burden rather than an acquisition," but Hanson still urged Byron not to relinquish his claims to it, because "many circumstances may arise to induce a wish that you had retained the option." Byron was not interested. He was willing to "wa[i]ve any pretension to it." This also ensured that there was no need for him to return to England to settle the business.[46]

The issue to be resolved by the arbitrators really concerned the future management of the property and the division of income from the estate. Byron wanted possession of the property, from which he would pay a suitable annuity to Lady Byron. In his view the arbitration was a simple matter that should be completed in days rather than months, hence his complaint to Kinnaird in April, "[W]hy don't you get on with the arbitration?"[47] Kinnaird was doubtless not amused by this show of naïveté, partly because Byron seemed to have forgotten the 1816 agreement. The two parties had to work together to agree on the income, which was to be divided between Byron and his estranged wife. For his part, Kinnaird had requested and received a rental of the Kirkby Mallory estate, which was the first step toward reaching an agreement. In mid-April Burdett met with Lady Byron's arbitrator, Lord Dacre, to sort out a suitable division of the spoils.

Byron meantime was frustrated by the lack of information reaching him: "[W]hen and how and where are the rents paid, or to be paid, when are they due, or are they ever due . . . I desire illumination," he told Kinnaird in May 1822.[48] By August he was so annoyed with the delays that he rather lamely threatened to refer the whole business to Chancery. When, he asked Kinnaird, could he expect some income from the property, and what was it likely to be? "I do not understand how Lady Noel who died in January can be entitled to rents beyond Lady Day, and I never heard of payments of rents except at Lady Day and Michaelmas. Do you mean to tell me that I should be entitled to the next half year's rent if Lady Byron was to be translated at present?" "I did expect," he told Kinnaird in September, "something better from the Kirkby property than has yet turned out." Kinnaird patiently explained that Lady Noel's "executors neither claim nor are entitled to any rent from and after the day of her death. But rents, unlike dividends from the funds, are not paid, nor by custom payable, till a long period after they become due."[49]

Byron's behavior was unpredictable. To Kinnaird's annoyance he agreed to John Hanson's proposal that his son Charles should be Byron's steward of the Leicestershire estates. "I think," Kinnaird responded, "Mr Hanson's attempt to be appointed your agent one of the most indecent things I ever heard of. He is no more fit for it than to write a 10th Canto to Don Juan." Kinnaird also rejected Byron's argument that Davidson, the current Kirkby steward, should be fired. Byron expressed himself in forcible terms: "I positively object to drunken Davidson," wrote Byron; "what, to sit down and be saddled with two hundred a year for an old superannuated toss-pot of Sir Ralph's; let him go back to Halnaby, as he has got drunk in Sir Ralph's service, let him provide for his liquid necessities." He would not be "saddled . . . with a drunken blackguard"; "Davidson shall not be steward at Kirkby, am I or am I not to have a voice in such matters? if not: the estate shall go into Chancery at once, the appointment of Davidson is an infamous plot to settle him there at my expence." The appointment made him "furious," but Byron's outrage made Kinnaird equally annoyed: "What! not consent to their exercising an equal privilege with yourself of naming a person to look after Lady B's interests?"[50]

Kinnaird's annoyance was partly sparked by the knowledge that whatever aspersions Byron might cast on Davidson's character, a report prepared by Richard Crabtree had shown the property to be in first-class condition. "I hear . . . that the tenants are very good indeed," Kinnaird told Byron in August 1822, "wealthy and capable of managing and paying for the land. Lady Noel, it appears, laid out £4,000 on the estate and it is in excellent order." For his part, Byron told Thomas Moore that the estates "are estimated at seven thousand a year, and rents very well paid, a rare thing at this time. It is, however, owing to their consisting chiefly in pasture lands, and therefore less affected by corn bills, etc., than property in tillage." In fact, the Kirkby Mallory estate turned out to yield £6,336 gross, of which (after deductions) Byron could expect to receive about £2,500 a year. But these were difficult years for farmers, and it was not easy to collect. In August 1822 Byron was already wondering when he would receive some rents from Leicestershire, and by February 1823 he was complaining that he had so far received only £900, of which £600 had been consumed in insurance premiums. During March 1823 he pointed out to Kinnaird that "we have now been a year in presumed possession of Kirkby Mallory," and according to his calculations he ought to have received £1,125, "but we shall see."[51] His pessimism was right: the sum turned out to be £900, just sufficient to pay the premiums on Lady Byron's life insurances and the fees required by the Heralds' Office for changing his name to Noel Byron.

For the first time since he sold Newstead, Byron's interest in landed property filtered through into his poetry. In canto 9 of *Don Juan*, which he wrote in August and September 1822, his frustrations over Kirkby Mallory spilled out into the intrepid hero:

> At least he pays no rent, and has best right
> To be the first of what we used to call
> "Gentlemen Farmers" — a race worn out quite,
> Since lately there have been no rents at all,
> And "gentlemen" are in a piteous plight,
> And "farmers" cant raise Ceres from her fall
> She fell with Buonoparte: What strange thoughts
> Arise, when we see Emperors fall with oats! [52]

In canto 11, written in October 1822, Byron's dual annoyance over the investment of his capital and the shortfall in Kirkby rents was reflected in the lines

> Where are those martyred Saints the Five per Cents?
> And where—oh where the devil are the Rents![53]

The subject of rent played on his mind throughout these months; hence the lines in *The Age of Bronze*, written around the turn of the year 1822–23. Rents, Byron perceived, had been in free fall since Waterloo.

> But where is now the goodly audit ale?
> The purse-proud tenant never known to fail?
> The farm which never yet was left on hand?
> The marsh reclaimed to most improving land?
> The impatient hope of the expiring lease?
> The doubling rental? What an evil's peace![54]

Byron was annoyed that despite his attention to business, he could not make the Kirkby accounts add up, and he asked Hobhouse to double-check his calculations with Kinnaird, since he was concerned that he was not being kept properly informed. From a rental of £6,336, even allowing for the known deductions and the need to divide the surplus with his estranged wife, £900 did not seem very much. He even wondered about selling his interest in the Noel property as a way of at least knowing where he stood financially. Several months later he was still worrying away at the figures. He asked Hobhouse to tell Douglas Kinnaird that I cannot make out from his statement whether the 950 deducted in the first year (1822) from the Kirkby Mallory rental on account of Lady Noel is to return to Lady Byron and to me or no, but whether it is or not, there was still better than £5,000 to divide between Lady B and myself the rental being £6,336 of which in all I have as yet received but nine hundred in two separate payments. There is therefore or ought to be in any case still due to me from the 1822 rental fully sixteen hundred pounds being my balance of two thousand five hundred. . . .[55]

Byron's inquiries continued: Were the tenants at Kirkby paying off their arrears? he asked Kinnaird in October 1823, and again in December and yet again in March 1824. By the time Byron died the following month, £2,000 of arrears had built up.[56]

The death of Lady Noel made one other change to Byron's finances. Sir Ralph Noel agreed to pay £4,000 toward Annabella's portion, the sum over and above the £16,000 that he had been required to make available for her in 1814. The money was paid in August 1822 and, as the terms of the marriage settlement demanded, invested by Kinnaird in 3 percent consols. Byron was not amused: "Why the deuce did you lodge the 4000 in the funds now, when they are at 80? could not one have got exchequer bills or some other security pro tempore. . . ." "Do not be afraid of the funds till I tell you," Kinnaird responded.[57] The transaction still left £9,800 outstanding on Annabella's portion, and this was unpaid when Byron died.

IV

While the Kirkby Mallory estate was being sorted out, Byron heard good news from Rochdale. As lord of the manor he received the market tolls, but these amounted to only about £12 a year. In November 1820 he told Kinnaird that he had received a representation from the town "to permit a new market place." He sent the relevant papers to Kinnaird for an opinion, adding that "I am full of philanthropy but must maintain my Manorial rights. Read, perpend, pronounce, or ask Spooney."[58] The intention was to enlarge the market in view of the additional business being generated in the fast-growing township. Hanson expected the Rochdale authorities to offer either to lease or buy the duties: "[I]t seems that I may obtain two thousand pounds more or less for permission to the town to take toll for the new Market place." Byron was too wise to Hanson's ways to expect to make £2,000 from the transaction, although he told Kinnaird that even if it was only £1,000 or even £100, "they be monies." The bill went through Parliament in May 1822, and Byron was eventually paid £500, which he considered to be "better than nothing." The money was paid to Hanson and assigned by Kinnaird in part payment of his outstanding legal bill.[59]

As for the news Byron really wanted to hear about Rochdale, silence once again descended after 1818. Hanson assured him that Dearden was desperate to win the case; indeed, he had been so anxious prior to the 1818 hearing

> not to lose the possession of his purchase that he had a person in readiness to set off immediately to your Lordship at Venice in case the decision of the Court of Exchequer had been against them to strike a bargain with your Lordship for the property to prevent any other person from getting it so little did they expect the decision would have been in their favour, but Mr Dearden should account for profits he has made before he is allowed to treat as a purchaser.[60]

Encouraged by Hanson's view of Dearden's commitment, in March 1822 Byron asked both Hanson and Kinnaird (in separate letters), "[W]ould not Dearden, think you, come to some terms without going through with the Appeal?"[61] Over subsequent months Byron continued to inquire occasionally if there was any further news of the Rochdale case. Hanson did not respond, and Byron started to worry that this was because he could not expect a fair hearing before the lord chancellor, Lord Eldon.[62] His concerns about Lord Eldon stretched back to the days when he attended the House of Lords, and two incidents stood out in his mind. One was his 1812 speech in the House of Lords in defense of the Luddites: "I spoke very violent sentences with a sort of modest impudence, abused every thing & every body, & put the Ld. Chancellor very much out of humour."[63] The other occasion was during a debate in the Lords on Catholic Emancipation when Byron was "sent for in great haste to a Ball which I quitted I confess somewhat reluctantly to emancipate five Millions of people." His appearance behind the Woolsack was spotted by Eldon, who recognized that the cause was lost.[64]

Byron decided that the matter could not be resolved in the courts while Eldon remained as lord chancellor, and in an attempt to break the deadlock he decided on a change of tactics. In November 1822 he sent Kinnaird "an open letter for Mr Deardon of Rochdale, which I request you to forward, and after perusing it to do all you can to forward an accommodation. I want the lawsuit concluded or off my mind." It was, he added subsequently, "a conciliatory gesture" reflecting a willingness on his part to "sacrifice any remote contingent or possible advantage." Kinnaird was impressed: the letter was "admirable," and he had sent it straight on to Lancashire—"it is excellent and cannot do harm."[65]

The letter was as honest as Byron felt he could be. It was, he stressed, written without taking legal advice:

> You and I have been now eighteen years at law with various success. I succeeded in two decisions and you in one. The appeal is now before the House of Lords. Of the original occasion of this suit I have no knowledge since I inherited it and was a child when it began and for aught I know may arrive at second childhood before it terminates.

Could they, he continued, ignore the lawyers, and try to find "an accommodation . . . either by arbitration or a mutual agreement"? He wanted to avoid further anxiety "to both sides"; indeed, he was willing to dispense with the undisputed part of the manor, "because I wish to invest the profit of that as well as other monies abroad since I do not reside in England and have thoughts of permanently settling in Italy or elsewhere."[66] While he awaited a response, Byron thought further of the Rochdale issue: "[I]s there no way," he asked Kinnaird,

> by which either in disposing of my part of the manor, or of having it surveyed and working the whole in partnership with [Dearden] he making some sacrifice also on his part of uniting the concern and healing all differences? I should be willing to make some outlay, were there any prospect of the collieries (of the unworked portion) being a safe and moderately profitable concern.[67]

Dearden did not take long to frame his reply, which he sent directly to Byron with a copy to Kinnaird in London. Dearden proposed to meet Kinnaird in London, because "I am free to admit that I am desirous of obtaining a release from the long litigation in which his Lordship and I have unfortunately for us both been so long engaged." Although Dearden was too ill to attend the proposed meeting, Kinnaird met with his son and brother-in-law on two occasions before Christmas, and they agreed that Byron's Leicestershire agent, Richard Crabtree, should go to Rochdale to value the property.[68] All this took place before Dearden's letter reached Byron early in January 1823. Byron, writing to Kinnaird, noted several material errors and concluded that "neither he nor I can be proper judges of the value, nor fit surveyors of the part in or out of litigation. The value of the unlitigated part, a manor of 40,000 acres, over uninclosed ground, depends also in some measure on the part to be allotted to the Lord of the Manor, in case of enclosure, and you know that they cannot enclose without this sanction." Byron questioned Dearden's recall of the legal suit, and noted that "he has uniformly refused to account for or state the profits of the last twenty-five years, the time from which the *claim* relates." Despite such cavils, Byron was still anxious to reach a settlement, and to this end was willing to have the property surveyed: "I would rather take Mr Deardon by the hand (at some expense) than go on with bickering lawsuits."[69]

Having expressed his views privately, Byron replied to Dearden, a letter for which he again requested Kinnaird's approval. He suggested that they each nominate a "friend" to arbitrate between them. For his part Byron proposed Sir Francis Burdett "or at any rate not a gentleman of the law." Once the valuation was complete they could consider selling the manor or, alternatively, they could enter into an agreement to become "joint proprietors of the whole" and, as such, to prospect for minerals on the property and to promote an enclosure: "[I]n case of there being any probability of the remainder of the manor being capable of being worked for coal with prospects of profit, I would of course make the requisite outlay on my part; always premising that this was previously justified by the report of the surveyors." Byron even suggested that he might return to England to complete the negotiations. Kinnaird assured him that would be unnecessary.[70]

For some weeks subsequently the subject of Rochdale was clearly never far from Byron's mind. "I am very anxious," he complained to Kinnaird on 24 February 1823, "to hear that you have received and forwarded my letter to Mr Deardon . . . as your not mentioning it keeps me not only in the uncertainty of its arrival, but of whether I am or am not to go to England to meet him." Three days later the same subject was still on his mind: "I confess I could wish that something was done with Deardon, what will he give for the Manor? It must produce something." Two days later he urged Kinnaird, "[D]o not forget Deardon's affair," and on 5 March he again wanted to know if Kinnaird had received the Dearden letter. He asked Hobhouse to find out from Kinnaird whether the letter had arrived. Eventually on 2 April he received Kinnaird's reply, sent on 21 March, from which he learned that nothing more would happen until Crabtree had been to Rochdale.[71]

Byron turned his thoughts once more towards the sale of his interests in Lancashire. If Dearden would buy them he was happy to take "a little . . . now, than more at another time," even if the sum was "scanty in proportion to it's actual value." As he had by now set his face towards Greece, more or less any sum would be helpful and the proceeds could be added to redeemed bonds and other outstanding credit. Information from Kinnaird was slow to arrive, to Byron's disgust—"I have neither time nor inclination to scold about it"—and when he did receive a letter in mid-April 1823 he was by no means pleased to find that Crabtree had yet to set out for Rochdale:

I merely want to hear the result, and settle the business, time and disappointments have made my expectations very moderate; but it is hard with

Deardon's wish to finish the affair and mine also that I cannot get a statement of any kind. Six months have now elapsed since I first wrote but . . .
with the exception of your and Mr Deardon's first epistle, every day seems
to put the period further off than it was before reversing the usual progress
of time.[72]

Kinnaird took the view—probably correctly—that not all his letters were
reaching Byron, but by late May Crabtree had been to Rochdale and the
results of his negotiations were favorable:

I have to congratulate you on the result of Mr Crabtree's proceedings with
Mr Deardon. I have agreed to receive £11,250 for your Rochdale property
and the suit into the bargain. This has been effected, I am quite satisfied,
solely by the spirit in which your letter was written and in which the negotiations has been carried on between us. The lawyers have had nothing to
do with it. . . .[73]

Kinnaird was too optimistic, since negotiations on the price continued for
some months. In August he told Byron he was likely to get between £10,000
and £12,000, and "we shall have done very well to get so much." The letter
reached Byron, by now in Cephalonia, only on 12 October, when he hurriedly scribbled a note on the end of a letter to Augusta asking her to tell
Kinnaird that he approved of the proposal, although he would like a greater
sum. He wrote to Kinnaird two days later, accepting the low price: "It is
probably less than a more skilful or lucky personage than myself might
have obtained, but anything is better than such a litigation, and as you have
full powers of attorney to act for me you can settle as soon as you please."[74]
Byron repeated the same message to Hobhouse for onward transmission to
Kinnaird, and a few days later he reiterated to Kinnaird that his only hope
was that "you will make the best of the business for me that you can."
Kinnaird was not inactive, but it was only on 2 November that he wrote to
confirm a sale price of £11,225.[75] In the end the price was finalized at
£11,250, and Dearden agreed to pay any outstanding legal bills of
Hanson's.[76] Byron happily concurred.

What sort of a deal had Kinnaird and Crabtree negotiated? The agreement was reached by circumventing Hanson, who was kept in the dark
until very late in the negotiations; indeed, he was still charging for his legal
work on the case even when Byron was negotiating behind his back.[77] Although Byron had given joint powers to Kinnaird and Hanson when he left
England in 1816, it was increasingly Kinnaird who had taken over dealing
with his financial affairs. A split with Hanson had long been in the cards,
but even Kinnaird had recognized the importance of avoiding such a final
move while Hanson remained tied up in his legal business: "[Y]ou know,"

he reminded Byron in April 1823, "that I have always told you that until I could see my way clearly through the Rochdale business I would not advise an open rupture with the Messrs. Hansons, although I have never disguised, nor obtruded, my opinion of those gentlemen in the character of your solicitors."[78] He had certainly made no effort to disguise his view; indeed, in letter after letter Kinnaird took the opportunity to warn Byron from having more than cursory dealings with the lawyer,[79] and he was delighted to be able to complete the Rochdale deal without his aid. Unfortunately, he could not dispense with Hanson's services altogether. In late May 1823 he reported to Byron that "at this moment I am writing to Hanson to prepare the title, but he knows nothing of the price." Hanson, who was still pressing on with the appeal to the House of Lords, was in for something of a surprise.[80]

We do not know how Hanson reacted to finding himself circumvented in this way, but Kinnaird's account of his own conduct needs to be treated with care. Kinnaird told Byron that "Mr Deardon was worried out of his life by the suit and jumped at an opportunity of closing the suit, of which he never had a hope as long as the Hansons had to do with it." Hanson was marching to a different tune. He was well aware that Dearden did not think he could win the case, and it had always been his view that the estate would sell for very little as long as litigation was ongoing. Even Kinnaird admitted that "Hanson did not value it, or expect to get for it above £6,000."[81] Since he believed Byron stood to gain a great deal by an appeal to the House of Lords, Hanson continued to press the case, and in any case he had no reason to take any other course of action, because he had not been instructed otherwise by Byron. Kinnaird's justification for accepting such a low price was carefully framed in a letter to Byron in which he claimed to have established two salient points. One was that Farebrother, the auctioneer, had assured him that there had been no bona fide bid for Rochdale above £10,000, and the other was that "Crabtree fished out of Deardon's brother-in-law that he would at that time have given £10,000 but not a sixpence more."[82] Kinnaird seems to have forgotten that in 1819 Farebrother had told him £17,000 had been bid for Rochdale.[83]

It is at least arguable that Kinnaird sold Byron short. In his anxiety to circumvent Hanson and to bring about a conclusion to the long-running legal battle, he agreed on behalf of Byron to drop the legal case—which Dearden expected to lose—in return for a purchase price only marginally above the highest genuine bid (if indeed £10,000 was the highest bid) made at the 1815 auction. This was not how Kinnaird saw things: he was simply elated that "you need have no more of lawyers," and "thank God we shall have no more law expenses." Subsequently he expressed a wish that Byron and Dearden would have met twelve years earlier, and joined in sorting things out, "as well as saving thousands in law expenses." Be that as it may, tying up the loose ends took longer than anticipated, and the papers were still unsigned when Byron died in April 1824. Byron had no opportunity to alter his will, in which Rochdale had been left to Hanson and Hobhouse as trustees, and the property was legally released from any claims they may have had over it only in 1828.[84]

V

With the Rochdale business we have run ahead of Byron's life in Italy. By the time Lady Noel died he was established in Pisa, and it was here that he lived for much of 1822. Naturally, he was devastated to hear in April of the death of Allegra, and he was further distressed in July when Shelley drowned in a boating accident. He was again contemplating travel, despite apparently being happily settled with Teresa. Byron considered, alternately, moving on to Greece or going to South America, but he was still in Pisa when Hobhouse joined him for a few days in September. While in Pisa he resumed writing *Don Juan*. He also had a splendid boat built, the *Bolivar*, although he took little interest in it subsequently. By August, in the wake of Shelley's death, he was preparing to leave Pisa for Genoa—although still with longer-term hopes of traveling further afield. Late in September he finally left Pisa, and a few days later he arrived at what was to be his last Italian home in Genoa. Teresa, with her father and brother, lived with him; and Mary Shelley, together with Leigh Hunt, his wife, and their six children, also traveled from Pisa to set up home close by.

To Byron's friends in Italy who knew nothing of the complications over Rochdale or of the size of his debts, the Noel inheritance and the Rochdale market agreement presaged financial salvation well beyond their limited means: "Lord Byron is a rich, a still richer man," noted Shelley. Living in Italy free of income tax, and with an apparently steady stream of sterling coming in his direction, the image of a wealthy aristocrat was clearly warranted.[85] Yet they must have been surprised that this influx of wealth made him, if anything, less generous than in the past. Even before Lady Noel's death Byron recognized that he was financially quite well off,[86] but ironically this seems simply to have made him more, rather than less, careful when it came to working out his accounts, although it did not prevent numerous small, local acts of charity on his part.

Kinnaird's work on his behalf was scrutinized with great care. On 24 August 1822 Byron accused him of siphoning off money for unknown causes. He ought to have remitted £2,525, the interest on the marriage portion, together with £190 from the Noel interest, but he had sent only

£2,400—"what have you done with those parings?" This, together with a series of other questions, was sent off to London with the request, "Reply, please your honour, on these financial matters." Kinnaird did, with "a copy of your account for last year and this year. You will thereby see what has been done with your monies." He was not, in other words, rising to the bait.[87] Subsequently Kinnaird was instructed to invest £1,000 from Byron's income in exchequer bills, and to set aside up to a further £1,000 toward debt repayment. He was also reprimanded for being insufficiently careful in detailing for Byron the state of his accounts. Byron then wrote to say, "I could wish to know exactly or nearly the probable state or rather statement of my budget in the ensuing year," and he added his own calculations. For 1823 he had calculated that he should receive £3,168 from the Kirkby Mallory estate, £2,715 "my own," £2,100 from Murray "for the 4 new Cantos and the volume already in press," making a total of £7,983. With £4,000 currently in the bank, he expected a surplus of £2,000 in 1822, which would give him £9,983 in 1823. Should his wife die, he would lose the Kirkby income, but he would be the gainer by £500 a year (interest on her unpaid portion) and a lump sum from the insurance on her life. It was a rather more accurate calculation than the methodology he used at Newstead prior to his engagement in 1814, but two weeks later he prepared a further list, this time estimating his 1823 assets at £12,825. Byron was happy to admit "my avarice" to Kinnaird.[88]

When, toward the end of September 1822, he received from Kinnaird "the banking account of assets and disbursements," although he complained of being "still ignorant of the sum total of my remaining bond debts" (which he thought were about £2,400) the detail was sufficient to enable him to draw up a further series of calculations:

> Besides your late credit of £2,000 in advance (which I do not mean to touch unless in some emergency) I have still £1,700 in your former circulars, and £1,200 in ditto lately received in all £2,900—also in the hands of Messrs. Webb of Leghorn £630 sterling (£3,580 in all between you) and about three or four hundred pounds cash in the house—total about £4,000—more or less.

From this he proposed to set aside £1,000 to pay for his move to Genoa, but he could not count on the other £3,000 as surplus because he had been "foolish enough to build a slight Schooner, which was to have cost £300 but which eventually cost nearly £800, her expences since . . . say about £180 sterling per annum including men's wages and sundries." This was the *Bolivar*. He had also given money to Leigh Hunt. Even so, he expected in 1823 to be well in surplus, and "if I knew pretty nearly what I was likely to have in all I could then settle with you how much debt we can afford to liquidate." "The moment I know the exact amount of outstanding demands, and also of probable assets," he added in October 1822, "I will tell you what to pay and what I wish done with the remainder, for I am economizing, have sold three horses and pay all bills in person, keeping a sharp look out, on the candle's ends." In this way he could see an end to repaying his debts, which Kinnaird had told him were "hardly two thousand pounds." "I suppose that you will laugh at all my pecuniary plans, but after having known the miseries of embarrassments, it is natural to try to provide against their recurrence."[89] Some of the immediacy of Byron's requests was lost on Kinnaird, who spent much of October 1822 in Paris.[90]

The flow of information back to Kinnaird was remorseless during the autumn of 1822. Perhaps ironically, Kinnaird congratulated him on being "so accurate a financier," and hoped that none of the sources of income he had detailed would fail.[91] Kinnaird must certainly have found the intensity of Byron's business letters sat uneasily with his lack of interest in such matters while he was in England and his admission in 1817 to Scrope Davies that he was not interested in matters of business. In late November 1822 Byron was back to an old theme: "[I]t is my intention when assets are at a certain height to liquidate the remaining debt but it is best to have double funds in hand first. About June [1823] if you have three thousand pounds of mine in hand, you can pay five or six hundred, and so on, in proportion, till the whole two thousand, or thereabouts . . . are liquidated. . . . I have carried my own economy into effect hitherto, even better than I expected. I have laid up my Schooner in the Arsenal (which stops that expence of wages &c) reduced my establishment, sold some horses, and mean to sell another, thereby keeping five instead of ten, and I wish if possible to live as simply as need be for some years though not sordidly. You will smile at all this tirade upon business, but it is time to mind it, at least for me to mind it, for without some method in it where or what is independence?" Unfortunately the figures were spoilt somewhat when on 10 December Hanson produced for Kinnaird a further list of Byron's debts, including £40 to a butcher near Newstead and several hundred pounds on an annuity raised before his coming of age. However, Kinnaird was "really and sincerely glad that you are taking the trouble to look after and understand your own affairs."[92]

Although Byron admitted on 30 November to Kinnaird that he had "lately written to you reams upon business," he started again the next day: "I cannot approve the paying away of considerable sums at once, which might leave me out of cash and consequently liable to incur new debts." In mid-December, perhaps fearing that not all his letters would arrive, Byron laid out the whole situation again:

I am living very economically. . . . I had calculated that with the surplus of this year (now in Coffers) the £6,000 and upwards (your computation) of the Kirkby and funds productions, that could you have sold the D[on] J[uans] tolerably and "Werner" bore a decent value, I should not have had less on the whole then twelve or even fourteen thousand pounds, as it is there are £9,000, aye nearly ten, i.e. £6,465 (your own account of the year 1823 and quarter of 1822 from Kirkby *added* of *course* to my own from the funds) also five hundred pounds from the Rochdale tolls, and my saving of three thousand three hundred pounds. From this of course must be deducted first the insurances, the remaining debt, and Hanson's remaining account, but I cannot decide what or how much I shall pay, till I know what we have to receive. I will do my best to live on a thousand or twelve hundred pounds per annum till I have realized. My present ordinary expenses do not in fact amount to *half* that sum.

Such attention to business was now the order of Byron's day—"I cast up my household accounts, and settle them daily myself."[93] "I am anxious," he reminded Kinnaird, "to get a few thousand pounds together, to pay off remaining debt, and invest any little remnant for my sister's family after my demise." He had suggested in October that she might move to Nice, where he would join her. Despite his offer to pay her traveling expenses, she did not take up the proposal.[94]

Through the winter of 1822–23, Byron continued with *Don Juan*. Cantos 10 to 12 were complete by December 1822, and cantos 13 to 15 by March 1823. Despite his literary activity, the stream of letters to Kinnaird, often repetitive in content, continued. Byron was reducing his expenses, reorganizing his household, and restructuring his finances in order to build up a surplus and at the same time pay his debts in an orderly manner. He calculated his savings for 1822 at £3,300, and insisted that Kinnaird could "depend on my using every exertion short of sordid to continue the temperate system which I have lately adopted . . . I think you will allow that the better half of the year 1822 I have been not unsuccessful." Byron could not resist justifying his actions: "You will perhaps wonder," he remarked to Kinnaird in January 1823,

at this recent and furious fit of accumulation and retrenchment, but it is not so unnatural. I am not naturally ostentatious, although once careless and expensive because careless, and my most extravagant passions have pretty well subsided, as it is time that they should on the very verge of thirty five.

Carelessness had been replaced by a love of "lucre, for one must love something."[95]

At the end of January 1823 he prepared to send Kinnaird £1,200 to invest in exchequer bills (£1,000) and use for debt repayment (£200). Additional interest due on his invested income would raise the latter figure to £500, "the whole of which may go to pay off any debts of mine still extant." The acknowledged debtors included Baxter, Hanson, and Widow Mealey, but he still disputed others, which he was not willing to recognize "till fully proved." After a long list of instructions he finally decided not to send the £1,200 but to wait and see if Kinnaird agreed with his proposals. When Kinnaird seemed to be unreasonably long in responding, Byron proposed the postponement of further debt payments and liquidations until the autumn or winter of 1823, since income from the Noel estate had failed to come up to expectations. A few days later the postponement was lengthened again to "probably for a year," as a result of the poor returns from the Noel estate:

> From my own income I have saved about £3,000 or better, but this must be kept in reserve to meet emergencies and usual expences. As soon as I have realized a sufficient sinking fund, I will pay the remaining creditors, a great deal has already been paid, as you know. The rest must wait. I do not choose to leave myself bare. Every sixpence which can be saved (after deducting my requisite credits with your bank) must be paid out in Exchequer bills, or at other interest, and that interest again at Compound interest, we shall then soon be able to cover the interest of Baxter's bond.[96]

In April 1823 he assured Hobhouse that he was "pretty well off. I have still a surplus of three thousand pounds of last year's income, a thousand pounds in exchequer bills in England, and by this time, as also in July, there ought to be further monies paid to my account in Kinnaird's bank."[97]

One debtor was a source of more trouble than most, and this was John Hanson. Byron's complaint as far as Hanson was concerned was that his bill was never presented in the itemized manner he anticipated. In 1813 Byron had given him £2,700 on account, and following the Newstead transaction another £5,000. To check that Hanson's claims were valid, Byron asked him to submit a properly itemized bill, but this apparently proved impossible. "Upon one point I insist," Byron told Kinnaird in October 1820, "and that is that he sends in his account. If not, at all risks, losses or hazards I will withdraw my affairs out of his hands, and this I beg you to state for and from me in plain and peremptory English." To Hanson he wrote in much the same terms: "[I]t is also surprising that you have never sent in your account to Mr Kinnaird; if it is not sent, how can we ever come to any final settlement?"[98] It did not appear. "Now surely," Byron told Kinnaird in September 1821, "we should have a bill before further payments." In September 1822 he told Kinnaird, "Do pray get Hanson's bill . . . I must really break with him if he don't send them in." He told Charles Hanson in November 1822 that "for years after years I have been urging for these accounts." He noted that in the aftermath of the Newstead sale "many thousands have been paid to you, and all on an unpresented account." "I am willing," he added, "and indeed desirous to settle accounts between us, if you will but present them to Mr D Kinnaird to be looked over as is usual I am told in all such transactions." He sent the letter to London via Kinnaird, and asked, "[H]ow much has Hanson had in all? and how much ought he to have?" In fact, Byron knew already that the sum the Hansons had received was nearly £8,000.[99]

The key issue was how much money was still outstanding. "I should be glad to know what he would have further, or what he is really entitled to have," Byron said to Kinnaird, "otherwise there seems to be no end to his demands. . . . I must and will have a regular account of the whole of his bill audited by a professional man of your choosing. It may not be my interest and it is not my wish to quarrel with him, but better do anything than have thousands asked for yearly without a bill or account to show for it."[100] Subsequently Hanson did submit a bill, which Byron examined with some care. He wrote to Kinnaird in January 1823: "Has Hanson's bill since 1817 received any liquidation, is it the £1,400 that I have to pay? or the balance of 6 or 700 as mentioned in your former letters as about the whole now due. Pray clear this up—an important point." Hanson had kept the £500 from the Rochdale tolls toward his bill—he had also charged £130 for his professional services in acquiring the £500—but Byron remained unclear about what he owed the lawyer. He asked Kinnaird in February 1823, "[I]s it the outstanding balance which is £600 or what? is this after the payment of the 500 R[ochdale] money, or before?"[101]

Kinnaird's view was that whichever figure was correct, it was too much: "If you correspond directly with Messrs. Hanson who take care to write to you without consulting me, recollect you are incurring a large annual bill . . . I can have no wish but to save your money from being thus squandered." By July Kinnaird was ever more forceful on this particular subject:

> I consider that the elder Hanson will never be able to show, if he ever should even make a claim against you. He never has delivered an account, and has confessed he could not make one out against you. He has to my knowledge received about £8000 from you without any account.

However, Hanson's bill remained unsettled shortly before Byron's death.[102] Hobhouse told him that "no more money will be paid to Hanson than he can fairly demand, and I hope that is none at all. The great thing is to get out of his books and to have done with him. I think it is well you did not lose your whole estate by him."[103]

Byron's attention to business in these months was remarkable. As a young man he wrote several poems about Newstead, but from the time of the first abortive sale of 1812 all reference to the estate, or more broadly to land and the concerns of a landed aristocrat, disappear from his work. The business of running an estate, collecting rents, and handling tenants was sufficiently alien to Byron that it did not feature in his poetry until 1822 when, in the wake of Lady Noel's death, he was once again a landowner with an interest in rents. In fact, he found himself in a position he had not previously experienced. From the time he inherited Newstead in 1798 wartime conditions were such that rents everywhere were rising. While he lacked the courage to raise the Newstead rents in 1811, Claughton showed no such sentiment after 1812. Yet, just as Claughton forfeited on the Newstead deal in 1814 when rents were no longer rising and postwar prospects were gloomy, so Byron in 1822 came for the first time face to face with falling rents and gloomy agricultural conditions, offset only by the relatively prosperous conditions enjoyed by his newly inherited tenants in pastoral Leicestershire. Perhaps it was because through 1822 and the early months of 1823 Byron was immersed in business matters to a degree he had never previously attained that his thoughts returned to Newstead in the later cantos of *Don Juan*. Perhaps for the first time what he had done by selling the ancestral home caught up with him; we cannot know.

11

Greece, Glory, and
Financial Security

While he was living in Genoa during the spring of 1823 Byron received a number of English visitors. They included Henry Fox, son of Lord Holland, and Lord and Lady Blessington with the French dandy Count d'Orsay. Lady Blessington had been anxious to meet Byron, and they conversed frequently over a period of two months.[1] These visitors provided Byron with interesting diversions, but in the longer term Byron's most significant callers came on 5 April. On that day he met two men whose conversation profoundly influenced the rest of his life. One was a young Irishman, Edward Blaquiere, who was one of the most active members of the London Greek Committee and who was on his way to Greece to investigate the state of affairs in the country on behalf of the committee. The other visitor was Andreas Luriottis, who was returning home to Greece from a visit to London to enlist support for the Greek uprising against the Turks. Byron was happy to meet them; indeed, he had told Blaquiere prior to their rendezvous that "I shall be delighted to see you and your Greek friend, and the sooner the better." He had been expecting them "for some time," and was anxious for news of events in Greece: "I cannot express to you how much I feel interested in the cause." The two men confirmed in Byron a lingering belief that his future lay in Greece: within hours or at most days he had made up his mind to break with Teresa, to quit Genoa, and to set forth to Greece. And he intended to support the Greek cause financially: "[Y]ou must be aware that it would not do to go without means into a country where means are so much wanted," he told Kinnaird.[2]

I

Since the fifteenth century Greece had been under Ottoman (Turkish) rule. A small Greek nationalist movement developed toward the end of the eighteenth century, and in 1814 Prince Alexander Ypsilantis (1792–1828) founded a secret nationalist organization, the Society of Friends. He recruited members among Greeks living abroad, and he began to plan an uprising. As a former general in the Russian army, he was well aware of the tension that existed between Turkey and Russia. The Russians had aspirations regarding Constantinople, which they saw as a gateway to Asia and the Black Sea. Consequently, he counted on the tsar's backing in the event of an uprising. The Greek cause also attracted sympathizers elsewhere in Europe. Members of the Philhellenic movement (scholars and intellectuals who had become passionately interested in classical Greece) gave their backing to the Greeks, viewing their resistance as a modern crusade for Christianity and independence against Turkish oppression of the birthplace of Western civilization. Hobhouse and Byron were naturally sympathetic. Both still had vivid memories of their visit to Greece during their European tour of 1809–11, and Byron's reputation as a poet was largely fashioned from *Childe Harold's Pilgrimage,* which he had written as a result of these travels.

Prince Alexander's preparations led in 1821 to a nationalist uprising, but neither the Romanians nor the Russians, both of whom he was counting on for support, came out in favor of the Greeks. The revolt was crushed, but the Greek spirit had been aroused, and subsequently uprisings against the Turks broke out in mainland Greece and on several Aegean islands. The brutality of the Turks in putting down these revolts appalled Western liberal thinkers. In 1822 the Turks massacred or enslaved the Greek population of the island of Chios, after executing the patriarch of Constantinople in his ecclesiastical robes on Easter Sunday 1821. Undaunted, and with no more than token support from elsewhere in Europe, the Greeks held out almost alone, aided by money and volunteers. Byron and Shelley were prominent in their espousal of the Greek cause.

News of the Greek uprising quickly spread through Europe, and Philhellenic societies and committees were formed to offer support. Hobhouse, visiting Byron in September 1822, discussed with him the foundation of a committee that would raise financial support for Greece. The "London Greek Committee" was set up in February 1823. Both Hobhouse and Kinnaird were members, and on 12 May Byron heard that on Hobhouse's recommendation he had also been elected a member. By then he had met Blaquiere, and he was actively planning to return to the country he had so much enjoyed visiting with Hobhouse during his earlier travels. Hobhouse had probably wanted Byron on the London Greek Committee only for his moral support and his reputation, but Byron was prepared to make his wealth as well as his person available to the Greeks. Hobhouse was disposed to encourage him: "[Y]our appearing among these poor fellows will have a great and beneficial effect." Having made up his mind that this was a cause that deserved his full support, Byron finished cantos 15 and 16 of *Don Juan*. He sent them to Kinnaird with instructions to find a new publisher, since he had fallen out with Murray. The break with Murray occurred on the publisher's part because he was embarrassed by *Don Juan*, and on Byron's part because of Murray's alleged meanness over royalties. Byron then began to plan his journey and his—necessary—break with Teresa.[3]

Byron was not destined to be a military hero, but he was in a position to help fund the Greek cause, and after the austerity of 1822–23 came a new liberal open-handedness as he planned his Greek adventure. Hobhouse instructed Kinnaird as to how he could open a credit for Byron in Greece, and Kinnaird forwarded £4,000 to him in Genoa. "Tell Douglas," Byron wrote in a letter to Hobhouse, "that when anything is settled I will let him know what sum I should like to take in Credit and on what houses." Writing two days later direct to Kinnaird, Byron proposed taking about £5,000 in credits with him. Fortunately, Kinnaird had anticipated his need and increased the credits en route to Genoa to £6,000.[4] During his closing weeks in Italy Byron was also replenishing his wardrobe for this latest and, as it transpired, last journey.[5]

Hobhouse's view was that a simple appearance by Byron in Greece would be sufficient: "I do not see the necessity of your staying long. . . . A few days or weeks in the Morea would be quite sufficient. . . . the Greeks here say they think your going to Greece would be of the utmost possible service to the cause." He added that the London Committee lacked the funding to do a great deal for the Greeks, and therefore the most they could offer was encouragement and sympathy, "of which no proof would be so decisive as your visit." By contrast, Byron had rather more ambitious plans, hence his request for money from London. He also began making preparations, including the purchase of medical stores for a thousand men for two years.[6] He told Kinnaird that he was anxious to have as much money available as possible, but "I should not like to overdraw, and yet may have occasion for all the means that I can muster, as I should not like to give the Greeks but a *half helping* hand, but rather aid them as much as I can." He was aware, partly from what he heard locally about the Greek cause, that funds were in short supply.[7]

By the time Byron was ready to set out Kinnaird had made available nearly £9,000 in cash and credits, and on 16 July, after two false starts, he set sail aboard the *Hercules*.[8] With him went five horses and two canoes, ten thousand Spanish dollars in cash, and bills of exchange from Kinnaird for forty thousand more. Byron's entourage included his business manager, Lega Zambelli, and the ever reliable Fletcher. After stopping briefly at Leghorn, he landed at Argostoli on the island of Cephalonia, off the west coast of the Greek mainland, on 3 August, where he was met by the British

Resident, Sir Charles James Napier. After spending some days exploring the island, in early September he took a house at Metaxata in southwest Cephalonia. The area was relatively safe, as it was legally British territory.[9] He settled down to try to find out exactly what was going on in Greece, particularly to try to assess the differing claims of the various factions who were competing for his own funds, and also those being gathered together by the London Greek Committee. He recruited a group of Souliote Pallikars as his suite.

Ironically, given Byron's checkered financial history, he found the Greeks anxious to have him as a figurehead in their struggle with the Turks, at least in part because they believed he would provide a significant portion of the funding. Byron responded positively. All his remaining creditors were relegated to a waiting list as he plunged his financial energies into battle. In July 1823 Kinnaird proposed paying off Baxter, the last of the bond creditors, but Byron would have none of it. "Tell Douglas Kinnaird," he wrote to Hobhouse from Metaxata on 27 September 1823,

> that except the payments to keep up the insurances, he must not let any monies of mine be converted to Hanson's or others' purposes . . . but to keep everything in bank for the Credits of mine of the present and ensuing year. Of all things to do anything amongst these fellows money is the most essential, and I have no wish to spare mine, though I will not allow a six-pence to be expended except to a public purpose, and under my own eye.[10]

Writing to Hobhouse a few days later Byron again urged him to encourage Kinnaird "to muster all my possible monies, as well for the present, as for the ensuing year, that I may take the field in force in case it should be proper or prospective of Good that I should do so." His open-handedness was not always matched by the ability of his bankers to convert credit notes and bills of exchange into ready cash, although the situation eased when Charles Hancock, an English merchant living in Cephalonia, and his part-ner Samuel Barff, who lived on the neighboring island of Zante, agreed to act as his bankers and to cash his bills of exchange. Byron also met Greek representatives on their way to England in search of an £800,000 loan.[11]

Byron had sufficient cash for the present, but he was less well served in terms of relevant intelligence. British, Greek, and other sources pro-vided him with a range of conflicting and contrasting information that was not easily interpreted. He gained the impression that the military was un-trustworthy, and he grew suspicious of the patriotic behavior of the Greeks, partly because he found a series of so-called provisional governments, to-gether with lesser bodies and individual chiefs, all claiming to embody the true spirit of Greek independence. Certainly he found them all more than ready to beat a path to the door of a wealthy English aristocrat whose funds they wished to deploy in their own preferred way. The petty rivalries they displayed annoyed Byron and led him to distrust the Greek leaders. To Prince Alexander Mavrocordatos he wrote on 2 December of how "it pains me exceedingly to hear that the internal dissensions of Greece still continue . . . if Greece wants to become forever free, true, and independent she had better decide now, or never again will she have the chance, never again."[12] He also found the unruly behavior of his Souliote warriors troublesome.

Byron gathered much of his information about events in Greece from James Hamilton-Browne, a Greek-speaking Scotsman who had traveled with him on the *Hercules* from Leghorn. After Byron settled at Metaxata, Hamilton-Browne went with Edward Trelawny, who had also traveled with him from Italy, to the Morea in order to make a fuller assessment of Greek affairs. Both sent back positive reports, and in November Hamilton-Browne returned with the Greek deputies John Orlandos and Andreas Luriottis, who negotiated with Byron a loan of £4,000 from his funds.[13] He anticipated being reimbursed in England by the London Greek Committee. With the money the navy was revitalized, and a squad of fourteen armed merchantmen from Hydra sailed to Missolonghi, attacked the Turks, and chased their scattered vessels to the neutral waters of Zante. Prince Mavrocordatos, who had been on board one of the Greek ships, disembarked on 11 December and established an administration at Missolonghi, on the mainland of Greece. Byron's money could, it appeared, be put to good use, and he christened the scholarly prince the George Washington of Greece.

Prince Mavrocordatos invited Byron to join him, and despite forebodings and misgivings on 29 December he set out for the mainland after dispatching one last message to Kinnaird: "[Y]ou must let me have all the means and credit of mine that we can muster or master, and that immediately, and I must do my best to the shirt or the skin if necessary. Stretch my credit and anticipate my means to their fullest extent. . . . Send me forthwith all the credits you can." Barff provided him with an additional eight thousand Levant dollars (c. £1,600). For his part, Hobhouse was full of praise: "I think you have done a very wise not to say a very spirited and honorable deed by going to Greece. It gives me the greatest satisfaction to find that your visit is properly appreciated by the people whom you go to encourage."[14]

Byron's boat was chased by a Turkish vessel but successfully eluded capture, and he arrived in Missolonghi on 3 January 1824. He arrived as a savior, a messiah with handfuls of dollars to support the cause of independence, and he was received "with all kinds of kindness and honours." For a man who disliked responsibility to find himself viewed as a potential national hero, and for Byron, of all people, to adopt a significant military role—he wore his red military uniform for the landing—must have seemed difficult for his friends to credit. But the Greeks, or more particularly Prince Mavrocordatos, were by now convinced that he would bankroll the war of independence, and that his status as an English aristocrat would make him an important rallying point. Byron agreed to provide for five hundred of the Souliote warriors in Missolonghi, and he pressed Kinnaird to provide all possible funds. In his enthusiasm, Byron committed himself financially in a manner that brooked no turning back. "I have undertaken to maintain the Souliotes for a year," he wrote in January 1824, and said that during the calendar year "besides the money already advanced to the Greek government, and the credits . . . from the income of 1823, I shall, or ought to have at my disposition upwards of an hundred thousand dollars." He needed it, since by February he was spending about two thousand Levantine dollars a week. He was prepared also to commit the purchase money he anticipated from Rochdale to the cause. "His house," wrote one observer, "was filled with soldiers; his receiving room resembled an arsenal of war, rather than the habitation of a poet."[15]

Byron did not find his new circumstances easy. Although the Greeks showered him with military titles, and plans were drawn up for him to lead two thousand soldiers in an attack on Lepanto, the almost constant rain turned everything to mud, made action impossible, and left the bored Souliotes to quarrel among themselves. Byron sought relief in the companionship of the fifteen-year-old Loukas Chalandritsanos, but found none; and he struggled with increasing ill health. He was certainly not prepared to sign a blank check. He was asked for a loan of twenty thousand to thirty thousand dollars to finance a campaign to secure Candia (Crete). "The government of the Morea and of Candia have written to me for a further advance from my own peculium of 20 or 30,000 dollars to which I demur for the present."[16]

Even so, Byron's general disposition was clear. In letter after letter he proclaimed a willingness to help out the Greek cause. He was determined to provide "all the monies I can muster," or, to another correspondent, "I must muster all the means in my compass as I am paymaster." He added that "I mean to stick by the Greeks to the last rag of canvas or shirt." He wrote urgently to Kinnaird in mid-March 1824 to the effect that "I require reinforcements," and he returned to a favorite theme to suggest how these might be forthcoming: "[I]t would be advantageous, nay even necessary for me or for my heirs that you should sell out of the 3 per cent Consols now while they are so high, it might make a difference of ten thousand in our favour on the original sum invested." Surely, he thought, Kinnaird's fellow marriage settlement trustee, Thomas Bland, would agree to such an arrangement, and the principal could be invested in a mortgage at 4 percent as soon as one became available. His plea was still the same, "I may possibly require all available sums for the assistance of the Cause here." By the end of March he reckoned he had advanced 30,000 Spanish dollars in the Greek cause "without counting my own contingent expences of every kind." Without his money, he told Kinnaird, "everything would have been at a stand still in Messalonghi," and although part of the money was due to be repaid, he was willing to "spend it in the cause." He was himself support-ing 225 "regular and irregular soldiers," and nearly 30 officers.[17]

By February 1824 there was news that his financial support was at last to be supplemented. A loan of £800,000 had been negotiated in London, and Hobhouse wrote to tell Byron the good news. The Greek community in London, he added, looked upon Byron as "a perfect Godsend." For his own part, he added in what was to be his last letter to Byron, "your present endeavour is certainly the most glorious ever undertaken by man."[18] Hobhouse's sentiments were laudable, but Byron was discovering the re-alities of life on the front line, and in particular the fact that he could not trust the very people he was funding. Although the first installment of the loan was already on its way, the requests for support still poured in. Byron half complained on 7 April that "the Greeks here of the government have been boring me for more money, as I have the brigade to maintain, and the campaign is apparently soon to open, and as I have already spent nearly 30,000 dollars [£4,000] in three months upon them in one way or another . . . I have given them a refusal, and as they would not take that, another refusal in terms of considerable sincerity." Kinnaird let him know that his initial £4,000 loan to the Greeks would be recovered through the London Greek Committee.[19]

Byron's days were now numbered. He suffered a seizure on 15 Febru-ary from which he never properly recovered. Although he continued to raise money, he was not destined to be the savior of the Greeks. However much he may have been lauded in London, he was suffering in Greece. Military plans had to be abandoned in the face of appalling weather, and his health continued to give grounds for concern. On 9 April he wrote what was to be his last letter, largely about his financial support for the Greek cause. On the same day, while out riding, he was caught in heavy rain and quickly developed feverish and rheumatic symptoms. He appeared to re-cover over the next day or two, but it was a temporary reprieve, and on 19 April he died: "[T]o terminate my wearisome existence I came to Greece," he reputedly told his physician, Dr. Julius Millingen, during his last hours; "my wealth, my abilities, I devoted to her cause."[20]

Byron was not destined to fall in battle. His involvement in the struggle for Greek independence was not a matter of enemies killed, fortresses cap-tured, and battles won, but of the encouragement he offered and, perhaps above all, the finance he provided by showing his willingness to sacrifice his fortune and risk his life for a country rich in history but poor and divided in its recent fortunes. The Greeks recognized his sacrifice. Missolonghi went into mourning, and there was widespread grief throughout the country: 5 May was appointed a national day of mourning. Nor was the sacrifice in vain. In 1827 Britain, France, and Russia signed the Treaty of London, threatening the Turks with military intervention if they did not accept an armistice. When the Turks refused, a combined naval force destroyed the Turkish fleet at Navarino. Russia declared war on the Ottoman Empire in 1828, and in 1832 the Greeks finally won their independence from the Turks. A Bavarian prince was chosen to be the king of Greece. The cause that took Byron to Greece for the last eight months of his life was finally successful. Byron has, ever since, been revered as a national hero in Greece: in the words of the Greek prime minister, speaking at Newstead Abbey in July 1931, "many are those who were convinced . . . that, if Byron had not come to die facing the lagoon of Missolonghi, during the Easter of 1824, there would not have been a Navarino in 1827. Childe Harold died like a Crusader."[21]

II

After an autopsy, Byron's body was embalmed and lay in state for six days in St. Nicholas's Church, Missolonghi. The body was then taken to Zante and handed over to Colonel Stanhope. There were many who wanted Byron to be buried in Greece, but in the event the English authorities in Zante insisted that he should be carried back to his native country. The coffin was loaded aboard the *Florida*, which set sail for England on 30 April. News of Byron's death reached Kinnaird on 14 May, and circulated rapidly. Hobhouse was relieved to find it announced in the *Times* on 15 May "in a manner which is, I think, a fair sample of the general opinion on the event." The coffin reached England early in July, when the *Florida* docked in London. It was taken by barge to Palace Yard Stairs, and then to Sir Edward Knatchbull's house in Great George Street, Westminster, covered with a black silk pall. Hobhouse failed in his bid to have Byron buried in Westminster Abbey, and at Augusta's suggestion it was agreed that he should be interred in the family vault at Hucknall. "He was buried like a nobleman, since we could not bury him as a poet," Hobhouse reflected, conveniently overlooking the fact that Byron no longer owned the estate associated with his nobility.[22]

The coffin was viewed by members of the nobility and gentry who had acquired tickets, on 9 and 10 July,[23] and on the twelfth the cortege set out north, finally reaching Nottingham on 15 July, where the coffin lay overnight at the Blackamoor's Head. The public were allowed to file past in groups of twenty in order to pay their last respects. Hobhouse reported the town "crowded in every street leading to the inn in which the coffin lay, and much feeling and sympathy were exhibited by all classes." The following morning the procession left for Hucknall: "[T]he Mayor and Corporation of Nottingham joined the funeral procession. It extended about a quarter of a mile, and, moving very slowly, was five hours on the road to Hucknall. . . . The churchyard and the little church at Hucknall were so crowded that it was with difficulty we could follow the coffin up the aisle." At 3:30 P.M. on 16 July 1824 Byron was laid to rest.[24] Apart from Hobhouse, present at the burial were Francis Hodgson, William Fletcher, Colonel Wildman, and the man who had greeted Byron at Newstead in August 1798—John Hanson.

Byron died unlanded. He had succeeded in 1798 to a depleted estate, but he had never really been interested in the intricacies of everyday property management. From 1812 he was actively attempting to relieve himself from the burdens it imposed. The remaining Norfolk properties were sold while he was on his first journey abroad. Newstead finally passed into other hands in 1819, and Rochdale only weeks before he died in 1824. To the seventh Lord Byron he bequeathed only a title. For the last eight years of his life Byron lived out of England, occasionally talking seriously or less seriously of returning, but never actually setting his sights toward his native shores. He still thought of Newstead, as is clear from canto 13 of *Don Juan*, but gradually his links with the family estate were severed. Hanson slowly disappeared from his affairs (Rochdale apart, and here he was effectively sidelined in 1823) and Hobhouse's activities faded once his political career took precedence. Kinnaird became the financial and literary linchpin of Byron's later years, and he had not visited Newstead during Byron's ownership.[25] His task was to pay off debts and fashion an income from interest on investments, interest on the Noel mortgage, Byron's literary earnings, and the rents of Kirkby Mallory. Ironically, when Byron died he owned no land, although a substantial part of his credits was constituted by unpaid rents from Leicestershire. Yet Byron was an English aristocrat, and wealthy or not there is still something poignant about the statement in his executors' accounts to the effect that "he had no real property, at least in this country at the time of his death having sold all his estates."[26]

III

The irony was that when Byron owned land he seemed perpetually short of cash, but once he disposed of the property—notably Newstead—

The Chancel of Hucknall Church, lithograph by S. Rayner after T. Barber, published by Alfred Barber, Nottingham, 30 November 1835. The plaque on the right-hand wall commemorates Byron. (Nottingham City Museums and Art Galleries [Newstead Abbey].)

his financial affairs began to improve almost out of recognition. He may have given his all in the Greek cause during his final months, but he died a relatively wealthy man. He cheerfully told James Dearden during the final Rochdale negotiations that "My debts have long been liquidated by the sale of Newstead and the purchase money settled and invested." This was not quite true, since both Hanson and Widow Mealey had still to be paid, but the general tenor of the comment was correct; indeed, less than a month before he died Hobhouse wrote to him in particularly upbeat tones: "Your monied matters, Kinnaird will tell you, are going on swimmingly. You will have, indeed you have, a very handsome fortune." "Your affairs," he noted in another letter, "go on prosperously."[27]

Byron's fortune was not to be his to enjoy, and new financial arrangements now had to be made and backdated to the date of Byron's death. Since the sale of Newstead, £66,200 had been invested in 3 percent consolidated annuities. The total investment at face value stood at £89,136 2s. 5d., paying £2,575 interest per annum after deductions. A further £13,800 outstanding on Annabella's portion was liable to 5 percent per annum interest, of which £500 was paid to Lady Byron and £190 to Byron. This sum had been reduced to £9,800 when in 1822 Sir Ralph Noel paid an additional £4,000 of Annabella's portion. With Byron's death the trustees became liable for Lady Byron's jointure of £2,000 a year, which replaced her £500 pin money, and £640 maintenance for Augusta Ada, the interest at 4 percent payable on her putative marriage portion of £16,000. This money was payable to Lady Byron for her daughter's maintenance, until the age of twenty-one. When the jointure and the maintenance had been paid, there was an annual surplus on the fund of £524, which the trustees permitted to accumulate as capital.[28]

What of the sums over and above those retained for Lady Byron and her daughter? Byron's effects were distributed under the terms of his will drawn up in 1815. To the surprise and indeed embarrassment of his friends, Byron was found not to have revised his will since he left England. When Hanson visited him in Venice in 1818 he added a codicil to his existing will in which he left £5,000 to Allegra.[29] Lady Blessington found him "making his will" one day during her visit to Genoa in 1823, but Byron did not update the will he made in London before departing for Italy in 1816.[30] Hobhouse, Kinnaird, and Hanson met at Kinnaird's office on 10 June 1824 and agreed, in Hobhouse's words, "that Hanson ought to deposit the original will in Doctors' Commons until every search had again been made in Italy for a later will, but I begin to entertain some doubts of any posterior will to that of 1815 and 1818. None was made in Greece, we know." In fact, none was made at all, an omission that concerned Byron during his final illness. Consequently, no provision was made for Byron's servants, notably Fletcher and Lega Zambelli, but Hanson and Hobhouse, his administrators, were to receive £1,000 each. The residue of his estate was left to Augusta Leigh and her children. Hobhouse, embarrassed by his old friend's largesse, told Augusta that his £1,000 would be at the disposal of one of her children.[31]

Augusta's share was estimated in 1826 at £15,377 (table 11.1). The money was to remain in the public funds during her lifetime, with the proceeds to be paid to her directly—Byron had been anxious to avoid them going to her spendthrift husband—and subsequently to her children. She was also entitled to receive the investments secured for Lady Byron's jointure (£63,993) should she survive her.[32]

The capital invested to produce Lady Byron's jointure and her daughter's portion had a face value of £100,548 by 1831. Hanson proposed as early as 1825 that £60,000 should be converted into a mortgage. It took time to arrange, but in 1831 the trustees sold consolidated annuities with a value of £61,162 14s. 6d., and placed £61,000 of this in the security of a Cheshire estate, paying 4½ percent interest (£2,745), which was sufficient to pay Lady Byron's jointure and her daughter's maintenance. Byron's wish in life had finally been satisfied after his death. Augusta Ada's portion of £16,000 became due when she married in 1835 William, eighth Lord King, and subsequently first earl of Lovelace (1805–93). To raise this sum the trustees sold consolidated annuities for £16,200. Ada died in 1852. In 1838 £3,000 of the £61,000 mortgage was repaid, and invested in £3,007 10s. 4d. 3 percent consolidated annuities. The total in consolidated annuities was now £4,526 15s. 5d. The residue of the mortgage, £58,000, remained out at interest but at 3½ percent (£2,030), which was sufficient to pay Lady Byron's jointure.

Table 11.1. Augusta Leigh's Inheritance from Byron

Estimated income from sale of the capital stock of 89,136 @ 96	85,570
Lady Byron's portion outstanding	9,800
	95,370
Loss	
Retained by trustees of the marriage settlement for Lady Byron's jointure (63,993) and Augusta Ada Byron's portion (16,000)	79,993
Surplus payable to Augusta Leigh	£15,377

Hobhouse and Hanson had also to dispose of Byron's liquid assets, notably his personal fortune at the time of his death, and any outstanding proceeds of the Rochdale estate. In total these assets were estimated at approximately £8,312. The sum comprised £3,900 with his bankers, £2,000 arrears of rent from the Noel estate, anticipated dividends of £837, and seven thousand dollars brought from Greece and estimated to be worth £1,575. The final tally from Rochdale is not known. If we add to this anticipated future profits from Byron's published works, copyrights, and royalties, he had almost certainly never been so well off in cash terms, hence Hobhouse's upbeat tone in his final letters. How much of this would have survived if Byron had lived and continued his open-handed support for the Greek cause is more problematic.

When the various effects were converted into money and outstanding debts were paid, the residue was invested:

£10,044	14s.	6d.	New 3½ percent consolidated annuities
2,873	4s.	0d.	Reduced annuities
1,085	11s.	2d.	3 percent consolidated bank annuities

These sums were still outstanding in 1853, when the Byron residue also included £6,087 5s. 7d. 3 percent consolidated annuities (the sum outstanding after the mortgage and portion had been paid, see above), £1,900 exchequer bills and £84 4s. 10d. cash. All of this personal estate was held in trust for Augusta and her family. A sale of Byron's manuscripts in 1830 produced good returns. Hanson told Hobhouse that Murray bought lot 1 for 3700 guineas.[33]

Augusta died in 1851, a year after her husband. Her half-brother's money seems to have done her little good, since she was perpetually in financial difficulty, and by the time she died only Emily of her seven children was still on friendly terms with her. George (b. 1812), in the army, and Frederick (b. 1816), in the navy, may well have borrowed on the reversion of the capital, but the two men did not speak to each other for twenty-five years and they were both deeply in debt when their mother died.[34] Lady Byron died in 1860, and the funds that had underwritten her jointure passed to Augusta's family under the terms of Byron's will. Byron's personal estate was in Chancery from 1853 in the search for an amicable distribution of the sums to Augusta's children. In the end, what was left passed to Ada Augusta Leigh, Frederick's daughter. She was still a ward in Chancery in 1868 when she married J. G. Stephenson of The Cleevelands, Bishop's Cleeve, Cheltenham, supposedly a man of fortune. She is described by Byron's godson, Captain Byron Drury, as "a considerable heiress" and "very beautiful." Chancery cannot have swallowed up all of the £63,993.[35]

IV

Who did *not* benefit? The most obvious loser was George Anson, Byron's cousin and his successor in title. George was the son of George Anson, younger brother of the sixth Lord Byron's father, and an almost exact contemporary. He was frequently at Newstead, but Byron fell out with him in 1816 when he took Lady Byron's side over the breakup of the marriage. The seventh lord was another navy man, rising to the rank of admiral and, besides this distinction, he was nonpolitical lord-in-waiting to Queen Victoria from 1837 to 1860. He married in 1816 Elizabeth Mary Chandos-Pole, but while in 1824 he became the seventh Lord Byron he did so as an English rarity, the nonlanded peer. George Anson Byron's inheritance was simply a title, although with a dash of irony Lady Byron—who now enjoyed the whole of the Kirkby Mallory income—made over her £2,000 jointure to him. Had the estates been settled in the normal way, Byron could not have deprived his cousin in this manner. After three hundred years at Newstead the family now had no established home, and the seventh lord had to look elsewhere. He subsequently lived at Park Hall, Barlborough, and he died in 1868 at Brighton and is buried at Kirkby Mallory. Later generations lived at Thrumpton Hall in Nottinghamshire, and in 1883 the family property, all in Nottinghamshire, totaled 2,196 acres and was valued at £3,729 gross. It passed out of the family in 1949 on the death of the eleventh Lord Byron. The present Lord Byron, the thirteenth, lives in Essex. The title has survived where the land and estate have gone, and the links with Nottinghamshire and Lancashire have been severed.[36]

The other losers in 1824 were all of those who had served Byron faithfully in the years after he made the will in 1815. None of his servants was mentioned, and Kinnaird also seems to have had nothing for his services, despite the enormous energy he had expended on Byron's behalf. He died in 1831. Hanson's £1,000 did not go far. His business failed, partly as a result of the lasting scandal arising from his daughter's marriage to the earl of Portsmouth, and by 1840 he was in considerable financial distress. He died in 1841. Bland, the other marriage trustee, died in 1847. Scrope Davies died five years later, but Hobhouse outlived all Byron's other friends. He became a cabinet minister and succeeded to his father's baronetcy. By the time he died in 1869, Byron's old home at Newstead, which Hobhouse had first visited more than sixty years previously, had been restored—and turned into a shrine.

12

Byron and Newstead:
The Myth

The confidence of Lord Byron in the good feeling and good taste of
Colonel Wildman has been justified by the event. Under his judicious
eye and munificent hand, the venerable and romantic pile has risen from
its ruins in all its old monastic and baronial splendour, and additions
have been made to it in perfect conformity of style. The groves and
forests have been replanted, the lakes and fish-ponds cleared out, and
the gardens rescued from the "hemlock and thistle" and restored to
their pristine and dignified formality.
—Washington Irving, *Abbotsford and Newstead Abbey*

Byron's last visit to Newstead was in 1814. He left England in 1816,
and following the sale in 1817 he told Wildman, "I should regret to trouble
you with any requests of mine in regard to the preservation of any signs of
my family which may still exist at Newstead, and leave everything of that
kind to your own feelings, present or future, upon the subject."[1] He had
removed any furnishings he valued, although these had probably been seized
by bailiffs at Piccadilly Terrace, yet there was still something rather heart-
less in abandoning the family portraits, the heirlooms which normally descended with the estate or at least the title.[2] Under other circumstances he
would have retreated into obscurity, shunned by aristocratic society for
demonstrating all too vividly the vulnerability of landed families to the
very swings and fortunes of market forces against which they believed
themselves to be immune. It was the fate every family dreaded. Yet—and
this is the irony—the man who sold the family patrimony is as closely
associated with Newstead today as when he walked in the grounds and
lived in the abbey nearly two hundred years ago. Both tacitly and deliberately, those who followed him promoted a myth that still connects the man
and the house.

I

When the Newstead transaction was finally completed early in 1819 the purchaser was Thomas Wildman (1787–1859). The Wildmans were a Lancashire family. Thomas Wildman Sr. (1740–95) was the third son of a yeoman from the Bowland Forest area. He trained as a solicitor, moved to London, and in 1773 he became a member of Lincoln's Inn. His eldest son, Thomas, was also brought up in London, mainly by his mother since his father died in 1795. He was sent to Harrow in 1798. Some of his surviving school letters from 1804 and 1805 mention Byron, although there is little evidence that their friendship was maintained after they left the school. Wildman went to Oxford in 1806, but left when he came of age in 1808 to join the Seventh Hussars and mapped out for himself a career in the army. He served in Spain in 1808 and 1809, then in Ireland, and again in Spain in 1813 and 1814 during Wellington's Peninsula campaign. At the Battle of Waterloo he was aide-de-camp to Lord Uxbridge (later marquess of Anglesey). He remained in the army following the conclusion of the French wars in 1815, but he then went on half-pay with the rank of brevet-colonel (1819). His active life in the regular army was over, but under the system then in operation he rose to the rank of lieutenant colonel in the Ninth Light Dragoons, and to full colonel in 1838. He married, in 1816, Louisa Preisig (c. 1802–77), whose Swiss father was domiciled in London. There were no children.[3]

Wildman took to Nottinghamshire in a way that Byron never had, and he held a number of positions reserved for the county gentry, including justice of the peace, deputy lord lieutenant, and, in 1821, high sheriff. With the death of Lord George Bentinck in 1828 he was asked by the duke of Newcastle, as lord lieutenant of the county, to take over the Mansfield troop of Yeomanry Cavalry, and he subsequently took command of the Sherwood Rangers.[4] Unfortunately for Wildman, his reputation with Newcastle plummeted in 1831. Following a protest meeting in Nottingham on 10 October that year a mob attacked and burnt down the castle, which was owned by the duke and lay just outside the town boundaries. Wildman was one of two county (as opposed to town) magistrates in Nottingham that afternoon. As a known sympathizer with the cause of parliamentary reform, he was held responsible by Newcastle for failing to take sufficient action to quell the disturbance and prevent the attack. Wildman defended himself vigorously, claiming he had done everything possible under the circumstances, but a combination of his radical views and an attack on his integrity launched by Newcastle's son, the earl of Lincoln, undermined his position. He was one of only a handful of local gentry to oppose the payment of compensation to the duke for the loss of his castle.[5]

Wildman's social progress was temporarily but by no means irretrievably damaged by the events of October 1831. By then he was heavily involved with what became his main interest from 1819, the Newstead estate. Since the 1817 Newstead auction was the third in only six years, and since once again the catalog was prepared by Farebrother, we have a good idea of what Wildman acquired when he decided to redirect his West Indian fortune into Nottinghamshire landed property. The estate was measured at 3,200 acres, and included the manor and lordship of Newstead, together with the abbey, the gardens, the fishponds, and the fifth Lord Byron's folly, described as a castle "standing on an eminence at the head of a great lake of 30 acres." Most of the land was divided into farms, described as good wheat and turnip land. The property also included mills, public houses, quarries, and limekilns. Table 12.1 details the farms on the property.

The position in 1817 was virtually the same as in 1815, although two tenancies had changed hands, and Robert Walker's farm had been divided between William Hebbard and Samuel Howet. How these figures converted

Table 12.1. Newstead Farms and Rents, 1817

Tenant	Acreage			Rent		
	a	r	p	£	s.	d.
In hand	1,079	3	3			
Thomas Heath	211	3	24	300		
Mr. Hodgkinson	67	0	12	200		
Mr. George Wightman	404	3	30	440		
Mr. John Hardstaff Jr.	184	3	23	200		
Mr. Lee	91	2	0	90		
Mr. William Hebbard	57	0	17	65		
Mr. Samuel Howett	59	0	31	62	14	
Mr. William Beardall	149	1	26	140		
Mr. John Hardstaff Sr.	178	0	24	200		
Mr. William Beardall	97	3	22	110		
	2,581	3	12	1,807	14	
Newstead Forest Farms						
Owen Mealey	13	1	18			
William Hibbert						
Robert Slaney	631	3	3			

Source: Reelig 700, 1817 Sale Catalogue

into real income is more difficult to ascertain. Landlords across the country were forced into rent abatements and later rent reductions in the immediate aftermath of the Napoleonic Wars. Claughton had raised the Newstead rents as high as they would go in 1814, and Wildman was probably forced to tolerate arrears, and perhaps to allow abatements at least in the years to 1820.[6]

Approximately one-third of the land was described in 1817 as being "in hand" (table 12.2). Although part of this was accounted for by the house, the lakes, and the remaining woodlands, the majority was described rather vaguely as lands and stone quarries. Whatever else this may imply, it suggests that despite Claughton's changes there was still room for an active landlord to reorganize and improve the farmsteads. Wildman seized the opportunity, particularly in respect of the remaining forest and heath land, which was not separately distinguished in 1817. As a solicitor noted in 1855, "the Forest has been divided into various Plantations and farms and the whole is now planted or brought into cultivation." Only the day before he died, Wildman was reported to have been "superintending the marking and numbering of some timber on the estate."[7]

Precisely what Wildman achieved among the tenants in these years can be reconstructed from three sets of material: the farm rents and acreages recorded in the 1817 sale particulars, a list of tenancies compiled in 1844 (table 12.3), and yet another set of sale particulars drawn up when

Table 12.2. Land "In Hand" at Newstead in 1817

| | Acreage | | |
	a	r	p
Mansion, abbey gardens, walks, etc.	12	0	0
Two homesteads	6	1	36
Woodlands	79	2	11
Lakes and ponds Reed Damstead	14	1	13
Ponds and yard	1	3	0
Mill and Great Lake	30	0	0
American Lake or Forest			
Dam	2	2	37
Slue	0	0	19
Nether Lake	18	1	0
Dam	0	2	26
Lands and stone quarries	913	3	21
	1,079	3	3

Source: Reelig, 700, 1817 Sale Catalogue

Table 12.3. The Newstead Abbey Estate in 1844

Tenant	Acreage			Rent		
	a	r	p	£	s.	d.
Col. Wildman in hand	1,254	2	34			
Col. Wildman-farm	376	0	37	300 (assumed)		
William Beardall	273	1	37	293		
Charles Cocks	350	0	17	277		
Samuel Taylor	259	0	15	176		
Mark Wilkinson	111	1	7	100		
John Hardstaff	100	1	25	86	18	
William Palin	79	0	6	60		
Charles Stubbins	208	2	35	80		
John Heath	90	2	11	70		
John Howis	61	3'	14	64	14	
William Smith	56	0	29	63		
Sundry occupations	7	2	6			
– House, Mr. Pickard				7		
– House, Mrs. Rushton				5	5	
– brick rent				6	11	8
– stone quarry				30		
– cottages				10	13	
	3,229	0	33	1,630	1	8

Source: Reelig, 717

Newstead was again advertised for sale in 1860 (table 12.4). Between 1817 and 1844 Wildman increased the land "in hand," but he himself was farming on a substantial scale, with a tenancy of 376 acres.[8] He had rationalized the Newstead Forest farms, so that there were now three farms exceeding three hundred acres (one in 1817), two exceeding two hundred acres (one in 1817), and two others of between one and two hundred acres. Beardall, Hardstaff and Heath survived among the tenant surnames, but none of the farms were of the same acreage in 1844 as in 1817. The rental, which was almost certainly too high to be sustained in 1817, had fallen to £1,630 despite Wildman's efforts at consolidation.

    Wildman was certainly active in reorganizing the estate, which suggests that Washington Irving, during his visit to Newstead in 1831, viewed things through something of a romantic haze:

Some of the families have rented farms there for nearly three hundred years, and, notwithstanding their mansions fell to decay, and everything about

Table 12.4. The Newstead Estate in 1860

Land and farms	Acreage		
	a	r	p
Abbey Park, gardens and pleasure grounds	636	3	11
Weeds and plantations in Park	196	2	7
Lakes and ponds	47	3	13
Woods, plantations, without the Park	628	0	8
Cottages, yard, gardens, keeper's house	8	1	15
Farms – Hutt Inn and Farm	80	1	21
Forest	237	2	3
Grange	259	0	15
Wire Mill	140	0	16
Abbey Field	301	1	17
Wighay	67	3	36
Hays	56	0	29
Hopping Hill	88	3	17
Hazleford	107	0	30
Monk Barns	294	3	11
Hagg Nook	73	1	37
Linby Quarry	2	0	35
	3,226	3	1

Source: Reelig, 707

them partook of the general waste and misrule of the Byron dynasty, yet nothing could uproot them from their native soil. I am happy to say that Colonel Wildman has taken these staunch loyal families under his peculiar care. He has favoured them in their rents; repaired, or rather rebuilt, their farm-houses; and has enabled families, that had almost sunk into the class of mere rustic labourers, once more to hold up their heads among the yeomanry of the land. . . . [T]he farms on the estate have been put in complete order; new farm-houses built of stone, in the picturesque and comfortable style of the old English granges; the hereditary tenants secured in their paternal homes, and treated with the most considerate indulgence; everything, in a word, gives happy indications of a liberal and beneficent landlord.[9]

Given the never-ending problems of controlling the tenants in the sixth Lord Byron's day, this blissful picture perhaps needs to be taken with a grain of salt, but Wildman was clearly an active, as well as a resident, landlord. He had no need to rely on Owen Mealey, and as a farmer himself he was able to pay particular attention to the needs and problems of his tenants in a manner quite alien to the previous owner of Newstead.

For the years after 1844 we can compare the 1844 and 1860 lists, although the position is complicated by the change to naming farms rather than using tenants' names for identification. However, two of the farms, Grange and Hays, were presumably equivalent to Samuel Taylor and William Smith in 1844, since the acreages were exactly the same. Almost everything else had changed. The land "in hand" and farmed by Wildman in 1844 totaled 1,630 acres, but the parkland, woods and lakes, came to 1,507 acres in 1860. The woods and plantations "without the park" in 1860 were the same as the Newstead Forest Farms in 1817, and it is not clear under what heading they appear in 1844. Otherwise, the impression is of acreages being adjusted perhaps at tenancy changes, or to suit individual needs. Wire Mill Farm was occupied by John Hardstaff Sr. in 1817 when it consisted of 178 acres, but the Hardstaff farm in 1844 had 100 acres, and Wire Mill in 1860 consisted of 140 acres. Wildman obviously made his farms suit the available tenants rather than the other way around—which had been Claughton's undoing.

II

Wildman's reorganization of the farms was important for his income, without which his legacy to future generations might not have been afforded. This was Newstead itself. The house had fallen into a state of serious disrepair under the fifth Lord Byron, and only cosmetic improvements had been carried out—mainly in 1808—by his successor. Further damage had occurred in the 1816 earthquake. Wildman's thoughts on first viewing the abbey in 1817 are not known. Hobhouse dined with him in 1819 and reported to Byron that "he adores you next to idolatry," and Augusta told Francis Hodgson: "Major Wildman has, I hear, soul enough to value the dear Abbey and its ruinous perfections: so much that he would not remove a stone and wishes to restore it as far as he can."[10] In fact, the restoration was virtually a rebuilding, and many stones were to be removed as Wildman rapidly became deeply immersed in his self-appointed task of restoring Newstead.

Wildman's first ideas for the restoration date from 1817, even before he took possession of Newstead, and they included a plan and elevation for alterations to the west front and the range behind it.[11] He was a competent draftsman, well equipped to turn his hand to architectural design. His original intentions for the exterior were quite moderate; he wanted to remove the outside staircase and porch built in 1631. The reerected porch was to be placed nearer ground level and further to the south. He intended to preserve the medieval character of the house, but was obviously dissatisfied with his own ideas, since in 1818 he employed the architect John Shaw (1776–1832), who worked extensively in the Norman and Gothic styles. Shaw's designs were intended to blend well with the oldest parts of the building, and Newstead today is much as Wildman and Shaw restored it between 1818 and the 1850s. The medieval undercrofts and ground-floor spaces were restored and brought into use. The upper floors were considerably altered and brought up to the comfort standards of the time with bathrooms, water closets, and oil lighting. Shaw also designed the Sussex tower, named after HRH the Duke of Sussex, a frequent visitor to Newstead. Wildman was, for many years, his equerry.[12] Outside a lake was made in front of the south range.

Wildman's extensive program of improvements met with almost universal approval. Hanson heard early in 1819 that Wildman had "now 200 workmen constantly at work," and when Hobhouse called at Newstead in 1823 he found so many workmen that he "had some difficulty in getting into the house. When I was admitted I was shown up into the old gallery, then refitted, and scarcely to be recognized." Byron, assuming that Shaw had talked Wildman into a scheme that went rather beyond the restoration to which Augusta referred, was not amused, and lampooned the building works in canto 16 of *Don Juan:*

> There was a modern Goth, I mean a Gothic
> Bricklayer of Babel, called an architect,
> Brought to survey these grey walls, which though so thick,
> Might have from time acquired some slight defect;
> Who, after rummaging the Abbey through thick
> And thin, produced a plan whereby to erect
> New buildings of correctest conformation,
> And throw down old, which he called *restoration.*

When Hobhouse returned to Newstead again in 1835, he was delighted to sleep in a room "which had no roof to it in my day."[13] William Howitt, visiting in the 1830s, commented that "the new stone-work is very substantially and well done; there is a great deal of modern elegance about the house; a fortune must have been spent upon it. The grounds before the new front are extremely improved; and the old gardens, with very correct feeling, have been suffered to retain their ancient character."[14]

Old Joe Murray, reported Washington Irving,

> rejoiced at the extensive repairs that were immediately commenced, and anticipated with pride the day when the Abbey should rise out of its ruins with renovated splendour, its gates be thronged with trains and equipages, and its halls once more echo to the sound of joyous hospitality. What chiefly,

however, concerned Joe's pride and ambition was a plan of the Colonel's to have the ancient refectory of the convent, a great vaulted room, supported by Gothic columns, converted into a servants' hall. Here Joe looked forward to rule the roost at the head of the servants' table.[15]

He was not to do so. Joe had endured a checkered career. Retained at Newstead following the fifth Lord Byron's death, he was dismissed by Mrs. Byron in 1804. Augusta then found him a place with the duchess of Leeds, from which he was given notice in 1807. He was reinstated at Newstead by Byron in 1808, and accompanied him on his first European travels.[16] He survived the turmoil of the various sales, and stayed on at Newstead after Wildman bought the estate. Byron was anxious in 1818 that he should "not be forgotten . . . let him above all have all possible comforts and requisites." By early 1820 he was reported to be "growing very feeble and is nearly blind, but his memory is much better than might be expected. Colonel Wildman is very fond of him and allows him to live in the old rooms in the Abbey." Charles Hanson proposed that Byron should pay off Murray's debts (£29 4s. 6d.) and allow him 10s. a week stipend, a proposal to which he enthusiastically agreed. Byron was saddened to hear in October 1820 that Murray had died: "Newstead and he went almost together."[17]

Wildman's improvements at Newstead were carefully thought out because he was passionately interested in Gothic architecture. One of the most notable features of Wildman's work at Newstead was the recreation of the original medieval great hall, which had been marred by previous alterations.[18] At the same time, Wildman had to live at Newstead, which he found not only dilapidated but also lacking greatly in comfort and convenience. He installed a bathroom, toilets, and colza-oil lighting. In other words, he was trying to maintain the ancient style of the house while ensuring that it functioned as a comfortable family home. Some Newstead visitors commented scornfully (and probably jealously) on his work: one Nottinghamshire lady, after a visit to Newstead in 1828, wrote scathingly that the chapter house was "new painted and gilded and overdone with modern innovations and luxuries and the owner not priding himself in ancestry and titles, but on the richness of his carpet and the costliness of his chairs."[19]

Doubters there may have been, but Wildman ensured Newstead's survival. Would any other purchaser have gone to such extraordinary lengths at Newstead? Certainly not Byron, who lacked the funding, or Claughton, who had never lived in the house. Other potential purchasers may have been put off in 1812, 1815, and 1817 by the potential cost of restoration. Any other purchaser might well have demolished all or part of it, to make way for a house that was more appropriate to the size of estate, and more

Southwest View of Newstead Abbey, by W. M. Fellows after R. T. Buttery, published by R. T. Buttery, Nottingham, 26 February 1827. By the time of this picture Wildman was busy renovating Newstead. While the picture was dedicated to Wildman, it was a sign of things to come that Byron's name was picked out in substantially larger lettering. The picture also locates "Byron's Oak," to the right of the abbey and standing alone on the lawn. It was commemorated by Byron in "To a Young Oak," written in 1807 but published only in 1832, after which the tree became much sought-after by visitors to Newstead. (Nottingham City Museums and Art Galleries [Newstead Abbey].)

financially manageable. And, of course, until 1824, Newstead was just another country house.

III

Wildman attended Byron's funeral, but he can scarcely have imagined the impact on him and his house of the poet's premature death. Byron's influence across Europe grew rather than waned with his death. Poets imitated him, painters illustrated him, musicians were inspired by his work, and liberal politicians saw his example as offering them powerful support.[20] Newstead, as a fixed point in the poet's universe, became a place of pilgrimage. Thomas Moore was one of the earliest to arrive in January 1828. He was fascinated by "the dining room which Byron used when he first took possession, the small apartment he afterwards occupied, dinner, sitting and bedroom." Wildman was himself the guide. Moore recorded: "Colonel Wildman out shooting but was sent for; [he] arrived; showed me all over the house."[21]

Wildman's restoration program was already well underway in 1824, but he soon recognized the implications of Byron's death for Newstead. Irving commented in 1831 on the "reverential care with which [Wildman] has preserved and renovated every monument and relic of the Byron family, and every object in anywise connected with the memory of the poet."[22] "The only objects in the interior, which can much interest strangers," wrote William Howitt in 1838, were those "connected with the history of Lord Byron." Howitt was sure that "Wildman is as desirous as any man can be not to obliterate any traces of his Lordship's former life here," but he was disappointed that *any* alterations had been made:

> I cannot help regretting that the poet's study should now be converted into a common bed-room; and most of all, that the antique fountain which stood in front of the abbey and makes so strong a feature in the very graphic picture of the place drawn in Don Juan, should be removed. It now adorns the inner quadrangle, or cloister court, and is certainly a very beautiful object there.

Howitt's point was that Byron had immortalized the fountain in canto 13 of *Don Juan*, and thus, "to every visitor of taste, the abbey front must be thus injured whilst it and the poet's description of it, last together."[23]

Wildman could not have been expected to recognize in 1819 what Newstead would become after 1824, and perhaps not surprisingly he was forced to develop one or two myths of his own. For visitors, the highlight of their tour of Newstead was Byron's bedroom, and they were assured that this had not been altered since Byron last stayed at Newstead in September 1814. Wilfrid Scawen Blunt noted after his visit to Newstead that "Byron's own little bedroom, with its simple furniture, is most interesting, unaltered since his time."[24] This was not quite accurate, since Wildman had replaced the earlier fireplace that had contained part of a medieval tombslab from the priory.[25] Another temptation was to over-elaborate: "Colonel Wildman possesses the Table (a round one covered with green baize)," wrote a visitor in 1849, "at which Lord Byron told him he had written the whole of *Childe Harold*. He keeps the table in his study."[26] Some of *Childe Harold* may well have been written at Newstead, but the later cantos were written after Byron left England in 1816. Wildman can perhaps be forgiven his little exaggerations, since he was, after all, more than willing and indeed happy to exploit his possession and indulge an early generation of Byronists by opening it up to visitors.

Perhaps such tampering with the truth did not matter, because most visitors were suitably respectful, awed, or sentimental, although one lady wrote that "we have just been seeing Lord Byron's room, but in horrid taste, nothing but the remembrance to make it interesting."[27]

The number of visitors to Newstead increased partly out of respect for Byron and partly because his death coincided with a growing interest in country-house visiting. As a combined result, by the middle of the century Newstead was one of about one hundred show houses that were advertised as being open on specific days of the week, or at any time in the absence of the family. Wildman encouraged visitors: Howitt noted that "it is fortunate for the public that the place has fallen into the hands of a gentleman who affords the utmost facility for the inspection of it by strangers. Nothing can exceed the easy courtesy with which it is thrown open to them." James Carter, writing in 1850, commented that "thousands" of visitors had, "by his courtesy, been permitted to traverse its spacious galleries and venerable halls."[28]

Newstead by mid-century had become a mecca for Byron pilgrims, and it may have been drawing at or near ten thousand visitors annually.[29] Samuel Collinson traveled from Nottingham to visit the abbey in June 1846. He joined "large numbers of visitors," and, in words more often associated with the late twentieth century than the mid-nineteenth, complained that he was "hurried through the rooms as quickly as possible to make way for fresh arrivals." It was all too much for the landlord of The Hutt, whom Collinson found "completely bewildered." By 1850 commercial instincts were taking over, and The Hutt was said to be able to accommodate "the numerous parties who arrive to visit the abbey."[30]

Visitors needed guidebooks, which offered them an opportunity of learning more about the house, the Byrons, the poet, and—sometimes—Wildman. Byron was the key figure, as the guidebooks, through their titles and contents, made clear. The emphasis was on Newstead as Byron's house: a guidebook of 1857 praised Wildman's "magnificent restoration," while noting how he had preserved "with almost filial reverence every memorial of his noble friend."[31] Subsequently Richard Allen produced an official souvenir guidebook, with considerable emphasis placed on Byron's bedroom, which was one of the few parts of the house that could be indisputably linked with the poet, partly because his bed was still to be seen.[32]

Wildman had set himself an ambitious program at Newstead that took many years to complete. The stained-glass windows in the Great Hall were not put in until the 1850s. It was also a costly program. Hobhouse heard in 1818 that Wildman had an income of £10,000 a year, and that he intended to live on £2,000 and "to lay out the remaining income on repairs to the Abbey." Irving noted in the 1830s that Wildman had already spent about

£80,000 and that work was still continuing.[33] Unfortunately Wildman's income did not stretch to meet the demands placed upon it. In 1817 he was a man of very considerable means, with a fortune derived from the activities of his late father and two of his uncles. They had been the not overscrupulous manager and agents running William Beckford's sugar plantations in Jamaica, and without much doubt they had considerably enriched themselves at Beckford's expense, acquiring estates and slaves of their own on the island. Over time Wildman suffered financially as his Jamaica income was severely reduced in line with the experiences of other absentees, particularly following slave emancipation.[34]

Despite a growing financial shortfall Wildman carried on, and in 1826 he began to mortgage parts of the estate, borrowing £7,000, then £4,000, and then a further £2,000. By 1844 he had run up mortgages of about £30,000. Wildman had no children and, as he had bought the estate after he married, it was almost certainly unsettled; hence his ability to raise mortgages in precisely the manner Hanson had failed to do for Byron. The restoration of Newstead and the creation of a memorial to the poet was his life's work: the expense could be secured on the equity of the estate and, if required, redeemed at a later stage by selling the property.[35] Only the abandonment in 1829 of the planned grand main entrance may have reflected what Shaw, the architect, referred to as the "fearful expenditure" at Newstead. By repute Wildman spent about £100,000 on the house.[36]

Wildman died in 1859, having rescued, and then restored and rebuilt, Newstead. The dilapidated abbey had been turned into a shrine to the poet, and Wildman's active role was widely appreciated. In the words of the *Mansfield Reporter:*

> As the owner of the seat of Lord Byron he always evinced the utmost anxiety to preserve its ancient associations and to sustain the venerable fabric intact. This he did in no selfish or ostentatious spirit, for whilst Newstead was the scene of constant reunions of that large circle of friends whose intercourse and esteem it was Colonel Wildman's happiness to enjoy, the edifices and all pertaining to it were generously thrown open to the public gratification, and its picturesque and romantic locale, with its interesting relics and reminiscences, have afforded delight to thousands of pilgrims, tourists, ramblers, and pleasure seekers, during the forty years the beautiful domain has been in the possession of Colonel Wildman.

Six thousand people were said to have followed his cortege to Mansfield cemetery, and shops in Mansfield closed for the occasion.[37] But while Wildman was locally popular, the future for Newstead was still uncertain. Lacking an heir, Wildman directed in his will that the estate should be sold by his trustees—John Wildman, Richard Wildman, and Jonathan Hardcastle.

IV

In June 1860, for the fourth time since 1812, Newstead came under the auctioneer's hammer, and as on each of the previous occasions it failed to reach its reserve price. However, as in 1812 and 1817, a private buyer was found after the sale. The purchaser on this occasion was William Frederick Webb of Pepper Hall in Yorkshire, who in February 1861 agreed to a price for Newstead of £147,000 including the timber. The transaction was completed on 9 April 1861.[38] The 50 percent increase in the price since 1817 must have reflected both rising land prices and Wildman's improvements in the house and on the estate. Subsequently, Wildman's executors held an auction of Byron effects at Newstead. Perhaps surprisingly, "many of the lots realised only moderate prices," but Webb purchased various items that he intended to retain at Newstead.[39]

Webb, his daughter later recalled, first saw Newstead "on a lovely May morning, fell in love with it at sight, and bought it on the spot. So little time did he lose over the transaction that before the month was out my mother and the whole family were installed there. The sudden step was the more remarkable, in that he habitually left all minor decisions to my mother." Fortunately, Pepper Hall had only been rented, but if it was her father's decision to purchase the Newstead estate it was her mother who set about maintaining the Byron myth:

> To be quite frank, none of us, with the exception of my mother, cared about Byron, for in our youthful days we heard too much of him not to be wearied by the subject, and the very familiarity deprived his history of romance. Happily my mother felt differently, and it is chiefly owing to her care on her first arrival at Newstead that every relic connected with him has been so religiously preserved. Her almost meticulous reverence for all that concerned the Byron family, and, of course, more especially the poet, even at times provoked ridicule, a clever relative remarking with some truth that my mother seemed "much less mistress in her own house, than caretaker for the Byrons." She regarded them, however, as an obligation, and in some sort as a duty that she owed to all the poet's admirers.

For Mrs. Webb it had been a matter for considerable deliberation before "she decided on her own responsibility to cut down part of the tree on which Lord Byron had carved his and his sister Augusta's name during his last visit to Newstead." Webb was not quite so sentimental. His first improvement to the house was to arrange for it to be lit by gas, which was looked upon "as an audaciously modern innovation applied to a private dwelling house."[40]

Webb and his wife followed where Wildman had led, preserving the Byron links, but accommodating change to suit the needs of a family home. The entrance to the southeast wing was changed in about 1870 and a bow window added. Numerous alterations were made within the southeast wing, including changes of floor levels and the insertion of a large staircase around a well. The chapel was decorated as a memorial to Wildman. In the grounds Webb built stables and lodges, and he and his wife made a great many alterations to the gardens. Mrs. Webb laid out the fern garden in about 1864 or 1865, constructed with Derbyshire tufa and stones taken from the ruins of the priory church. The grand herbaceous border was created sometime before 1876, and the Spanish garden in about 1896. Geraldine Webb, her daughter, created about 1895 the Rockery with its tiny stream and tunnel grotto, supposedly based on the heroine's wild garden in Disraeli's *Venetia* (1837). Despite these changes, the Webbs treasured Newstead's link with the poet: Wilfrid Scawen Blunt noted when he visited in 1909 that they were "proud of their family possessions . . . and of its connection with the poet."[41]

Where the fifth and sixth Lords Byron had lacked the income to live in the manner to which they aspired, and Wildman had run out of cash partly because the income from his Jamaica properties dwindled over time, Webb was an altogether more substantial landowner. In 1883 his holdings totaled 13,458 acres, of which 7,599 were in the North Riding of Yorkshire, and 5,859 were in Nottinghamshire. The gross annual value of the property was put at £11,770.[42] As such he was one of a group of just over three hundred greater English landowners with estates exceeding ten thousand acres, and for once Newstead was in the hands of someone who could well afford its upkeep.

Webb died in 1899 having two years earlier made a will leaving Newstead in trust to his daughters Geraldine and Ethel.[43] Geraldine, with her husband, Sir Herbert Chermside, and Ethel lived at Newstead. Geraldine had no children, and following her death in 1910 Newstead passed to Ethel. Sir Herbert remarried, and moved to Pepper Hall.[44] Ethel Webb converted the large room in the extreme southeast corner of the house from an orangery into a billiard room and added a bay window. She was probably responsible also for the subtropical or bamboo gardens, and the Japanese garden was laid out for her in 1907 by a Japanese landscape architect with plants and ornaments brought from Japan.

Ethel Webb died in 1915 and Newstead passed to trustees acting on behalf of Webb's son, Captain Roderick Webb. However, he was killed on active service in 1916, and Newstead passed to William Webb's eldest daughter, Mrs. Augusta Fraser of Reelig, Inverness-shire. She died in 1925, leaving the property to her son, Mr. Charles Ian Fraser.

V

By this time the future was looking less encouraging for Newstead than in the days of Wildman and Webb. Country-house visiting faltered in the later nineteenth century, and Byron's reputation suffered at the hands of the more prudish later Victorians. Byron had acquired a scandalous reputation, both because of suspicions about his personal life that partly provoked his flight in 1816, and because of the nature of some of the poetry he wrote while living abroad. It was this reputation which reputedly encouraged the Nottinghamshire gentry and local clergy to stay at home when he was buried at Hucknall in 1824.[45] Hobhouse and Kinnaird had preferred to maintain a dignified silence about their old friend, but Moore wrote his biography partly because

> If we could get all the world to preserve silence on the subject of Byron's private character, I agree with Hobhouse that it would be better to let him in future live only in his works; but if every rascal that ever broke bread with him is to be suffered to depreciate and villify his character, while his friends stand by in (what they think) dignified silence, this, I do not hesitate to say, is to surrender tamely, if not faithlessly, the memory of the man we all loved, undefended, into the hands of his enemies.[46]

Moore was only partially successful. Byron's reputation as a rake, and probably most importantly the rumors of his relationship with Augusta, offended the Victorians, who preferred to love the poetry and hate, or even ignore, the man. Such attitudes persisted into the twentieth century. When the Nottingham Mechanics' Institute held a Byron exhibition in 1915, the event was opened with a lecture by Marie Corelli entitled "Byron: The Man and the Poet." In fact, despite the title, Corelli insisted that "it is not my intention to discuss the private faults and follies of so brilliant a genius. I consider that a man's work is a man's true self."[47] Through the interwar years Byron continued to be ostracized by literary scholars. T. S. Eliot, writing in 1937, claimed to address only "the qualities and defects visible in his work," not "the private life, with which I am not concerned." Scholars tried to ignore the biographical context of Byron's work, and since this was clearly nonsensical they tended to denigrate the verse as aesthetically "impure."[48] Schoolchildren were warned not to be too inquisitive. In Geoffrey Trease's words: "Generations of boys and girls at school, while expected to study and appreciate his poems, have been discouraged from asking awkward questions about his life." Byron was not approved of, not an example to set before the young.[49]

In these circumstances, interest in Newstead waned. The house remained open to visitors in the later nineteenth century, but only on a restricted basis. After 1918 its fate hung in the balance. Country houses were out of fashion. Some were pulled down, especially in the years after about 1926; others were converted for alternative uses such as schools or even hospitals; and yet others—a possibility considered for Newstead—were turned into apartments.[50] All around the demolition men were moving in, often with scarcely disguised local enthusiasm. This was all too evidently the case when Nuthall Temple, no more than ten miles from Newstead, and one of the four or five English descendants of Palladio's Villa Rotonda, came down in 1929. On 31 July that year it was simply torched by a local property developer "without protest from the village constable or any of the spectators." The *Nottingham Evening News* reported that the blaze was "a wonderful sight."[51] Newstead was of nothing like such architectural significance; indeed, the National Trust considered it insufficiently important to take over. Fortunately, a Byron devotee appeared who was willing to take what was obviously a risk by associating himself with the poet. This was Sir Julian Cahn, a local businessman and philanthropist, who in 1931 bought the house from Charles Fraser and then presented it to Nottingham City Council as a memorial to the poet: "I shall have the pleasure of knowing that Newstead, which is of such great interest to the lovers of Byron's works, will for all time be in safe hands."[52] Cahn may have been motivated by seeing the way in which Nottingham City Council had acquired Wollaton Hall from Lord Middleton in 1924 and succeeded both in retaining the house and making the transaction profitable by selling off part of the park for housing development.

Fraser, following in his family's tradition of seeing themselves as guardians of the Byron legacy, offered to the city various pictures, including the 1813 Phillips portrait, and other artifacts that he considered "properly the complement" of Newstead. As Fraser subsequently told the audience who attended the handing-over ceremony, his family, "ever since they had been at Newstead had regarded the possession of these treasures as in the nature of a public charge. . . . They were merely the guardians of them." Noticeably the emphasis during the ceremonies was placed firmly on Byron's links with Greece. None of his poetry was read or, indeed, even mentioned, although the Greek prime minister did accurately predict that the "ancestral home of Byron might continue as a shrine of pilgrimage for devotion to ideas and poetry . . . liberty and sacrifice."[53] Nottingham City Council subsequently reopened Newstead to the public.

Since the 1930s a great deal has changed. The threat posed to country houses has been lifted; indeed, today the emphasis is on conservation, rather than destruction. Changing social attitudes have meant that the Victorian veil drawn over Byron's personal life has been lifted, largely through the publication in 1957 of Leslie Marchand's three-volume biography and G. Wilson

Newstead today. (Private collection.)

Knight's *Lord Byron's Marriage*, which made what were still at the time sensational claims about Byron's sexuality. Westminster Abbey finally agreed in 1969 to a Byron memorial in Poet's Corner. These changes have been significant, because today Newstead is a Grade I listed building, with its future assured, and no one suffers the same prurient worries of earlier generations about allowing themselves and their children to be sullied by an acquaintance with the memory of Lord Byron.

Today Byronic pilgrims and local people happily gather during the summer months at Newstead Abbey, the unofficial shrine of George Gordon, sixth Lord Byron. It was his poetry, not his estate management, which made Byron famous, a fact recognized by Lady Blessington as early as 1823: "Were he but sensible how much the *Lord* is overlooked in the *Poet* he would be less vain of his rank."[54] Subsequently it has been the international fame of the poet and his poetry that has protected Newstead from destruction, and that led to its coming into public hands during the 1930s. It is because of the sixth Lord Byron that in truth the Byrons have never left Newstead, and yet there is something remarkably ironic about this situation. Byron inherited Newstead by accident. Had William Byron not died at the Siege of Calvi in 1794, things might well have been quite different. If William Byron had lived, and if he had married and raised children, George Gordon Byron could have expected no more than a quiet upbringing in Scotland on whatever his mother's income would buy. He would have had to earn his own living, perhaps in a profession. By temperament he would probably have written poetry, but would literary London have read the works of an obscure Scot? And would he ever have had the resources to travel, and to enjoy the experiences that he poured into *Childe Harold, Don Juan,* and his other literary works? The accident that left Byron in possession of an aristocratic title and a landed estate also helped to open up to him channels into literary society. Through friendships forged in his school and university days, and because he was at leisure to write poetry (despite his cash-flow problems), he was able to move in the sort of circles that in 1812 catapulted him to fame and success in literary society.

Byron did not respond well to his success. In 1811 he refused to entertain Hanson's proposals for the sale of Newstead, and he had made a will strictly settling Newstead on his successor in title. As such he acted like an aristocrat, but not for long. After 1812 he considered himself a Londoner, for whom Newstead was an occasional retreat from the perpetual whirl of his newfound social life. He could not bring himself to worry about the business of an estate, and agreed to sell the family patrimony that he had inherited through no merits of his own but from which he now cut off the Byrons, notably George Anson Byron, his successor in title. Although from the perspective of his finances this may have been the most sensible course of action, it was not what was expected of a landed gentleman. When in 1816 he ran into trouble with his newfound friends because of suspicions about his relationships with Augusta and Annabella, he fled not to Newstead, where he could (like his great uncle in 1765) have found the peace and security of tranquil Nottinghamshire while he worked his passage back into society, but abroad. He went with no desire other than to sell his estates, pay his debts, and live out the rest of his days writing what he wanted on a secured investment income. His credibility as a landowner was gone. Most families would have tried to bury his memory in decent obscurity as the disastrous generation who, left to his own devices by not inheriting the estate in settlement, had run them out of funds and land.[55]

While his mother lived, Byron appreciated, or at least claimed to, his great good fortune in 1794: his title, his land, his money, his entrée into London literary circles. These were lessons he forgot, or chose to abandon, in 1812, and yet ironically it is his fame as a poet, perhaps never more so than in the ringing stanzas of canto 13 in *Don Juan,* which means Byron is more closely associated with Newstead today than ever. The thirteenth Lord Byron lives in relative obscurity in Essex: he might be forgiven for refusing to have anything whatsoever to do with his predecessor in title: after all, even the fifth Lord Byron left the family with an estate and a great house. The sixth Lord Byron left them with nothing—but he left us all with a collection of poetry that might never have been written but for the fatal cannonball fired by an unknown gunner at Calvi in 1794, and with a house—Newstead Abbey—which might not have survived but for its links with the poet.

THE BYRON FAMILY

WILLIAM
1636-95
3rd Lord Byron
= Elizabeth Chaworth
(1632-83)

WILLIAM
(1670-1736)
4th Lord Byron
= (1) 1703 Mary, dau. Earl of Bridgewater (d. 1703)
(2) 1706 Frances Williamina, dau. Earl of Portland (d. 1712)
(3) 1720 Frances, dau. Lord Berkeley (d. 1757) = (2) 1740 Sir Thomas Hay

Katherine = Sir Arthur Cole

Juliana (d.1731)

George = Frances Levett
(1730-89)

Charles
(1726-31)

John = 1748 Sophia Trevanion
(1723-86)   (d. 1790)

Richard
(1724-1811)

Charlotte = Admiral
Parker

Sophia Maria

George = Augusta Byron

Robert John Wilmot
(1784-1841)

Juliana = (1) (1771) William Byron
(d.1788)   (2) (1783) Sir Robert
                  Wilmot
                  (c.1752-1834)

Frances = General
            Charles
            Leigh

GEORGE ANSON =
(1789-1868)
7th Lord Byron
Elizabeth
Chandos
Pole (d. 1873)

GEORGE ANSON = 1843 Lucy Westcomb
(1818-70)   (d. 1912)
8th Lord Byron

George Anson = Charlotte
                  Dallas

George Gordon
of Gight (1765-1811)

WILLIAM
(1722-98)
5th Lord Byron
= 1747 Elizabeth
       Shaw (d.1788)

Isabella = (1) 1743 Earl of Carlisle
(1721-94) (2) 1759 Sir Wilfrid Lawson

Frances
(1711-24)

George
(1707-20)

Caroline
(1755-84)

John = (1) 1779 Lady Carmarthen
(1757-91) (2) 1785 Catherine Gordon
                  of Gight (1765-1811)

GEORGE GORDON = 1815 Annabella
(1788-1824)   Milbanke
6th Lord Byron   (d. 1860)

Augusta Ada
(1815-52)

Augusta Mary = 1807 Col.
(1784-1851)   George Leigh
                         (1st cousin)

Henrietta
(1751-60)

Juliana
(d.1788)

William
(1749-76)

William
(1748-9)

William John
(1772-94)

Notes

BL   British Library
Lovelace   Bodleian Library, Lovelace-Byron Mss.
BLJ   *Byron's Letters and Journals*, ed. Leslie A. Marchand, 13 vols. (London: John Murray, 1973–94)
Murray Mss. Papers held by John Murray, Publishers, Albemarle Street
NAC   Newstead Abbey Collection
N.A.O.   Nottinghamshire Archives Office
N.U.M.D.   Nottingham University Manuscripts Department
P.R.O.   Public Record Office
Reelig   Papers of Trower, Still, and Keeling, Solicitors, now in the possession of the Fraser family of Reelig Glen, Inverness-shire
TTS   *Transactions of the Thoroton Society*

PREFACE

1. W. S. Blunt, *My Diaries, 1888–1914* (London: Secker, 1932), 663–64.

INTRODUCTION

1. Washington Irving, *Abbotsford and Newstead Abbey* (London: Henry G. Bohn, 1850), 60.

2. Sir Julien Cahn to the Lord Mayor of Nottingham, 19 Sept. 1930, in *The Roe-Byron Collection: Newstead Abbey* (Nottingham, U.K.: Corporation of Nottingham, 1937), 21.

3. Peter Mandler, *The Fall and Rise of the Stately Home* (New Haven: Yale University Press, 1997), 245–46. The National Trust refused the house.

4. Thomas Moore, *Letters and Journals of Lord Byron with Notices of his Life,* 2d ed. (London: John Murray, 1830), 11.

5. *Nottingham Journal,* 17 July 1931; *Nottingham Guardian,* 17 July 1931. Both newspapers carried long reports and several pictures of the handing-over ceremony. A black-and-white silent film made on the occasion is now in Nottingham City Library.

6. Pamphlet commemorating the gift of Newstead to City of Nottingham by Sir Julien Cahn, and of Byron furniture and relics by Mr. Charles Ian Fraser, 16 July 1931.

7. Phyllis Grosskurth, *Byron: The Flawed Angel* (London: Hodder & Stoughton, 1997), 305.

8. Leslie A. Marchand, *Byron: A Biography*, 3 vols. (London: John Murray, 1957), 1:266.

9. H. M. Swartz and M. Swartz, eds., *Disraeli's Reminiscences* (London: Hamilton, 1975), 129–36.

10. John Bateman, *The Great Landowners of Great Britain and Ireland* (1883; reprint, Leicester: Leicester University Press, 1969).

11. In later chapters I have, I hope gently, pointed to some of the problems arising from Doris Langley Moore's book (*Lord Byron: Accounts Rendered* [London: John Murray, 1974]). I have no desire whatsoever to be thought critical of her pioneering research in this area, but having studied the fortunes of many English landed families I am aware that there are shortcomings in her approach.

12. Marchand, *Byron: A Biography*, vii.

13. Mandler, *Fall and Rise of the Stately Home,* 401–18.

CHAPTER 1. THE BYRONS AND NEWSTEAD

1. A. Hamilton Thompson, "The Priory of St Mary of Newstead in Sherwood Forest," *TTS* 23 (1919): 33–141.

2. D. Bewley, "Newstead Priory," in *Sanctity and Scandal,* ed. D. Marcombe and J. Hamilton (Nottingham: Continuing Education Press, University of Nottingham, 1998), 65; R. Howard et al., "Tree-Ring Dates for Some East Midlands Buildings: 3," *TTS* 89 (1985): 36.

3. Quoted in Bewley, "Newstead Priory," 66.

4. This account of Newstead is largely based on Hamilton Thompson's study (see note 1, above).

5. The family background is given in V. W. Walker and M. J. Howell, *The House of Byron: A History of the Family from the Norman Conquest, 1066–1988* (London: Quiller Press, 1988).

6. Maurice Howard, *The Early Tudor Country House* (London: George Philip, 1987), chap. 7.

7. H. T. Fishwick, ed., *Survey of the Manor of Rochdale, 1626,* Chetham Society Remains, 71 (Manchester: Chetham Society, 1913), xiv.

8. Walker and Howell, *House of Byron*, 46–48.

9. Fishwick, *Survey of the Manor of Rochdale*, xvi, et seq.; Walker and Howell, *House of Byron*, 66.

10. T. Wildman to Miss Cursham, 20 Aug. 1831, N.A.O. M 509. See chap. 12 for Wildman's work at Newstead.

11. Murray Mss. Box A1.

12. T. Wildman to Miss Cursham, 20 Aug. 1831, N.A.O. M 509.

13. W. Webster, ed., *Nottinghamshire Hearth Tax Returns, 1664, 1674,* Thoroton Society Record Series, 37 (Nottingham, U.K.: Thoroton Society, 1988), xxxiii.

14. BL, Addit. Mss. 32,686, fol. 102; 32,687, fol. 188; Walker and Howell, *House of Byron*, 116–18.

15. Rosalys Coope, "Newstead Abbey in the Eighteenth Century: The Building Works of the Fourth and Fifth Lords Byron," *TTS* 83 (1979): 56–62.

16. Sidney Evelyn to Sir John Evelyn, 30 Sept. 1738, BL, Evelyn Papers, SJE12.

17. Peter Tillemans (1684–1734) spent several years at Newstead. Many of his paintings were sold in the 1770s, but have occasionally been recovered for the modern collection. Two paintings, which have been in the Bute Collection of Sporting Pictures since the 1930s, were bought for Newstead in August 1999: *Nottingham Evening Post*, 27 Aug. 1999.

18. P.R.O. C 108/4. Some of the family portraits at Newstead listed in 1762 have subsequently been lost, although the present Lord Byron owns many of those which have survived: BL, Addit. Mss. 5726 F(3): ff. 1–3.

19. Sidney Evelyn to Sir John Evelyn, 30 Sept. 1738, BL, Evelyn Papers, SJE12; Coope, "Newstead Abbey," 50.

20. N.U.M.D. P1 E12/3/1/13/1–2. For the family tree, see the appendix.

21. "Abstract of the Title of Lt. Col. Wildman to the Newstead Estates, 1847," Reelig, 717.

22. Byron to the Duke of Portland, 31 Jan. 1722, N.A.O. M 18061–2.

23. G. E. Cokayne, *The Complete Peerage of England, Scotland, Ireland, Great Britain, and the United Kingdom, Extant, Extinct, or Dormant,* 13 vols. (London: St. Catherine Press, 1910–): 2:456; N.U.M.D. P1 E12/3/1/18.

24. BL, Addit. Mss. 36,686, fols. 424, 432.

25. The 1692 figures are from N.U.M.D. P1 E12/3/1/64. The 1720 rental is in the Murray Mss.

26. N.U.M.D. P1 E12/3/3/7–9, E12/3/4/9/1–2.

27. P.R.O. PROB 11/679, fol. 213; 20 George II, c.18, "An Act for Settling the Estates of William, Lord Byron and Elizabeth Shaw, Spinster" (1747).

28. N.U.M.D. P1 E12/3/1/20–3, 26.

29. Historical Manuscripts Commission, *Dartmouth Mss.* 3:158; Parish Register abstracts, Murray Mss. Box A1.

30. P.R.O. C 11/139/4.

CHAPTER 2. WILLIAM, FIFTH LORD BYRON: LANDOWNING ARISTOCRAT, 1743–70

1. *Cobbett's Complete Collection of State Trials* (London: Longman & Co., 1809–26), 19:1175; *Account of the Tryal of Lord William Byron* (London: n.p., 1765).

2. Moore, *Letters and Journals of Lord Byron,* xxx.

3. Irving, *Abbotsford and Newstead Abbey,* 55.

4. *People's Journal* 56 (1847), Murray Mss.

5. Cokayne, *Complete Peerage,* 2:456; *Dictionary of National Biography,* 3:584.

6. André Maurois, *Byron* (London: Jonathan Cape, 1930), 19–24.

7. Marchand, *Byron: A Biography,* 7–10.

8. Elizabeth Longford, *Byron* (London: Weidenfeld and Nicolson, 1976), 5.

9. Grosskurth, *Byron,* 6–7. See also Benita Eisler, *Byron: Child of Passion, Fool of Fame* (London: Hamish Hamilton, 1999), 8, and Keith Train, "The Byron Family: From the Conqueror to the Poet, Most Gifted of Them All," *Byron Journal* 2 (1974): 39. In fairness, Miss Walker has commented that following the trial "far from retiring from the world he continued to divide his time between town and country as before," and "the welfare of the estate was emphatically not being neglected as yet": Walker and Howell, *House of Byron,* 133–34; Rosalys Coope, "Newstead Abbey in the Eighteenth Century: The Building Works of the Fourth and Fifth Lords Byron," *TTS* 83 (1979): 57.

10. Keele University Archives, M 72/31/2; N.A.O. M 24,194; Walker and Howell, *House of Byron*, 119, 123.

11. P.R.O. C 11/139/4; C 108/4. Since George Bowes was lessee of Newstead, it was not possible to prepare a new inventory, and the listing used on this occasion was a copy of the one prepared when Bowes leased the estate in 1738: Keele University Library, M72/31/2. The role of Chancery in respect of a minor is discussed in chap. 4.

12. Quoted in Walker and Howell, *House of Byron*, 124.

13. N.U.M.D. P1 E12/3/1/32–4.

14. N.U.M.D. P1 E12/3/1/24–5, 27, 28.

15. N.A.O. M 5443. I have been able to discover little about the East Anglian holdings either in the Norfolk Record Office or in the surviving Byron papers. Noel Boston and Eric Puddy, *Dereham: The Biography of a Country Town* (Dereham, U.K.: privately printed, 1952), 278, suggest Byron was a tenant of the Crown as late as 1787. I am grateful also to Dr. Susannah Wade Martins for help in tracking down the Norfolk manors. The rental figures are from the 1747 estate act.

16. 20 George II, c. 18, 1747. The estates were subject to the £300 jointure of Elizabeth's mother, Frances: Deeds, Murray Mss., Box A23.

17. Reelig, 717.

18. N.A.O. M 2569/5; M 2570/16.

19. W. S. Lewis, ed., *The Yale Edition of Horace Walpole's Correspondence* (New Haven: Yale University Press, 1941–), 9:299, 35:105.

20. Historical Manuscripts Commission, *Verulam Mss.* (London: H.M.S.O., 1906), 233.

21. Arthur Young, *The Farmers' Tour through the East of England*, vol. 1 (London: W. Strahan, 1771), 142–48.

22. N.A.O. M 2571/281, M 2572/325, 374. Daws was paid expenses for a visit to Gainsborough and Stockwith to buy materials for the ship: M 2567, 28 Nov. 1764; Young, *Farmers' Tour*, 141.

23. Coope, "Newstead Abbey," 56–57. This third lake, today always known as "the Lower Lake," is distinct from Byron's lower lake, the Sherwood, which is now buried in trees and largely forgotten.

24. N.A.O. M 2566–67; Walker and Howell, *House of Byron*, 127; Irving, *Abbotsford and Newstead Abbey*, 74; Historical Manuscripts Commission, *Verulam Mss.*, 233; Paul Sandby, *The Virtuosi's Museum* (London: G. Kearsly, 1778), plate 61; Lord Byron, *The Complete Poetical Works*, ed. J. J. McGann, 7 vols. (Oxford: Clarendon Press, 1980–93), 5:541.

25. N.A.O. M 2569/26, 6; M 2570/153.

26. N.A.O. DD 721/1/145; Reelig, 716.

27. N.A.O. M 2570/156; M 2567; M 2569/13, 14, 21.

28. N.A.O. M 2569/92; M 2567 Apr. 1761.

29. N.A.O. M 2570/160; M 2567–68.

30. N.A.O. M 2572/349, 353, 363, 387; M 2568.

31. N.A.O. M 2569/16.

32. N.U.M.D. P1 E12/3/1/42/1–2, 43; N.A.O. M 2570/105, 145, 146, 157, 162; M 2566.

33. N.A.O. M 2570/142, 187.

34. Reelig, 716.

35. N.U.M.D. P1 E12/3/5/3; Charles Slater held a farm of 152 acres 2 roods, paying a rent of £60 a year: N.U.M.D. P1 E12/3/1/60/2.

36. N.A.O. M 2570/120, 124.

37. N.A.O. M 2570/181, 267. The act was passed in 1771 and the award was in 1775 (for 3,143 acres).

38. N.A.O. M 2571/247, 252, 253, 295; M 2567.

39. N.A.O. M 2569/72, 75, 90.

40. N.A.O. M 2570/107, 119.

41. N.A.O. M 2570/134, 142, 144, 148.

42. N.A.O. M 2570/160, 170, 175, 185, 188. I am grateful to Dr. Colin Phillips for help in tracking down details of the Rochdale enclosure.

43. N.A.O. M 2569/9, 13, 19a.

44. N.A.O. M 2569/20, 21, 24.

45. N.A.O. M 2569/49.

46. N.A.O. M 2567, March–May 1760.

47. N.U.M.D. P1 E12/3/5/3–17; E12/3/1/60/2.

48. "Newstead Leases," Murray Mss.; Walker and Howell, *House of Byron*, 137; N.A.O. Violet Walker's Mss. notes. The Besthorpe sale is mentioned in a letter of Peter Stoughton to William Daws of February 1769, but I have been able to find no other direct evidence relating to it: M 2570/157. Particulars of the estate, drawn up apparently prior to sale c. 1752, show an annual rental of £715: N.A.O. M 5443–48,

49. N.U.M.D. P1 E12/3/2/14/3.

50. N.A.O. M 2567.

51. N.U.M.D. P1 E12/3/1/35/1–2.

52. N.U.M.D. P1 E12/3/1/37/1–2, 38.

53. Lewis, *Yale Edition of Horace Walpole's Correspondence* 9:299.

54. N.A.O. M 2569/44, 96; Reelig, 705, 719; Murray Mss. Box A23 Deeds; Young, *Farmers' Tour*, 141.

55. N.U.M.D. P1 E12/3/2/1/1.

56. N.U.M.D. P1 E12/3/1/39/1–3, 40/1–3.

57. N.U.M.D. P1 E12/3/2/2/3–4; E12/3/2/3/3.

58. N.U.M.D. P1 E12/3/2/21/1; E12/3/2/25/1–2; E12/3/2/4/1–2.

59. N.U.M.D. P1 E12/3/2/5/1; E12/3/1/50/1–2.

60. N.A.O. M 2570/101, 174; M 2572/356.

61. N.A.O. M 2570/177.

62. N.A.O. M 2570/182.

63. N.U.M.D. P1 E12/3/2/6/1–2.

64. N.A.O. M 2569/87, 50; M 2570/137.

65. N.A.O. M 2571/225. The fourth Lord Byron's holdings in government stock had long gone by this time, except for £4,000 in lottery annuities resubscribed into South Sea Stock, which was to be part of his daughter's portion.

66. N.A.O. M 2569/11, 29, 83, 91.

67. N.A.O. M 2569/40.

68. N.A.O. M 2569/66, 78; M 2570/164, 167, 172, 184; M 2571/221.

69. N.A.O. M 2569/32.

70. N.A.O. M 2569/43.

71. N.A.O. M 2569/86; M 2571/211, 212.

72. N.A.O. M 2569/77.

73. N.A.O. M 2570/178; M 2572/303.

74. N.A.O. M 2569/45; M 2571/238; M 2572/319.

75. N.A.O. M 2570/102, 112, 123, 161.

76. N.A.O. M 2571/216, 279, 293; M 2572/314.
77. These details are reconstructed from Reelig, 705–6.

Chapter 3. William, Fifth Lord Byron: The Man and the Myth, 1770–98

1. N.A.O. M 2570/136.
2. Hanson Narrative, Murray Mss.
3. N.A.O. M 2570/100, 108, 128.
4. N.A.O. M 2570/166, 173, 187, 194.
5. N.A.O. M 2571/219, 230, 235.
6. N.A.O. M 2571/239, 240, 242, 246, 259.
7. N.U.M.D. P1 E12/3/2/19/1; E12/3/2/7/1; E12/3/1/52; Reelig, 719.
8. Affidavits re the family descent of the sixth Lord Byron, Reelig, 698; Hanson Narrative, Murray Mss.
9. Irving, *Abbotsford and Newstead Abbey,* 55.
10. Lovelace, Box 161, fols. 1–3, 7. In October 1771 William Byron agreed to settle a jointure of £100 on Juliana, and to set aside portions of £4,000 for any younger children of the marriage, but only when he came into the property following the fifth lord's death. These putative arrangements were superseded in the 1773 resettlement.
11. N.U.M.D. P1 E12/3/2/8/1; E12/3/2/10/1, 11/1.
12. N.A.O. M 2570/158, 163; M 2571/283, 286; M 2572/299, 300, 310, 312; N.U.M.D. P1 E12/3/1/42/3.
13. N.A.O. M 2572/301.
14. N.A.O. M 2572/311, 320; M 2571/297.
15. N.A.O. M 2591/289.
16. Rosalys Coope, "Newstead Abbey in the Eighteenth Century: The Building Works of the Fourth and Fifth Lords Byron," *TTS* 83 (1979): 58; Walker and Howell, *House of Byron,* 136–37.
17. N.A.O. M 2572/343, 339, 355.
18. N.A.O. M 2572/346; Reelig, 705. Mather had paid Byron the whole rent for Bulwell Forge (£945) in 1762 by way of a bond, but once Byron sold the property he needed to reclaim £615 (rent plus interest no longer payable to Byron, since Devonshire now owned the forge).
19. Deeds, Murray Mss. Box A23; N.U.M.D. P1 E12/3/1/41, 45, 47.
20. N.U.M.D. P1 E12/3/1/46.
21. N.U.M.D. P1 E12/3/1/52; E12/3/1/60/2. A total of 3,200 acres is the figure given in subsequent sale catalogs, although the figures given here cannot be reconciled.
22. N.A.O. M 2572/354.
23. N.A.O. M 2572/372, 378, 384, 388; M 2571/267, 287; M 2567.
24. "Abstract of Title of George Gordon, Lord Byron," reciting the various settlements, Reelig, 719; Copy Deed of Covenants, 19 Feb. 1774. The numerous settlement documents are outlined in Murray Mss. Box A23 Deeds, Appeal Documents, House of Lords.
25. N.U.M.D. P1 E12/3/1/58/1–2.
26. N.A.O. M 164
27. N.U.M.D. P1 E12/3/7/21; E12/3/6/26, 27; M 2568.
28. N.U.M.D. P1 E12/3/1/54/1–3, 55–63.
29. Accounts of Brackley Kennett and John Heaton, Reelig, 705; Lists of Judgments in the King's Bench, 706; N.U.M.D. P1 E12/3/1/64.

30. N.A.O. M 2572/386; Reelig, 706, 719.

31. N.U.M.D. PwF 2928.

32. Rochdale rental 1795, Murray Mss. Box A23.

33. Coope, "Newstead Abbey," 58.

34. Reelig, 716; BL, Addit. Mss. 18,551, fol. 10; 62,910. Byron was looking to raise the rent to £600 in 1787: BL, Addit. Mss. 18,551, fol.10.

35. Hanson Narrative, Murray Mss. (Newton Hanson's narrative was intended as a running commentary on the sixth lord's early life to supplement Moore's *Life*, but it was never published).

36. Robert Thoroton, *The Antiquities of Nottinghamshire*, ed. and enl. by John Throsby (Nottingham, 1790–96), 2:289.

37. F. C. Laird, *The Beauties of England and Wales* (London: Verner & Hood, 1813), vol. 12, pt. 1, 401.

38. Irving, *Abbotsford and Newstead Abbey,* 60.

39. Robert Lowe, *General View of the Agriculture of the County of Nottingham* (London: printed for G. Nicol, 1798), 23.

40. Thoroton, *Antiquities,* 2:289–90.

41. BL, Addit. Mss. 62,910.

42. Baptism certificate, Murray Mss. Box A1.

43. Irving, *Abbotsford and Newstead Abbey,* 55–56.

44. The 1778 auction catalog, NAC.

45. A. Henstock, ed., *The Diary of Abigail Gawthern,* Thoroton Society Record Series, 33 (Nottingham, U.K.: Thoroton Society, 1980), 34.

46. Byron to Dawes, 6 Apr. 1779, Murray Mss. Box A1.

47. N.A.O. M 2568.

48. N.A.O. M 24195; M 1923; M 2567; N.U.M.D. P1 E12/3/6/20, 24–6; Walker and Howell, *House of Byron,* 140–41.

49. N.A.O. M 1924.

50. Coope, "Newstead Abbey," 58.

51. N.A.O. M 2568; M 10361.

52. N.A.O. M 2572/308.

53. N.A.O. M 2572/317.

54. N.A.O. M 2657.

55. N.A.O. M 5603, M 5604; M 507; Miscellaneous Papers, 12; Papers of Violet Walker.

56. A. Tayler and H. Tayler, eds., *Lord Fife and His Factor: Being the Correspondence of James, Second Lord Fife, 1729–1809* (London: Heinemann, 1925), 172–73.

57. N.U.M.D. P1 E12/3/7/19, 22.

58. N.A.O. M 2568.

59. Tayler and Tayler, *Lord Fife,* 172–73; *Nottingham Journal,* 14 May 1785.

60. *Nottingham Journal,* 8 August 1790; Nan Greatrex, "The Robinson Enterprises at Papplewick, Nottinghamshire," *Industrial Archaeology Review* 9, pt. 1 (1986): 37–56, pt. 2 (1986): 119–39; Reelig, 701; Tayler and Tayler, *Lord Fife,* 172–73.

61. N.A.O. M 2568.

62. Aisley appears on legal documents as early as 1781: Reelig, 716.

63. Will of Lord William Byron, d. 1798, Borthwick Institute, York.

64. N.A.O. Violet Walker notes; the fifty-six-acre farm was let to him in 1755 for twenty-one years at £30 a year: N.U.M.D. P1 E12/3/5/2, 3/1/60/2. The farm was part of the property sold in 1774 to the duke of Devonshire, and following subsequent reorganization by 1790 he was farming 118 acres: N.U.M.D. P1 E12/3/7/22.

65. Deed, 17 Feb. 1794, Shawe-Brown Mss.

66. Lovelace, Box 161, fols. 62–70.

67. The case is recorded in *Notes and Queries* 8, no. 192 (2 July 1853): 2, where Haselden noted that the law had subsequently been changed to prevent such a situation from recurring: BL, Egerton 2612, fols. 5–6.

68. A rental of estates in the parish of Rochdale, 1795, Murray Mss. Box A23; BL, Egerton 2611, fols. 2–10.

69. Irving, *Abbotsford and Newstead Abbey,* 75.

70. Hanson Narrative, Murray Mss.; Henstock, *Diary of Abigail Gawthern,* 73; Administration Papers of Lord William Byron, d. 1798, Borthwick Institute, York. Aisley knew of Byron's death on 1 June, but he did not agree to act until 9 June, and he did not attend the funeral: Hanson's Account, Murray Mss. Box A23.

71. Hanson Narrative, Murray Mss.

72. Hanson Narrative, Murray Mss.

73. Grosskurth, *Byron,* xiv; Marchand refers more vaguely to the estate being "encumbered": Marchand, *Byron: A Biography,* 49, but in *Byron: A Portrait* (London: John Murray, 1971), 16 he makes the spurious claim about burial costs quoted here; in fact, burial could and did take place before debts were paid; Eisler, *Byron,* 30.

74. Bell to Hanson, 25 July 1802, BL, Egerton 2612.

CHAPTER 4. THE ESTATE DURING THE MINORITY, 1798–1809

1. When, for legal purposes, it was necessary in 1809 to establish the sixth Lord Byron's title to the family estates, Thomas France, the clerk deputed to do the work, searched for evidence of the marriage of Sophia Trevanion of Carhays, Cornwall, at the parish church and in parishes in London and elsewhere but was not able to trace anything. However, he learnt from old people that the marriage took place in the chapel, by then in ruins, belonging to the lady's father at Carhays. No registers were kept: Parish Register abstracts, Murray Mss. Box A1; Reelig, 698/5, 699.

2. BL, Addit. Mss. 39,992, fols. 330–31. The marital and financial problems of Admiral John Byron and his wife are recorded in A.L. Rowse, *The Byrons and the Trevanions* (London: Weidenfeld & Nicolson, 1978); Walker and Howell, *House of Byron,* 156–66.

3. BL, Addit. Mss. 39,992, fols. 330–35; Parish Register abstracts, Murray Mss. Box A1.

4. Marriage Certificate, Murray Mss. Box A1; Megan Boyes, *My Amiable Mamma: A Biography of Mrs. Catherine Gordon Byron* (Derby, U.K.: privately published, 1991), 11–14.

5. John Byron Gordon to ?, 26 Jan. 1788, Murray Mss. Box A1.

6. Mrs. Byron to James Watson, 22 Feb. 1788, Murray Mss. Box A1.

7. Charles Gould to James Sykes, 25 Aug. 1790, Murray Mss. Box A1.

8. Will of John Byron, 1791, Murray Mss. Box A1; Langley Moore, *Lord Byron,* chap. 1.

9. Marriage Settlement and related papers of Byron and Miss Gordon, 1786–88; Hanson Narrative, Murray Mss. Box A23; Marchand, *Byron: A Portrait,* 10.

10. Mrs. Byron to Mrs. Leigh, 23 Aug. 1791, Murray Mss. Box A1.

11. BL, Addit. Mss. 31,037, fol. 11.

12. James Farquhar to John Hanson, 28 Mar. 1793, Lovelace, Box 161, fol. 98.

13. Hanson's Account, Hanson Narrative, Murray Mss. Box A23.

14. Boyes, *My Amiable Mamma,* 15–53; BL, Egerton 2612, fol. 7.

15. Henstock, *Diary of Abigail Gawthern,* 74; Walker and Howell, *House of Byron,*

174–75; *To an Oak in the Garden of Newstead Abbey,* in Byron, *Complete Poetical Works,* ed. McGann, 1:204.

16. "My father had made me understand that I was a caretaker for future generations," the duke of Westminster told the *Sunday Times* on 20 February 1983.

17. *BLJ,* 7:204; Mrs. Byron claimed descent from Princess Annabella Stewart, the daughter of King James I of Scotland. On this basis in 1799 she petitioned for a civil list pension. Subsequently she received £300 a year, reduced in 1805 to £200: J. Birch to J. Hanson, 2 Dec. 1799, Murray Mss. Box A1. Mrs. Byron reckoned her income at £700 to £900 a year: *BLJ,* 13:86.

18. Moore, *Letters and Journals of Lord Byron,* 13.

19. No records have survived of Hanson's practice among the archives of The Law Society, nor is there any relevant material in the Hampshire Record Office.

20. BL, Egerton 2611, fols. 211–13; *BLJ,* 4:224. Newton Hanson recalled that "After Lord Byron came of age he was still the constant visitant at our house and whether at home or abroad was either personally or by letter in constant unreserved communication either with my father or myself": Hanson Narrative, Murray Mss.

21. J. D. Gross, ed., *Byron's "Corbeau Blanc": The Life and Letters of Lady Melbourne.* (Houston, Tex.: Rice University Press, 1997), 194.

22. Hanson held minor government office as "the Government solicitor of the stamp office . . . put in by Lord Grenville": *BLJ,* 4:217–18. Byron congratulated him on "the accession of Dignity . . . from your official appointment." His patrons were in the coalition ministry that was dismissed in March 1807: *BLJ,* 1:113.

23. *BLJ,* 2:94; 4:217–18. Byron regretted knowing so little of his father, and could never quite accept Hanson as the substitute he so obviously was:

> Stern Death, forbade my orphan youth to share,
> The tender guidance of a Father's care;
> Can Rank, or ev'n a Guardian's name supply,
> The love, which glistens in a Father's eye?

Childish Recollections (1806), first published in *Hours of Idleness* (1807): Byron, *Complete Poetical Works,* ed. McGann, 1:165.

24. *BLJ,* 3:248; 4:230; 8:208.

25. *BLJ,* 6:87.

26. Hanson Account, Murray Mss. No copy of this survey has survived, but sale particulars prepared in 1815 and 1817 were based on it.

27. *BLJ,* 4:276.

28. Hanson Account, Murray Mss. BL, Egerton 2612, fols. 37–38. For a similar example of a London-based steward controlling properties around the country, see Howard Erskine-Hill, *The Social Milieu of Alexander Pope* (New Haven: Yale University Press, 1975), chap. 4. A major landowner might have a man of business operating from London, and controlling the whole range of properties: see R. A. Kelch, *Newcastle: A Duke without Money, Thomas Pelham-Holles, 1693–1768* (London: Routledge and Kegan Paul, 1974).

29. BL, Egerton 2612, fols. 10–11; Hanson Account, 18 Sept. 1798, Murray Mss. The fifth lord's effects were still at Newstead in 1803: Hanson Account, 20 July 1803, Murray Mss. Although dilapidated, Newstead was not the ruin suggested by some more imaginative writers: Maurois, *Byron,* 42.

30. C. J. Tyerman, "Byron's Harrow," in *Byron: The Harrow Collection,* ed. P. D. Hunter (Harrow, U.K.: Harrow School, 1994), 27–35. The medical treatment in Nottingham was for his deformed foot: A. B. Morrison, "Byron's Lameness," *Byron Journal* 3 (1975): 24–30.

31. BL, Addit. Mss. 62,910; Boyes, *My Amiable Mamma*, 96.

32. BL, Egerton 2612, fols. 22–23, 30–31, 37–40, 43–44, 84–85.

33. Hanson Narrative, Murray Mss.

34. BL, Egerton 2612, fols. 75–77.

35. Rosalys Coope, "Lord Byron's Newstead: The Abbey and Its Furnishings during the Poet's Ownership, 1798–1817," *TTS* 91 (1987): 133.

36. BL, Egerton 2612, fols. 47–48, 54–55, 75–77, 78–81.

37. BL, Egerton 2612, fols. 88–89, 92–93, 100–102, 104–5.

38. BL, Egerton 2612, fols. 108–9, 112–13, 126–27; 2611, fols. 11–12; C. J. Wright, "The Miss Launders: A Brief Chapter in the History of Newstead Abbey," *Byron Journal* 7 (1979): 104–11; Boyes, *My Amiable Mamma,* 85.

39. BL, Egerton 2612, fols. 121–23, 140–41.

40. BL, Egerton 2612, fols. 49, 52–53. Hanson's statement suggests that Elizabeth Longford was being rather too imaginative when she wrote that "Newstead had to be let if it was to be restored in time for [Byron's] 21st birthday": Longford, *Byron*, 9.

41. Hanson to Mrs. Byron, 29 Jan. 1803, Murray Mss. Box A1.

42. BL, Egerton 2612, fols. 73–74, 94–95, 130–31. The annual rent was thirty-five guineas.

43. BL, Egerton 2612, fols. 82–83, 123, 128, 130–31.

44. He did not, however, take Miss Chaworth with him to Rochdale, although William Robertson subsequently created such an imaginary visit: *Rochdale and the Vale of Whitworth: Its Moorlands, Favourite Nooks, Green Lanes, and Scenery* (Rochdale: privately published, 1897), 217–45.

45. BL, Egerton 2612, fols. 126–27, 132–33, 136–37. Many of Mealey's comments may be taken as spite. Lord Grey is most unlikely to have shot pheasants at roost.

46. Byron, *Complete Poetical Works,* ed. McGann, 1:35.

47. Ibid., 1:204–5.

48. BL, Egerton 2612, fols. 149–50, 163–64.

49. BL, Egerton 2612, fols. 134–35, 213–14; 2611, fols. 19–21. The break with Grey has been much debated: See, for a general discussion of the various theories, Grosskurth, *Byron,* 27–28 and Eisler, *Byron,* 72–74.

50. BL, Egerton 2612, fols. 149–50.

51. BL, Egerton 2612, fols. 171–72.

52. BL, Egerton 2612, fols. 190–91, 194–95, 196–97, 200–204.

53. BL, Egerton 2612, fols. 205–6, 207, 224–28, 261.

54. BL, Egerton 2612, fols. 171–72, 177–78, 185–87.

55. BL, Egerton 2613, fols. 10–11, 21–22; Hanson to Mrs. Byron, 21 Dec. 1807, Murray Mss. Box A1.

56. BL, Egerton 2613, fols. 31–32, 47–48, 59–60; 2611, fols. 55–56. Grey was still at Newstead on 4 July (BL, Egerton 2611, fols. 66–67), although apparently not by the 28th (BL, Egerton 2613, fol. 54). Grey married Anna Maria Kelham in 1809, and died the following year at the age of thirty.

57. BL, Egerton 2612, fols. 24–25, 26–27, 28–29, 30–31, 34–35, 39–42, 49; Addit. Mss. 62,910.

58. BL, Egerton 2612, fols. 94–95, 103, 116, 130–31, 142–46; Addit. Mss. 62,910.

59. BL, Egerton 2612, fols. 148, 175, 167–68, 183–84; Addit. Mss. 62,910.

60. BL, Egerton 2612, fols. 147–48.

61. BL, Egerton 2612, fols. 56–57, 163–64. Captain Byron was the son of George Byron, youngest brother of the fifth Lord Byron. He lived in Nottingham.

62. BL, Egerton 2612, fols. 167–68.

63. Lowe, *General View of the Agriculture of the County of Nottingham*, 23; D. V. Fowkes, "Nottinghamshire Parks in the Eighteenth and Nineteenth Centuries," *TTS* 71 (1967): 83. Some of the reorganization probably dates from 1812–15, when Thomas Claughton was at Newstead: see chap. 7.

64. Hanson to Kinnaird, 7 Sept. 1819, Hanson's Account, Murray Mss.; Reelig, 700.

65. BL, Egerton 2612, fols. 56–57, 145–46, 155–57, 169–70, 177–84, 188–89; Addit. Mss. 62,910; Hanson Narrative, Mrs. Byron to Hanson, 26 Apr. 1804, Murray Mss.

66. BL, Egerton 2612, fols. 30–31, 36.

67. BL, Egerton 2612, fols. 56–57, 94–95, 185–87, 218–19, 222–23.

68. BL, Egerton 2612, fols. 207, 215–17.

69. Reelig, 700; BL, Egerton 2612, fols. 45–46, 62–63.

70. BL, Egerton 2612, fols. 73–74.

71. BL, Egerton 2612, fols. 196–99, 218–19.

72. BL, Egerton 2612, fols. 233–38.

73. BL, Egerton 2612, fols. 239–42.

74. BL, Egerton 2613, fols. 2–3, 10–11, 15–16; 2611, fol. 145; 2612, fols. 233–34.

75. BL, Egerton 2613, fols. 6–7, 35–37, 39–40.

76. BL, Egerton 2612, fols. 237–38.

77. BL, Egerton 2613, fols. 2–3, 6–7, 10–11, 17–18, 31–32.

78. BL, Egerton 2613, fols. 25–28, 38–40.

79. BL, Egerton 2613, fols. 6–7, 19–20; Hanson to Mrs. Byron, 9 Aug. 1807, Murray Mss. Box A1.

80. Hanson's Account, Murray Mss.

81. Hanson to Mrs. Byron, 28 July 1803, Murray Mss.; Charles Hanson to Byron, 20 May 1820, Hanson's Account, Murray Mss.; BL, Addit. Mss. 62,910; *BLJ,* 1:99, 107.

82. Hanson to Mrs. Byron, 9 Aug. 1807, Murray Mss. Box A1.

83. BL, Egerton 2611, fols. 30–32, 36–38; Hanson to Mrs. Byron, 21 Dec. 1807, Murray Mss. Box A1.

84. BL, Egerton 2611, fols. 39–40.

85. BL, Egerton 2611, fols. 52–54.

86. BL, Egerton 2611, fols. 55–56.

87. BL, Egerton 2611, fols. 57–58.

88. BL, Egerton 2613, fols. 13–14, 49–50.

89. Hanson to Mrs. Byron, 26 May 1808, Murray Mss. Box A1.

90. BL, Egerton 2611, fols. 59–61, 66–69; 2613, fol. 54.

91. BL, Egerton 2611, fols. 75–77, 81–82. Eisler, *Byron,* 159, who adopts the conventional anti-Hanson viewpoint in discussing Byron's fortunes, doubts if this visit to Rochdale actually occurred. In fact Hanson went on to Rochdale from Newstead, and subsequently returned to Nottinghamshire en route to London.

92. BL, Egerton 2611, fols. 83–84; 2613, fols. 66–68.

93. BL, Egerton 2611, fols. 85–86, 93–94.

94. The returns for 1802–6 are in BL, Addit. Mss. 62,910. There may be other material in the Chancery Papers, but these have proved elusive. Classes C 103-C 106 in the Public Record Office, the Chancery Masters' Exhibits, contain accounts in cases where guardians discharged their responsibilities unaided by Chancery appointees. The lists do not indicate the survival of any Byron material in these classes. Classes C 117-C 126 of the Chancery Masters Documents contain records of the processes whereby the activities of guardians were subsequently examined by officials of the court. Unfortunately there are no lists, and with millions of documents involved it is quite impractical to search for a particular case. C 101, Chancery accounts, is indexed, but there are no Byron materials. I am grateful to Dr. David Crook for advice on this point.

95. Hanson Narrative; Hanson Account; Charles Hanson to Byron, 11 Jan. 1820, Murray Mss.

96. *BLJ*, 4:276.

97. N.A.O. DD 721/1/145

98. P. Roebuck, "Post-Restoration Landownership: The Impact of the Abolition of Wardship," *Journal of British Studies* 18 (1978): 67–85; R. A. C. Parker, *Coke of Norfolk* (Oxford: Clarendon Press, 1975), 1–11.

CHAPTER 5. LORD BYRON COMES OF AGE: FUNDING THE HEIR, 1803–9

1. *Nottingham Journal*, 28 Jan. 1809.

2. Boyes, *My Amiable Mamma*, 145.

3. BL, Egerton 2611, fol. 97.

4. Hanson to Byron, 12 Jan. 1809, Murray Mss. Hanson, on hearing that Byron was not going to be present tried to excuse himself the journey to Nottinghamshire—without success.

5. The money was borrowed from John Davy through Mealey, and Mrs. Byron paid interest until her death. The debt came to light only in 1820: Charles Hanson to Byron, 11 Jan. 1820, Murray Mss.

6. *BLJ*, 1:84–85.

7. *BLJ*, 1:90–91.

8. Hanson to Byron, 10 Dec. 1805; Hanson to Mrs. Byron, 11 Jan. 1806, Murray Mss. Box A1.

9. *BLJ*, 1:86, 87.

10. Byron, *Complete Poetical Works,* ed. McGann, 5:109.

11. *BLJ*, 1:86; Langley Moore, *Lord Byron,* 44–45.

12. *Times Literary Supplement*, 26 July 1974, 801.

13. *BLJ*, 1:82, 87, 88; 9:28; Mrs. E. H. Massingberd to Byron, 16 Jan. 1807, Murray Mss. Box 14. For Byron's statement as to his arrangements with Mrs. Massingberd, which provides much of our knowledge of the transactions, see *BLJ,* 2:154–55, and Langley Moore, *Lord Byron,* 153–63.

14. BL, Egerton 2611, fols. 19–21; *BLJ*, 9:37.

15. BL, Egerton 2611, fols. 22–25.

16. *BLJ*, 1:116.

17. Hanson to Byron, 22 Apr. 1807, Murray Mss.; *BLJ*, 13:87. Langley Moore has described Hanson's activities as "entirely unhelpful" (*Lord Byron,* 86), but she seems not to have appreciated the extent to which his hands were tied by Chancery.

18. *BLJ*, 1:120–21, 128n.

19. Hanson to Mrs. Byron, 9 Aug. 1807, Murray Mss. Box A1; *BLJ*, 13:7.

20. BL, Egerton 2612, fols. 28–35.

21. BL, Egerton 2611, fols. 41–42.

22. *BLJ*, 1:142, 144; BL, Egerton 2611, fols. 26–27; Hanson to Mrs. Byron, 21 Dec. 1807, Murray Mss. Box A1.

23. BL, Egerton 2611, fols. 44–48; *BLJ*, 1:150–51, 164.

24. *BLJ*, 1:162.

25. T. A. J. Burnett, *The Rise and Fall of a Regency Dandy: The Life and Times of Scrope Berdmore Davies* (London: John Murray, 1981), 71–75; *BLJ*, 9:39.

26. *BLJ*, 1:162.

27. Byron, *Complete Poetical Works,* ed. McGann, 1:107–12.

28. BL, Egerton 2611, fols. 39–40.

29. *BLJ,* 1:170–71.

30. *Nottingham Journal,* 28 Jan. 1809; *BLJ,* 1:172; Moore, *Letters and Journals of Lord Byron,* 82.

31. Coope, "Lord Byron's Newstead," 135, 141; Rosalys Coope, "Lord Byron's Bath at Newstead," *Byron Journal* 13 (1985): 68–72.

32. Lady Byron's Diary, 1818, Lovelace, Box 118, fol. 4.

33. Coope, "Lord Byron's Newstead," 142–44; Laird, *Beauties of England and Wales,* vol. 12, pt. 1, 403–4; 1812 Sale Particulars, NAC.

34. William Howitt, *Rural Life of England* (London: Longman, Orme, Brown, Green, & Longmans, 1838), 1:378–79.

35. Joe Murray to Byron, Mar. 1816, Murray Mss. Box A23. Langley Moore exaggerated when she wrote that the house was "no longer old-fashioned and dilapidated," and that Byron had "done up a good part of the house in a most handsome modern style," thereby giving it "up-to-date elegance": *Lord Byron,* 151, 474–80.

36. BL, Egerton 2611, fols. 73–74.

37. *BLJ,* 1:172, 176–77, 180–81, 187.

38. *BLJ,* 1:175, 181; BL, Egerton 2611, fols. 85–86. Hobhouse's poem, "Epistle to a Young Nobleman in Love," written after his visit to Newstead, appears to represent a friendly warning not only that marriage will put an end to their travel plans, but that a wife would have her own ideas about alterations to the house and grounds: "And quite transform, in every point complete, / Your Gothic abbey to a country seat."

39. Because the two men were together at Newstead there is no record of their discussions, but we may deduce Hanson's advice from Byron's draft of a letter he wrote to him on 8 February 1809, which included the comment (subsequently crossed through): "I will not sell Newstead, let my embarrassments be what they may, but I would willingly relinquish my Rochdale claim to be out of debt" (BL, Egerton 2611, fols. 101–2). He would have had no reason to make such claims if the matter had not previously been under discussion.

40. Lovelace, Box 154, fol. 136.

41. Hanson Narrative, Murray Mss.; Walker and Howell, *House of Byron,* 200. See chap. 12.

42. *BLJ,* 1:175, 179.

43. A. H. John, "Insurance Investment and the London Money Market in the Eighteenth century," *Economica* 20 (1953): 157.

44. BL, Egerton 2611, fol. 107. All these arrangements were straightforward and had been part of Byron's planning since 1805. He had no intention of "skipping the country to flee his creditors, with the prospect of debtors' prison waiting on his return": Eisler, *Byron,* 171. This claim suggests a misunderstanding of his financial position.

45. BL, Egerton 2611, fols. 43, 78, 95–96.

46. Hanson to Mrs. Byron, 13 Mar. 1809, Murray Mss. Box A1.

47. BL, Egerton 2611, fols. 93–94, 97.

48. BL, Egerton 2612, fol. 128.

49. BL, Egerton 2611, fols. 39–40.

50. BL, Egerton 2613, fols. 85–86.

51. BL, Egerton 2611, fols. 87–88. No correspondence has survived between Mealey and Hanson for most of 1808, and the next letters from the bailiff date only from September 1809: BL, Egerton 2613, fols. 73–74, 85–86.

52. BL, Egerton 2611, fol. 145; J. V. Beckett, "Absentee Landownership in the Later Seventeenth and Early Eighteenth Centuries: The Case of Cumbria," *Northern History* 19 (1983): 87–107.

53. BL, Egerton 2611, fol. 176.

CHAPTER 6. LORD BYRON AS LANDLORD, 1809–12

1. *BLJ,* 1:151, 171, 175.
2. BL, Egerton 2611, fols. 99–100; *BLJ,* 1:175; 9:28.
3. *BLJ,* 1:192.
4. BL, Egerton 2611, fols. 110–11.
5. Hugh Watson to Mrs. Byron, 13 Nov. 1808, 12, 22 Feb. 1809, Murray Mss. Box A1.
6. *BLJ,* 1:165.
7. *BLJ,* 1:175, 191, 195. According to Marchand, in the final version of his will signed on 14 June 1809, Byron left his lands and property to Hobhouse and Hanson: *BLJ,* 1:202n. Almost certainly Marchand is mistaken, and they were the trustees of the will, with the property settled on George Anson Byron: BL, Egerton 2611, fols. 115–16.
8. Moore, *Letters and Journals of Lord Byron,* 83; Richard Allen, *The Home and Grave of Byron: A Souvenir of Newstead Abbey, Nottinghamshire* (London: Longman & Co., 1874).
9. John Cam Hobhouse (Lord Broughton), *Recollections of a Long Life,* ed. Lady Dorchester (his daughter), 6 vols. (London: John Murray, 1909–11), 3:29.
10. Irving, *Abbotsford and Newstead Abbey,* 77–78.
11. BL, Egerton 2611, fols. 108–13.
12. BL, Egerton 2611, fols. 115–16. Hammersleys was an international banking house.
13. BL, Egerton 2611, fols. 112, 114, 119–23; *BLJ,* 1:201, 203. The £1,000 outstanding on Gringley was paid on 2 June 1809: N.U.M.D. P1 E12/3/6/27.
14. Reelig, 717, 719.
15. BL, Egerton 2611, fols. 127–31.
16. *BLJ,* 1:214; Byron was issued with a letter of credit on Hammersleys, on 23 June, permitting him to draw for up to £2,000 during his travels: Murray Mss. Box 14, file 1a.
17. *BLJ,* 1:213.
18. BL, Egerton 2611, fols. 130–31; Burnett, *Rise and Fall of a Regency Dandy,* 75–79.
19. BL, Egerton 2611, fol. 132.
20. BL, Egerton 2611, fols. 137–38.
21. Byron, *Complete Poetical Works,* ed. McGann, 2:13.
22. BL, Egerton 2611, fol. 173.
23. BL, Egerton 2611, fols. 137–38.
24. BL, Egerton 2611, fols. 139–40.
25. Letters of John Hanson, 21, 27, 31 July, 11 Aug. 1809, NAC.
26. BL, Egerton 2611, fols. 143–44.
27. BL, Egerton 2611, fols. 146–51.
28. BL, Egerton 2611, fols. 155–61.
29. BL, Egerton 2611, fols. 171–73, 178–79.
30. BL, Egerton 2611, fols. 181–82, 197; Byron wrote regularly to his mother: BL, Egerton 2611, fol. 175, and some of the letters certainly reached her at Newstead.
31. BL, Egerton 2611, fols. 189–91.
32. BL, Egerton 2611, fols. 221–25, 229–32; *BLJ,* 13:11.
33. Hanson to Byron, 5 Mar. 1811, Murray Mss. Box 14/2.
34. BL, Egerton 2611, fols. 236–38; Lovelace, Box 154, fol. 134.
35. *BLJ,* 1:171; BL, Egerton 2611, fols. 124–25.
36. Hobhouse, *Recollections,* 3:49; BL, Egerton 2611, fols. 124–25, 133–34; the bear died in May 1810.

37. BL, Egerton 2611, fols. 137–38; Hanson to Mrs. Byron, 26 Sept. 1809, Murray Mss. Box A1.

38. BL, Egerton 2611, fol. 126.

39. BL, Egerton 2611, fols. 153–54; *BLJ,* 1:214.

40. BL, Egerton 2611, fol. 145; 2613, fols. 73–74.

41. Lowe, *General View of the Agriculture of the County of Nottingham*, 16.

42. BL, Egerton 2611, fols. 153–54; Langley Moore, *Lord Byron,* 113, claims inaccurately that "leaseholding farmers placed a landowner at a great disadvantage if he was obliged to sell." In fact, new owners traditionally respected existing agreements when purchasing a property.

43. BL, Egerton 2611, fols. 189–91; 2613, fols. 85–86.

44. BL, Egerton 2613, fols. 75–76.

45. BL, Egerton 2611, fols. 211–12.

46. BL, Egerton 2613, fols. 77–78, 91–92; 2611, fols. 162–69.

47. BL, Egerton 2611, fols. 167, 194; 2613, fols. 94–95, 103–9.

48. BL, Egerton 2611, fols. 153–54, 170, 176, 183–88.

49. *BLJ,* 1:234–36, 243; BL, Egerton 2611, fols. 187–88.

50. BL, Egerton 2613, fols. 136–37; *BLJ,* 1:245; 2:51–52.

51. BL, Egerton 2613, fols. 116, 120–21.

52. Lovelace, Box 154, fol. 136.

53. Reelig, 706.

54. BL, Egerton 2613, fols. 79–82, 96–102, 112–15, 134–35; 2611, fols. 203–4.

55. Hanson to Mrs. Byron, 8 Jan. 1811, Murray Mss. Box A1.

56. BL, Egerton 2613, fols. 122–23; 2611, fols. 227–28; Hanson to Mrs. Byron, 31 Dec. 1810, 15 Jan. 1811, Murray Mss. Box A1.

57. BL, Egerton 2611, fols. 217–20.

58. Hanson to Mrs. Byron, 15 Jan. 1811, Murray Mss. Box A1.

59. BL, Egerton 2611, fols. 233–35; Hanson to Mrs. Byron, 28 May 1811, and a subsequent undated letter, Murray Mss. Box A1. Mrs. Byron's annoyance with Hanson for not answering her letters is not surprising in view of the subject matter, but Hanson had other things on his mind: his eldest son died on 30 April.

60. Hanson's accounts with Byron, 8, 27 July 1811, Murray Mss. Box A23. Many of the other bills from the 1808 refurbishment were still outstanding in 1819.

61. BL, Egerton 2611, fols. 213–14, 224–25, 229–30, 236–38.

62. Lovelace, Box 154, fol. 136.

63. *BLJ,* 2:45–46, 51–52, 59; Peter W. Graham, ed., *Byron's Bulldog: The Letters of John Cam Hobhouse to Lord Byron* (Columbus: Ohio State University Press, 1984), 69, 71.

64. BL, Egerton 2611, fols. 236–38.

65. Hanson to Mrs. Byron, 8 July 1811, Murray Mss. Box A1.

66. Dallas had arranged the publication details of *English Bards and Scotch Reviewers* in 1809: Marchand, *Byron: A Portrait*, 56, 101, 102.

67. BL, Egerton 2611, fols. 239–48; *BLJ,* 2:60–61.

68. *BLJ,* 2:69.

69. Byron, *Complete Poetical Works,* ed. McGann, 1:341–42, 455. Byron began the poem on 26 August.

70. *BLJ,* 2:81–96.

71. Byron, *Complete Poetical Works,* ed. McGann, 5:259, 708.

72. *BLJ,* 2:105, 114–15. It is not clear whether this rent increase ever took place. The only secure evidence we have of rents being raised is from 1813, when Thomas Claughton "owned" the estate: BL, Egerton 2613, fols. 188–89.

73. *BLJ,* 2:71–73; Bolton and Payne's account with Lord Byron, Aug. 1811, Murray Mss. Box A23; NAC, NA 961.

74. BL, Egerton 2611, fols. 252–58; *BLJ,* 2:66. "A List of Sundry Articles of Jewellery valued for Hanson Esq by Rundle, Bridge and Rundle, 23 Aug. 1811," Murray Mss. Box A1. This firm had supplied Mrs. Byron with jewelry—see bills in same bundle, and their letter to her of 1 Mar. 1811 (Hanson's account with Byron, 31 Aug. 1811, Murray Mss. Box A23).

75. *BLJ,* 2:75, 88, 114.

76. Thomas Medwin, *Journal of the Conversation of Lord Byron Noted during a Residence with His Lordship at Pisa in the Years 1821 and 1822* (London: Henry Colburn, 1824), 48.

77. Murray Mss. Box A1.

78. BL, Egerton 2613, fols. 89–90, 93.

79. Lovelace, Box 154, fol. 136.

80. *BLJ,* 2:93.

81. *BLJ,* 2:109. In view of this letter it is not clear why Eisler, *Byron,* 302, claims Hanson did not go to Rochdale with Byron.

82. *BLJ,* 2:114, 127; Murray Mss. Box A 23; Sarah Markham, *A Testimony of Her Times: Penelope Hind's Diaries and Correspondence, 1787–1838* (Salisbury, U.K.: M. Russell, 1990), 98–99, Hanson's account with Lord Byron, Oct. 1811. Byron's attention to detail both in this instance and throughout these months is at variance with Langley Moore's claim that he was "without the slightest knowledge of estate management": *Lord Byron,* 150.

83. Sir John Habakkuk has written that "the general difficulty of borrowing substantial sums on mortgages in most of the years between 1797 and 1810 is hardly open to doubt": *Marriage, Debt, and the Estates System: English Landownership, 1650–1950* (Oxford: Clarendon Press, 1994), 522–24; BL, Egerton 2611, fols. 266–70; 2613, fols. 155–60, 164–65, 168–71; *BLJ,* 11:160–61.

84. BL, Egerton 2611, fols. 264–65, 278–79; *BLJ,* 2:156.

85. BL, Egerton 2613, fols. 172–77, 184–85.

86. Michael Foot, *The Politics of Paradise: A Vindication of Byron* (London: Collins, 1988), 135–39.

87. *BLJ,* 1:256–57; Grosskurth, *Byron,* 78.

88. J. V. Beckett, "Elizabeth Montagu: Bluestocking Turned Landlady," *Huntington Library Quarterly* 49 (1986): 149–64.

CHAPTER 7. THE ABORTIVE SALE, 1812–14

1. Hobhouse, *Recollections,* 1:45. "The second" lot was Rochdale.

2. *BLJ,* 2:188–89.

3. W. Neale to Byron, 26 Feb. 1812, Murray Mss. Box 14/8; *BLJ,* 2:161–63.

4. BL, Addit. Mss. 36,456, fol. 44; Graham, *Byron's Bulldog,* 101. Hobhouse's meticulous accounts, kept while the two men were traveling in the East, are in the Murray Mss.

5. Langley Moore, *Lord Byron,* 182, 191; Burnett, *Rise and Fall of a Regency Dandy,* 89. Byron's willingness to put off repaying his indebted friend may explain why Davies found him "very agreeable and clever, but vain, overbearing, conceited, suspicious and jealous": C. Hibbert, ed., *Captain Gronow* (London: Kyle Cathie, 1991), 180.

6. Graham, *Byron's Bulldog,,* 101; Moore, *Letters and Journals of Lord Byron,* 173.

7. *BLJ,* 11:167; Langley Moore, *Lord Byron,* 241.

8. William Le Blanc to M. R. Boulton, 18 July 1812, and Boulton to Le Blanc, 23

July 1812, Birmingham City Archives, Matthew Boulton Papers, MBP 450, Land Speculations Portfolio No. 1. This collection also includes a copy of the 1812 sale particulars. Boulton eventually bought Great Tew, Oxfordshire, in 1815.

9. Joseph Bennett of Tutbury to James Watt, 13 Aug. 1812, in ibid.

10. Ibid.

11. Habakkuk, *Marriage, Debt, and the Estates System,* 525–29; C. Clay, "The Price of Freehold Land in the Later Seventeenth and Eighteenth Centuries," *Economic History Review* 27 (1974): 173–89; M. E. Turner, J. V. Beckett, and B. Afton, *Agricultural Rent in England, 1690–1914* (Cambridge: Cambridge University Press, 1997), 218; Norton, Trist and Gilbert, "A Century of Land Values," *The Times,* 20 April 1889.

12. *BLJ,* 5:271–72; Hanson to Byron, 14 Aug. 1812, Murray Mss.

13. Hanson to Byron, 15 Aug. 1812, Murray Mss.

14. F. Byron to Byron, 25 Oct. 1812, Murray Mss. Box A1.

15. Hobhouse, *Recollections,* 1:160.

16. Byron's biographers have paid the Claughton episode little attention. Marchand recorded simply that "Hanson had written that Claughton had finally agreed to sacrifice £25,000 of the down payment and give up the contract for Newstead": *Byron: A Portrait,* 173. More recently Grosskurth has commented merely that "on August 3 . . . Claughton forfeited £25,000; and Newstead—with all its problems—was again in Byron's hands": Grosskurth, *Byron,* 197. Langley Moore's explanation (*Lord Byron,* 203–8) is unconvincing. Eisler, *Byron,* 433, also glosses over the episode.

17. B. L. Anderson, "The Attorney and the Early Capital Market in Lancashire," in *Capital Formation in the Industrial Revolution,* ed. F. Crouzet (London: Methuen, 1972), 223–55; Hanson to Byron, 24 Aug. 1812, Murray Mss.; *BLJ,* 3:77; 4:43–44. In 1954 Mrs. Winifred Whittington, Claughton's great-granddaughter, repeated the claim that Claughton bought the property "acting as agent for his wife's people": Letter of 16 Mar. 1954, NAC.

18. *The Times,* 14 Aug. 1812; 1812 Sale Particulars, NAC.

19. Claughton to Hanson, 26 Aug. 1812, Murray Mss.

20. Hanson to Byron, 29 Aug. 1812, Murray Mss.; *BLJ,* 2:190; 3:77. Byron had not disposed of the furniture as he had proposed the previous February.

21. *BLJ,* 4:39; Gross, *Byron's "Corbeau Blanc,"* 162.

22. A. R. Griffin, *Mining in the East Midlands, 1550–1947* (London: Frank Cass, 1971), 97, 105; Indenture, 8 Oct. 1872, Shawe-Brown Mss.

23. The coal-mining explanation was the one preferred by Claughton's family. See Mrs. Whittington's letter cited above, note 17. Whether Claughton ever attempted to mine on the Newstead estate is not known.

24. Articles of Agreement, 17 Aug. 1812, (copy), NAC; Hanson to Byron, 5 Jan. 1813, Murray Mss.; *BLJ,* 2:189–90, 215.

25. *BLJ,* 2:194–95, 201, 233, 238.

26. Burnett, *Rise and Fall of a Regency Dandy,* 91, 93. Byron subsequently arranged for the £1,500 to be paid from Claughton's first installment of the deposit.

27. Hanson to Byron, 7 Sept. 1812, Murray Mss.

28. Hanson to Byron, 21 Oct. 1812, Murray Mss.

29 *BLJ,* 2:241, 248, 255. On 31 October Byron opened an account with Hoare's, the Fleet Street banker, into which the first credit was the £5,000 from Claughton. The account is reproduced in David Buttery, "Lord Byron's Account at Hoare's Bank," *Byron Journal* 26 (1998): 98–111, which is the source used here, with minor transcription errors corrected by Peter Cochran.

30. Claughton to Byron, 22 May 1819, Murray Mss.

31. Hanson to Byron, 21 Oct. 1812, Murray Mss.; Reelig, 717.

32. Hanson to Byron, 5 Jan. 1813, Murray Mss.

33. *BLJ,* 3:6–7; Buttery, "Lord Byron's Account at Hoare's Bank."

34. Graham, *Byron's Bulldog,* 107; *BLJ,* 11:182.

35. *BLJ,* 3:22, 24.

36. *BLJ,* 3:29.

37. *BLJ,* 3:29–39.

38. *BLJ,* 3:55; 5:173; Byron's Bills, Murray Mss.; Marchand, *Byron: A Portrait,* 146; Buttery, "Lord Byron's Account at Hoare's Bank." His bank account was credited early in June 1813 with £1,541, sold out of exchequer bills, which was probably the returned deposit on the Rochdale tithes.

39. Hanson to Byron, 3, 5, 9 July 1813, Murray Mss.; Reelig, 717.

40. *BLJ,* 3:77–78.

41. The money was paid into his account with Hammersley's on 10 July 1813. I am grateful to Peter Cochran for help with Byron's Hammersley Account.

42. Reelig, 717; Langley Moore, *Lord Byron,* 202; Hammersley's Account.

43. *BLJ,* 3:99.

44. *BLJ,* 3:138.

45. BL, Egerton 2613, fols. 188–89; *BLJ,* 3:136, 138.

46. *BLJ,* 3:187; Hammersley's Account.

47. *BLJ,* 3:217; 4:21.

48. Hanson to Byron, 22 Jan. 1814, Murray Mss.; *BLJ,* 4:38–39, 43–45, 54.

49. Burnett, *Rise and Fall of a Regency Dandy,* 93–96; *BLJ,* 4:86, 89; 11:162; Claughton to Hanson, 6, 10 Apr. 1814, Murray Mss.; Buttery, "Lord Byron's Account at Hoare's Bank."

50. Byron, *Complete Poetical Works,* ed. McGann, 3:220; *BLJ,* 4:83, 106, 115, 121; Charles Hanson to Byron, 24 May 1814, Murray Mss.

51. *BLJ,* 4:138–41.

52. R. J. Colyer, "The Haford Estate under Thomas Johnes and Henry Pelham, Fourth Duke of Newcastle," *Welsh History Review* 8 (1977): 273–74.

53. *BLJ,* 4:143.

54. Hanson to Byron, 15, 17 Apr. 1813, Murray Mss.

55. Hanson to Byron, 17 July 1814, Murray Mss.; *BLJ,* 4:147.

56. Hanson to Byron, 2, 6 Aug. 1814, Murray Mss.; Reelig, 700; *BLJ,* 4:218.

57. The calculations are necessarily speculative, but this figure is derived from the 1813 rental revision (£1,784) and the 1814 figure of rent per acre—see below—halved, since Claughton did not collect the Michaelmas rents (£1,613).

58. BL, Egerton 2613, fols. 178–81, 186–89; Claughton to Hanson, 26 Aug. 1812, Hanson to Byron, 27 Sept. 1812, Murray Mss.

59. BL, Egerton 2613, fols. 178–79, 182–83.

60. No substantial body of Claughton papers has survived. My inquiries drew a blank at the Greater Manchester County Record Office, Lancashire Record Office, Cheshire Record Office, Wigan Record Office, Warrington Library, and St. Helens Local History Library. There are a handful of letters in the Legh of Lyme collection in the John Rylands Library, Manchester, but none relate to Claughton's property transactions.

61. Hanson to Byron, 13 Oct. 1813, Murray Mss.; Box A23/6 for the 1811 rental, and BL, Egerton 2613, fols. 188–89, for Mealey's account of the 1813 agreements. The calculation assumes that Rushton and Bowman paid their existing rents for the year. The 1812 sale particulars did not include rental figures.

62. Claughton to Hanson, 6 Mar. 1814, written from Newstead, Murray Mss.

63. *Nottingham Journal,* 11 Dec. 1813, 1 Jan. 1814.

64. William Marshall, *On the Landed Property of England* (London: n.p., 1804), 389.

65. N.A.O. DD 721/1/145.

66. Hanson to Byron, 22 Jan. 1814, Murray Mss.

67. *BLJ*, 4:41.
68. *BLJ*, 4:190, 199.
69. This is actually a false assumption, because 645 acres were retained in what were called the Forest Farms. No rent figures are known for these before or after 1814. The first record we have of them being accounted within the overall Newstead farms dates only from 1844 (see chap. 12).
70. Hanson to Byron, 2 Aug. 1814, Murray Mss.
71. *BLJ*, 4:152, 161; Graham, *Byron's Bulldog*, 133; Marchand, *Byron: A Portrait*, 174.
72. *BLJ*, 4:150, 160, 163. Hanson told him £1,500 was too much: Hanson to Byron, 5 Sept. 1814, Murray Mss.
73. N.A.O. DD 721/1/145.
74. Augusta Leigh to Francis Hodgson, 14 Sept. 1814, NAC, RB E35.

Chapter 8. Marriage and Debt, 1814–15

1. *BLJ*, 4:165, 166, 168.
2. *BLJ*, 4:170; Hanson to Byron, 5, 30 Sept. 1814, Murray Mss.
3. BL, Egerton 2611, fol. 286; 2613, fols. 198–205.
4. *BLJ*, 3:227; 4:202; Marchand, *Byron: A Portrait*, 176.
5. *BLJ*, 4:235; Cokayne, *Complete Peerage*, 10:612; Langley Moore, *Lord Byron*, 459–71 for an extended discussion of the Portsmouth case.
6. *BLJ*, 4:170–71, 174–75, 190.
7. Hanson to Byron, 13 Oct. 1813, Murray Mss.; *BLJ*, 4:275.
8. *BLJ*, 4:115. The money for Augusta seems to have been paid from his Hammersley's account, of which records for May 1814 do not survive.
9. *BLJ*, 4:259–60, 266.
10. *BLJ*, 4:242, 259; Buttery, "Lord Byron's Account at Hoare's Bank"; Reelig, 706; Graham, *Byron's Bulldog*, 153.
11. *BLJ*, 4:175.
12. *BLJ*, 4:150.
13. *BLJ*, 4:189–90.
14. Walker refers to Byron being "forced to sell Newstead to pay the marriage settlement" (Walker and Howell, *House of Byron*, 200). Marchand says Byron had "to get Hanson to arrange the sale of Newstead so that he could make a proper settlement on his bride-to-be": *Byron: A Portrait*, 179. Others have written of this period that Newstead "had to be sold" (Stephen Coote, *Byron: The Making of a Myth* [London: Bodley Head, 1988], 68); that the Newstead sale "was forced on him" (Boyes, *My Amiable Mamma*, 146); and "Newstead had to be sold in order for a settlement to be made on Annabella" (Grosskurth, *Byron*, 211). In fact, Newstead was not even offered for sale again until six months after the wedding.
15. *BLJ*, 4:190, 215, 274.
16. Lovelace, Box 118, fol. 4.
17. Hobhouse, *Recollections*, 2:200.
18. *BLJ*, 4:188–90, 200.
19. *BLJ*, 4:199; Claughton to Hanson, 5, 9 Dec. 1814, Murray Mss.
20. *BLJ*, 4:241; Hanson to Claughton, 9 Dec. 1814, Murray Mss.
21. *BLJ*, 4:241.
22. *BLJ*, 4:199; Malcolm Elwin, *Lord Byron's Wife* (London: Macdonald, 1962), 243–45.

23. Grosskurth, *Byron*, 217.

24. Hobhouse, *Recollections,* 2:198. His words were repeated in Byron's *Dictionary of National Biography* entry: 3:592.

25. *BLJ,* 4:179, 202.

26. *BLJ,* 4:179, 218. Eisler, *Byron,* 372, underestimates Annabella when she comments that she was "of no vast fortune."

27. *BLJ,* 4:186.

28. *BLJ,* 4:204.

29. *BLJ,* 9:109.

30. *BLJ,* 4:192; S. H. Romilly, ed., *Romilly-Edgeworth Letters, 1813–1818* (London: John Murray, 1936), 92–93.

31. Gross, *Byron's "Corbeau Blanc,"* 185.

32. Hanson to Byron, 23 Oct. 1814, Murray Mss.; *BLJ,* 4:223, 225.

33. *BLJ,* 4:213; George Anson Byron to Byron, 14 and 24 Oct. 1814, Murray Mss. Box A1. Marchand, *Byron: A Portrait,* 182 wrongly surmises that Byron visited Newstead on his way to Seaham, presumably on the grounds that Byron said he would be calling: *BLJ,* 4:228. The error is repeated in Grosskurth, *Byron,* 214.

34. Hanson to Byron, 31 Oct. 1814, Murray Mss.; *BLJ,* 4:235.

35. *BLJ,* 4:186; BL, Addit. Charters 72,108.

36. *BLJ,* 4:199; Reelig, 717; Marriage Settlements, Murray Mss. Box A23/4.

37. *BLJ,* 4:254. Grosskurth, *Byron,* 215–16, writes incorrectly that "By the laws of the time Annabella could not inherit Newstead which was strictly destined to go to the heir George Byron." In fact she could have inherited Newstead if Byron had chosen to settle it on her, but she could not have inherited the *title,* which was destined to go to George Byron.

38. Graham, *Byron's Bulldog,* 171–72.

39. Byron spent some days paying off friends with whom he had bet that he would never marry, including one hundred guineas each to his cousin John Hay and to Martin Hawke: *BLJ,* 4:256, 260; 9:102n; Buttery, "Lord Byron's Account at Hoare's Bank." He recalled the wedding in *The Dream*; in *Complete Poetical Works,* ed. McGann, 4:27.

40. Gross, *Byron's "Corbeau Blanc,"* 288. Elizabeth Harvey married the fifth duke of Devonshire after the death of Georgiana, his first duchess. After he died in 1811 she spent most of her life in Rome: Amanda Foreman, *Georgiana: Duchess of Devonshire* (London: HarperCollins, 1998), 394–99.

41. Hobhouse, *Recollections,* 1:194; *BLJ,* 4:251; Graham, *Byron's Bulldog,* 143, 148, 151.

42. Graham, *Byron's Bulldog,* 152, 165–66; *BLJ,* 4:272–73.

43. *BLJ,* 4:276–79; Graham, *Byron's Bulldog,* 174–75, 178.

44. BL, Egerton 2613, fols. 210–11.

45. Hanson to Byron, 10 Jan., 11 Feb. 1815, Murray Mss.; *BLJ,* 4:261, 265, 270.

46. Hanson to Byron, 2 Mar. 1815, Murray Mss.; *BLJ,* 4:271; Graham, *Byron's Bulldog,* 175.

47. *BLJ,* 4:278–79, 282; Claughton to Hanson, 15 Mar. 1815, Murray Mss.

48. Hanson to Byron, 9, 25 Mar. 1815, Murray Mss.

49. *BLJ,* 4:282, 283. Papplewick Hall was built in the 1780s by the Hon. Frederick Montagu, a friend of the poet Thomas Gray. The family owned more than 300 acres in Nottinghamshire.

50. Lovelace, Box 132, fol. 9.

51. BL, Egerton 2613, fols. 190–91.

52. BL, Egerton 2613, fol. 206; 2611, fol. 286. William Hibbert held one of the Forest farms, and was the local tax collector. The meaning here presumably is that his rent money had gone to pay taxes that Byron (or Claughton) had failed to pay.

53. *BLJ*, 4:247, 248.

54. BL, Egerton 2613, fols. 207–11; *BLJ*, 4:264–65.

55. *BLJ*, 4:293, 300; BL, Egerton 2613, fols. 213–16.

56. *BLJ*, 4:264–65.

57. *BLJ*, 4:264, 288, 289, 291, 326, 333; Byron to Sir James Burgess, 22 Apr. 1815, NAC. Grosskurth, *Byron*, 236 states incorrectly that Byron was "dumbfounded" by the will because he expected Annabella to inherit the property.

58. Lovelace, Box 132, fols. 3, 7, 13, 14. Colonel Dalbiac had still to pay for Moulton Hall Farm.

59. *BLJ*, 4:291, 292, 298–99; Hanson to Byron, 1 July 1815, Murray Mss.

60. *The Times*, 19 July 1815; *The Roe-Byron Collection*, NAC, A 13; BL, Addit. Mss. 6715, fols. 113–19; Hobhouse, *Recollections*, 1:322; *BLJ*, 5:246. It is not clear if this was the Mr Fountayne Wilson who had shown an interest in the estate prior to the auction.

61. Marchand, *Byron: A Portrait*, 203; Elwin, *Lord Byron's Wife*, 309–10; Hobhouse, *Recollections*, 2:200; *BLJ*, 4:186, 188; 9:189; Hanson to Byron, n.d. (Sept. 1815), Murray Mss.

62. Elwin, *Lord Byron's Wife*, 314: Annabella must have meant that the farmers wanted smaller tenancies, i.e., a return to the pre-Claughton situation; Hanson to Byron, n.d. but contextually early Sept. 1815, Murray Mss.

63. BL, Egerton 2613, fols. 217, 220–21.

64. BL, Egerton 2613, fols. 192–93, 220–27.

65. *BLJ*, 4:317; George Anson Byron to Byron, 4 Oct. 1815, Murray Mss. Box A1; Mealey to Byron, 13 Oct. 1815, Murray Mss. Box A23.

66. Claughton to Hanson, 26 Aug. 1812, Murray Mss.; George Anson Byron to Byron, 4 Oct. 1815, Murray Mss. Box A1. The catalog turned out to be expensive to prepare. When Byron read it through he was astonished to find the contents of the wine cellar rather depleted. Joe Murray explained that the valuer employed to draw up the sale catalog had, with his associates, drunk fifty bottles of Madeira, and ten bottles of different sweet wines, as well as charging to Byron's account at The Hut two bottles of brandy and two of rum: Murray to Byron, 27 Oct. 1815, Murray Mss. Box A23. Even so, George Byron counted in the cellar 794 bottles, 489 of which were light wine, and the rest port: George Byron to Byron, 23 Oct. 1815, Murray Mss. Box A1.

67. *Nottingham Journal*, 30 Sept. 1815; NAC, NA 325.

68. Murray to Byron, 27 Oct. 1815, Murray Mss. Box A23; Claughton to Byron, 8 Jan. 1816, 22 May 1819; "T Claughton 1814–16 and Legal Documents"; BL, Egerton 2613, fols. 224–25; Elwin, *Lord Byron's Wife*, 320. Marchand, *Byron: A Portrait*, 206 mistakenly thought the sale took place, and Langley Moore, *Lord Byron*, 212–13 fails to recognize that two sales were planned, house and then contents.

69. BL, Egerton 2613, fols. 226–27, 234–35.

70. Moore, *Letters and Journals of Lord Byron*, 289–90.

71. Elwin, *Lord Byron's Wife*, 320, 327; *BLJ*, 4:333, 336, 337.

72. Reelig, 717; BL, Addit. Charters 72,100; Lovelace, Box 132, fols. 15–46; *BLJ*, 4:317, 327, 337.

73. Mealey to Byron, 8 Dec. 1815, Joseph Murray to Byron, 3 Oct. 1814, Murray Mss. Box A23/3. Byron's Hoare's account shows that £5,200 was paid in on 19 December, but none of these outflows are recorded. Some money may have been dispensed in cash.

74. For parallel examples see David Spring, "Ralph Sneyd: Tory Country Gentleman," *Bulletin of the John Rylands Library* 28 (1956): 535–55; B. English, "Patterns of Estate Management in East Yorkshire, c. 1840–c. 1880," *Agricultural History Review* 32 (1984): 29–48.

CHAPTER 9. THE SALE OF NEWSTEAD

1. *BLJ*, 5:70; Hobhouse, *Recollections*, 3, 56.
2. *BLJ*, 5:70.
3. D. Buttery, "Lord Byron's Account at Hoare's Bank"; *BLJ*, 5:15, 20–26.
4. *BLJ*, 5:33, 38–40, 44, 46.
5. Doctors' Commons was the name given to the society of advocates in the civil law prior to 1858, and also the name of the buildings close to St. Paul's Cathedral where they had their offices and the registry of wills. Those who practiced in Doctors' Commons held a monopoly of the practice of ecclesiastical law, and the ecclesiastical courts in which they operated still had powers in matrimonial cases and the probate of wills: S. M. Waddams, *Law, Politics, and the Church of England: The Career of Stephen Lushington, 1782–1873* (Cambridge: Cambridge University Press, 1992), 4; and G. D. Squibb, *Doctors' Commons: A History of the College of Advocates and Doctors of Law* (Oxford: Clarendon Press, 1977).
6. *BLJ*, 11:169; Andrew Nicholson, ed., *Lord Byron: The Complete Miscellaneous Prose* (Oxford: Clarendon Press, 1991), 95–97.
7. Lovelace, Box 132, fols. 92ff.; Buttery, "Lord Byron's Account at Hoare's Bank"; Marchand *Byron: A Portrait*, 230; Nicholson, *Lord Byron: The Complete Miscellaneous Prose*, 231–45.
8. Hanson to Lushington, 30 Mar. 1816, Lovelace, Box 90, fol. 52.
9. Hanson to Lushington, 17 Mar. 1816, Lovelace, Box 90, fol. 50.
10. Hanson to Byron, 30 Mar. 1816, Murray Mss.; Lovelace, Boxes 90, fol. 63; 133, fols. 32, 80, 153. This account of the separation proceedings is partly based on Waddams, *Law, Politics and the Church of England,* 100–134. Lushington, it is worth noting, did not accept Byron's suggestion that financial embarrassments had caused the separation. Such a claim was "repugnant to all my notions of truth, justice & liberal feeling," he told Lady Byron: 121.
11. Kinnaird to Byron, 7 July 1818, 14 July 1823, Murray Mss. Unfortunately, no records of financial transactions at Ransoms survive for these years; my thanks to Josephine Horner of Barclays Bank for searching the relevant archives.
12. Lovelace, Box 132, fol. 208; Buttery, "Lord Byron's Account at Hoare's Bank"; *BLJ*, 5:73.
13. Byron, *Complete Poetical Works,* ed. McGann, 4:38. Leman is, of course, the Swiss name for Lake Geneva. Byron, *Complete Poetical Works,* ed. McGann, 4:98, 462–65.
14. The fullest account of Byron's travels in Switzerland is in Elma Dangerfield, *Byron and the Romantics in Switzerland, 1816* (London and Nashville: Ascent Books, 1978).
15. *BLJ*, 5:53; Murray to Byron, 22 Mar. 1816, Murray Mss. Box A23/1.
16. BL, Egerton 2613, fols. 228–31.
17. BL, Egerton 2613, fols. 226–27, 232–33.
18. The 1817 sale catalog, Reelig, 700; BL, Egerton 2613, fols. 238–45. Perhaps surprisingly Wightman not only survived but by 1817 was paying more rent than in 1815 (£440 as opposed to £300), suggesting that he had taken on more land: 1815 and 1817 catalogs.
19. N.A.O. DD 721/1/145. Beardall died in Apr. 1822.
20. Hanson to Byron, 6 Dec. 1816, Murray Mss.; *BLJ*, 5:160–61, 225, 236.
21. Hanson to Byron, 18 July 1816, Murray Mss.; *BLJ*, 5:70, 134, 139, 151, 160–61.
22. R. Thorne, ed., *The House of Commons, 1790–1820* (London: Secker and Warburg, 1986), 3:445–46; Colyer, "Haford Estate," 257–84; Hanson to Byron, 6 Dec. 1816, Murray Mss.
23. Claughton to Byron, 22 May 1819, Murray Mss.

24. Charles Hanson to Byron, 11 Jan. 1820, Murray Mss. Since furnishings mentioned in the 1815 catalog are still at Newstead, it can be assumed that he sold the contents to Colonel Wildman. If so, the details have not survived.

25. Bond 20 Aug. 1814, Harrow School Collection; *BLJ*, 9:217–19; 10:48; Kinnaird to Byron, 16 Feb., 6 Apr., 7 Oct. 1819, Murray Mss.

26. *BLJ*, 8:62–63, 101, 208; 9:73, 82, 219; Kinnaird to Byron, 16 Dec. 1821, Murray Mss.

27. *BLJ*, 5:222, 225–26.

28. *BLJ*, 5:230, 236–37; 11:167.

29. *BLJ*, 5:245.

30. *BLJ*, 5:246.

31. *BLJ*, 5:225, 230, 261.

32. Reelig, 707; Claughton to Byron, 22 May 1819, Murray Mss.

33. *BLJ*, 5:261, 271–73, 277.

34. *BLJ*, 5:261; Hanson to Byron, 3 July 1818, Murray Mss.

35. *BLJ*, 5:70, 277; 6:49, 59, 87; Coope, "Lord Byron's Newstead," 133–54; Langley Moore, *Lord Byron,* 474–80.

36. *BLJ*, 1:195.

37. *BLJ*, 5:161; 6:62.

38. *BLJ*, 6:65.

39. Marchand, *Byron: A Portrait,* 268, 362; *BLJ*, 5:254, 266.

40. *BLJ*, 5:277.

41. F. Byron to Byron, 21 Feb. 1814, Murray Mss. Box A1; *BLJ*, 6:189; Lovelace, Box 84, fols. 239–44.

42. *BLJ*, 5:277–78.

43. Lovelace, Box 133, fol. 52; Graham, *Byron's Bulldog,* 240; *BLJ*, 6:53, 74.

44. *BLJ*, 6:31–32, 36, 37, 48.

45. *BLJ*, 6:7.

46. *BLJ*, 6:50; Graham, *Byron's Bulldog,* 232. Spooney was Byron's nickname for Hanson: Graham, *Byron's Bulldog,* 58.

47. *BLJ*, 6:54, 56, 60; Graham, *Byron's Bulldog,* 236, 240, 242. Kinnaird was also using whatever influence he could to "encourage" Hanson: Kinnaird to Byron, 7 July 1818, Murray Mss.

48. *BLJ*, 6:71, 72, 74, 78, 82; Charles Hanson to Byron, 2 Sept. 1818, Murray Mss. Newton Hanson's account of the Venice meeting is in R. E. Prothero, ed, *The Works of Lord Byron* (London: John Murray, 1922), 4:266–67.

49. Kinnaird's letters to Byron, Murray Mss. The series is incomplete but it provides considerable evidence of Kinnaird's work on Byron's behalf.

50. *BLJ*, 5:261.

51. *BLJ*, 6:59, 60, 63, 87; Kinnaird to Byron, 24 Nov. 1818, Murray Mss.

52. *BLJ*, 5:160–61.

53. *BLJ*, 7:69–70; 8:208; 10:48.

54. Prothero, *Works of Lord Byron,* 4:267.

55. Kinnaird to Byron, 22 Dec. 1818, Murray Mss.

56. Hanson to Kinnaird, 7 Sept. 1819, Murray Mss.; Hanson to Byron, Jan. 1820; Charles Hanson to Byron, 20 Feb. 1820; *BLJ*, 10:46.

57. Hanson to Hobhouse, Jan. 1819, Murray Mss.; Hanson to Byron, 30 Jan. 1819.

58. Deed of 14 Nov. 1818, Murray Mss. Box A23; Reelig, 705, 706. Hanson prepared various lists at different times, and because they reflect an ongoing debt redemption process they are not usually compatible.

59. Prothero, *Works of Lord Byron,* 4:267.

60. Lovelace, Box 133, fols. 58–65.
61. Kinnaird to Byron, 16 Feb. 1819, Murray Mss.
62. *BLJ*, 6:78–79.
63. Kinnaird to Byron, 22 Dec. 1819, Murray Mss.
64. Kinnaird to Byron, 29 Dec. 1818, Murray Mss.; BL, Addit. Mss. 56,540, fols. 38–39; Graham, *Byron's Bulldog*, 254.
65. Hanson to Byron, 30 Jan., 18 Feb. 1819, Murray Mss.
66. Kinnaird to Byron, 16 Feb., 19 Mar. 1819, Murray Mss.; *BLJ*, 6:101, 102.
67. Kinnaird to Byron, 6 Apr. 1819, Murray Mss.; Hanson to Byron, 30 Jan., 18 Feb. 1819, Jan. 1820.
68. Claughton's £970 was his unpaid rent for the Newstead home farm (less property tax and interest payable on the £3,000 owed to him), and £150 outstanding on his purchase of the abbey furnishings: Hanson to Byron, Jan. 1820, Murray Mss.
69. Hanson to Kinnaird, 7 Sept. 1819, Murray Mss.
70. Kinnaird to Byron, 7 Oct. 1819, Murray Mss.
71. *BLJ*, 6:97–100.
72. Graham, *Byron's Bulldog*, 256–60; Langley Moore, *Lord Byron*, 244–90.
73. Byron to Kinnaird, 5 Sept. 1819, Murray Mss.; *BLJ*, 6:222. Hopkinson's bill was for £42 5s.
74. Byron to Kinnaird, 5 Sept. 1819, Murray Mss.; Charles Hanson to Byron, 11 Jan. 1820.
75. Kinnaird to Byron, 15 Nov. 1822, 1 May, 14 July 1823, 19 Mar. 1824, Murray Mss.; *BLJ*, 9:55; 10:47; Will of Owen Mealey, proved 22 Aug. 1823, Borthwick Institute, York. My thanks to Philip Jones for this reference.
76. *BLJ*, 5:277–78; 6: 225, 232; Byron to Hanson, 11 Dec. 1817, Murray Mss. Box A23/6.
77. Byron, *Complete Poetical Works*, ed. McGann, 4:38.
78 *BLJ*, 6:6.
79. James T. Hodgson, *Memoir of the Rev. Francis Hodgson* (London: n.p., 1878), 2:50.
80. *BLJ*, 7:208.
81. Medwin, *Journal of the Conversation of Lord Byron*, 39, 48. In fairness, Medwin is often considered to have been an unreliable witness.
82. Byron's biographers have been divided on his attitude to the Newstead sale: Marchand, *Byron: A Biography*, 2:744, wrote that "It may be surmised that part of his anxiety to conclude the bargain with Major Wildman stemmed from the pain of parting with a property that held so many memories of his youth, and which he had early associated with the pride of his ancestry and dreams of an expansive baronial life. Augusta, who still had sentimental recollections of Newstead, and had always protested against his intention to sell it, now felt herself so cut off from her brother than she did not remonstrate with him." By contrast, Grosskurth has written that "Byron indicated no regret at the loss of the abbey": *Byron*, 319.
83. Byron, *Complete Poetical Works*, ed. McGann, 5:541–44.
84. Quoted in J. B. Firth, *Highways and Byways in Nottinghamshire* (London: Macmillan & Co., 1916), 197.

CHAPTER 10. AN EXILED ARISTOCRAT, 1818–23

1. *BLJ*, 6:65
2. BL, Egerton 2611, fols. 229–30.
3. Lovelace, Box 133, fol. 63; Graham, *Byron's Bulldog*, 272.

4. *BLJ*, 6:49
5. Thomas France to Hanson, 16 Oct. 1808, Murray Mss. Box A23; *BLJ*, 2:114; *The Times*, 19 July 1815.
6. Kinnaird to Byron, 18 May 1819, 6 May 1823, Murray Mss.
7. *BLJ*, 6:6, 25, 42, 43.
8. Hanson to Byron, 3 July 1818, Murray Mss.; Kinnaird to Byron, 6 Apr. 1819; *BLJ*, 6:79.
9. *BLJ*, 6:222, 225, 228, 232; Kinnaird to Byron, 7 Oct. 1819, Murray Mss.
10. *BLJ*, 7:70–75, 85, 94, 110; Charles Hanson to Byron, 11 Jan. 1820, Murray Mss.
11. *BLJ*, 7:119.
12. *BLJ*, 7:122, 136; Charles Hanson to Byron, 12 June 1820, Murray Mss.
13. Charles Hanson to Byron, 20 May 1820, Murray Mss.; *BLJ*, 7:144–45.
14. *BLJ*, 7:146, 168, 202, 220, 239, 240; 8:96.
15. Quoted in Grosskurth, *Byron*, 327.
16. *BLJ*, 5:254.
17. *BLJ*, 6:48.
18. *BLJ*, 12:71; 9:73; 10:48–49; 8:159; Kinnaird to Byron, 1 May 1823, Murray Mss.
19. *BLJ*, 6:113–14, 91.
20. Graham, *Byron's Bulldog*, 288; *BLJ*, 7:144; 9:82.
21. *BLJ*, 9:82; Kinnaird to Byron, 16 Dec. 1821, Murray Mss.
22. *BLJ*, 6:100, 107, 109, 136.
23. Kinnaird to Byron, 19 Mar., 4 May 1819, 28 Mar. 1821, Murray Mss.
24. Graham, *Byron's Bulldog*, 266.
25. Lovelace, Box 132, fol. 26, 95, 150, 153.
26. *BLJ*, 6:100, 102.
27. *BLJ*, 6:247; 7:68; Kinnaird to Byron, 19 Mar., 6 Apr. 1819, Murray Mss.
28. *BLJ*, 7:69, 72.
29. Kinnaird to Byron, 18 Jan., 20 Feb. 1820, Murray Mss.; *BLJ*, 7:116–17.
30. *BLJ*, 7:202, 214.
31. *BLJ*, 7:116–17, 202; Hanson to Byron, 9 Nov. 1820, Murray Mss.; Lovelace, Box 133, fols. 2, 95, 150.
32. *BLJ*, 8:62. The parenthesis referred to the Portsmouth case.
33. *BLJ*, 8:91, 137, 171; Kinnaird to Byron, 28 Mar., 31 July, 18 Aug. 1821, Murray Mss.
34. Kinnaird to Byron, 16 Dec. 1821, Murray Mss.
35. Kinnaird to Byron, 3 May, 5 Dec. 1822, Murray Mss.; Charles Hanson to Byron, 6 Sept. 1822; BL, Addit. Mss. 70,949, fols. 136–37.
36. *BLJ*, 9:209; 10, 38.
37. *BLJ*, 8:145, 146, 202, 240; 8:62. Given his increasing concern with money in these years, it is worth pointing out that while at Ravenna Byron gained something of a reputation for his charitable giving: Eisler, *Byron,* 689.
38. *BLJ*, 6:138, 232.
39. *BLJ*, 7:214; 9:72, 120; Kinnaird to Byron, 8 Apr. 1822, Murray Mss.
40. *BLJ*, 9:84.
41. Hanson to Byron, Mar. 1822, Murray Mss. Byron rather liked having the same initials, NB, as Bonaparte.
42. Byron's appointment of Burdett was on 20 January 1822, prior to Lady Noel's death: *BLJ*, 9:105. Burdett had been his preferred choice in 1818: BL, Addit. Mss. 56,540, fols. 38–39.
43. Lovelace, Box 133, fol. 173; *BLJ*, 9:113.
44. Kinnaird to Byron, 29 Mar. 1822, Murray Mss.; *BLJ*, 9:141, 187. Lady Byron's

reputed milk diet may explain Byron's lines in *Don Juan,* canto 15, stanza 41, which is about Annabella:

> Love's riotous, but Marriage should have quiet—
> And being Consumptive, live on a Milk Diet.

45. Kinnaird to Byron, 16 Apr., 15 Oct., 15 Nov., 22 Dec. 1822, Murray Mss.; *BLJ,* 9:158, 166, 176, 196, 211; 10:20, 35, 38, 49.

46. Lovelace, Box 90, fols. 68, 70; *BLJ,* 9:105–9; Hanson to Byron, Mar. 1822, Kinnaird to Byron, 5 Apr. 1822, Murray Mss.; Marchand, *Byron: A Portrait,* 366–67. Rebuilt in 1774, Kirkby Mallory was demolished in 1952.

47. *BLJ,* 9:110–13, 137.

48. Kinnaird to Byron, 4 Apr. 1822, Murray Mss.; *BLJ,* 9:144–45, 152–53, 155, 166.

49. *BLJ,* 9:194–96, 198–99, 203; Kinnaird to Byron, 15 Oct. 1822, Murray Mss.

50. Lovelace, Box 90, fols. 68, 72, 75; *BLJ,* 9:177; Kinnaird to Byron, 15 Oct. 1822, Murray Mss.; *BLJ,* 9:209, 211, 212, 219.

51. *BLJ,* 10:114–15; Kinnaird to Byron, 9 Aug. 1822, Murray Mss.

52. Byron, *Complete Poetical Works,* ed. McGann, 5:418.

53. Ibid., 5:489.

54. Ibid., 7:19–20. McGann suggests that Byron was dealing in this section of the poem with recent debates in Parliament about the agricultural distress since the conclusion of peace in 1815. Byron's own experience arising from Kirkby Mallory must have loomed just as large in his thinking.

55. *BLJ,* 10:118, 119, 149, 150, 155; 11:42.

56. *BLJ,* 9:110, 195, 199, 201; 10:110; 11:50, 74, 144; Lovelace, Box 83, fols. 62–65.

57. *BLJ,* 9:209; Kinnaird to Byron, 9 Aug., 7 Sept. 1822, Murray Mss.

58. *BLJ,* 7:220.

59. Hanson to Byron, 30 Jan. 1822; Charles Hanson to Byron, 14 May 1822, Murray Mss.; *BLJ,* 9:106, 108, 165, 177; 10:60; Kinnaird to Byron, 3 May 1822, Murray Mss.

60. Hanson to Byron, 7 Mar. 1822, Murray Mss.

61. *BLJ,* 9:127, 128.

62. *BLJ,* 9:177, 188–89, 191, 201, 206, 211, 214.

63. *BLJ,* 2:167; 11:49.

64. *BLJ,* 9:28. Eldon opposed Catholic Emancipation, and the event described here must refer to an occasion early in 1812 when the opposition managed to divide both Houses on the Irish question: Ian R. Christie, *Wars and Revolutions: Britain, 1760–1815* (London: Edward Arnold, 1982), 293.

65. *BLJ,* 10:35, 49, 53; Kinnaird to Byron, 5 Dec. 1822, Murray Mss. The correct spelling of Dearden's name was with an "en," but both Byron and Kinnaird insisted on spelling it "on." I have left their spelling in quotations but given the correct spelling elsewhere in the text.

66. Byron to James Dearden, 18 Oct. 1822 (transcript), Rochdale Local Studies Library, Dearden Mss. Box 1. This, and the subsequent correspondence, is discussed in Andrew Nicholson, "'That Suit in Chancery': Two New Byron letters," *Byron Journal* 26 (1998): 50–56.

67. *BLJ,* 10:59, 61, 73–77.

68. Kinnaird to Byron, 17, 22 Dec. 1822, Murray Mss.

69. *BLJ,* 10:84, 86.

70. Byron to James Dearden, 22 Jan. 1823 (transcript), Rochdale Local Studies Library, Dearden Mss. Box 1; Kinnaird to Byron, 15 Apr. 1823, Murray Mss. Box A23; *BLJ,* 10:88–89.

71. *BLJ,* 10:108–11, 114, 118, 124, 126, 135. There is no copy of Kinnaird's letter in the Murray archive, although he mentions the Crabtree visit to Rochdale in his letter of 31 Jan. 1823.

72. *BLJ,* 10:150, 151, 153–55.

73. Kinnaird to Byron, 1 May 1823 and an undated letter that must, from context, be late May 1823, Murray Mss.

74. Kinnaird to Byron, 14 Aug., 2 Nov. 1823, Murray Mss.; *BLJ,* 11:47, 48

75. *BLJ,* 11:51, 57.

76. *BLJ,* 1:110; 11:116, 135; Kinnaird to Byron, 23 Nov. 1823, Murray Mss.; Nicolson, "That Suit in Chancery," 51.

77. Kinnaird to Byron, 23 Dec. 1822, Murray Mss.; *BLJ,* 10:90–91.

78. Kinnaird to Byron, 7 Apr. 1823, Murray Mss.

79. Kinnaird to Byron, 7 Oct. 1819, 20 Feb., 27 Oct. 1820, 28 Aug. 1821, 8 Apr. 1822, Murray Mss.

80. Kinnaird to Byron, n.d. (from context, late May 1823), Murray Mss.; *BLJ,* 11:25.

81. Kinnaird to Byron, 1 May 1823 and n.d. (late May 1823), Murray Mss.

82. Kinnaird to Byron, 18 May 1819, Murray Mss.

83. Kinnaird to Byron, 2, 23 Nov. 1823, 19 Mar. 1824, Murray Mss.

84. Kinnaird to Byron, 19 Mar. 1824, Murray Mss. This information comes from a legal document drawn up between the trustees of the sixth Lord Byron, deceased, and James Dearden and his trustees. It was prepared by C. Deane of Lincoln's Inn Fields, 8 July 1828. The document was offered for sale by Maggs (Modern Books and Mss. catalog 1122); Draft assignment, Hanson to Deane, 8 July 1828, Murray Mss. Box A23.

85. Quoted in Grosskurth, *Byron,* 398; see also Langley Moore, *Lord Byron,* 250.

86. *BLJ,* 9:92.

87. *BLJ,* 9:195; Kinnaird to Byron, 7 Sept. 1822, Murray Mss.

88. *BLJ,* 9:200, 201, 205–7, 214.

89. *BLJ,* 9:217–18; 10:19–20.

90. Kinnaird to Byron, 15 Oct. 1822, Murray Mss.

91. Kinnaird to Byron, 15 Nov. 1822, Murray Mss.

92. *BLJ,* 10:42–43; Kinnaird to Byron, 10 Dec. 1822, Murray Mss.

93. *BLJ,* 10:47, 60–61. Langley Moore, *Lord Byron,* 362–63 suggests Byron was keeping his own accounts in these weeks rather than relying on Lega Zambelli, due to some concerns about his honesty.

94. *BLJ,* 10:15, 110, 111, 119.

95. *BLJ,* 10:73–74, 78, 85, 87–88.

96. *BLJ,* 10:91–92, 96, 114–15, 118, 153.

97. *BLJ,* 10:143–44.

98. *BLJ,* 7:198, 202; Langley Moore, *Lord Byron,* 202, 240.

99. *BLJ,* 8:208; 9:219; 10:46–48.

100. *BLJ,* 10:47–48, 51.

101. *BLJ,* 10:90, 110; Kinnaird to Byron, 22 Dec. 1822, Murray Mss.

102. Kinnaird to Byron, 21, 31 Jan., 14 July 1823, 19 Mar. 1824, Murray Mss.

103. Graham, *Byron's Bulldog,* 343–44.

CHAPTER 11. GREECE, GLORY, AND FINANCIAL SECURITY

1. E. J. Lovell Jr., ed., *Lady Blessington's Conversations of Lord Byron* (Princeton: Princeton University Press, 1969).

2. *BLJ,* 10:139, 143–44, 168–69, 199; Harold Nicolson, *Byron: The Last Journey* (London: Constable, 1924).

3. Graham, *Byron's Bulldog,* 329; Kinnaird to Byron, 10 June 1823, Murray Mss.

4. Graham, *Byron's Bulldog,* 329; Kinnaird to Byron, 6 May, 10 June 1823, Murray Mss.; *BLJ,* 10:177.

5. Langley Moore, *Lord Byron,* 366–68.

6. Graham, *Byron's Bulldog,* 333; *BLJ,* 10:186, 187; Kinnaird to Byron, 3 June 1823, Murray Mss.

7. *BLJ,* 10:199, 211.

8. Marchand, *Byron: A Portrait,* 402, 405; he had sold his schooner *Bolivar* to Lord Blessington.

9. Langley Moore, *Lord Byron,* 375–88.

10. *BLJ,* 11:28. Kinnaird paid Baxter early in 1824; Kinnaird to Byron, 19 Mar. 1824, Murray Mss.

11. *BLJ,* 11:42, 65; Marchand, *Byron: A Portrait,* 423.

12. *BLJ,* 11:71.

13. *BLJ,* 11:60–63.

14. *BLJ,* 11:86; Marchand, *Byron: A Portrait,* 427: Graham, *Byron's Bulldog,* 337–38.

15. *BLJ,* 11:92, 93; Coote, *The Making of a Myth,* 170; Ransoms to Byron, 10 Feb. 1824 [copy], Murray Mss.

16. *BLJ,* 11:94.

17. *BLJ,* 11:96, 97, 135, 136, 144–46; Marchand, *Byron: A Portrait,* 441.

18. Graham, *Byron's Bulldog,* 346, 350, 352.

19. *BLJ,* 11:152; Kinnaird to Byron, 19 Mar. 1824, Murray Mss.; Langley Moore, *Lord Byron,* 414.

20. *BLJ,* 11:153; Marchand, *Byron: A Portrait,* 457.

21. *Nottingham Journal,* 17 July 1931.

22. Hobhouse, *Recollections,* 3:41.

23. *The Times,* 10 July 1824.

24. T. Bailey, *Annals of Nottinghamshire* (London: Simpkin, Marshall & Co., 1852–55), 4:332; Walker and Howell, *House of Byron,* 215–16: Langley Moore, *Lord Byron,* 419; Hobhouse, *Recollections,* 3:66, 68, 69. Hobhouse's record was slightly different from that of William Howitt, who recalled that "the church was by no means crowded," and that most of those who attended were villagers and "a certain number of people from Nottingham of a similar class": William Howitt, *Rural Life of England,* 3d ed. (London: Longman & Green, 1862), 269–74.

25. Kinnaird to Byron, 15 Apr. 1817, Murray Mss. mentions simply that "I saw Newstead lately. . . . I had been hunting."

26. Marriage Settlements, Murray Mss. Box A23/4.

27. Byron to Dearden, 22 Jan. 1823, Rochdale Local Studies Library; Graham, *Byron's Bulldog,* 348, 352.

28. Marriage Settlements, Murray Mss. Box A23/4.

29. BL, Addit. Charter 72103.

30. Lovell, *Lady Blessington's Conversations,* 61.

31. Hobhouse, *Recollections,* 3:47, 67; Marchand, *Byron: A Portrait,* 459.

32. P.R.O. PROB 12/216. The will was proved in the Province of Canterbury on 6 July 1824. The codicil Byron added to take account of Allegra's interests had lapsed with her death in 1822.

33. BL, Addit. Charters 72,103; Langley Moore, *Lord Byron,* 348, 361, 372, 389–90, 393–94.

34. Doris Langley Moore, *The Late Lord Byron* (London: John Murray, 1961), chap. 4.

35. Letters to John Murray 3, Sept 1868; Marriage Settlements, Murray Mss. Box A23/4.

36. BL, Addit. Mss. 36,466, fol. 18; Walker and Howell, *House of Byron.* Personal Communication, Dr. Rosalys Coope.

CHAPTER 12. BYRON AND NEWSTEAD: THE MYTH

1. *BLJ,* 6:81.

2. Many of the family portraits are now in the possession of the 13th Lord Byron, and several were reproduced in Walker and Howell, *House of Byron.* Quite what happened to them is unclear. Wildman asked Byron for a portrait of himself, which suggests that the portraits had been removed by 1819. They could have been taken to Piccadilly Terrace in 1815, in which case Annabella would have had their custody, perhaps passing them on to the heir in title, the seventh Lord Byron, after 1824. Byron supplied Wildman with a copy of the Phillips's portrait of 1813, and this is still at Newstead. I am grateful to Annette Peach for help on this point.

3. Rosalys Coope, "The Wildman Family and Colonel Thomas Wildman of Newstead Abbey, Nottinghamshire," *TTS* 95 (1991): 53–58.

4. N.U.M.D. NeC 4853–54, 4860, 4863–65, 4869–70, 4872–73, 4876–77, 4879–80, 4882, 4884, 4892.

5. Wildman to Miss M.A. Cursham, 22 Oct. 1831, N.A.O. M 510; Letter to Duke of Newcastle, unsigned, 19 Oct. 1831, N.U.M.D. NeC 5026; John Sherbrooke Gell to Duke of Newcastle, 18 Oct. 1831, NeC 5025; Earl of Lincoln to Duke of Newcastle, 20 Oct. 1831, NeC 5028; Edward Unwin to Newcastle, 8 Jan. 1833, NeC 5035.

6. No estate papers from Wildman's days at Newstead have survived, except for some legal documents in the Reelig collection.

7. Reelig, 718; *Mansfield Reporter,* 23 Sept. 1859.

8. Reelig, 717: The figure for his farm was 460 according to the 1851 census.

9. Irving, *Abbotsford and Newstead Abbey* 59–60, 72–73.

10. Graham, *Byron's Bulldog,* 264; Hodgson, *Memoir of the Rev. Francis Hodgson,* 2:251.

11. This and subsequent paragraphs are based on Rosalys Coope, "Colonel Thomas Wildman and the Transformation of Newstead Abbey, Nottinghamshire, 1817–1859," *TTS* 101 (1997), 157–73. I am particularly grateful to Dr. Coope for her help in guiding me through some of the more complex problems involved in reconstructing Newstead in Wildman's day.

12. For life at Newstead when Wildman was entertaining the duke of Sussex, see A. B. Reid, ed., "The Leah Gossip Diary and Letters," *TTS* 25 (1931): 117–48.

13. Hanson to Byron, 18 Feb. 1819, Murray Mss.; Hobhouse, *Recollections,* 3:29; 5:29; Byron, *Complete Poetical Works,* ed. McGann, 5:637.

14. Howitt, *Rural Life of England* (1838), 1:389.

15. Irving, *Abbotsford and Newstead Abbey,* 76.

16. Marchand, *Byron: A Portrait,* 54; Hanson Narrative, Augusta Byron to John Hanson, 19 Mar. 1807, Murray Mss.

17. Charles Hanson to Byron, 11 Jan. 1820, Murray Mss.; *BLJ,* 6:41; 7:70, 208.

18. Mark Girouard, *The Return to Camelot* (New Haven: Yale University Press, 1981), 69–76. Renovations to the Great Hall were completed only in the 1850s.

19. N.A.O. M 5616.

20. Coote, *Byron: The Making of a Myth,* 174–87.

21. Quoted in Firth, *Highways and Byways in Nottinghamshire,* 197.

22. Irving, *Abbotsford and Newstead Abbey,* 60.

23. Howitt, *Rural Life of England* (1838), 1:385–87.

24. Blunt, *My Diaries, 1888–1914,* 664.

25. Coope, "Lord Byron's Newstead," 141.

26. N.A.O. DD 1251/13/1a.

27. Quoted in Coope, "Colonel Thomas Wildman," 167.

28. Howitt, *Rural Life of England* (1838), 1:386; [James Carter], *A Visit to Sherwood Forest including the Abbeys of Newstead, Rufford and Welbeck; Annesley, Thoresby, and Hardwick Halls; Bolsover Castle and Other Interesting Places in the Locality with a Criticial Essay on the Life and Times of Robin Hood* (London: Longman & Co., 1850), 29.

29. Mandler, *Fall and Rise of the Stately Home,* 76, 207, 442.

30. N.A.O. M 382; Carter, *Visit,* 26.

31. Thomas Bailey, *Handbook to Newstead Abbey* (London: Simpkin, Marshall & Co., 1855); *Newstead Abbey. Lord Byron. Colonel Wildman. A Reminiscence* (Leeds: n.p., 1856); *Newstead Abbey: Its Present Owner, with Reminiscences of Lord Byron* (London: n.p., 1857).

32. Richard Allen, *The Home and Grave of Byron: A Souvenir of Newstead Abbey, Nottinghamshire* (London: Longman & Co., 1874). Allen's guide came in several forms, including the "richly bound" version at two guineas, the slightly less luxurious volume with fewer illustrations at one guinea, and the "popular edition" at 2s. 6d. with only one illustration.

33. BL, Addit. Mss. 56,540, fols. 38–39; Irving, *Abbotsford and Newstead Abbey,* 60.

34. *Mansfield Reporter,* 23 Sept. 1859; J. R. Ward, "The Profitability of Sugar Planting in the British West Indies, 1650–1834," *Economic History Review* 31 (1978): 197–213; Boyd Alexander, *England's Wealthiest Son: A Study of William Beckford* (London: Centaur Press, 1962).

35. Reelig, 717; Coope, "Wildman Family," 63–64.

36. This seems to be the accepted figure. It was common knowledge when, for example, Wilfrid Scawen Blunt was at Newstead in 1909: Blunt, *My Diaries, 1888–1914,* 663.

37. *Mansfield Reporter,* 23, 30 Sept. 1859.

38. Reelig, 707.

39. *The Times,* 8 July 1861.

40. A. Z. Fraser, *Livingstone and Newstead* (London: John Murray, 1913), 61–66.

41. Blunt, *My Diaries, 1888–1914,* 662. There is no evidence to suggest that the Webbs were affected by the revived interest in Byron following the publication in 1870 of Harriet Beecher Stowe's *Lady Byron Vindicated,* with its claim that the poet had been guilty of incest: A. Elfenbein, *Byron and the Victorians* (Cambridge: Cambridge University Press, 1995), 79–80.

42. John Bateman, *The Great Landowners of Great Britain and Ireland* (London: Harrison, 1883), 469.

43. Copy of W. F. Webb's will dated, 23 April 1897, Shawe-Brown Mss.

44. Information courtesy of Dr. Rosalys Coope, who is preparing a detailed study of the Webb family's years at Newstead.

45. Howitt, *Rural Life of England* (3d ed., 1862), 269–74.

46. BL, Addit. Mss. 36,464, fol. 259.

47. N.A.O. M 5700.

48. Ann Barton, "Byron Lives!" *New York Review of Books,* 10 June 1993.

49. Geoffrey Trease, *Byron: A Poet Most Dangerous to Know* (London: Macmillan, 1969), 7.

50. Mandler, *Fall and Rise of the Stately Home,* 221, 246.

51. *Nottingham Evening News*, 1 Aug. 1929.

52. *Roe-Byron Collection*, 21. Cahn had bought what were referred to as the historic parts of the abbey and a considerable part of the protective land, including the Upper Lake. The corporation later acquired the rest of the abbey and the grounds.

53. *Nottingham Journal*, 17 July 1931; C. J. Fraser to Lord Mayor of Nottingham, 17 Sept. 1930, Shawe-Brown Mss.

54. Lovell, *Lady Blessington's Conversations*, 63.

55. The marchioness of Londonderry, in her four-hundred-page memoir of her father, Henry Chaplin of Blankney in Lincolnshire, written in 1926, managed to write at length about his numerous interests in foxhunting, public affairs, deer stalking, and racing, but with only one sentence, hidden away on p. 115, to the effect that due to his financial embarrassments he had sold the family estate in 1896. The Marchioness of Londonderry, *Henry Chaplin, a Memoir* (London: Macmillan, 1926).

Bibliography

PRIMARY SOURCES

Birmingham City Archives
    Matthew Boulton Papers

Bodleian Library
    Byron-Lovelace Papers

Borthwick Institute, York
    Will and Administration papers, fifth Lord Byron

British Library
    Egerton MSS, 2611–13
    Additional MSS 62,910. Account of Newstead and Rochdale estates, 1802–6
    Evelyn Papers, SJE12

Fraser of Reelig, Inverness-shire (private hands)
    Legal papers, estate plans, leases, and abstracts of title, formerly belonging to family
    solicitors, Trower, Still, and Keeling of Lincoln's Inn Fields

John Murray (Publishers) Archive, Albemarle Street, London
    Legal documents, accounts, deeds, and correspondence

Keele University Archives
    Inventory

Newstead Abbey Collection
    1778 auction catalog
    Byron letters

Nottingham University Manuscripts Department
  PwF 2928 Abstract of Byron estate rentals, 1776
  Newcastle Papers
  Portland (London) Papers

Nottinghamshire Archives Office
  Sixteenth- and Seventeenth-Century Deeds
  General Accounts of the Newstead Estate, 1748–98
  Estate Correspondence, 1763–73

Public Record Office
  Papers relating to the Legal Case involving Newstead, 1738
  Wills, fourth and sixth Lords Byron

Rochdale Local Studies Library
  Dearden MSS

Shawe-Brown Papers (private hands)
  Deeds and other papers

Printed Primary Sources

Account of the Tryal of Lord William Byron. London: n.p., 1765.

Allen, Richard. *The Home and Grave of Byron: A Souvenir of Newstead Abbey, Nottingham-shire*. London: Longman & Co., 1874.

Bailey, T. *Annals of Nottinghamshire*. London: Simpkin, Marshall & Co., 1852–55.

Bailey, Thomas. *Handbook to Newstead Abbey*. London: Simpkin, Marshall & Co., 1855.

Blunt, W. S. *My Diaries, 1888–1914*. London: Secker, 1932.

Buttery, David. "Lord Byron's Account at Hoare's Bank." *Byron Journal* 26 (1998): 98–111.

[Carter, James.] *A Visit to Sherwood Forest including the Abbeys of Newstead, Rufford, and Welbeck; Annesley, Thoresby, and Hardwick Halls; Bolsover Castle and Other Interesting Places in the Locality with a Critical Essay on the Life and Times of Robin Hood*. London: Longman & Co., 1850.

Cobbett's Complete Collection of State Trials. 33 vols, London: Longman & Co., 1809–26.

Fishwick, H. T., ed. *Survey of the Manor of Rochdale, Lancashire, 1626*. Chetham Society Remains, vol. 71. Manchester: Chetham Society, 1913.

Graham, Peter W., ed. *Byron's Bulldog: The Letters of John Cam Hobhouse to Lord Byron*. Columbus: Ohio State University Press, 1984.

Gross, Jonathan David, ed. *Byron's "Corbeau Blanc": The Life and Letters of Lady Melbourne*. Houston, Tex.: Rice University Press, 1997.

Henstock, A., ed. *The Diary of Abigail Gawthern*. Thoroton Society Record Series, vol. 33, Nottingham, U.K.: Thoroton Society, 1980.

Historical Manuscripts Commission, *Verulam MSS*. London: H.M.S.O., 1906.

Hobhouse, John Cam (Lord Broughton). *Recollections of a Long Life*. Edited by Lady Dorchester (his daughter). 6 vols. London: John Murray, 1909–11.

Hodgson, James, T., ed. *Memoir of the Rev. Francis Hodgson*. 2 vols. London: n.p., 1878.

Howitt, William. *Rural Life of England*. 2 vols. London: Longman, Orme, Brown, Green, & Longmans, 1838.

Irving, Washington. *Abbotsford and Newstead Abbey*. London: Henry G. Bohn, 1850.

Laird, F. C.. *The Beauties of England and Wales*. Vol. 12, part 1. London: Verner & Hood, 1813.

Lewis, W. S., ed. *The Yale Edition of Horace Walpole's Correspondence*. New Haven: Yale University Press, 1941–.

Lovell, E. J., Jr., ed. *Lady Blessington's Conversations of Lord Byron*. Princeton: Princeton University Press, 1969.

Lowe, Robert. *General View of the Agriculture of the County of Nottingham*. London: printed for G. Nicol, 1798.

Mansfield Reporter

Marchand, Leslie A., ed. *Byron's Letters and Journals*. 13 vols. London: John Murray, 1973–94.

Markham, Sarah. *A Testimony of Her Times: Penelope Hind's Diaries and Correspondence, 1787–1838*. Salisbury, U.K.: M. Russell, 1990.

Marshall, William. *On the Landed Property of England*. London: n.p., 1804.

McGann, J. J., ed. *Lord Byron: The Complete Poetical Works*. 7 vols. Oxford: Clarendon Press, 1980–93.

Medwin, Thomas. *Journal of the Conversation of Lord Byron Noted during a Residence with His Lordship at Pisa in the Years 1821 and 1822*. London: Henry Colburn, 1824.

Moore, Thomas. *Letters and Journals of Lord Byron with Notices of His Life*. 2d ed. London: John Murray, 1830.

Murray, John, ed. *Lord Byron's Correspondence*. London: John Murray, 1922.

Newstead Abbey: Its Present Owner, with Reminiscences of Lord Byron. London: n.p., 1857.

Newstead Abbey. Lord Byron. Colonal Wildman. A Reminiscence. Leeds: n.p., 1856.

Nicholson, Andrew. "'That Suit in Chancery': Two New Byron Letters." *Byron Journal* 26 (1998): 50–56.

———, ed. *Lord Byron: The Complete Miscellaneous Prose*. Oxford: Clarendon Press, 1991.

Norton, Trist, and Gilbert. "A Century of Land Values." *The Times*, 20 April 1889.

Nottingham Guardian

Nottingham Journal

Prothero, R. E., ed. *The Works of Lord Byron*. 6 vols. London: John Murray, 1922–24.

Reid, A. B., ed. "The Leah Gossip Diary and Letters." *TTS* 35 (1931): 117–48.

The Roe-Byron Collection: Newstead Abbey. Nottingham, U.K.: Corporation of Nottingham, 1937.

Romilly, S. H., ed. *Romilly-Edgeworth Letters, 1813–1818.* London: John Murray, 1936.

Sandby, Paul. *The Virtuosi's Museum*. London: G. Kearsly, 1778.

Tayler, Alastair, and Henrietta Tayler, eds. *Lord Fife and His Factor: Being the Correspondence of James, Second Lord Fife, 1729–1809*. London: Heinemann, 1925.

Thoroton, Robert. *The Antiquities of Nottinghamshire*. Edited and enlarged by John Throsby. 2d ed. 1790–96. Reprint, Wakefield, U.K.: E. P. Publishing, 1972.

The Times (London)

Times Literary Supplement

Webster, W., ed. *Nottinghamshire Hearth Tax Returns, 1664, 1674.* Thoroton Society Record Series, vol. 37. Nottingham, U.K.: Thoroton Society, 1988.

Young, Arthur. *The Farmers' Tour through the East of England.* Vol. 1. London: W. Strahan, 1771.

SECONDARY SOURCES

Alexander, Boyd. *England's Wealthiest Son: A Study of William Beckford.* London: Centaur Press, 1962.

Anderson, B. L. "The Attorney and the Early Capital Market in Lancashire." In *Capital Formation in the Industrial Revolution,* edited by F. Crouzet. London: Methuen, 1972.

Barton, Ann. "Byron Lives!" *New York Review of Books,* 10 June 1993, 30–35.

Bateman, John. *The Great Landowners of Great Britain and Ireland.* 1883. Reprint, Leicester: Leicester University Press, 1969.

Beaumont, Gwen. "Supporting the Under-Dog: Lord Byron's Influence in Nottinghamshire." *Nottinghamshire Historian* 21 (1978): 2–3.

Beckett, J. V. "Absentee Landownership in the Later Seventeenth and Early Eighteenth Centuries: The Case of Cumbria." *Northern History* 19 (1983): 87–107.

———. "Byron's Nottingham." *The Newstead Byron Society Review,* July 2000, 49–59.

———. "Elizabeth Montagu: Bluestocking Turned Landlady." *Huntington Library Quarterly* 49 (1986): 149–64.

Boston, Noel, and Eric Puddy. *Dereham: The Biography of a Country Town.* Dereham, U.K.: privately printed, 1952.

Boyes, Megan. *My Amiable Mamma: A Biography of Mrs. Catherine Gordon Byron.* Derby, U.K.: privately published, 1991.

Brent, Peter. *Lord Byron.* London: Weidenfeld & Nicolson, 1974.

Burnett, T. A. J. *The Rise and Fall of a Regency Dandy: The Life and Times of Scrope Berdmore Davies.* London: John Murray, 1981.

Chapman, Stanley. "The Robinson Mills: Proto-Industrial Precedents." *Industrial Archaeology Review* 15 (1992): 58–61.

Clay, C. "The Price of Freehold Land in the Later Seventeenth and Eighteenth Centuries." *Economic History Review* 27 (1974): 173–89.

Cokayne, G. E. *Complete Peerage of England, Scotland, Ireland, Great Britain, and the United Kingdom, Extant, Extinct, or Dormant.* 13 vols. London: St. Catherine Press, 1910–.

Colyer, R. J. "The Haford Estate under Thomas Johnes and Henry Pelham, Fourth Duke of Newcastle." *Welsh History Review* 8 (1977): 257–84.

Coope, Rosalys. "Colonel Thomas Wildman and the Transformation of Newstead Abbey, Nottinghamshire, 1817–1859." *TTS* 101 (1997): 157–73.

———. "Lord Byron's Bath at Newstead." *Byron Journal* 13 (1985): 68–72.

———. "Lord Byron's Newstead: The Abbey and Its Furnishings during the Poet's Ownership, 1798–1817." *TTS* 91 (1987): 133–54.

———. "Newstead Abbey in the Eighteenth Century: The Building Works of the Fourth and Fifth Lords Byron." *TTS* 83 (1979): 50–66.

———. "The Wildman Family and Colonel Thomas Wildman of Newstead Abbey, Nottinghamshire." *TTS* 95 (1991): 50–66.

Coote, Stephen. *Byron: The Making of a Myth*. London: Bodley Head, 1988.

Crouzet, F., ed. *Capital Formation in the Industrial Revolution*. London: Methuen, 1972.

Dangerfield, Elma. *Byron and the Romantics in Switzerland, 1816*. London and Nashville: Ascent Books, 1978.

Dictionary of National Biography

Eisler, Benita. *Byron: Child of Passion, Fool of Fame*. London: Hamish Hamilton, 1999.

Elfenbein, A. *Byron and the Victorians*. Cambridge: Cambridge University Press, 1995.

Elwin, Malcolm. *Lord Byron's Wife*. London: Macdonald, 1962.

English, B. "Patterns of Estate Management in East Yorkshire, c. 1840–c. 1880." *Agricultural History Review* 32 (1984): 29–48.

Firth, J. B. *Highways and Byways in Nottinghamshire*. London: Macmillan & Co., 1916.

Fleming, Anne. *The Myth of the Bad Lord Byron*. Cuckfield, U.K.: Old Forge Press, 1998.

Foot, Michael. *The Politics of Paradise: A Vindication of Byron*. London: Collins, 1988.

Fowkes, D. V. "Nottinghamshire Parks in the Eighteenth and Nineteenth Centuries." *TTS* 71 (1967): 72–89.

Fraser, A. Z. *Livingstone and Newstead*. London: John Murray, 1913.

Girouard, Mark. *The Return to Camelot*. New Haven: Yale University Press, 1981.

Greatrex, Nan. "The Robinson Enterprises at Papplewick, Nottinghamshire, Part One." *Industrial Archaeology Review* 9 (1986): 37–56.

———. "The Robinson Enterprises at Papplewick, Nottinghamshire, Part Two." *Industrial Archaeology Review* 9 (1986): 119–39.

Griffin, A. R. *Mining in the East Midlands, 1550–1947*. London: Frank Cass, 1971.

Grosskurth, Phyllis. *Byron: The Flawed Angel*. London: Hodder & Stoughton, 1997.

Habakkuk, John. *Marriage, Debt, and the Estates System: English Landownership, 1650–1950*. Oxford: Clarendon Press, 1994.

Hibbert, C., ed. *Captain Gronow*. London: Kyle Cathie, 1991.

Howard, Maurice. *The Early Tudor Country House*. London: George Philip, 1987.

Howard, R., et al. "Tree-Ring Dates for Some East Midlands Buildings: 3." *TTS* 89 (1985): 30–36.

Hunter, P. D., ed. *Byron: The Harrow Collection*. Harrow, U.K.: Harrow School, 1994.

John, A. H. "Insurance Investment and the London Money Market in the Eighteenth century." *Economica* 20 (1953): 157.

Longford, Elizabeth. *Byron*. London: Weidenfeld & Nicolson, 1976.

Mandler, Peter. *The Fall and Rise of the Stately Home*. New Haven: Yale University Press, 1997.

Marchand, Leslie A. *Byron: A Biography*. 3 vols. London: John Murray, 1957.

———. *Byron: A Portrait*. London: John Murray, 1971.

———. "Byron's Letters." *Byron Journal* 1 (1973): 34–46.

Marchioness of Londonderry. *Henry Chaplin, a Memoir*. London: Macmillan, 1926.

Marcombe, David, and John Hamilton, eds. *Sanctity and Scandal.* Nottingham, U.K.: Continuing Education Press, University of Nottingham, 1998.

Marshall, J. D. "Early Application of Steam Power: The Cotton Mills of the Upper Leen." *TTS* 60 (1956): 34–43.

Maurois, André. *Byron.* London: Jonathan Cape, 1930.

Milbanke, R. G. N. *Lady Noel Byron and the Leighs.* London: W. Clowes & Son, 1887.

Moore, Doris Langley. *Accounts Rendered.* London: John Murray, 1974.

———. *Ada, Countess of Lovelace.* London: John Murray, 1978.

———. *The Late Lord Byron.* London: John Murray, 1961.

Morrison, A. B. "Byron's Lameness." *Byron Journal* 3 (1975): 24–30.

Nicolson, Harold. *Byron: The Last Journey.* London: Constable, 1924; reprint, London: Prior Books, 1999.

Nottinghamshire County Council Leisure Services. *Lord Byron and Nottinghamshire, 1788–1824.* Nottingham, U.K.: Nottinghamshire County Council, 1974.

Page, N., ed. *Byron: Interviews and Recollections.* London: Macmillan, 1985.

———. *A Byron Chronology.* Basingstoke, U.K.: Macmillan, 1988.

Parker, R. A. C. *Coke of Norfolk.* Oxford: Clarendon Press, 1975.

Peach, Annette. "Portraits of Byron." *The Walpole Society* 62 (2000).

Raizis, M. B., ed. *Byron and the Mediterranean World.* Athens: Hellenic Byron Society, 1995.

Robertson, William. *Rochdale and the Vale of Whitworth: Its Moorlands, Favourite Nooks, Green Lanes, and Scenery.* Rochdale, U.K.: privately published, 1897.

Roebuck, P. "Post-Restoration Landownership: The Impact of the Abolition of Wardship." *Journal of British Studies* 18 (1978): 67–85.

Rowse, A. L. *The Byrons and the Trevanions.* London: Weidenfeld & Nicolson, 1978.

Spring, David. "Ralph Sneyd: Tory Country Gentleman." *Bulletin of the John Rylands Library* 28 (1956): 535–55.

Squibb, G. D. *Doctors' Commons: A History of the College of Advocates and Doctors of Law.* Oxford: Clarendon Press, 1977.

Swartz, H. M. and M. Swartz, eds. *Disraeli's Reminiscences.* London: Hamish Hamilton, 1975.

Thompson, A. Hamilton. "The Priory of St. Mary of Newstead in Sherwood Forest." *TTS* 23 (1919): 33–141.

Thorne, R., ed. *The House of Commons, 1790–1820.* Vol. 3. London: Secker & Warburg, 1986.

Train, Keith. "The Byron Family: From the Conqueror to the Poet, Most Gifted of Them All." *Byron Journal* 2 (1974): 35–40.

Trease, Geoffrey. *Byron: A Poet Most Dangerous to Know.* London: Macmillan, 1969.

Turner, M. E., J. V. Beckett, and B. Afton. *Agricultural Rent in England, 1690–1914.* Cambridge: Cambridge University Press, 1997.

Waddams, S. M. *Law, Politics and the Church of England: The Career of Stephen Lushington, 1782–1873.* Cambridge: Cambridge University Press, 1992.

Walker, V. W., and M. J. Howell. *The House of Byron: A History of the Family from the Norman Conquest, 1066–1988.* London: Quiller Press, 1988.

Ward, J. R. "The Profitability of Sugar Planting in the British West Indies, 1650–1834."
    Economic History Review 31 (1978): 197–213.

Wheeler, P. T. "The Grounds of Newstead Abbey." Unpublished paper, 1988.

Wright, C. J. "The Miss Launders: A Brief Chapter in the History of Newstead Abbey."
    Byron Journal 7 (1979): 104–11.

Index

339